AMERICAN LITERATURE IN TRANSITION, 1990–2000

EDITED BY
STEPHEN J. BURN
University of Glasgow

CAMBRIDGE
UNIVERSITY PRESS

University Printing House, Cambridge CB2 8BS, United Kingdom

One Liberty Plaza, 20th Floor, New York, NY 10006, USA

477 Williamstown Road, Port Melbourne, VIC 3207, Australia

314–321, 3rd Floor, Plot 3, Splendor Forum, Jasola District Centre, New Delhi – 110025, India

79 Anson Road, #06-04/06, Singapore 079906

Cambridge University Press is part of the University of Cambridge.

It furthers the University's mission by disseminating knowledge in the pursuit of education, learning, and research at the highest international levels of excellence.

www.cambridge.org
Information on this title: www.cambridge.org/9781107136014
DOI: 10.1017/9781316477069

© Cambridge University Press 2018

This publication is in copyright. Subject to statutory exception and to the provisions of relevant collective licensing agreements, no reproduction of any part may take place without the written permission of Cambridge University Press.

First published 2018

Printed in the United States of America by Sheridan Books, Inc.

A catalogue record for this publication is available from the British Library

Library of Congress Cataloging-in-Publication data
Names: Burn, Stephen J., editor.
Title: American literature in transition, 1990–2000 / edited by Stephen J. Burn.
Description: New York : Cambridge University Press, 2017.
Identifiers: LCCN 2017026525 | ISBN 9781107136014 (hardback)
Subjects: LCSH: American literature – 20th century – History and criticism. | Literature and technology. | Literature and society – United States – History – 20th century.
Classification: LCC PS228.T42 A44 2017 | DDC 810.9/356 – dc23
LC record available at https://lccn.loc.gov/2017026525
ISBN 978-1-107-13601-4 Hardback

Cambridge University Press has no responsibility for the persistence or accuracy of URLs for external or third-party internet websites referred to in this publication and does not guarantee that any content on such websites is, or will remain, accurate or appropriate.

AMERICAN LITERATURE IN TRANSITION, 1990–2000

Written in the shadow of the approaching millennium, American literature in the 1990s was beset by bleak announcements of the end of books, the end of postmodernism, and even the end of literature. Yet as conservative critics marked the century's twilight hours by launching elegies for the conventional canon, American writers proved the continuing vitality of their literature by reinvigorating inherited forms, by adopting and adapting emerging technologies to narrative ends, and by finding new voices that had remained outside that canon for too long. By reading 1990s literature in a sequence of shifting contexts – from independent presses to the AIDS crisis, from angelology to virtual reality – *American Literature in Transition, 1990–2000* provides the fullest map yet of the changing shape of a rich and diverse decade's literary production. It offers new perspectives on the period's well-known landmarks (Toni Morrison, Thomas Pynchon, David Foster Wallace), but also overdue recognition to writers such as Ana Castillo, Evan Dara, Steve Erickson, and Carole Maso.

STEPHEN J. BURN is the author of two other books (and editor of three more) about contemporary literature, which have been translated into Finnish, Italian, Portuguese, and Spanish. In 2010, he was picked as one of the best critics under the age of forty by the *New York Times* and was invited to write the essay that opened their feature on "Why Criticism Matters."

AMERICAN LITERATURE IN TRANSITION

American Literature in Transition captures the dynamic energies transmitted across the 20th- and 21st-century American literary landscapes. Revisionary and authoritative, the series offers a comprehensive new overview of the established literary landmarks that constitute American literary life. Ambitious in scope and depth, and accommodating new critical perspectives and approaches, this series captures the dynamic energies and ongoing change in 20th- and 21st-century American literature. These are decades of transition, but also periods of epochal upheaval. These decades – the Jazz Age, the Great Depression, the Cold War, the sixties, 9/11 – are turning points of real significance. But in a tumultuous century, these terms can mask deeper structural changes. Each one of these books challenges in different ways the dominant approaches to a period of literature by shifting the focus from what happened to understanding how and why it happened. They elucidate the multifaceted interaction between the social and literary fields and capture that era's place in the incremental evolution of American literature up to the present moment. Taken together, this series of books constitutes a new kind of literary history in a century of intense cultural and literary creation, a century of liberation and also of immense destruction too. As a revisionary project grounded in pre-existing debates, American Literature in Transition offers an unprecedented analysis of the American literary experience.

Books in the series

American Literature in Transition, 1910–1920 edited by MARK W. VAN WIENEN
American Literature in Transition, 1920–1930 edited by ICHIRO TAKAYOSHI
American Literature in Transition, 1930–1940 edited by ICHIRO TAKAYOSHI
American Literature in Transition, 1940–1950 edited by CHRISTOPHER VIALS
American Literature in Transition, 1950–1960 edited by STEVEN BELLETTO
American Literature in Transition, 1960–1970 edited by DAVID WYATT
American Literature in Transition, 1970–1980 edited by KIRK CURNUTT
American Literature in Transition, 1980–1990 edited by D. QUENTIN MILLER
American Literature in Transition, 1990–2000 edited by STEPHEN J. BURN
American Literature in Transition, 2000–2010 edited by RACHEL GREENWALD SMITH

Contents

List of Contributors — *page* viii

Introduction: American Literature Under the Shadow of the Millennium — 1
Stephen J. Burn

PART I ENDTIMES

1. American Literature and the Millennium — 17
Jeremy Green

2. Angels, Ghosts, and Postsecular Visions — 32
Brian McHale

3. Aging Novelists and the End of the American Century — 48
Marshall Boswell

4. Violence — 63
Sean Grattan

5. The End of the Book… — 76
David Ciccoricco

6. The End of Postmodernism — 91
Ralph Clare

PART II FORMS

7. Encyclopedic Fictions — 107
Stephen J. Burn

8	Historical Fiction *John N. Duvall*	124
9	Lyrical Thinking in Poetry of the 1990s *Thomas Gardner*	140
10	Story Cycles *Paul March-Russell*	154
11	Materiality in the Late Age of Print *Mary K. Holland*	169
12	Manifestos *Rachel Greenwald Smith*	185
13	Revisionary Strategies *Christian Moraru*	199

PART III INTERCONNECTIVITY

14	Borders and Mixed-Race Fictions *Aliki Varvogli*	217
15	Globalization *Paul Giles*	233
16	The Two-Cultures Novel *Jon Adams*	249
17	Ecosystem *Heather Houser*	263
18	Virtual Reality *Joseph Conte*	279

PART IV PUBLIC AND PRIVATE LIFE

19	Trauma *Patrick O'Donnell*	297
20	Family *Kasia Boddy*	312
21	AIDS *Lesley Larkin*	329

PART V INSTITUTIONS

22 The University "After" Theory 347
    Daniel Punday

23 Independent Presses 362
    Jeffrey R. Di Leo

Index 378

Contributors

JON ADAMS, Research Video Producer, London School of Economics

KASIA BODDY, Lecturer, Fitzwilliam College, University of Cambridge

MARSHALL BOSWELL, Professor, Rhodes College

STEPHEN J. BURN, Reader in Post-45 American Literature, University of Glasgow

DAVID CICCORICCO, Senior Lecturer, University of Otago

RALPH CLARE, Associate Professor, Boise State University

JOSEPH CONTE, Professor, State University of New York Buffalo

JEFFREY R. DI LEO, Professor and Dean of the School of Arts and Sciences, University of Houston-Victoria

JOHN N. DUVALL, Margaret Church Distinguished Professor of English, Purdue University

THOMAS GARDNER, Alumni Distinguished Professor, Virginia Tech

PAUL GILES, Challis Professor of English, University of Sydney

SEAN GRATTAN, Lecturer in American Literature, University of Kent

JEREMY GREEN, Associate Professor, University of Colorado Boulder

MARY K. HOLLAND, Professor, State University of New York New Paltz

HEATHER HOUSER, Associate Professor, University of Texas at Austin

LESLEY LARKIN, Associate Professor, Northern Michigan University

PAUL MARCH-RUSSELL, Associate Lecturer in Comparative Literature, University of Kent

List of Contributors

BRIAN MCHALE, Distinguished Arts and Humanities Professor, Ohio State University

CHRISTIAN MORARU, Class of 1949 Distinguished Professor in the Humanities, University of North Carolina, Greensboro

PATRICK O'DONNELL, Professor, Michigan State University

DANIEL PUNDAY, Professor, Mississippi State University

RACHEL GREENWALD SMITH, Associate Professor, Saint Louis University

ALIKI VARVOGLI, Senior Lecturer in English and Associate Dean for Learning and Teaching, University of Dundee

Introduction
American Literature Under the Shadow of the Millennium
Stephen J. Burn

American Literature in Transition, 1990–2000 gathers twenty-three essays to present a collaborative map of the decade's shifting literary forms, obsessions, and crises. It does not attempt to curate the memory of a sequence of isolated literary works or authors, but instead tries to see the decade in motion, thinking through both the ways American literature evolved in the period and the dynamic contexts that incubated such changes. Relentless change is figured as the default status of American history writ large in one of the decade's key texts when, near the end of *Mason & Dixon* (1997), Thomas Pynchon describes his two surveyors glimpsing a "a ceaseless Spectacle of Transition"[1] after they have marked the divide between the country's north and south. Settling a colonial boundary dispute and marking the border between what would be the free and slave states, Pynchon's characters might conceive of transition as encompassing large-scale, national ruptures: the War of Independence, the Civil War. Yet on smaller scales, *transition* can also mean succession in time, a localized metamorphosis, or adaptation to new conditions. These various resonances, working at both macro and micro levels, inform and shape the chapters that follow as they document the unusual diversity of literary production in a decade that Daniel T. Rodgers describes as an "age of fracture."[2]

"Time has no divisions to mark its passage," Thomas Mann noted in *The Magic Mountain* (1924), "there is never a thunder-storm or blare of trumpets to announce the beginning of a new month or year. Even when a new century begins it is only we mortals who ring bells and fire off pistols."[3] Although American literary and cultural history "has perennially" been conceived "in terms of decades,"[4] to abbreviate the "ceaseless Spectacle of Transition" to the dynamics of a single decade might seem to risk the kind of empty ceremony Mann identifies. The 1990s are particularly vulnerable to this charge, not just because of the vast cultural and historical weight that was placed on the arbitrary moment when the clock ticked past midnight on December's last day in 1999, but also because the two signal historical events that bookend the decade lie beyond its boundaries: the fall of the Berlin Wall in early November 1989, and the terrorist attacks on the World Trade Center and Pentagon on September 11, 2001. The latter pair of events provides the frame for several earlier studies of the period.[5] The former calls for much larger temporal perspectives that can take in the long arc of the American writer's fascination with the millennium.

The approach of the millennium exerted a magnetic attraction for American writers long before the last decade of the twentieth century. As Douglas Robinson has shown, because America was "settled by millenarian religious groups," apocalyptic imagery – not simply the end of the world, but in eschatological terms, "the unveiling of the future in the present, the encroachment of a radically new order into a historical situation that has disintegrated into chaos"[6] – has always run through American literature, especially in cohort with reflections on time and judgment. American history reminds us that such doctrines of last things need not be tied to the calendar's signal dates – William Miller's 100,000 followers famously expected a millennial conflagration on October 22, 1844 – yet the year 2000 remained compelling for many writers.

Edward Bellamy's speculative fiction, *Looking Backward: 2000–1887* (1888), is a particularly representative carrier of the millennial infection. Bellamy's novel tells the story of Julian West, who goes to bed in May 1887, amid reports of imminent labor disputes, and awakens more than a century later in a tranquil Boston that embodies the utopian dream of perfect solidarity. Mingling the suspicion that this futuristic world has authentically "entered upon the millennium"[7] with a quasi-Darwinian explanation for the newly peaceful society, Bellamy's vision of the future at times comes chillingly close to unintentional cultural prophecies: West wakes up on the "tenth day of September in the year 2000," a year and a day before the first landmark moment for America's new century.[8] But his relevance, here, is in the way that the imagined millennial future acts as a rhetorical tool to highlight and displace the inequities of Bellamy's present day through a series of inversions: the selfish nineteenth-century's "age of individualism" has been replaced by "that of concert"; class distinctions and the rise of "ever larger monopolies" are supplanted by a total redistribution of wealth, where business is "conducted in the common interest for common profit"; and even the "horrible babel" of advertising is succeeded by an age without billboards.[9] Or rather, this world *almost* displaces the past, for in the book's last pages Bellamy suddenly returns West to the squalor and clamor of his nineteenth-century origins, before restoring him to the year 2000, as if, through this final narrative juxtaposition, to remind the reader that the need to grapple with realities of the past should not be completely forgotten amid dreams of the millennial "solidarity of the race and the brotherhood of man."[10]

The millennium, then, performed narrative labor for American novelists long before the twentieth century's last years, but to think of the 1990s as a coherent transitional moment does not mean that the decade's literature must be thought of in isolation from this longer history. John Updike's *Toward the End of Time* (1997), for instance, rewards being read from such a dual temporal perspective. Just as Bellamy mined the past for the conceit that drives his novel – *Looking Backward* is effectively an exponential rewrite of Washington Irving's "Rip Van Winkle" (1819) – so, in this long view, does Updike seem to deliberately revise and update Bellamy's model in his late, millennial fiction. Not only does Updike imagine his narrator, Ben Turnbull, living in the twenty-first century as "a nineteenth-century-minded custodian of... Dickens" (West's "prime favorite among the book writers"),[11] but the books are also united by a sequence of parallels. Following Bellamy, Updike's vision of a postmillenial future (the book is set in 2020) measures time's passage by having his protagonist move around a reimagined Boston. Both authors estrange us from our contemporary moment by replacing the economic status quo with new monetary systems (Updike has "welders" replace dollars; Bellamy imagines an equitable system of credit). Finally, just as Bellamy brusquely returns West to the nineteenth century late in the book, so at key points does Updike's future world suddenly drop away to put Ben in earlier moments of historical transition: Ancient Egypt, Late Rome, Monastic Ireland, "Poland in early 1944."[12] Time is uncertain in both books, and the past tugs each character backwards into the "abysmal well of time" in unpredictable ways.[13]

Yet while Updike's novel might be read as echoing earlier instalments in the long history of American millenarianism, it can equally be set in its specific 1990s context, a process that marks differences, rather than continuities, from Bellamy. While *Looking Backward* can manage its dramatic shifts in time through the quaint narrative mechanism of "mesmeric sleep" and the "extraordinary dream,"[14] Updike instead draws on late twentieth-century quantum physics and its "Many Worlds Interpretation" to underwrite its sudden leaps beyond calendrical succession. In what Judie Newman calls a "syncretic and creative" elaboration on "the idea of many universes,"[15] Updike invokes the "little fork in reality when a quantum measurement is made" to allow "another universe, thinner than a razor blade" to slice into and potentially destabilize the authority of any given narrative moment.[16] This approach parallels the work of a distinct strand of 1990s writers who set their novels in the quantum realm of parallel universes (notably Don DeLillo, Helen DeWitt, Thomas Pynchon, and David Foster Wallace),[17] but Updike is arguably most characteristic of his 1990s moment – and most different from Bellamy – in his insistence that the postmillenial world's transitions will involve incremental decline rather than revolutionary breakthrough. From a purely pragmatic perspective, this difference partly reflects relative proximity to the year 2000: the millennial threshold, for Updike in 1997, is now too near to permit the total reversal and renewal of society that Bellamy allows. In place of the strategic inversions that characterize Bellamy's future world, Updike instead extrapolates his future from an extension and acceleration of current conditions. *Toward the End of Time*'s America has, for instance, been devastated by a Sino-American conflict that, as Newman has shown, "closely resembles" arguments predicting a coming conflict with China that were developing in the 1990s.[18] The logical conclusion of Updike's extrapolations is a decline whose scope is neatly encapsulated by a final comparison with *Looking Backward*. While Bellamy's novel can imagine millennial Boston made up of "public buildings of a colossal size and ... architectural grandeur," set next to the "sinuous Charles" like a "blue ribbon winding away to the sunset,"[19] more or less the same view is rendered in much bleaker terms in Updike's novel: "Looking back at the city's profile from ... above the Charles, we saw the blue-glass, postmodern downtown buildings darkened in their post-war desolation, and rusty stumps of projected construction that had been abruptly abandoned, as too expensive for our dwindled, senile world."[20] Visions of waste and detritus were not always coded so negatively in the decade. A. R. Ammons's riffs that "garbage is spiritual,"[21] and the trash artists in DeLillo's *Underworld* (1997) spring to mind. But Updike's vision of decline is apocalypse in the 1990s vulgate, a vision dominated by the rhetoric of endtimes that becomes the keynote in much of the decade's literature and broader cultural discourse.

Published in the middle of the decade, John Barth's "The End: An Introduction" directly addresses the proliferation of such end-oriented discourse in the period. Barth's deft fiction is presented in the form of an introductory speech delivered to an audience who awaits the arrival of the main speaker, a writer-under-threat partly modeled on Taslima Nasrin and Salman Rushdie. As the speaker's arrival is delayed and delayed, the introducer starts to meditate on what Barth will later call "those fin-de-siècle and millenarian currents, more or less apocalyptic, much astir by the mid-1990s,"[22]

> [A]s we end our century and millennium... it is no surprise that the "terminary malady" afflicts us... not long ago, believe it or not, there was an international symposium on "The End of *Post*modernism" – just when we thought we might be beginning to understand what the term describes! In other jurisdictions, we have Professor Whatsisname on the End of History, and Professor So-and-So on the End of Physics (indeed, the End of Nature), and Professor Everybody-and-Her-Brother on the End of the Old World Order with the collapse of the Soviet Union and of international Communism.
>
> In short and in sum, endings, endings everywhere; apocalypses large and small.... The end of this, the end of that; little wonder we grow weary of 'endism,' as I have heard it called.[23]

As is typical of Barth's late fiction, what may seem mere rhetorical performance is a densely encoded distillation of the times that permits and rewards annotation. The sequence of *End of* titles begins with literary fiction, referring to the August 1991 Stuttgart seminars on "The End of Postmodernism," which featured Barth himself.[24] His reflection that in the early 1990s "we might be beginning to understand what the term describes" on one level surely refers to the more formal updates on his seminal essays on literary exhaustion and replenishment that he presented in Stuttgart, yet from our perspective this phrase might also be linked to the appearance of Fredric Jameson's landmark volume, *Postmodernism, or the Cultural Logic of Late Capitalism*, in 1991. "Professor Whatsisname" is Francis Fukuyama, cited here for his 1992 book-length expansion of his earlier claim that we had reached not simply the end of the Cold War but "the end of history as such: that is, the end point of mankind's ideological evolution and the universalization of Western liberal democracy as the final form of human government."[25] "Professor So-and-So" is presumably David Lindley, whose *The End of Physics* (1993) argued that speculative superstring theorists had become a branch of aesthetic theory, "because their theories could never be validated by experiments,"[26] while "the End of Nature" points to Bill McKibben's 1989 account of global warming and the worsening environmental crisis. Barth reminds us that such apocalyptic musings and their attendant political upheavals are not new, through his sly echo of a work from a different fin-de-siècle: "The Rime of the Ancient Mariner" (1798), which Coleridge wrote through the last years of the French Revolution. Yet the range of parallel fields – moving from the literary, through global politics and advanced science, to emerging environmentalism – that are each arcing toward endings and perhaps renewal speaks to the way the proximate millennium's shadow gathered an unusual concentration of transitional moments within the decade. In light of these intersecting discourses, Jay Prosser's claim in *American Fiction of the 1990s* (2008) that "the figure for the 1990s may be trans: transnational, transhistorical, and *transitional*" seems apposite.[27]

The decade certainly featured works that ask – like *Toward the End of Time* – to be read in the longer history of a specifically millennial transition: Richard Powers's *Gain* (1998) retells the story of William Miller's belief that the millennium would arrive in 1844[28]; Wallace's *Infinite Jest* (1996) plays with the etymology of millennial apocalypse through its multiple veils and games of eschaton[29]; and DeLillo's research materials for *Underworld*'s vision of "Last Things"[30] include documents that helpfully explain "How Should I Prepare to Be Raptured?" But as the chapters gathered in this book illustrate, while millennial energies are rife, the period's literary trigger points often stem from the larger end-oriented debates that Barth glossed in his short fiction. Part I maps different iterations of the millennial sense of an ending across 1990s American literature. Chapter 1 considers the intermingling of hope and terror in the decade's developing apocalyptic imagination, as represented by Jorie Graham, Steve Erickson, and Don DeLillo. As Jeremy Green shows, in some cases (Tim LaHaye's and Jerry Jenkins's *Left Behind* series, for example), such visions are explicitly based in Biblical writings, yet with notable exceptions (Norman Mailer's mild expansion of Biblical sources in *The Gospel According to the Son* [1997]), the period typically saw such staples of millennial religion as the appearance of angels or the return of the dead float free of their traditional religious valence. In Chapter 2, Brian McHale examines the presence of such angels, in particular, through a wide-ranging discussion of works by Ana Castillo, Tony Kushner, and Thomas Pynchon.

Moving beyond the accoutrements of millenarianism, the next four chapters trace literary shifts in relation to various end-oriented discourses. The end of the twentieth century seemed to overlap with the ends (either real or imagined) of a sequence of aging male writers' careers. While some of these writers released final books that had been decades in the making (Ralph Ellison's posthumous *Juneteenth* [1999] is a key example), others (Saul Bellow, Philip Roth, Norman Mailer) turned toward retrospection after enormously prolific careers. Marshall Boswell examines such late works in Chapter 3. Rhetoric of approaching end-times was often accompanied by iconic visual footage of escalating violence in the period, but the period's specifically literary explorations of violence might be classified into two tracks. On the first track, writers were drawn magnetically to signal instances of earlier twentieth-century violence (James Ellroy and

Mailer on Lee Harvey Oswald; John Edgar Wideman on the 1985 bombing of a Philadelphia row home in *Philadelphia Fire* [1990]). On the second track, there were meditations on what seemed to be specifically 1990s manifestations of violence (Anne Deveare Smith's one-woman play response to the Rodney King beating; Chuck Palahniuk and Bret Easton Ellis on crises in masculinity; Joyce Carol Oates's near-encyclopedic sequence of books on rape, serial killers, child murder, and so on). In Chapter 4, Sean Grattan reads the LA riots as crystallizing larger violent social changes in the period, setting the events of 1992 alongside later works by Octavia Butler, Toni Morrison, and Dennis Cooper.

While the 1990s saw the fundamental staples of a postmodern metafiction that many critics had almost solely associated with white, male writers,[31] adopted and adapted by a much broader swathe of multiethnic writers (so Sherman Alexie's superb *The Lone Ranger and Tonto Fistfight in Heaven* [1993] revels in funhouse imagery, stories-embedded-within-stories, and traces the ubiquity of television's "white noise"), it has nevertheless become commonplace to see literary postmodernism abruptly coming to an end in the decade, to be simplistically succeeded by some successor movement that abandons all trace contamination of its literary ancestors. This move is no doubt related to the increasing prominence of orphans in millennial work (Lethem's *Motherless Brooklyn* [1999], Eggers's *Heartbreaking Work* [2000], Foer's *Everything is Illuminated* [2002]), even as it ignores the continued productivity of writers such as Robert Coover, John Barth, and William Gass in the twenty-first century. What it also ignores (as Ralph Clare demonstrates in Chapter 6) is that narratives of the end of postmodernism were themselves a narrative propounded by a postmodernist fiction that had been "playing posthumous" for much of the decade. One of the central figures in early constructions of American postmodernism – Robert Coover – was also (perhaps unwittingly, as David Ciccoricco shows in Chapter 5) one of the key architects of the decade's fascination with the end of the book and the corresponding rise of electronic fictions.

Part II shifts the focus to changing forms in the decade, though in many ways this topic retains a millennial flavor. The "formal sense of millennium," DeLillo has noted, "not only looks ahead to the year 2000 but recollects as well."[32] In Bellamy and Updike this dual temporal perspective is manifest in the way both books shuttle between different eras, but a comparable effort to look forward by dwelling on the past is manifest throughout this section. Chapter 7 traces the encyclopedic novel's development in the hands of the younger writers whose apprenticeship was indebted to ancestor texts by DeLillo, Gaddis, and Pynchon. The historical novel has always worked the hinge between recollection and speculation, but – as John Duvall demonstrates in Chapter 8 – the unusual centrality of historical fiction in the decade stems from a post–Cold War intellectual climate that made history the time's "key cultural issue." One of the key binaries, for Duvall, is represented by the divergent interpretations offered by Linda Hutcheon and Fredric Jameson of history in novels from the 1970s; for lyric poets in the 1990s, Thomas Gardner (Chapter 9) identifies a different opposition whose resolution finds echoes throughout the decade. Gardner reads the changing form of 1990s lyric poetry as the result of a hybrid aesthetic that spliced the previous decade's opposed camps – poets committed to a program of realist self-expression and those pursuing more avant-garde strategies – into a fertile union. Similar hybrids are charted in Paul March-Russell's account of the revival of the story cycle (Chapter 10), which moves from Tim O'Brien, through Louise Erdrich, to A. M. Homes, and in Mary K. Holland's discussion of the competing claims of physicality and textuality in Mark Z. Danielewski, William Gass, and Carole Maso (Chapter 11).

Part II ends with two chapters that explicitly engage with the split temporal perspective that DeLillo accords the formal millennium. In Chapter 12, Rachel Greenwald Smith examines debates about self-expression that stem from the way the decade's fiction manifestoes often looked to the future by looking backwards. In Chapter 13, Christian Moraru examines the revisionary strategies that we have seen employed by Bellamy and Updike, in a much wider context that carries into the book's later explorations of globalization.

If the 1990s were rife with millennial imagery that, as Douglas Robinson has argued, stemmed back to "the Puritans in the Massachusetts Bay Colony,"[33] the legacy of the European arrival in the New World inevitably carried a different valence for different segments of American society. Danzy Senna's 1998 passing novel, *Caucasia*, for instance, satirizes the equation of American history and whiteness not just in her choice of title but also by having her mixed-race central character, Birdie, be ferried around the country in a car that's a near echo of Christopher Columbus's *La Pinta*. Ironically replaying America's colonization in a fashion comparable to Gerald Vizenor's *The Heirs of Columbus* (1991), these scenes typically insulate Birdie from the world around her rather than bringing genuine contact: "[S]ometimes when we drove around in the back of my mother's Pinto, I would stare at the children outside with newfound interest, wondering which one of them I would become."[34] Growing recognition of America's long-standing plurality brought an overdue critique not just of the illusory racial neutrality of the American literary canon (notably by

Toni Morrison's *Playing in the Dark* [1992]) but more generally of the category of national identity. As Katha Pollitt reported in 1994, "Sheldon Hackney of the National Endowment for the Humanities wants to fund what he calls a 'national conversation' to determine what it means to be an American. Hackney himself acknowledges that he does not know the answer, but believes the question is worth pursuing."[35] Part III begins with the pressing need to think of both American identity and 1990s American literature in more expansive terms, both in terms of the period's changing conception of "borders" (addressed by Aliki Varvogli in Chapter 14's discussion of Cormac McCarthy, Karen Tei Yamashita, and Jhumpa Lahiri) and in the increased prominence of globalizing forces (as mapped by Paul Giles in Chapter 15, with an eye on Jessica Hagedorn, Bob Shacochis, and DeLillo). Emphasis on globalization and interconnectivity often functioned – at the largest scale – in terms of emerging debates about the ecosystem, which Heather Houser takes up in Chapter 17's discussion of Leslie Marmon Silko, Richard Powers, and David Foster Wallace. As Houser's references to biology and geology show, addressing ecology in the 1990s often required interdisciplinary perspectives. The wider blurring of the line, between what was once the clear domain of the literary and the scientific, in the 1990s is addressed in Jon Adams's discussion of "the Two-Cultures Novel" (Chapter 16), a designation that ranges from Barbara Kingsolver's *Animal Dreams* (1990) to Jonathan Lethem's *Motherless Brooklyn* (1999). The different kinds of interconnectivity explored in this chapter were variously enabled, studied, or imagined during the period by emerging computer networks and technologies. This section ends with Joseph Conte's assessment of the way the decade's literature (by Neal Stephenson, Richard Powers, and Pat Cadigan) responded to the various utopian promises offered by virtual reality, which once seemed to represent the leading edge of such technologies.

While globalizing technologies reshaped America at the largest scale, those same technologies were often also implicated in reshaping life at much smaller levels. While many major social networking platforms only emerged after the millennium – *MySpace* in 2003, with *Facebook* appearing the following year – the foundations of the social media revolution are strongly rooted in the nineties, with, for instance, the 1995 development of Classmates.com in the United States. If social media provides a membrane through which the once private becomes public, then its emergence in the 1990s might be seen in the context of a cluster of other intersections of the public and private whose literary ramifications are considered under the umbrella of the book's fourth section. Near the start of the decade, Madonna published her coffee-table book *Sex* (1992), and its implicit meditation on the relationship of sex and power proved unintentionally prophetic as the decade saw a sequence of scandals that brought private sex acts into the public domain of specifically political power as, first the Bill Clinton and Monica Lewinksy scandal, and then the Hemings-Jefferson controversy unfurled. Such major news stories provide the backdrop for literary reflections on both the reputed demise of the quintessential American family and its attendant mythology (in Chapter 20, Kasia Boddy's wide-ranging study triangulates the family, television, and writers from Edwidge Danticat to Junot Díaz), and for the prominence of AIDS narratives as a representative example of one way that the private world of sex was brought into wider public discourse in the decade (Lesley Larkin's account of Tony Kushner, Rabih Alameddine, and Jamaica Kincaid, in Chapter 21). As Patrick O'Donnell observes, the public revelation of sexual offenses was also at the heart of the outpouring of recovered memory debates in the period, and this shift is considered in concert with the rise of Trauma theory in the academy in Chapter 19.

The book's final section considers the decade's changing institutional foundations. The 1990s were rife with typically end-oriented accounts of the deleterious impact of specifically academic institutions on literature. Alvin Kernan announced *The Death of Literature* (1990), charging that academic culture wars had "emptied out" canonical works "in the service of social and political causes that are considered more important than the texts themselves."[36] Moving in parallel, Harold Bloom's *The Western Canon* (1994) offered "an elegy for the canon," as "the ages of reading ... now reach terminus" leaving an "almost wholly ... oral and visual culture."[37] John W. Aldridge blamed the rise of creative writing programs for producing a generation of writers whose work was "technically conservative, stylistically bland, and often extremely modest in intention."[38] Both Kernan's and Bloom's positions have been read as reactionary responses to the unsettling of white male power in the university, something like the critical equivalent of the struggle David Mamet dramatized in *Oleanna* (1992). Many voices, of course appropriately celebrated the unsettling of the conservative canon: Jay Clayton's *The Pleasures of Babel*, for instance, welcomed the creation of a "literature without masterpieces," a pluralistic vision where no single "writer or style" could "hold sway"[39]; Henry Louis Gates, Jr.'s address, "Canon-Formation, Literary History, and the Afro-American Tradition," similarly saw "wondrous" potential for black canon formation (a widely discussed topic across the decade) at the decade's start.[40] But while it was often reactionary complaints that made the decade's news (the *New York Times* responded to *The Western Canon*'s publication by christening Bloom "a colossus among critics"),[41] as Daniel Punday illustrates in

Chapter 22, axial changes to the university took place away from the headlines, and need to be read in relation to economics rather than the canon.

Massive economic and institutional changes also provide the backdrop for the final chapter's discussion of independent presses. Corporate consolidation across all areas of American life characterizes the 1990s, and in literary publishing the power and influence of a small group of publishers expands greatly by decade's end. In spite of such imperial expansion, Jeffrey Di Leo nevertheless documents the resilient vitality of independent presses in the decade, which served as a home and an incubator for both avant-garde experimenters and multi-ethnic writers (Chapter 23). While (as earlier chapters demonstrate) there is a strong eschatological flavor running through much of the decade's thinking, independent presses and affiliated magazines were often home to more forward-thinking currents. In October 1992, for instance, the University of Kentucky's *ANQ* acknowledged the prevailingly "bleak commercial conditions," yet gathered a sequence of writers and critics to speculate on the future of American fiction, identifying such younger figures as Susan Daitch, Steve Erickson, William T. Vollmann, David Foster Wallace, and Mark Leyner as writers-to-watch in the coming decade.[42] Four years later, the *Review of Contemporary Fiction* followed suit, asking Wallace to edit a forum called "The Future of Fiction," drawing in such writers as Franzen, Vollmann, Bradford Morrow, and Carole Maso.

That so many of these writers might be associated with independent publications and yet be published by mainstream presses before the decade ended points to the prevailing trend in the 1990s for what was once marginal to become mainstream. In music, Nirvana and grunge displace Michael Jackson. In cinema, *Pulp Fiction* breaks records for an "indie" film.[43] In literature, not only is this shift manifest in the arc of Dave Eggers's career, moving from early work within the model of the "little magazine"[44] to the mainstream success of *A Heartbreaking Work of Staggering Genius* (2000), but also – in larger terms – in the fate of African-American writers who, as Prosser notes, "began their careers in the 1970s and 1980s redefining the canon" and then "became central to it and set the trends for their times."[45] No single figure reflects this shift more completely than Toni Morrison, who, in 1993, became the first African-American writer to win the Nobel Prize.[46]

The 1990s are still close enough for recent memory to make the decade available for nostalgic consumption,[47] but they have receded sufficiently for the difference between our millennial reflections on the decade and the time's judgment on itself to be revealing. At times, such differences are simply terminological: the Gulf War of 1990–1991, for instance, must now be known as the *first* Gulf War. In other cases, they involve wholesale reevaluations. In 1996, for example, *Granta* ran its first special issue devoted to picking the "Best of Young American Novelists." The list was noted even at the time for its tame selection – David Lodge (in terms that echo Aldridge's attack on Creative Writing programs) diagnosed "nothing very startling or ambitious" in the work chosen, but rather a "certain sameness" amid "a high standard of technical competence"[48] – and the passing of years has not often endorsed the judges' cultural speculations, especially in their narrow preference for a kind of well-behaved dirty realism. Preparing a new list in 2007, even *Granta*'s editor – Ian Jack – wisely repudiated the 1996 list, lamenting "judges with God-knows-what axes to grind in California or Kansas."[49] At times the essays gathered in this book return to debates current in the decade about key transitions – the emergence of hypertext fiction, the end of postmodernism, and so on – but they also rely on the wisdom of distance to identify shifts that were less remarked at the time – the prevalence of AIDS narratives, the role of independent presses, the changing shape of the lyric. In doing so, they cover many of the widely recognized key works from the decade, but they also seek out less familiar names, deliberately aiming not just to enlarge our sense of *how* literature changed in this decade-in-transition, but also of *who* helped drive those transitions.

NOTES

1 Pynchon, *Mason & Dixon* (London: Cape, 1997), 713.
2 In *The Age of Fracture* (Cambridge, MA: Harvard University Press, 2011), Rodgers traces the gradual fragmentation in the 1980s and 1990s of the mid-century ideas that shaped American life in the realms of politics, economics, and society. Fracture also sums up much of the 1990s zeitgeist, with the Y2K bug's combination of advanced technology and atavistic fear typifying the hybrid moods that inform much of the period's literature.
3 Mann, *The Magic Mountain* (New York: Vintage, 2011), 223.
4 O'Donnell, "A Rough Decade," *American Literary History* 24.2 (2012): 404.
5 Both Samuel Cohen and Phillip E. Wegner take this frame, and (in different ways) see the decade as a momentary pause, rich in possibility, from the remorseless logic of the surrounding year. Cohen's *After the End of History* (Iowa City: University of Iowa Press, 2009) frames the 1990s as an "interwar decade," marked by a preoccupation with history that he reads against end-historical arguments raised by Francis Fukuyama, Fredric Jameson, and Walter Benn Michaels (4); Wegner's *Life Between Two Deaths* (Durham, NC: Duke University Press, 2009) influentially names the same years "the long nineties," and – by way of Lacan and Žižek – sees the fall of the World Trade Center

echoing the fall of the Berlin Wall in a way that belatedly destroyed "the symbolic universe of the Cold War... and thus marked the opening of a new period in global history" (9). This makes the 1990s a "transitional phase" "between an ending (of the Cold War) and a beginning (of our post-September 11 world)" (ibid).
6 Robinson, *American Apocalypses* (Baltimore: Johns Hopkins University Press, 1985), xi, xii.
7 Bellamy, *Looking Backward: 2000–1887* (Harmondsworth: Penguin, 1986), 153.
8 Ibid., 51.
9 Ibid., 122, 64–65, 219.
10 Ibid., 111.
11 Updike, *Toward the End of Time* (London: Hamilton, 1997), 247. Bellamy, *Looking Backward*, 120.
12 Ibid., 241.
13 Ibid., 313.
14 Bellamy, *Looking Backward*, 47, 216.
15 Newman, *Utopia and Terror in Contemporary American Fiction* (New York: Routledge, 2013), 107.
16 Updike, *Toward the End*, 16, 241.
17 In *American Postmodernist Fiction and the Past* (New York: Palgrave, 2011), Theophilus Savvas insightfully explores how "Pynchon's re-inscription of the subjunctive" in *Mason & Dixon* invokes an analogy to "the 'Many Worlds Interpretation' of quantum mechanics" (86); DeWitt's use of similar ideas is discussed in Chapter 7 of the present volume; although it was not published until 2001, DeLillo spent the late 1990s working on *The Body Artist*'s many-worlds narration: "She stood nude in the workout room... Or sat cross-legged... Or went about on all fours" ([New York: Scribner, 2001], 73); finally, Marshall Boswell argues in *Understanding David Foster Wallace* (Columbia: University of South Carolina Press, 2003) that we should see the counterfactuality that marks "the world of *Infinite Jest*" as a "parallel universe" created when "a quantum physicist makes a determination whether or not an observed proton is a particle or a wave" (125).
18 Newman, ibid., 105. Such a conflict had, of course, been prophesied at least as far back as Jack London's "The Unparalleled Invasion" (1910), which imagines a late twentieth-century conflict between China and the United States.
19 Bellamy, *Looking Backward*, 55.
20 Updike, *Toward the End*, 40.
21 Ammons, *Garbage* (New York: Norton, 1993), 18.
22 Barth, *Coming Soon!!!* (Boston: Houghton, 2001), 58.
23 Barth, *On with the Story* (Boston: Little, 1996), 14–15. Early drafts of the story come closer to attributing the phrase "endism" to Salman Rushdie, while they also omit "The End of Physics" and deny the unnamed speakers professorships.
24 I explore the resonance of these seminars and other 1990s debates over the "end of postmodernism" in chapter one of *Jonathan Franzen at the End of Postmodernism* (London: Continuum, 2008).

25 Fukuyama, "The End of History?" *National Interest* 16 (1989): 4.
26 John Horgan, *The End of Science* (New York: Broadway, 1996), 70.
27 Prosser, "Introduction," in *American Fiction of the 1990s*, ed. Prosser (Abingdon: Routledge, 2008), 10.
28 Powers, *Gain* (New York: Farrar, 1998), 81–83.
29 As Robinson notes, "the apocalypse is an unveiling (*apo* [from or away], *kalupsis* [covering] from *kalupto* [to cover], and *kalumma* [veil]) . . . [and] the veil is the *eschaton*, that which stands between the familiar and whatever lies beyond" (xii).
30 DeLillo, *Underworld* (New York: Scribner-Simon, 1997), 577.
31 Madhu Dubey's *Signs and Cities* (Chicago: University of Chicago Press, 2003) and W. Lawrence Hogue's *Postmodern American Literature and Its Other* (Urbana: University of Illinois Press, 2009) notably buck this trend.
32 DeLillo, "Silhouette City: Hitler, Manson, and the Millennium," *Dimensions* 4.3 (1988): 30.
33 Robinson, *American Apocalypses*, xi.
34 Senna, *Caucasia* (New York: Riverhead-Penguin, 1998), 31.
35 Pollitt, "Subject to Debate," *Nation*, April 18, 1994, 513.
36 Kernan, *The Death of Literature* (New Haven: Yale University Press, 1990), 212.
37 Bloom, *The Western Canon* (London: Macmillan, 1994), 15, 519.
38 Aldridge, *Talents and Technicians* (New York: Scribner's, 1992), 30.
39 Clayton, *The Pleasures of Babel* (New York: Oxford University Press, 1993), 148.
40 Gates, Jr., in *Afro-American Literary Study in the 1990s*, ed. Houston A. Baker, Jr., and Patricia Redmond (Chicago: University of Chicago Press, 1989) 14.
41 Adam Begley, "A Colossus Among Critics," *New York Times*, September 25, 1994, http://www.nytimes.com/books/98/11/01/specials/bloom-colossus.html.
42 Lance Olsen, "The Michael Jacksonization of American Fiction," *ANQ* 5.4 (1992): 177.
43 As Colin Harrison notes in *American Culture in the 1990s* (Edinburgh: Edinburgh University Press, 2010), however, "what counts as 'independent'" in 1990s cinema "is by no means clear-cut" (114).
44 Alexander Starre, *Metamedia* (Iowa City: University of Iowa Press, 2015) 67.
45 Prosser, "Introduction," 2.
46 At the time, Henry Louis Gates Jr. put this transformation in even stronger terms, noting in the *New York Times* (Oct. 8, 1993) that "just two centuries ago, the African-American literary tradition was born in slave narratives . . . Now our greatest writer has won the Nobel Prize."
47 Kurt Anderson, for instance, calls it "the happiest decade of our American lifetimes" in his short essay, "The Best Decade Ever? The 1990s, Obviously," (*New York Times*, February 6, 2015, SR6).
48 Lodge, "O Ye Laurels," *New York Review of Books*, August 8, 1996, 20.
49 Jack, "Best of Young Novelists 2: Introduction," *Granta* 97 (2007), https://granta.com/introduction-boyan-2/.

PART I
Endtimes

CHAPTER 1

American Literature and the Millennium

Jeremy Green

Midnight is never far away. Since 1947, the *Bulletin of the Atomic Scientists* has published a "Doomsday Clock" to show how close the world stands to global catastrophe. Through the decades of the Cold War, the clock's minute hand edged back and forth as nuclear war seemed more or less likely depending on the state of the arms race and the promise of test ban treaties, coming as close as two minutes to midnight in 1953. With the collapse of the Soviet Union, tension eased and the minute hand withdrew in 1991 to a comparatively comfortable seventeen minutes from disaster. Although the promise of 1991 did not hold – nuclear arms proliferated once again, the peace dividend failed to materialize – the decade following the end of the Cold War appears in hindsight as a period of cautious optimism, in spite of the growing awareness of irreversible climate change and continued international tensions and conflicts. Yet the countdown to the end of the century and the millennium excited both millennial hopes and apocalyptic anxieties as the year 2000 approached.

Portentous as these dates once appeared – 1999, 2000 – they had only the significance projected onto them in response to hopes and fears that had nothing to do with the calendar. In *The Sense of an Ending*, a study of eschatology and narrative, Frank Kermode writes, "The century and other fundamentally arbitrary chronological divisions – we might simply call them *saecula* – are made to bear the weight of our anxieties and hopes."[1] The last decade of the twentieth century saw remarkable social, cultural, and political changes, among them a new post-Soviet geopolitical reality, the rapid emergence of new digital technologies (including the arrival of the Internet), and the unchecked ascendancy of neoliberal social and economic policies. The confused apprehension of such changes seized on the calendar to cast millennial and apocalyptic figures, whether fantasies of a dawning new age or fears of a cataclysmic ending.

Events unfolded during the 1990s that appeared to highlight the menacing power of the millennial imagination. The Waco Branch Davidians, an explicitly apocalyptic religious cult led by David Koresh, came to a fiery end in the disastrous 1993 ATF-FBI raid on their Texas compound; and in 1997, the nightly appearance of the Hale-Bopp comet prompted the Heaven's Gate UFO cult to commit mass suicide in pursuit of a millenarian sci-fi fantasy. As the decade drew to a close, calendrical fears took on a curiously specific form with media-driven trepidation about the Y2K bug, the alarming prospect that a worldwide computer failure would result in apocalyptic chaos – airplanes falling out of the sky, nuclear missiles launching themselves. What these events shared, very different though they were, was a sense of imminent chaos and change associated with the century's end. In the case of the Branch Davidians, prophecies derived from the Book of Revelations provided an important source of inspiration. Religious cults and popular movements alike, associated with a tradition of eschatological prophecy and dispensationalist fundamentalism, have deep roots in American culture. Even at the end of the twentieth century, biblical prophecy retained a powerful popular appeal. Tim LeHaye and Jerry Jenkins's *Left Behind* series of novels (1995–2007), for example, presented a Revelations-inspired premillennial vision of the battle between good and evil in thriller format. The series – along with spinoffs in other media, including video games, movies, and graphic novels – proved wildly popular, regularly topping the bestseller lists.

Such a full-fledged eschatological conception of the present and immediate future gives a narrative shape to inchoate anxieties. As Kermode argues, this narrative shape establishes a consonance between origins and promised endings, and fits apparent chaos – often the chaos of a transitional period – into a comprehensible structure. Premillennialist prophecy seizes on evidence of perceived social and political disarray and converts it into a privileged set of signs legible in terms of a biblical master-text. Otherwise unrelated events – the rise of a political leader, an earthquake, a pandemic – become linked figures in a narrative, and not just any narrative, but the narrative to end all narratives. A menacing present can thus be resolved into a future-oriented – and future-ending – story of the last days of humanity before God's final wrath.

Secular millennialism has structural affinities with eschatological prophecy. Kermode writes: "The notion of an End-dominated age of transition has passed into our consciousness, and modified our attitudes to historical pattern."[2] As the century came to a close, calling up *fin de siècle* images of decadence and confusion, as well as notions of epochal change, a deeper uncertainty about historical patterning in general could also be detected, a sense of permanent transition that called the present into question. What Fredric Jameson has called our "inverted millenarianism" – the end of one thing after another (grand narratives, the subject, the human, ideology) – gives a priority to competing and contradictory narratives that would lay hold of a moment of incessant transition or crisis in which rapid change appeared to threaten the present as an intelligible unit of time distinct from future and past.[3] The appeal of apocalyptic thinking, even to the secular imagination, stems from the prospect of a restored narrative pattern, no matter how dark in aspect.

Francis Fukuyama's notorious end-of-history thesis expressed something of the temper of the times, at once triumphalist and morose. His controversial claim that free-market liberal democracy, best represented by the United States, had emerged from the struggles of the twentieth century as the only social system capable of securing freedom and prosperity sought to capitalize on the collapse of the Soviet Union to advance the supposedly Hegelian thesis of the end of history. Of course, events would continue to occur, but the essential problem facing states would henceforth be technical or managerial – how best to arrive at the condition of a functioning liberal democratic society. But the mood of *The End of History* is, as Krishan Kumar notes, hardly celebratory: "Fukuyama is concerned at the selfishness and excessive individualism of liberal societies, their relentless erosion of all forms of community and social morality . . . If the whole world is becoming liberal, the whole world is also becoming amoral."[4] This sobering conclusion suggests less the dawning of a new age of liberal capitalism than the long twilight of civil society decaying from within.

Jean Baudrillard's mournful discourse of simulation gave a postmodern flavor to the millennial talk of the end of history. In what he called the "hysteresis of the millennium," a condition seemingly inescapable in the 1990s, the end of history turned out to be one more simulation, a staged event designed to conceal the long-vanished possibility of real change. Although it may have seemed at the start of the decade that the rapid unfolding of events in Eastern Europe and the Persian Gulf promised to kick-start the historical process, Baudrillard saw this as one more illusion: "This revival of vanished – or vanishing – forms, this attempt to escape the apocalypse of the virtual, is a utopian desire, the last of our utopian desires."[5] For Baudrillard, countdown to the end of the millennium awakens the desire for a true end, a genuine apocalypse, and hence a nostalgia, he claims, for the dread-filled nuclear stalemate of the Cold War. But now it seems we are alienated even from the prospect of our own annihilation, which, Baudrillard muses, continues to orbit us like a forgotten cosmonaut.

"The apocalyptic myth," writes Kumar, "holds, in an uneasy but dynamic tension, the elements of both terror and hope. The apocalyptic ending will also signal the millennial beginning. However frightful the contemplation of the end, there is no need to despair: a new world will be born."[6] Although these interrelated elements of destruction and inception continued to have a powerful hold on the imagination, a more characteristic mood in the last years of the century involved a sense that the dynamic tension of which Kumar writes had slackened, with a consequent confusion of endings and beginnings, the sense, in a phrase cited from Derrida, of "an end without an end."[7]

Such a confusion of beginnings and endings, and of endings that fail to end, inflected the writing of the 1990s with a distinctive poetics of hesitation and suspension. The title poem of Jorie Graham's 1997 collection *The Errancy* begins:

>   Then the cicadas again like kindling that won't take.
>   The struck match of some utopia we no longer remember
>   the terms of –
>   the rules. What was it was going to be abolished, what
>   restored?

The poem opens with the difficulty of beginnings and the confusion of criteria. Utopia no longer lives in the imagination as an anticipated millennial conflagration; such hopes have faded, along with the idea of utopia itself. Instead of the flames of destruction, or the plague of insects – or even the bright light of utopia imagined – the poem's speaker hears only "the foghorn in the harbor, / the hoarse announcements of unhurried arrivals, / the spidery virgin-shrieks of gulls." The present continues, dimly heralded, obscurely sensed, but it is a present that has lost the shape, the orientation or direction, that utopia once promised:

>   But here, up on the hill, in town,
>   the clusterings of dwellings in balconied crystal-formation,
>   the cadaverous swallowings of the dream of reason gone,
>   hot fingerprints where thoughts laid out these streets, these braceletings
>   of park and government – a hospital – a dirt-bike run –
>   here, we stand in our hysteria with our hands in our pockets,
>   quiet, at the end of day, looking out, theories stationary,
>   while the freight, the crazy wick, once more slides down –
>   marionette-like its being lowered in –
>   marionette-strung our outwaiting its bloody translation . . .[8]

Graham evokes a pause or space, a *caesura*, in which a dismayed but oddly becalmed subject stands between "the dream of reason" and an incalculable, menacing future. For the dream of reason may have mapped out the livable city on a hill – an avatar of the New Jerusalem – or, as the echo of Goya's phrase reminds us, it may have bred monsters. Characteristically, Graham's lines stretch out, tendril-like, suspending the closure of image or syntax, and enacting the searching yet unresolved movement of the post-utopian condition – a condition, it seems, of unavoidable error, as the poem's title indicates.

Graham carefully reworks the notion of hysteria. As the poem continues to extend its "spidery" network of images, linking the "struck match" of the opening lines to a "christened bonfire" and "scorched comprehension," it begins to convey the sense, as well as the cognitive and ethical challenge, of a far-flung global space, which seems to offer a glimpse of apocalypse just beyond the confines of the writer's page:

> spidery gestures, tongued-over the molecular whiteness,
> squared out and stretched and made to resemble emptiness,
> will take down the smoldering in the terms of her passion
> – sunglasses on the table, telephone ringing –
> and be carried across the tongue-tied ocean,
> through dusk, right through it, over prisons, over clapboard houses
> to which the bartender returns, exhausted, after work,
> over flare-ups of civil strife, skeletons rotting in the arms of
> skeletons, the foliage all around them gleaming[9]

Hysteria suggests an extreme affective response, an over-response, to conditions that tax the subject's comprehension; it also implies that suffering stems from memory, as Freud famously observed. In the case of millennial hysteria, the threat of intoxication by images, reminiscent of Baudrillard's post-historical melancholia, is offset by the haunting memory of utopia, now irretrievably lost.

Graham's poetry of the 1990s offers a compelling and beautifully deliquescent picture of the millennial sensibility, in all its confusion, disappointment, and apprehension. Her poised qualifications evoke the loss of meaning invested in large narrative structures, whether progress, historical consciousness, or utopian desires. The lyric mode, as Graham practices it, sustains the pathos of reservation and privation. For novelists of the decade, the challenge of shaping narratives under the spell of suspended endings remained provocative and pressing.

Don DeLillo's 1991 novel *Mao II* sets millennial anxieties under a clear heading: "The future belongs to crowds."[10] Through several spectacular scenes of crowds, the novel conveys the impression that the future is collapsing into the present and threatening the liberal individualism of late twentieth-century America. The first of these crowds has a threateningly regimented structure and clear apocalyptic dimension. In the prologue, "At Yankee Stadium," DeLillo describes a Unification Church mass wedding officiated by the Reverend Sun Myung Moon himself, an event of stunning strangeness taking place in an archetypically familiar American setting. To the participants, the massed brides and grooms, the Reverend Moon is literally the Messiah, the Second Coming of Christ, his life a parable of suffering and miraculous endurance: "This is a man who lived in a hut made of U.S. Army ration tins and now he is here, in American light, come to lead them to the end of human history." Through mass marriage, the Unification Church pursues a millenarian doctrine: the members of the Church are joined in matrimony in order to establish a world family that, free from the taint of original sin, can live out the promise of God's Kingdom on earth. DeLillo emphasizes the uncanniness of this event by jump-cutting to the bewildered parents scattered around the stands trying to make sense of what they are seeing, not knowing what they should feel. These then are the two sides of millennial hysteria in DeLillo's novel: the overwhelming certainty that amalgamates a crowd, and the fretful doubts, dismay, and isolation of those who witness the crowd.

Following the prologue, *Mao II* takes shape around the figure of a reclusive novelist, Bill Gray. After many years working on a novel he cannot finish, Bill has grown tired of isolation, and tries tentatively to find his way back to the world, first by inviting a photographer to his hideaway, and then by getting caught up, more or less willingly, in a plot involving terrorists and a hostage in Beirut. Bill's secretary, Scott, reports Bill's thoughts about the Moonie mass wedding:

> Mass-married. Married in a public ceremony involving thousands of others. Bill calls it millennial hysteria. By compressing a million moments of love and touch and courtship into one accelerated mass, you're saying that life must become more anxious, more surreal, more image-bound, more prone to hurrying its own transformation, or what's the point? You take marriage, the faith of the species, the means of continuation, and you turn it into catastrophe, a total implosion of the future.[11]

According to Bill, mass-marriage programmatically folds the future – figured as marriage – into the present; it also transforms intimacy into spectacle. As Malcolm Bull has argued, one characteristic feature of the apocalyptic, from the Bible forward, has been the collapse of socially significant distinction and a bewildering or alarming resurgence of the undifferentiated.[12] In Bill Gray's account, the social bond of marriage becomes an image of mutation or disintegration, a portentous sign of things to come.

The mass-marriage is only the first of several such scenes in which a loss of scale, differentiation, and perspective present themselves to characters gripped by confusion. The Moonie bride, Karen, now living in Bill Gray's household, watches the Hillsborough football stadium disaster unfold on the TV screen. The late night newsfeed offers terrible images of football fans crushed against the security fence, pictures that resemble "a religious painting [...] a fresco in a tourist church [...] a crowded twisted vision of a rush to death as only a master of the age could paint it."[13] Such a comparison suggests the aestheticizing nature of the medium of television, which introduces an element of spectatorship, a contemplative detachment, thereby converting a scene of horror into a consumable image. It also hints at the apocalyptic frame the spectator's gaze imposes on the events: the fresco, by implication, might very well be a scene of the Last Judgment, a reminder to the faithful of the final revelation promised in the Bible. But there is an uncomfortable mismatch between the scene of horror and its apocalyptic framing. Watching TV in bed, Karen "sees the crowd pushed toward the fence and people at the fence pressed together and terribly twisted. It is an agony of raised and twisted arms and suffering faces. They show men calmly watching."[14] As a media spectacle, the scene evokes the imagery of apocalypse, even as it desublimates the apocalyptic as a meaningful eschatological patterning. Karen finds herself suspended between alarming significance and a troubling absence of affect.

Other crowds follow: the pro-democracy protests in Tiananmen Square, Beijing; the funeral of Ayatollah Khomeini; the crowds of homeless people in lower Manhattan. Less visible, but no less important for the novel, is the implied crowd of watchers, that disaggregated mass of people gazing at TV screens, rapt or disengaged – it seems hardly to matter. Increasingly, the vast open-air crowds come to represent a particular threat – to the individual, and, by implication, to American sovereignty, as the critic John McClure has observed.[15] At the same time, the novel stresses the symbiosis between the media, gripped by catastrophic news, and the terrorists who work in secret to seize the attention of the West. Terrorists, Bill argues, understand this symbiosis and act accordingly. Novelists, by contrast, are sidelined by the media appetite for spectacle and disaster, and so the rise of the terrorist portends the eclipse of the novelist. *Mao II* eventually flattens the dialectic between the individual and the crowd to the point where the arch-individualist, the writer whose work is expressive of singular identity, is pitted against the terrorist in a zero-sum game. Where the novelist works painstakingly in isolation to express his or her essence through the grain and heft of well-formed sentences, the terrorist sinks identity into a single, violent purpose, or at the very least into the image of a leader – a latter-day avatar of Mao Zedong, a second Mao that doubles the Andy Warhol sketch for which the novel is named. This comparison between writer and terrorist pushes the plot to its logical conclusion – the disappearance of the writer: Bill is inveigled, perhaps in answer to a suicidal impulse, into a haphazard plot to exchange himself with a prisoner held in Beirut. He dies before any exchange can take place, and his passport is stolen from his corpse by one of the nameless indigents who hover on the margins of the narrative. The writer disappears into the crowd. The author's death appears to confirm the dominance of the new era of terror and crowds, even though the epilogue holds out a modestly optimistic symmetrical mirror-image of the mass-marriage when a bride and groom celebrate their wedding in war-torn Beirut. This rather too tidy symmetry and the implausible pairing of novelist and terrorist highlight the novel's tendency to schematize its intuitions. But in so doing, DeLillo introduces a theme – the marginalization of literature by a culture of media and technology – that will assume increasing importance for a number of writers throughout the course of the decade.

Even more than Don DeLillo, the underrated novelist Steve Erickson has forged, through several books, a contemporary millennial mythology. From the beginning of his career he has trafficked in the apocalyptic scenarios and postapocalyptic settings that run through 1990s culture. He has imagined various precipitous declines for his home city, Los Angeles, among them cataclysmic sandstorms (*Days Between Stations*), authoritarianism and ruinous desolation (*Rubicon Beach*), and inexplicable flooding (*Our Ecstatic Days*). He returns over and again to locations and motifs – the vacant hotel, the isolated visionary or madman, the lost girl – to make the city and the time over into his preferred dreamscape, an alternate Los Angeles dominated by bizarre occurrences and obsessions, tenuously anchored to a recognizable reality by references to modern history and popular culture. Of his novels of the 1990s, Erickson's *The Sea Came in at Midnight* focuses most closely on the turn of the millennium; the book marshals an abundance, almost an overabundance, of apocalyptic figures and plotlines.

The Sea Came in at Midnight proceeds by way of flashbacks, memories retrieved and related in a time when the faculty of memory itself seems impaired. One thread of the text, for example, deals with the central character's brief career as a Tokyo "memory girl," one who exchanges memories in confidence with a paying client, an organized response to the disappearance of memory that apparently afflicts postwar Japan. Similarly, characters get caught up in the smuggling of time capsules; these are canisters filled with mementoes and souvenirs, material emblems of memory that are stolen and shipped across the Pacific to an amnesiac nation. The novel's imagined present – the last days of 1999 and the first of 2000 – seems suspended between an inaccessible past and an unimaginable future. Kristin, the protagonist, is propelled in part by a desire for dreams. Unable to dream, she imagines dreams to be memories projected back from the future, and fantasizes that nocturnal sex with sleeping men will somehow give her access to the dreams of others. But as the novel unfolds she stumbles into the millennial fantasies of others, fantasies that are shaped to close off the future – to hasten the end, or render it unthinkable. Leaving her hometown in central California in the closing days of 1999, she gets caught up in a doomsday cult that is in the process of compelling two thousand women to march to their deaths over a cliff into the Pacific Ocean. Narrowly escaping this fate – she was to have been the two-thousandth victim – she finds her way to Los Angeles, where she shelters in the house of a self-styled "apocalyptologist." This individual – he is known only as the Occupant – has spent years plotting a map of the times and locations of the "Age of Apocalypse." He explains:

> Modern apocalypse was no longer about cataclysmic upheaval as related to divine revelation; modern apocalypse, the Occupant told Kristin, speaking with more passion than she had ever heard him express before, was 'an explosion of time in a void of meaning,' when apocalypse lost nothing less than its very faith – and in fact the true Age of Apocalypse had begun well before 31 December 1999, at exactly 3:02 in the morning on the seventh of May, in the year 1968.[16]

The Age of Apocalypse resembles an inverted Age of Aquarius, the New Age of peace and love announced in the 1960s. Rather than peace and love, the last decades of the twentieth century have been dominated, Kristin gathers, by senseless horrors, by a movement away from ideologically motivated violence, typified by the assassination of Martin Luther King, Jr., to meaningless acts of murder, random disasters, and a grotesque amnesia. The Occupant has numerous examples ready at hand – the murders of Alberta King and Martin Luther King's mother, the Manson murders, Bhopal, Chernobyl, the Heaven's Gate suicides. In sum, "the crucial reference points of the Apocalyptic Calendar were moments of nihilistic derangement no scheme could accommodate."[17] At the center of the Occupant's calendar, "the true vortex where all meaning collapsed into blackness," are two events from the spring of 1985 notable for their folly and banality: President Reagan laid a wreath on the tomb of an S.S. officer in Germany; and Coca-Cola chose to discontinue its most successful product, "in order to produce in its place a bad imitation of its obviously inferior competitor."[18] Coming at the end of a litany of horrors, the crashing misstep of the soft drink company hints at the dark absurdity of the Occupant's mad project, as though unreason has no limits, and all kinds of inexplicable events, however banal, can be cast into the web of apocalyptic unmeaning.

The novel follows several paths that lead out of, but also back into, this nihilistic labyrinth. Various plotlines diverge, only to intersect much later, suggesting that the character arcs, often involving fruitless searches and obsessive quests, resemble the geometry of the Occupant's calendar. One such narrative follows a notorious pornographer, Lulu Blu, and uncovers her connection with the filming of a fake "snuff movie," supposedly the inspiration for a rash of genuinely murderous porn films. Consumed with guilt over her role in unleashing such atrocities, Lulu spends decades tracking down and destroying every copy of the movie she helped make, abandoning her daughter (Kristin) along the way. A second thread traces the Occupant's career back to the inaugural moment of the Age of Apocalypse, aged eleven, when he lived in Paris at the time of the May '68 events, and a gunshot from his parents' bedroom precipitated citywide rioting. It is this outcome – an act of violence with enormous, unintended consequences – that sheds light on the portentous phrase the Occupant applies to the modern apocalypse: "an explosion of time in a void of meaning." For the gunshot from a crime of passion (the Occupant's mother shoots her rival) occurs at a moment of maximum tension between the police and the student protesters in the streets of Paris, a spark that ignites the chaotic conflict that engulfs the city.

The Occupant's story suggests that predictions and the retrospective plotting of events might be equally inadequate. Instead, the meaning of historical narrative disappears punctually with the irruptive and anarchic force of events. Erickson's mythology of the millennium lays claim to a historical period – from 1968 until the end of the century, and perhaps beyond – but also challenges the idea that these decades can be understood except as a series of implosive events that defy understanding, that, indeed, swamp understanding with senseless horror – an apocalyptic deluge at the level of comprehension.

For DeLillo and Erickson alike, the menacing scenes of millennial confusion are inescapably connected with media technologies. Lulu Blu, for example, tries to undo the damage her pornography career has done by burning the offending videotapes and daubing the ashes on television satellite dishes, a form of apotropaic magic enacted against the new technologies that typified the 1990s. The technologies of satellite television, home computing, and the Internet produced the new media landscapes of the end of the century; they presented an important source of the millennial anxieties with which novelists, anticipating cultural change, grappled as the year 2000 approached.

Indeed, as the clock ticked down toward the end of the millennium, widespread uncertainty and anxiety arose in connection with the Y2K computer bug. All sorts of software coded during the previous decade had, as it turned out, been built on existing systems that had saved the then-scarce memory by shortening dates; when the calendar turned over to the year 2000, experts feared the dating code would not recognize the new date or recognize it wrongly, perhaps jumping back to 1900. So the apprehensiveness associated with the turn of the millennium took on a strangely literal quality: it was the date itself that would cause chaos, not what it signified in our "centurial" imaginings.[19] Although the problems caused by the date conversion turned out to be minor – no planes fell out of the sky, no missiles launched in error – the fears of mayhem caused by a widespread software glitch gave a vivid illustration of the condition of living in what Ulrich Beck has called "a risk society."[20] Fear of the Y2K bug stemmed from the sense that we now live in a society so networked and interconnected that a seemingly small computer error might have enormous consequences. It highlighted the extent to which our safety and security depend on the digital technology that now pervades the entirety of social life.

For writers the awareness of the digitalization of society and culture increased sharply during the 1990s. Computers and the Internet changed patterns of marketing and consumption, and as new venues for sales and the promotion of books opened up, along with new spaces for reviewing and discussion, the existing institutions of literature often perceived the emerging digital landscape as a threat. For some novelists this perceived problem felt overwhelming, a threat to the production of novels as well as a threat to reading in general. In a well-known essay published in *Harper's* in 1996, Jonathan Franzen stated the problem, as he saw it, in blunt terms. American novelists face a culture dominated by "technological consumerism:" "to ignore it is to court nostalgia. To engage with it, however, is to risk writing fiction that makes the same point over and over: technological consumerism is an infernal machine, technological consumerism is an infernal machine."[21] Franzen's essay recounts his rethinking of the novel, his approach to writing fiction, and his eventual embrace of what he saw as fundamental and perennial novelistic concerns.

Nonetheless, the challenge of writing fiction that would reflect the rapid social and cultural changes brought into being by digitalization encouraged some writers to investigate the narrative potential of new technologies. John Barth, another postmodern writer deeply invested in the long history of the novel, made use of the external features of hypertext to explore the possibilities of fiction in an imaginary new space in the story "Click," and then, on a much larger scale, in his 2001 novel *Coming Soon!!!*, which dramatized the overlap, or border war, between old-fashioned postmodern intertextuality and new-fangled hypertext fiction – a self-consciously millennial drama, with the trappings of biblical apocalypse and Y2K thrown in for good measure. In novels involving computer networks, artificial intelligence, and virtual reality, Richard Powers in *Galatea 2.2* and *Plowing the Dark* fashioned narratives that captured some of the breathless promise and disturbing implications of the new digital technologies.

These novels established a place where science fiction and more traditional modes might usefully interact. Among the most ingenious of such novels to adopt this approach is *The Walking Tour* by Kathryn Davis. Davis's novels are intricate, elliptical, and often uncanny or magical. In *The Walking Tour* Davis achieves an intriguing fusion of unlike genres; she mixes travel narrative, dystopia, and folk tale to tell an apocalyptic story of insidious technological menace. She imagines a technology, inspired by the Internet, that would allow readers to rewrite anything they read, opening texts to limitless changes and undermining any principle of ownership or fidelity to the written word. To picture the consequences, the novel draws from the early Welsh narrative collection *The Mabinogion*, particularly the story of Manawydan and the magical fall of mist that swallows up his lands and people. In *The Walking Tour* the sinister enchantment comes from the new text-sharing software. Davis tracks her characters on a walking tour of Wales just before they lose everything, and long after, when the central characters' daughter, living in a bleak future of technological backwardness and species mutation, tries to make sense of the last days of her parents and their friends. The novel leaves us with the uncertainty of what is to come and with the mystery of transformations – one world has become another, but art as the bearer of memory offers a fragile thread connecting them across a period of cataclysm.

Davis's imagined future in the novel is a dark world of random genetic mutation and climatic disaster. This, too, is the currency of the millennial imagination. As Bruno Latour points out, 1989 was not only notable for the fall of the Berlin wall and the revolutions that swept through Eastern Europe; it was also a year in which Paris, Amsterdam, and London held the first international conferences on the state of the global environment.[22] Through the remaining years of the twentieth century, awareness of the crisis of anthropogenic climate change, depletion of the ozone layer, and the destruction of habitats around the world only grew stronger. This too contributed to the millennial concerns of American writing, though in ways that now, in the second decade of the twenty-first century, seem surprisingly oblique. DeLillo's major novel of the 1990s, *Underworld* (published in 1997) sifts through the wreckage and waste of the Cold War, examining cultures of memory and environmental toxicity, the processing of garbage, and the keeping of secrets. The novel ends with a vision of the Internet as a millennial space in which the living and the dead comingle, and everything floats free of time and space, each thing connected to every other. Sister Edgar, a nun who plays a small but important role in the novel, finds herself in cyberspace, the afterlife of a new century, and learns that the unearthly presence implied throughout the web is not God but the atomic bomb, the apocalyptic vision at the beginning and end of all the teeming linked nodes of the web.

DeLillo's sense of interconnectedness, thematized in *Underworld* as paranoia, has an ecological dimension as well. The paranoid characters of postmodern fiction fear the plots that seem to enmesh a range of events, but the millennial imagination might also perceive the connections as evidence of the inextricable links between human beings and their environment. Richard Powers makes this point forcefully in his 1998 novel, *Gain*. The novel has a simple but effective structure. It intersperses two narratives, one concerning the growth and expansion of an American company from its nineteenth-century roots in soap manufacture to its late twentieth century expansion into foods, fertilizers, and pharmaceuticals; the other concerns a middle-aged woman living at the end of the century who is diagnosed with ovarian cancer, endures grueling treatments, and finally faces her unavoidable demise. Although there are crude parallels to be drawn between the runaway growth of a business and the metastases of cancer, the important connection between the narratives lies in the recognition that the success of the corporation has been achieved at the expense of the environment, human and non-human alike, in which it has flourished. Just as the Clare Company has myriad enterprises and a global reach, so soil, air, water, and human bodies are contaminated by the chemicals the company produces. Capitalism, it seems, is now inseparable from nature.

In the first decades of the third millennium, narratives of global disaster and postapocalyptic survival have proliferated to the point of cliché. Popular novels and movies, as well as some serious fiction, have dealt time and again with the ultimately numbing spectacle of our demise, a sign of the ineluctable fact of environmental catastrophe – but also of a corresponding failure of the imagination. George Saunders, currently one of American fiction's sharpest satirists, published during the nineties a highly prescient novella, "Bounty," which details a brutal postapocalyptic environment that turns out to be a theme park for the rich, a pleasure garden staffed by the unfortunate mutant victims of the very disaster they stage on a daily basis for paying guests. In the wake of the year 2000, it seems that we have not lost our taste for apocalypse; indeed, we now perhaps have learned to take an ominous and oppressive pleasure in the spectacle of catastrophe. As signs of environmental catastrophe become increasingly obvious, challenging the literary imagination, we are obliged to wonder whether a Doomsday Clock can measure the dawning understanding that it is already too late.

NOTES

1. Frank Kermode, *The Sense of an Ending: Studies in the Theory of Fiction* (New York: Oxford University Press, 2000), 11.
2. Ibid., 13–14.
3. Fredric Jameson, *Postmodernism: Or, the Cultural Logic of Late Capitalism* (London: Verso, 1991), 1.
4. Krishan Kumar, "Apocalypse, Millennium and Utopia Today," in *Apocalypse Theory and the Ends of the World*, ed. Malcolm Bull (Oxford: Blackwell, 1995), 206.
5. Jean Baudrillard, *The Illusion of the End,* trans. by Chris Turner (Stanford, CA: Stanford University Press, 1994), 117.
6. Kumar, "Apocalypse, Millennium and Utopia Today," 202.
7. Ibid., 207.
8. Jorie Graham, *The Errancy* (Hopewell, NJ: Ecco, 1997), 4.
9. Ibid., 5.
10. Don DeLillo, *Mao II* (New York: Viking, 1991), 16.
11. Ibid., 80.
12. Malcolm Bull, *Seeing Things Hidden: Apocalypse, Vision and Totality* (London: Verso, 1999), 84.
13. DeLillo, *Mao II*, 33–34.
14. DeLillo, *Mao II*, 33.
15. John A. McClure, *Late Imperial Romance* (London: Verso, 1994), 145–148.
16. Steve Erickson, *The Sea Came in at Midnight* (New York: Avon, 1999), 49.

17 Ibid., 51.
18 Ibid., 52.
19 Kermode, *The Sense of an Ending*, 189.
20 Ulrich Beck, *Risk Society: Towards a New Modernity*, trans. Mark Ritter (London: Sage, 1992).
21 Jonathan Franzen, "Perchance to Dream: In the Age of Images, a Reason to Write Novels," *Harper's Magazine*, April 1996, 43.
22 Bruno Latour, *We Have Never Been Modern*, trans. Catherine Porter (Cambridge, MA: Harvard University Press, 1993), 8.

CHAPTER 2

Angels, Ghosts, and Postsecular Visions

Brian McHale

Angelicism

In the 1990s, there were angels in America. Some of the most conspicuous of them appeared right at the hinge between the eighties and nineties, in Tony Kushner's two-part epic drama of that title. By the second decade of the new millennium, they were mostly gone. Kushner's *Angels in America* returned at the end of 2003 as an all-star cable television adaptation directed by Mike Nichols, but the most conspicuous pop-culture angels of the new millennium might have been the ones in Danielle Trussoni's bestselling novel, *Angelology* (2010), and its sequel *Angelopolis* (2013). (A third volume, to round out the inevitable trilogy, is promised.) *Angelology* reveals how attenuated the angel motif had become by the 2010s. A kitsch product, it echoes – weakly and belatedly – not only Father Andrew Greeley's theological angel romances of the eighties and nineties (*Angel Fire* [1988], *Angel Light* [1995], *Contract with an Angel* [1998]), but also other bestselling genre fictions of the era: J. K. Rowlings' Harry Potter novels (1997–2007), Stephenie Meyer's *Twilight* series (2005–2008) of vampire romances, and Dan Brown's *The Da Vinci Code* (2003). But it is the sheer volume of this novel's angel lore, clumsily transmitted via encyclopedia entries, lectures by learnéd angelologists, and other thinly veiled data-dumps, that reveals the exhaustion of the angel motif. Once there were angels everywhere, in pop culture and aesthetically ambitious literature alike; now there is only *Angelology*.

Harold Bloom, who dubbed the popular obsession with angels "angelicism," regarded it as a kind of "populist poetry."[1] He plausibly dated its onset to 1990, when Sophy Burnham's *A Book of Angels* became a surprise bestseller, inaugurating a publishing boom in angel books.[2] The angel-book craze swept along in its wake a flock of angel narratives in various media, from the CBS television series *Touched by an Angel* (1994–2003) through the big-screen John Travolta vehicle *Michael* (1996), to the

Hollywood remake of Wim Wenders and Peter Handke's art film *Der Himmel über Berlin* [*Wings of Desire*] (1987) under the title of *City of Angels* (1998). The craze also created or reinforced a market for collectible angels – posters, calendars, mantelpiece tchotchkes, garden statuary, etc. – as well as wearable ones – T-shirts, jewelry, even lingerie in the "Angel" line introduced by the undergarment retailer Victoria's Secret in 1997. The highwater mark of popular culture's angel obsession might be said to have been symbolically reached on or about February 7, 1995, when Judge Lance Ito, presiding over the intensively televised and racially charged "trial of the century" – that of O. J. Simpson, for a double murder – reprimanded prosecutor Marcia Clark for wearing an angel pin similar to one worn by the murdered wife's relatives.

But angels were not just a pop-culture phenomenon; they flourished also in ambitious and cutting-edge art of the nineties. They enjoyed, says Roger Gilbert, "a special ubiquity" in serious poetry of the decade,[3] and he lists, by way of confirmation, no fewer than twenty-five books of American poetry published in the nineties with "angel" in their titles. Kushner's *Angels in America*, a touchstone of serious drama in the nineties, is typical of the era; so, too, is the crossover artist Laurie Anderson's 1989 CD *Strange Angels* and her angel-filled *Empty Places* world tour (1989–1990) in support of the CD. Markedly different, but just as typical in its own way, was Don DeLillo's story "The Angel Esmeralda" (1994), later incorporated in his major megafiction of the late nineties, *Underworld* (1997). This short story narrates a case of collective delusion – or vision? – when an entire South Bronx community sees, or thinks it sees, the face of a murdered girl in a billboard advertisement for orange juice. Is DeLillo being ironic, or does he actually spot a glimmer of transfiguration in the folds of consumer culture? It is impossible to say.[4]

DeLillo's Esmeralda reflects one type of nineties angel, Kushner's angels another type; they mingle strangely throughout the decade. Orthodox Christian angelology conceived of angels as beings of a different order from our own – divine intermediaries created separately from us at the beginning of the world, sublime and radically alien. This is the basis for Kushner's angels, whom he ironizes without, however, ever degrading or demeaning them. The alternative, heterodox model, which crept into the popular imagination during the nineteenth century, originated with the Swedish scientist and visionary, Emanuel Swedenborg (1688–1772). In Swedenborg's visions of heaven, the angels aren't beings of a different order but rather spirits of the human dead. In place of the angelic hierarchy of orthodox angelology, Swedenborg substituted a kind of spiritual career-ladder that the dead could ascend as they achieved ever-higher levels of posthumous spiritual perfection.[5] Traces of this Swedenborgian model are visible among the South-Bronx visionaries of DeLillo's story, and in many other quarters of both popular and high-art angelology.

The question implied by this juxtaposition of models is this: are angels basically ourselves transfigured, or are they radically other? Popular culture can blithely live with such contradictions, as the nineties abundantly illustrate, but more serious artistic expression strives to reconcile them somehow. On the brink of the decade, for instance, Wenders and Handke approached it one way in *Wings of Desire*, where angels yearn for human experience to the point of abandoning their angelhood for the privilege of *being us*. Joseph McElroy, in his 1200-page meganovel of the same year, *Women and Men* (1987), approached it another way. Here angels seem to hover above the characters, monitoring them from outside, slipping from one to another in defiance of time and space, and sometimes dipping into their minds. They behave, in other words, much like the omniscient narrators of nineteenth-century fiction,[6] ontologically superior to human characters, investing them at will with their own angelic consciousness.

The poet Jorie Graham, in her late-nineties collection *The Errancy* (1997), approaches it yet another way. One strand in the complex weave of this difficult book is a set of six "guardian angel" poems distributed irregularly across the volume. In some of these poems, the angel is ourselves, in others it is radically alien, and in still others it aspires to become us. It is the wholly human hostess who is the metaphorical guardian of the "little utopia" of her party in the poem of that title ("The Guardian Angel of the Little Utopia"), like all-too-human Clarissa Dalloway in Virginia Woolf's novel. In "The Guardian Angel of Self-Knowledge" and "The Guardian Angel of Private Life," by contrast, the voice and point of view are that of utterly non-human angels, casting an estranged eye on human experience. In "The Guardian Angel of Not Feeling," the inhuman and perhaps malevolent angel seems to apostrophize a human being, presumably the poet, directing her to perform a strange, ritualistic parody of the act of writing.[7] But in "The Guardian Angel of Point of View," as in Wenders and Handke's *Wings of Desire*, the angel expresses envy for the very limitations of the merely human point of view, "the limits of the single aperture" as distinct from the boundless, all-over perspective that angelic experience evidently entails.[8]

"*The Errancy* may have been the decade's most representative book of poems," Gilbert writes, "both in its distinctive mix of religion, myth, and philosophy and in its crossing of traditional lyric modes... with the disjunctive forms developed by Language poets."[9] "Representative," yes, but is it really appropriate to attribute "religion" to Graham's poetry, exactly? For all its allusions to theological thinkers such as St. Anselm and Pascal, and despite the fact that the volume climaxes in an "Easter Morning Aubade," it is not clear that *The Errancy* actually embraces religious ideas or sentiments. In this respect, it resembles many of the other cultural products of nineties angelicism. They are all, perhaps, less religious or even spiritual than postsecular – which is not quite the same thing.

Postsecularism

A distinctive feature of the angels of the nineties, high as well as low, is their dissociation from orthodox religious contexts and their affiliation instead with other metaphysical phenomena and violations of physical law – with ghosts, hauntings, and unsanctioned miracles. There are, for instance, no angels in Thomas Pynchon's novel *Vineland* (1990), as might have been expected from the author of *Gravity's Rainbow* (1973), a text top-heavy with angels – or rather, no *actual* angels, only discredited and metaphorical ones.[10] Nevertheless, even in the absence of angels, close encounters of a metaphysical kind abound: intimations of "messages from beyond"[11]; visits to the afterlife, actual realms of death immediately adjacent to our own world, near enough that passage between the worlds is easy; even traces of what can only have been an incursion by the sci-fi movie-monster Godzilla.[12] It is even possible in the *Vineland* universe to earn a living as a "karmic adjuster," working out the injustices of guilty and aggrieved ghosts who remain in limbo, dead but lingering on. Pynchon calls the undead of *Vineland* "Thanatoids," which we learn "means 'like death, only different'"[13] – dead-*ish*.

Similarly, in Ana Castillo's *So Far from God* (1993), miracles, hauntings, and apparitions familiar from magical realist fiction of the Latin American *Boom* and other global postcolonial literatures mingle with channeling, psychic healing, and other phenomena of North American New Age spirituality. Strongly reminiscent of magical realism, for instance, is an inexplicable rain of starlings,[14] which recalls the plague of butterflies in Salman Rushdie's *Satanic Verses* (1988), but also recalls the tabloidesque incredible-but-true phenomenon of frogs or other animals falling from the sky, as they do at the climax of Paul Thomas Anderson's film *Magnolia* (1999).[15] The matriarch figure of Castillo's novel, Sofi, has four doomed daughters, all of them miracle-prone. The daughter called La Loca, miraculously resurrected from the dead, flies to the church roof.[16] Another daughter, Caridad, runs away to live as a hermit in a cave in the Sangre de Cristo mountains, but when she's finally captured she has miraculously become too heavy to lift.[17] Later she will leap suicidally from a mesa hand-in-hand with her beloved, Esmeralda, and their bodies will miraculously disappear into thin air, never to be recovered.[18]

Sofi's daughters are also haunted and ghost-ridden, or they are themselves the ghosts who do the haunting. La Loca is visited by La Llorona, the Weeping Woman of Mexican legend who haunts the earth seeking the children she drowned in order to elope with her lover. La Loca's sister Esperanza, kidnapped and killed in Saudi Arabia with her TV crew during the First Gulf War, haunts their mother; later on, so does La Loca herself.[19] Hilariously, when the three strange siblings attend their sister Fe's wedding, they each do so in a different, ontologically ambiguous present/absent state – there but not there:

> [The bride's family] more or less attended. Her parents were present. Loca watched the ceremony from outside the church, peering in through the open door. Caridad was not physically present but "channeled" in her aura. And Esperanza was seen there by some, but not by everybody.[20]

Castillo and Pynchon, together with the other writers mentioned in this chapter, are symptoms of what John McClure has called "postsecuralism." By this he means *not* reactionary fundamentalism, the retreat to scriptural literalism and other forms of religious certainty reflected in, e.g., James Redfield's New Age adventure novel *The Celestine Prophecy* (1993), the *Left Behind* series (1995–2007) of the fundamentalist novelists Tim LaHaye and Jerry Jenkins, or Mel Gibson's sado-pious film *The Passion of the Christ* (2004). McClure is thinking, rather, of forms of artistic expression (narrative fiction in particular) that register disenchantment with mere secularism and a yearning for spirituality without fleeing to faith, whether orthodox or heterodox. The "signature" of such fiction is "the rearticulation of a dramatically 'weakened' religiosity with secular, progressive values and projects."[21] Postsecular writers are practitioners of "weak religion" or "weak ontology," in the spirit of the Italian philosopher Gianni Vattimo's "weak thought," a modest, self-limiting alternative to the robust metaphysics of Heidegger and the Western philosophical tradition generally.[22] Typically in such fictions, "a fundamental element of a specific religious ontology is weakened but retains a certain shaky power: it is taken out of its original context and combined with alien elements, challenged, and revised."[23] "[P]eople are born again, the dead are brought back to life, gods walk the Earth, and windows open in the walls of the secular world."[24] "[T]the walls of the visible world come down," McClure writes, doors open, angels break through, zones... are suddenly opened to one another. But the openings are, without exception, emphatically partial and the world revealed complex... [T]he openings that occur extend [characters'] vision in limited ways, disclose unmapped zones and require them to practice, if they can, the difficult arts of discernment.[25]

Angels break through, as in Kushner's *Angels in America* or Graham's "guardian angel" poems; zones open to one another, as in the neighboring worlds of the living, the dead, and the dead-ish in Pynchon's *Vineland;* characters peek through loopholes in the visible, as the sisters do from their various ambiguous vantages in Castillo's *So Far from God;* La Loca is brought back from the dead; starlings and frogs rain from the sky. The world begins to pivot from secular to postsecular, and everyone practices, with difficulty, the arts of discernment. Difficulty of discernment is in part a consequence, no doubt, of the heightened ontological pluralism of an early-nineties world disoriented by the abrupt disappearance of Cold War alignments, its disorientation further aggravated by the onset of new technologies that multiplied realities, and bored holes between worlds. These new technologies included cellular telephony, ripe with opportunities for uncanny bilocation; the World Wide Web, still a novelty in the early- to mid-nineties; and the interfaces of personal computers, through whose windows one peered into other planes, other spaces.

Plague Angels

One dimension of postsecularism in the nineties was the struggle to come to terms, imaginatively and otherwise, with the specter of mortality raised by the AIDS epidemic. Still untreatable in 1990, posing an existential threat especially to America's gay communities, AIDS, though then as now incurable, was brought increasingly under control as the decade advanced. Angels came to be associated with the discourse surrounding the AIDS epidemic, a phenomenon that Kushner's *Angels in America* both reflects and reinforces. The connection was an obvious one to make, given angels' traditional association with death on the one hand (not least through their ubiquity in cemetery statuary and war memorials), and their appropriation by the gay community on the other. Twentieth-century gay subcultures "queered" the figure of the angel, which had been "feminized" in the Victorian era but in traditional iconography of earlier times had been male or androgynous.[26] The term "angel" is itself gay slang for a male homosexual, an affirmative alternative to the insulting or self-deprecating "fairy."[27] A gay subtext is readily discernible in many later twentieth-century angel texts,[28] from Beat iconography (Kerouac's "desolation angels," Ginsberg's "angel-headed hipsters"[29]) down to the angel figures of gay writers such as James Merrill and Tony Kushner and the angel logo of the gay graffiti artist Keith Haring (1958–1990).

"Not surprisingly," Roger Gilbert writes, "AIDS was a significant presence in much nineties poetry and undoubtedly played a role in the widespread turn to religious themes and tropes."[30] One of the angel titles that Gilbert calls attention to is Reginald Shepherd's *Angel, Interrupted* (1996). Like other poetry collections of the decade, this one makes a connection between angels and the AIDS plague, but it does so subtly and obliquely. These are explicitly homoerotic poems, frankly expressing the desire of a black man for white men. At least one of these poems confronts the AIDS epidemic head-on: "A Plague for Kit Marlowe," an elegy for the gay British filmmaker Derek Jarman, who died of AIDS in 1994.[31] Shepherd's poems are perfused with classical mythological allusion, and some of the classical figures are winged: "In Plato the soul has wings (strange irritations/at the shoulder blades)." Does this count as an angel? Apart from a mordantly ironic "angel of apostate spectators," the only angels identifiable as such are the one in the title and in a related prefatory poem, "The Angel of Interruptions." The book's title surely derives from that of Susan Kayser's bestselling memoir *Girl, Interrupted* (1993; film adaptation, 1999), in which Kayser tells of her life's interruption by mental illness. In the spirit of Kayser's memoir, Shepherd's "Angel of Interruptions" is a poem of unmaking or erasure, its angel a deconstructive angel.[32] The ultimate reference here, unspoken and perhaps unspeakable, seems to be the AIDS crisis, interrupter of lives – arguably the subtext of the entire book.

Also mentioned by Gilbert in his survey are the angel figures in Mark Doty's *My Alexandria* (1993). Doty's poetry of the gay experience reflects both the pre-AIDS days and the AIDS crisis as it impacted his personal life through his partner's infection. Doty is in dialogue with gay predecessor poets (as well as straight ones, it goes without saying), including Hart Crane ("Almost Blue"), and the Greek-language poet Constantine Cavafy ("Days of 1981," "Chanteuse," and the title *My Alexandria*), perhaps others as well. Conspicuously present, though unacknowledged, is James Merrill, whose trilogy of book-length poems, *The Changing Light at Sandover* (1976–82), cannot help but be evoked by the Ouija-board episodes of spirit communication in Doty's poems "Fog" and "Lament-Heaven."

Merrill famously (or maybe notoriously) obtained the visionary texts around which he constructed his *Changing Light* trilogy from Ouija-board sessions with his life-partner David Jackson.³³ A Ouija board, of course, is a game board printed with letters and numbers on which a pointer of some kind – traditionally a teacup – slides easily, guided by the fingers of two or more collaborators to spell out messages, letter by letter; or rather, the collaborators rest their fingers on the pointer *without* consciously guiding it, and spirits from beyond allegedly take control of the pointer and pick out the messages. In Doty's case, the pivotal Ouija moment occurs in "Fog." Here the spirits that he and his partner are in touch with over on the other side of death seem to be contending among themselves for the right to communicate through the Ouija board with their living interlocutors:

> It seems a cloud of spirits
>
> numerous as lilac panicles vie for occupancy –
> children grabbing for the telephone,
>
> happy to talk to someone who isn't dead yet?
> Everyone wants to speak at once, or at least
>
> these random words appear, incongruous
> and exactly spelled: *energy, immunity, kiss.*
>
> Then: *M. has immunity. W. has.*
> And that was all.³⁴

M., presumably Mark, has immunity, while his partner W. has – what? AIDS? Like the spirits competing to be heard, "word[s] that [begin] with P" keep bubbling up into the poem – *porcelain, planchette, peony, porch, public, phantom* – all except the one P-word that Doty cannot bear to think or say: "positive," as in HIV positive.

In common with the spirits who communicate through Ouija boards or automatic writing, angels are otherworldly figures of communication between worlds – divine messengers, bearers of annunciations. Glimpsed already in the very first poem of *My Alexandria* ("Demolition"), the angel finally emerges fully into view in the poem that directly addresses Doty's partner's positive test results: "The Wings," a poem explicitly in dialogue with Wenders and Handke's *Wings of Desire*, and implicitly with Doty's precursors, Merrill and Kushner. The angel here is a product of poetic making, literally a work of the imagination, willed into existence by the poet to protect his threatened beloved.³⁵ Our final glimpse of the angel comes in the last of these poems, "Lament-Heaven," another text animated by messages transmitted through the Ouija board. As heard by the poet, music played by a young violinist in a church is "a crowd of wings":

> I heard it, the music
> that could not go on without us,
> and I was inconsolable.[36]

"Inconsolable" is literally the book's last word.

Reality Deficits

Postsecular angels of the nineties, then, among their other functions, serve as an imaginative tool for thinking about and perhaps coming to terms with the AIDS epidemic. Other metaphysical beings serve other urgent functions. The undead, for instance – ghosts and other liminal beings – correlate with the perceived "deficit of reality" in American culture of the era.[37] In the decades leading up to the nineties, commentators had been persistently calling attention to the way that actual lived reality was being leached out of American culture, displaced by simulacra and hyperreality. Celebrities were displacing real people, and staged pseudo-events, real events. Theme parks substituted for real history and real community. Reality television, still in its infancy (the MTV series *The Real World* premiered in 1992), was poised to siphon off whatever remained of lived experience; society itself was becoming spectacle.[38] In this landscape of ersatz experience, the undead sometimes functioned as symptoms of pervasive hyperreality but sometimes, perhaps more surprisingly, as compensations for it.

One premonitory vision of the rising tide of hyperreality is to be found in Pynchon's *Vineland*. The world of *Vineland* is saturated with mass-media popular culture, especially *televised* pop culture. Inhabitants of this world consume TV continually, in all kinds of contexts; they interpret their world in terms of TV genres and conventions, and they shape their lives to conform to televisual models.[39] None are better adapted to this regime of the hyperreal than the undead. Reality, for the undead Thanatoids, is entirely simulacral: they "watch a lot of Tube" in their limbo state.[40] Television having trivialized death, why should the undead not be TV addicts? "If mediated lives," reasons the karmic adjuster, "why not mediated deaths?"[41] Thanatoids figure here not exactly as metaphors of simulacral reality, but more like metonymies of it – simulation displaced onto human lives (and deaths). The undead turn out to be exemplary citizens of a mass-mediated world where TV preempts and devalues the real.

Akin in some ways to Pynchon's vision of the undead vegging out in front of the tube is Castillo's ghost-haunted *So Far from God*. Here ghosts of lost children attend conferences of their bereaved mothers – and what is more of a pseudo-event than a conference? Even more tellingly, the ghost of Sofi's daughter Esperanza lingers on posthumously after having lost her life in the very war that Jean Baudrillard once characterized as entirely simulacral. The First Gulf War, Baudrillard controversially asserted, "did not take place," not in the sense that people didn't die – they did, of course, horribly – but in the sense that the entire operation, from beginning to end, was stage-managed with its television coverage in mind: war as reality TV.[42] An "embedded" TV reporter missing in action in a ghost-war, Esperanza is ideally qualified to return as a ghost herself.

Pynchon's and Castillo's undead are simulacra, indigenous to a simulacral world. George Saunders' ghosts are somewhat different. It is not television and its simulacral realties that fascinate Saunders in his inaugural story collection, *CivilWarLand in Bad Decline* (1996), but rather theme parks and the way they preempt and evacuate history and lived experience. Apart from the title story, which takes us behind the scenes of the CivilWarLand park, theme parks also feature in "The Wavemaker Falters," the novella "Bounty," and, with a slight variation (an interactive museum instead of a theme park proper) "Downtrodden Mary's Campaign of Terror."[43] Strikingly, in two of these stories, the title story and "The Wavemaker Falters," the theme park is haunted. In "CivilWarLand in Bad Decline," ghosts of actual Civil War–era inhabitants haunt the ersatz Civil War–themed amusement park and reenact their violent last moments, while in "The Wavemaker Falters" the narrator is haunted by the ghost of a boy he accidentally crushed in a wavemaking machine. In "CivilWarLand," the narrator is himself killed and actually joins the dead; in "Wavemaker," the narrator is threatened with death but spared. Death, ghostly revenants, and theme-park simulation: what is the connection? It seems that in Saunders' wacky version of the postsecular vision, the undead aren't just *symptoms* of the deficit of reality, reflecting or signifying it, as in Pynchon and Castillo; they also to some degree serve to *compensate* for it. Figures of the reality that theme parks are designed to exclude and occlude, they prove to be realer than the theme park's simulacral reality.

The most complex of all these reflections on the relation between ghosts and simulation appears in David Foster Wallace's immense and multifarious novel, *Infinite Jest* (1996). The near-future world of *Infinite Jest* deviates from mid-nineties reality in a number of striking ways – for instance, the whole of North America has been unified under a single federal government, toxic waste is being dumped on a massive scale in a forbidden zone in the far Northeast, Quebecois terrorists are wreaking havoc, etc. – but most of them can be naturalized in science-fictional terms as more or less rational extrapolations, "realistic" at least in the limited sense of not violating physical laws. Not until almost the end of this 1,000-plus-page novel does it swerve abruptly into the fantastic and supernatural – or, let's say, into the postsecular.

Gately, one of the novel's two main protagonists, hospitalized with a gunshot wound, is visited by a "ghostish figure" glimpsed first in his peripheral vision but then, during a fever dream, fully materializing as a "wraith" whose monologue reveals him to be the filmmaker James O. Incandenza (or J.O.I.), the late father of the novel's other main character, Hal Incandenza.[44] More precisely, the wraith is revealed *to the reader* to be J.O.I.; Gately himself does not know J.O.I., and knows nothing about him, and so could not be expected to recognize him. The wraith is troublingly "specific"; for instance, he brings with him a can of Coke with "Oriental-type writing on it" in a language that Gately can't even identify.[45] More troublingly still, he uses diction that Gately *does not know* and would never voluntarily use. Gately experiences this diction as a violation, "a sort of lexical rape," and some of these alien "ghost words" – e.g., "dextral" – actually lodge themselves in Gately's own vocabulary.[46] All of these details disqualify the apparition of J.O.I. from being a mere hallucination emanating from Gately's own mind. We are forced to conclude that the apparition really *is* a ghost and that Gately really *is* being haunted, in blatant violation of everything we have heretofore assumed about the basically realist norms of Wallace's world.

What is the *point* of Gately's "epiphanyish visitation"?[47] Why does the novel swerve so belatedly into ghost-story mode, and what is the apparition of J.O.I. doing here in Gately's hospital room? There are many ways we could begin unpacking this dense episode, but one correlation strikes me as particularly salient. James O. Incandenza, the ghost who haunts Gately and by his very presence reroutes the whole novel in a different, unanticipated generic direction, is responsible for having directed the video cartridge that gives the novel its title: *Infinite Jest*. This video is reported to be so entertaining that it preempts reality in the most literal sense: its viewers become terminally absorbed in it, to the point of dying. Literally unable to take their eyes from it, they dehydrate and starve themselves to death, later to be discovered (like Pynchon's Thanatoids) stone dead in front of their televisions. A hyperbolic figure of the risks of reality's preemption by simulacral entertainment, *Infinite Jest* (the video, not the novel) is appropriately associated with an auteur whose only actual appearance in Wallace's novel is as a ghost.[48] Here, as in Pynchon, Castillo, and Saunders, ghostly haunting correlates with hyperreal simulation.

Toward a Typology of Para-Humans

What do angels, ghosts, and other metaphysical or liminal beings *mean*? What are they *for*? I have entertained here a number of hypotheses about what they meant and what they were for in the American nineties. Angels, I have proposed, were tools for imaginatively confronting the AIDS epidemic that was then ravaging gay communities. Ghosts and the undead reflected, but also sometimes compensated for, the perceived evacuation of reality in an age of simulations. All of these beings, and the miracles and other metaphysical phenomena with which they were affiliated, were means of envisioning a postsecular condition on the far side of monodimensional secularism, but also on the far side of orthodox religious faith.

Other hypotheses are equally plausible. Angels and ghosts have of course meant many different things over the course of human history, and even in recent times their meanings have been shifting and various. Angels are metaphors for mediation and information flow in an era of light-speed communication.[49] They compensate for what might be perceived as a loss of spirituality in contemporary culture, or maybe they offer an alternative to religious orthodoxy more palatable to New Age sensibilities. They reflect anxiety about the approaching millennium, or conversely they capture the longing for apocalyptic change and renewal. Ghosts, for their part, function as figures of traumatic history, a history that whether personal, collective, or both – as in Toni Morrison's *Beloved* (1987) – is as intolerable as it is indispensable, and so on.

In addition, all of these strange beings also figure what Fredric Jameson once memorably called the "reality-pluralism" of postmodernism.[50] They signify the existence, or at least the possibility, of other worlds and other planes of being, of alternative subcultures, lifestyles, values systems, enclaves of meaning, psychological realities – of alternative realities, in an extended sense. Their impact is comparable to the experience identified by the renegade Harvard psychologist John E. Mack, who coined the term "ontological shock" to characterize the testimony of people who claimed to have been abducted by Unidentified Flying Objects (UFOs). Whether the encounter is with angels, ghosts, or aliens, the experience is similar: what one undergoes is the shock of recognizing that there are other worlds besides this one, other orders of being beyond our own.[51]

"Angels are New Age spiritualism's version of cyborgs," writes Maria Damon.[52] True, no doubt; but also, the other way around, cyborgs are techno-culture's version of angels. Just as angels and aliens are in some sense functionally equivalent in popular culture of the nineties,[53] so too are angels and cyborgs, or angels and online avatars. American culture, high and low, has since at least the late 1960s (and no doubt long before) deployed a small repertoire of liminal types, figures poised just across the borderline from humanity – posthumous humans, other-than-humans, greater-than-humans, simulated humans. Collectively, these para-human types serve to define the fully human by their difference – their respective differences – from humanity. Among these types have figured, from time to time, not just the angels and ghosts that I have been discussing here and not only the aliens and cyborgs that are in many ways interchangeable with them, but also other types of the undead – vampires, zombies – and other types of posthumanity – superheroes, clones, replicants, AIs. Among them they form a miniature "ontological ecosystem," in which the types are continually shuffling and realigning themselves, changing their significance and function relative to one another, duplicating and replacing each other, surging into the foreground relative to the others or receding into the background.

Angels seized the cultural center stage in the early nineties, but by the 2010s they had waned in importance, first displaced gradually by vampires (from Anne Rice's vampires to *Buffy the Vampire Slayer* to *Twilight*), then more decisively by zombies. A conspicuous para-human type since George Romero's first *Night of the Living Dead* movie (1968), zombies had all but eclipsed the other types in importance by 2010, their cultural dominance ratified by the appearance the next year of Colson Whitehead's hyperliterate zombie apocalypse novel, *Zone One* (2011). Cyborgs and replicants, posthuman types to be reckoned with since at least *Blade Runner* (1982), have arguably ceded the high ground in the new millennium to clones, as reflected in Kazuo Ishiguro's *Never Let Me Go* (2005) and its elegiac film adaptation (2010). Types change or lose their functions, others compensate; new figures are added to the repertoire. The totality of the ontological system reflects the difficulty of achieving even provisional stability in a period of ontological instability such as the era stretching from the nineties down to the present. "What is human?" the para-humans ask, and they imaginatively empower us to envision an answer – indeed multiple answers, if only provisional ones, subject to continual revision.

NOTES

I want to express my gratitude to Yonina Hoffman for coaching me in the ways of *Infinite Jest*, a novel she knows more about than I ever will. I would like also to thank Elana Gomel for coining the phrase "ontological ecosystem."

Angels, Ghosts, and Postsecular Visions 45

1 Harold Bloom, *Fallen Angels* (New Haven: Yale University Press, 2007), 59.
2 Ibid., 4.
3 Roger Gilbert, "Awash with Angels: The Religious Turn in Nineties Poetry," *Contemporary Literature* 42.2 (2001): 240.
4 See John McClure, *Partial Faiths: Postsecular Fiction in the Age of Pynchon and Morrison* (Athens: University of Georgia Press, 2007), 93–97.
5 Colleen McDannell and Bernhard Lang, *Heaven: A History* (New York: Vintage/Random House, 1990), 181–227; Harold Bloom, *Omens of Millennium: The Gnosis of Angels, Dreams, and Resurrection* (New York: Riverhead Books, 1996), 40.
6 Brian McHale, *Constructing Postmodernism* (London: Routledge, 1992), 203–205.
7 See Gilbert, "Awash in Angels," 262–263.
8 Jorie Graham, *The Errancy* (Hopewell NJ: Ecco, 1997), 78.
9 Gilbert, "Awash in Angels," 260–261.
10 Frenesi Gates, the disgraced heroine of *Vineland*, is metaphorically an outcast angel: moonlight falling across back casts "shadows of her shoulder blades, like healed stumps of wings ritually amputated once long ago, for some transgression of the Angels' Code"; Thomas Pynchon, *Vineland* (Boston: Little, 1990), 261.
11 Ibid., 122, 124.
12 Ibid., 142–145, 186–187, 379–380.
13 Ibid., 170.
14 Ana Castillo, *So Far from God* (New York: Norton, 1993), 172.
15 See Takayuki Tatsumi, "Planet of the Frogs: Thoreau, Anderson, and Murakami," *Narrative* 21.3 (2013): 346–356.
16 Castillo, *So Far from God*, 22–23.
17 Ibid., 86–87.
18 Ibid., 211.
19 Ibid., 160–164, 248, 251.
20 Ibid., 176.
21 McClure, *Partial Faiths*, 3.
22 Ibid., 12–13, 129–130.
23 Ibid., 41.
24 Ibid., 3–4.
25 Ibid., 128–129.
26 David Jones, *Angels: A History* (Oxford: Oxford University Press, 2010), 34–36.
27 Maria Damon, "Angelology: Things with Wings," in *Mass Culture and Everyday Life*, ed. Peter Gibian (New York: Routledge, 1997), 206–207.
28 Suzanne Hobson, "A New Angelology: Mapping the Angel through Twentieth-Century Literature," *Literature Compass* 42 (2007): 503.
29 Damon, "Angelology," 208.
30 Gilbert, "Awash with Angels," 256.
31 The poem features a catalogue of AIDS drugs: "I tramp through a closed garden of cures, Foscarnet, Retrovir,/Zovirax, gaudy bouquets which wilt

expensively/before ever reaching you. Roferon, Sporonox,/Leukine and Cytovene..."
32 Gilbert, "Awash with Angels," 258–259.
33 As with W. B. Yeats before him and the spirit-dictated texts the latter received through his wife George's automatic writing, Merrill depended on the Ouija sessions to yield "metaphors for poetry."
34 Mark Doty, *My Alexandria* (Urbana: University of Illinois Press, 1993), 33.
35 Gilbert, "Awash in Angels," 254–257.
36 Doty, *My Alexandria*, 89.
37 See Andreas Killen, *1973 Nervous Breakdown: Watergate, Warhol, and the Birth of Post-Sixties America* (New York: Bloomsbury, 2006), 5–6, 45–76.
38 Jean Baudrillard, "Les précession des simulacres," in *Simulacres et simulations* (Paris: Galilee, 1981), 9–68; Daniel J. Boorstin, *The Image: A Guide to Pseudo-Events in America* (New York: Atheneum, 1985 [1961]); Louis Marin, *Utopics: Spatial Play*, trans. Robert A. Vollrath (Atlantic Highlands NJ: Humanities Press, 1984 [1973]), 239–257; Umberto Eco, "Travels in Hyperreality," in *Travels in Hyperreality: Essays*, trans. William Weaver (San Diego: Harcourt Brace Jovanovich, 1986 [1975]), 3–58; Guy DeBord, *The Society of the Spectacle*, trans. Donald Nicholson-Smith (New York: Zone Books, 1995 [1967]).
39 McHale, *Constructing Postmodernism*, 115–141.
40 Pynchon, *Vineland*, 170.
41 Ibid., 218.
42 Jean Baudrillard, *The Gulf War Did Not Take Place*, trans. Paul Patton (Bloomington: Indiana University Press, 1995 [1991]).
43 Another variant occurs in "Offloading for Mrs. Schwartz," whose narrator produces virtual-reality modules at the expense of wiping the memories of those he "offloads," simulacral experience substituting for and preempting the real thing.
44 David Foster Wallace, *Infinite Jest* (Boston: Little, 1996), 828, 829, 833.
45 Ibid., 830, 833.
46 Ibid., 832; 884; 887, 919–920, 922; 836, 839, 843, 845.
47 Ibid., 833.
48 Unless, that is, J.O.I. is actually *everywhere*, and the entire novel (or large portions of it, anyway) is ghostwritten, or rather ghost-narrated, by the wraith of J.O.I. "*Infinite Jest*," argues J.T. Jacobs, "is a ghost story told by a ghost"; J.T. Jacobs, *The Eschatological Imagination: Mediating David Foster Wallace's* Infinite Jest (Ph.D. Thesis, Department of English, McMaster University, July 2003), 55. According to Jacobs, J.O.I. mediates much of *Infinite Jest* as a surrogate or "author-proxy" (Ibid., 64) for David Foster Wallace himself, allowing the latter to both circumvent the "death of the author" doctrine and ironically to literalize it. I'm not fully persuaded, but the argument is tantalizing, adding a layer of narratological complexity to a novel that is already plenty complex enough.
49 Michel Serres, *Angels: A Modern Myth*, trans. Francis Cowper (Paris: Flammarion, 1995 [1993]), 154.

50 Fredric Jameson *Postmodernism; or, The Cultural Logic of Late Capitalism* (Durham NC: Duke University Press, 1991), 372.
51 John E. Mack, *Abduction: Human Encounters with Aliens* (New York: Scribner's, 1994), 26, 44; see Damon, "Angelology," 207.
52 Damon, "Angelology," 206.
53 Bloom, *Fallen Angels*, 59.

CHAPTER 3

Aging Novelists and the End of the American Century

Marshall Boswell

Endings inspire retrospection. For Normal Mailer, Saul Bellow, John Updike, and Philip Roth, the four white male writers who dominated the postwar American literary landscape, the end of the American century was a moment to take stock of their time. Throughout the 1990s, all four writers produced ambitious, wide-ranging work that, each in its own way, sought to render a fulsome, encompassing assessment of the postwar American experience and, in one case, the entire century. Throughout their illustrious careers, these writers produced work that, in various and ingenious ways, sought to make connections between the private experience of contemporary Americans and the great geopolitical trends of the broader globe – all part of their attempt to take on the challenge of chronicling what was already being called The American Century. The work they produced in the 1990s continued this project of connecting the private with the public, with a new added note of closure and final assessment. Mailer titled his commemorative "greatest hits" collection of essays and excerpts *The Time of Our Time* (1998). Bellow titled his 1994 nonfiction collection *It All Adds Up*. Between 1997 and 2004, Roth would publish two books with the word "America" in the title. Updike, meanwhile, wrapped up his Rabbit tetralogy, which he began in 1959 and finished in 1990, declaring, in his introduction to *Rabbit Angstrom* (1995), the 1500-page omnibus edition of the entire work, "[T]he character of Harry 'Rabbit' Angstrom was for me a way in – a ticket to the America all around me."[1] He also opens the introduction by invoking *Moby-Dick* and *Huckleberry Finn*, indicating not only his hopes for the long-term literary prospects of his crowning achievement but also his continued belief in the notion of a representative novel and a representative character: the great novelist speaking for all men.

This boundless confidence to speak for all ran firmly against the grain of the decade's burgeoning embrace of identity politics and multiculturalism. Novelist David Foster Wallace laid down the gauntlet in his infamous 1998 excoriation of Updike's *Toward the End of Time*, wherein he dubbed

Mailer, Roth, and Updike the "Great Male Narcissists," or the GMNs. For Wallace, these writers represent "the single most self-absorbed generation since Louis XIV," and, as he notes, it is "no coincidence that the prospect of [the Great Male Narcissists's] own deaths appears backlit by the approaching millennium and online predictions of the death of the novel as we know it. When a solipsist dies, after all, everything goes with him."[2] While the work Mailer and Bellow produced during this decade seems unruffled by such criticisms, both Updike and Roth pointedly moved beyond the narrow trough of autobiographical self-absorption that Wallace identifies as their default mode. What's more, even as these aging novelists take one more swing at singing "America," they also, in various ways, address the limitations of this same undertaking. Their 1990s output, for all its ambition, is also marked at times by a diffidence that discloses the vast differences between history and politics, on the one hand, and literature, on the other hand, a gap best captured by Leo Glucksman, a teacher in Roth's 1998 novel *I Married a Communist*, who tells Nathan Zuckerman, "Politics is the great generalizer, and literature the great particularizer, and not only are they in an inverse relationship to each other – they are in an antagonistic relationship."[3] All of the works addressed in this essay – Mailer's *The Time of Our Time*, Bellow's *Ravelstein* (2000), Updike's *In the Beauty of the Lilies* (1996), and Roth's *American Pastoral* (1997) – affirm the particularizing impulse of literature over the generalizing dehumanization of politics or the abstract leveling of history.

Though not a novel, per se, *The Time of Our Time* has been designed by its author to read like one. Meant to commemorate both his seventy-fifth birthday and the fiftieth anniversary of *The Naked and the Dead* (1948), Mailer's breakthrough debut novel, the volume collects more or less the best discrete pieces from Mailer's novels, essays, and "new journalism" works from the late 1960s. Rather than arranging the pieces in the order of their publication, however, Mailer instead chose to arrange the pieces according to "the year [he] had been writing about."[4] As a result, the book's table of contents begins, after two "Preludes," with "The Second World War," and then moves through "The Cold War," "Hollywood," "Convention Time," "Cuba," "Kennedy, Castro, and Oswald," and so on before petering out sometime after "Watergate," after which Mailer's output becomes much more spotty, the monumental *Executioner's Song* notwithstanding. In justifying this curious arrangement, Mailer explains, "Re-reading the bulk of my work in the course of a spring and summer, one theme came to predominate – it was apparent that most of my writing was about America."[5] To the charge – unleveled by himself but implied – of narcissism in assuming this mantle as a national spokesman, Mailer insists, "I hope that this book may stimulate your sense of our time," before going on to affirm that "this is a book nearly all of us have created in our own minds."[6] Mailer here insists that his unique take on the events that have shaped his life should not be read as provisional and positioned by race, class, and gender but rather seen as representative, a part of some collective national whole, a confidence shared in various ways by his fellow GMNs, whether that representative is Updike's Rabbit Angstrom, or the Wilmots of *In the Beauty of the Lilies*, or Roth's assimilated all-American sports hero, Swede Levov.

But Mailer's project, like that of his contemporaries, is not without awareness of its limitations. As early as 1959's *Advertisements for Myself*, Mailer's first collection of bits and pieces and the first prequel to *The Time of Our Time*, Mailer declared, "The sour truth is that I am imprisoned with a perception that will settle for nothing less than making a revolution in the consciousness of our time," a statement reprinted in the recent volume.[7] In order perhaps to avoid too much repetition with the earlier collection, Mailer populates the section of *The Time of Our Time* devoted to the Fifties and Sixties with excerpts from his 1991 novel *Harlot's Ghost*, a late novel epic shipped out into the world long after Mailer had left center stage in the literary limelight. But this strategy also recognizes, whether consciously or unconsciously, how badly much of his early work has dated, a fact borne out by the early work he *does* include, such as: "The White Negro," his existentialist analysis of the 1950s hipster; "The Time of Her Time," the beatnik erotica that gives the entire volume its title ("a salacious object in its time" Mailer reminds us[8]); or the mean-spirited attacks on Kate Millet and 1970s feminism that occupy most of the early '70s material here – all examples that disclose the degree to which Mailer's perceptions, by the 1990s at least, were in fact vastly out of sync with his own time.

Also a figure out of step with his time, Saul Bellow surveys the end of the decade from his position as a member of the neoconservative right, thanks to his connection with Allan Bloom, author of *The Closing of the American Mind* (1987), an extended diatribe against political correctness and multiculturalism in American higher education that became a surprise bestseller in 1987 before going on to inspire a host of imitative volumes, including Robert Kimbell's *Tenured Radicals* (1990) and Dinesh D'Souza's *Illiberal Education* (1991). All of these books date the decline in American values with the countercultural politics of the 1960s, a diagnosis Bellow made in real time, as it were, in his novel *Mr. Sammler's Planet* (1970), the book that first signaled the author's conservative turn. Fittingly, Bellow, who encouraged his friend Bloom to write down his ideas and publish them for the masses, supplied a foreword to *The Closing of the American Mind*, giving the book a prestigious intellectual seal of approval. *Ravelstein*, his final novel of the decade, of the millennium, and of his career, is a *roman a clef* about his friendship with Bloom.

The novel's title character, Abe Ravelstein, has written a bestselling book, which, though unnamed, is clearly meant to invoke Bloom's *Closing*. According to the novel's narrator, a Bellow-like character named Chick, Ravelstein's tome "took you from antiquity to the Enlightenment, and then – by way of Locke, Montesquieu, and Rousseau onward to Nietzsche, Heidegger – to the present moment... He gave you a picture of this mass democracy and its characteristic – woeful – human product."[9] This brief outline captures a bit of Bloom's thesis, which asserts that American liberal democracy, in its embrace of multiculturalism and "openness" to other cultures, has "closed" itself off from the true source of its identity: the Great Books of Ancient Greek and other key works from the Western philosophical canon. This closure also represents a crisis similar to what confronted liberal-minded Germans of the Weimar Republic, just before Hitler's rise. Bloom's thinking was directly influenced by Leo Strauss, the problematic political philosopher whose "esoteric" thinking exerted such an indelible influence over the neoconservative movement that *Time* magazine, in 1996, listed Strauss as "perhaps one of the most influential men in American politics."[10] Similarly, Ravelstein was trained under a one "Professor Davarr" and continued to use "his esoteric vocabulary."[11] Ravelstein's late-career success has also put him direct contact with what he calls "Great Politics," leading to weekend visits with Margaret Thatcher and dinner with Ronald Reagan, while many of his former students "now held positions of importance on national newspapers" and "quite a number served in the State Department."[12] Similarly, Bloom's actual students included Paul Wolfowitz, U.S. Deputy of Defense under George W. Bush and a major architect of the Iraq War, and Francis Fukuyama, author of *The End of History and the Last Man* (1992).

Although Ravelstein's direct access to Great Politics would appear to be a perfect conduit by which Bellow could connect the private with the public, Bellow's two main characters have precious little to say about Great Politics, per se. Rather, the one political thing they do try to address is the Holocaust, or what Ravelstein calls "The Jewish question."[13] Rather than rehearse Bloom's argument in *The Closing* linking the flabby "openness" of pre-Hitler Weimar with contemporary American culture, Chick simply observes that when Ravelstein speaks of "History," he meant the word in "large Hegelian terms... With him gloomy conversations on the 'full particulars' were extremely rare."[14] At the end of his life, however, these Olympian abstractions no longer explain the facts on hand. While trying to understand the Jewish question, Ravelstein concludes, despite his lifelong advocacy for the fundamental importance of abstract, a historicized political thought, "that it is impossible to get rid of one's origins, it is impossible not to remain a Jew. The Jews... were historical witnesses to the absence of redemption."[15] What's more, Chick decides on his own – because Ravelstein "was not able to deliver his conclusions" – that his dear friend decided in the end that a "Jew should take a deep interest in the history of the Jews," while at the same time realizing that "not every problem can be solved."[16] It is no accident that Ravelstein arrives at this concrete conclusion while his body is wasting. As Adam Phillips argues, the "world-historical ringside seats" that Ravelstein inhabits throughout his life and at various points within the novel "keep running up against the centering image of the book, Ravelstein's increasingly dying body."[17] What's important for Bellow here is not abstract politics, but the unendurable biological fact of death. In this regard, Ravelstein's late turn to his Jewish particularity discloses the limits of political philosophy to account for the horrors of human existence.

After surveying the range of responses to the novel, and determining that reviewers tended to like or dislike the book in accordance with their approval or disapproval of Bloom's own politics, John Uhr avers that Bloom's politics per se are not what is at issue; rather, "we should see *Ravelstein* as an important new document on the relationship between literature and politics."[18] As Roth's Leo Glucksman would argue, that relationship is necessarily antagonistic. "Generalizing suffering:" Leo argues, "there is Communism. Particularizing suffering: there is literature. In that polarity is the antagonism."[19] Whereas Ravelstein regarded great issues as solvable when viewed from the heady heights of the Hegelian mountaintop, Chick, and by extension Bellow, ends the novel by insisting that, in the end, those great problems prove ephemeral in light of the obdurate prospect of one's own death. While such a view might fulfill Wallace's charge of solipsism, from a different angle it also confirms Bellow's belief in the superior power of fiction to articulate the human truth that transcends the political, a belief shared by Mailer as testified by the latter's decision to let his fictional account of the CIA's postwar adventures, *Harlot's Ghost*, represent his final word on the great events of the Fifties and Sixties. If, by the late 1990s, the novel was on its deathbed, as Wallace darkly suggested, then these old lions were not about to let it die without a fight.

John Updike also clearly took the "online predictions of the death of the novel" in stride, for his 1990s output, while uneven in quality, showed no flagging in his faith in the medium as an effective means by which to address the times. After completing his great Rabbit tetralogy in 1991, he took one last stab at the Great American Novel via *In the Beauty of the Lilies*, a 500-page, multigenerational saga that charts the spiritual decline of a single American family, the Wilmots, against the rise of Hollywood and televised mass culture. In keeping with Roth's dictum, Updike amplifies this fairly simple and univocal thesis via his sumptuous attention to detail and to the concrete particulars of the Wilmots' representative American experience. In the process, *Beauty* stages a sustained "moral debate" about the social utility of religion – this in keeping with Updike's desire, as spelled out early in his career, to fashion all of his novels as "moral debates with the reader," with the books tending toward what he calls a "yes, but" quality – that is a sustained ambiguity, or at the very least a qualified affirmation.[20] Updike conceived this credo in the early 1960s, at a time when, as Stacey Olster argues, the literary established could "presume[] that Updike's perspective typified the American perspective"; conversely, in the 1990s world of multicultural ascendency and second-wave feminism, such diffidence left Updike "distinctly out of sync with his culture."[21] Perhaps sensing as much, Updike described himself in 1990 as "a sort of helplessly 50s guy."[22] Nevertheless, he never lost faith in the power of fiction to capture what he viewed until the end of his career as the inherent ambiguity of most social problems, and *In the Beauty of the Lilies*, an old-fashioned and unfashionable novel about America and God, represents his last major attempt to weigh in on the major movements of the national experience.

In the opening section, the book's best, Clarence Wilmot, an intellectually ambitious minister in Paterson, New Jersey, feels "the last particle of his faith leave him" at the exact moment that Mary Pickford, filming D.W. Griffin's *The Call to Arms* (1910) across town, faints while on set.[23] James Schiff points out that "the plot of the movie concerns a 'lost jewel beyond price,' which suggests the plot of Updike's novel: the loss of faith."[24] In depicting Clarence's loss, Updike invokes his own early story of religious doubt, "Pigeon Feathers," in which a twelve-year-old Updikeean hero named David Kern (with his "kernel" of faith) accidentally stumbles upon H. G. Wells' secularized, agnostic account of the life of Jesus in the *Outline of History* (1920), an experience that opens up the possibility that *There is no God*, a phrase Updike repeats, often in italics, more than a dozen times in the novel's opening pages. The doubts David feels aren't entirely new to him: rather, "it was as if a stone that for weeks and even years had been gathering weight in the web of David's nerves snapped them."[25] Similarly, Clarence's crisis is brought on by his reading of Robert Ingersoll's *Some Mistakes of Moses* (1879), which he "had been reading in order to refute it for a perturbed parishioner"; and, as with David's spiritual musings, Clarence's own "thoughts had slipped with quicksilver momentum into the recognition, which he had long withstood, that Ingersoll was quite right: the God of the Pentateuch was an absurd bully, barbarically thundering through a cosmos entirely misconceived. There is no God, nor should there be."[26]

Perhaps nowhere is Updike's "yes-but" quality of negative capability more in evidence than in his portrayal of Clarence's spiritual crisis. With the zeal of a fellow atheist, Updike enthusiastically rehearses all of Clarence's intellectual objections to the existence of God. He also stages a series of debates within the novel in which believers of various stripes try, and fail, to lure Clarence back into the fold. In all of these cases, Updike suggests, as a counter to Clarence's intellectual "clarity" (hence his first name), a pragmatic approach to religious faith grounded in the work of William James, who is cited by name by Clarence's affable higher up in the church, Thomas Dreaver, an intellectual himself who serenely doubts the resurrection but who nevertheless, drawing upon Husserl's phenomenology, advises Clarence to regard God as something "we make . . . with our minds, our minds and wills."[27] In all of these debates, Clarence remains steadfast in his non-belief, even as he refuses to push back and undermine his interlocuters' zeal.

Exiled from his church and his vocation, Clarence begins selling encyclopedias door to door, and takes his solace in the movies, whose "[i]mages of other shadows in peril and torment lifted his soul out of him on curious wings, wings of self-forgetfulness."[28] For Clarence and his progenitors, the cinema house becomes "a church with its mysteries looming brilliantly, undeniably above the expectant rows," while the luminous figures on screen emerge as new, modernist gods.[29] Clarence's granddaughter, Esther (or Essie) becomes one of those gods, or rather goddesses – an ascent from small town to Hollywood that Updike based on the real lives of Marilyn Monroe and Doris Day, as evidenced by the list of works adumbrated in his detailed afterword. Conversely, Essie's son, Clark (named after Clark Gable), is left adrift amid the decadent pop culture wasteland of 1980s America and finds meaning only after joining a religious cult based on the Branch Davidians. Both Clark's life and the novel end in a scene of spectacular, apocalyptic violence, all of it captured on CNN. For James Schiff, the exchange of churchgoing with cinema attendance means that "the grand spiritual yearning of American religion has been reduced, through movies and television, to cheapened images on a small box," while the "void created by the absence of God... has triggered the lunacy of contemporary times, in which listless questors like Clark seek redemption by following crazed false messiahs."[30] In its sweeping survey of the twentieth century – the novel deftly touches upon WWI, the "lost generation," the Jazz Age, the Depression, WWII, the sixties, and Reagan – *In the Beauty of the Lilies* tries to make a summative statement about trajectory of American life, and, as Schiff intuits, that trajectory, if one were compelled to generalize, is clearly down.

On closer inspection, however, the novel offers up a much more nuanced portrait, as Updike is careful throughout to address long-standing inequalities and flaws in the Wilmots' America. For instance, in the opening section, as Clarence struggles with his faith, factory workers in his hometown of Patterson push for better wages and are defeated by the factory owners who continue to exploit them. Years later, in the throes of the Depression, Essie waits in line to go see *Lost Horizon* (1937) and overhears a group of white cinemagoers make threatening, racist threats in response to Joe Lewis's boxing victories.[31] By ending the novel with an episode of mass violence borne from crazed religious fundamentalism, Updike was both prescient and eerily prophetic, yet the novel also continually asks us to consider if that closing violence is any worse (or better) than the violence inflicted on turn-of-the-century workers on strike or on African Americans under the yoke of Jim Crow.

What's more, the novel is teasingly ambivalent about the benefit of religious faith in general. Although Clarence ends his life as a hollowed man paralyzed by tuberculosis, his intellectual case against the existence of God is never adequately challenged in the novel. Similarly, if the book has a hero, it is Clarence's son, Teddy, who shares his father's atheism but also distrusts the capitalist ethos of his erumpent country. After training to be an accountant, he finds that "in the maze of borrowing and hidden assets and leveraged debt which is the digestive guts of capitalism Teddy began to feel confined and squeezed... and a little panicky."[32] In contrast with his go-getter brother Jared, who loses everything in the 1929 stock market crash, Teddy chooses small-town life with a crippled wife. He has no God and does not necessarily feel the lack; rather, he experience what Schiff admits is "one of the few successful marriages in the novel."[33] Teddy's "specimen life," as Updike describes his own in the foreword to *Self-Consciousness* (1989), is humble, purely secular, and successful, and, as such, confirms what Peter Bailey has identified as "the reluctantly expanding secularism of Updike's aesthetic."[34] Although God is an absence in the novel, that absence does not necessarily chart a steady decline; rather, Updike offers alternatives along the way to living a secular American life outside the strictures of both spiritual and secular "religion."

A year after its 1996 publication, Michael Wood would see direct connections between *Lilies* and Philip Roth's then new novel, *American Pastoral*, noting that both novels are "hefty and self-consciously American, ... both deal in painstaking and slightly mind-numbing realism, [and] both begin in New Jersey and end in hell."[35] *American Pastoral* would go on to function as the first of a trilogy that also included *I Married a Communist* and *The Human Stain* (2000), the whole of which Roth regarded as "a thematic trilogy, dealing with the historical moments in postwar American life that have had the greatest impact on my generation. I'd say the greatest impact on me, except I don't believe my response is singular."[36] The "historical moments" in mind are the Vietnam War, the McCarthy trials of the 1950s, and the Clinton-Lewinsky scandal, respectively. In each novel, Nathan Zuckerman, Roth's perennial fictional doppelganger, tells the story of an American who has been caught up in one of these historical moments. In language that echoes Updike's description of Rabbit's role in his own fiction, Roth "just wanted these historical debacles to enter into and pass through the characters – I just wanted to find out what that would be like."[37] The best of these remains the first.

According to Claudia Roth Pierpont, Roth originally began *American Pastoral* in 1970, and based it on the case of Kathy Boudin, a member of the Weather Underground who had been arrested for robbery. Roth wrote "fifty or sixty pages and got as far as the explosion, but he didn't know where to go from there," and abandoned the book.[38] When he returned to the novel in the mid 1990s, he made the daughter the antagonist and her father the protagonist, at which point, to quote Updike, Roth had found "his way in – a ticket to the America all around." Updike appears to have been on Roth's mind, for the novel *American Pastoral* most resembles is less *In the Beauty of the Lilies* than *Rabbit Redux* (1971), the second novel in the Rabbit Tetralogy. Both novels are set in the closing years of the Sixties and address the hippie movement, the protest against the Vietnam War, and the general dismantling of the 1950s American bourgeois middle. What's more, both novels focus on an All-American high school athlete who is undone by the cultural revolution occurring all around him. Both novels also feature a female runaway radical. In his memoir, *Self-Consciousness*, Updike recalls heated arguments he had with Roth in the late 1960s about the Vietnam War.[39] Roth later insists that "one of their arguments, somewhat transmogrified, made it into *Rabbit Redux*, with Updike – a defender of the war – in the role of the politically conservative Rabbit, and Roth's views emerging from a black revolutionary character called Skeeter."[40] Roth's original draft of the novel would have been written in the wake of those arguments and in the context of *Rabbit Redux*'s 1970 publication. It is inviting, then, to read *American Pastoral* as Roth's response both to Updike's novel and to Updike himself. In other words, the novel resumes the argument with Updike from the 1960s, but recasts it in a dialogic mirror.

American Pastoral also expands the bounds of what is possible in metafiction. Wallace's inclusion of Roth in his pantheon of Great White Narcissists should also be read within Wallace's own career-long critique of metafiction itself, which, in Wallace's reading, is a form of linguistic narcissism. As Wallace explains in "Westward the Course of Empire Takes its Way" (1989), "Metafiction is untrue" because "[i]t can only reveal. Itself is its only object. It's the act of a lonely solipsist's self-love."[41] By the early 1990s, Roth had clearly written himself into a solipsistic corner, beginning with his 1988 biography *The Facts* and culminating in 1993's *Operation Shylock*, a novel about a novelist named Philip Roth who discovers that someone named Philip Roth is giving lectures in Israel urging the Jews to return to Europe. As Updike observed in his review of the novel, "[T]here has been too much Philip Roth in the writer's recent books," a charge that Roth took personally, according to Claudia Roth Pierpont.[42] But the charge also appears to have challenged Roth to expand his metafictional palate, with remarkable results.

For the novel is in dialogue not only with other novels but also itself, a fact the book's readers overlook at their peril. When it first appeared, many readers read the book as a searing indictment of the Sixties writ large, and hence a conservative about-face on the part of its transgressive author. Conservative writer David Horowitz observed, "Who would have thought that the author of *Our Gang*, an unforgiving '60s satire of the Nixon era, would, in 1997, write a passionate defense of the American way of life, a paean to the America that the '60s had ransacked?"[43] Similarly, Mark Schechner, even after a second reading, described the book as "a screed against the sixties," even comparing it to Bellow's *Mr. Sammler's Planet*.[44] "Has Roth . . . gone NeoCon at last?" Schecter asks.[45] It's true enough that the damage inflicted on Roth's "good man" by the turbulence of the 1960s is shocking, and few readers have failed to note the book's combination of nostalgia and rage. What's more, Roth encourages us to read his fully assimilated hero as a metonymy for America writ large: as a star-struck high school student, Swede possesses an "unconscious oneness with America," while later in life Swede marries a former contestant in the Miss

American contest.[46] The titles he bestows on the novel's three sections – "Paradise Remembered," "The Fall," and "Paradise Lost" – suggest that Roth reads the Sixties as the end of an American paradise.

But those readings would be wrong. A determined atheist and a Jew as well, Roth employs Milton's Christian myth ironically. The paradise that is lost in *American Pastoral* is a paradise *remembered*, a paradise born from nostalgia: as Swede's brother Jerry says of nostalgia, "It's bullshit."[47] Zuckerman encounters Jerry at their high-school reunion, where Jerry goes on to say, "What they sit around calling the 'past' at these things isn't a fragment of a fragment of the past. It's the past undetonated – nothing is really brought back, nothing."[48] The past that Swede's daughter obliterates with her protest bomb isn't an American Eden, but the "bullshit" nostalgic version of America that has excised from its self-portrait what Zuckerman calls "the indigenous American berserk"; Merry, and Roth, detonate that false past, "the daughter and the decade blasting to smithereens [Swede's] particular form of utopian thinking, . . . transport[ing] him out of the longed-for American pastoral and into everything that is its antithesis and its enemy, into the fury, the violence, and the desperation of the counterpastoral."[49]

Why do so many of the book's readers miss this crucial element of Roth's portrait? Partly because Roth deliberately designed the novel to invite just such a misreading. After all, he titled one of his Philip Roth novels *Deception* (1990). The novel we read isn't a novel about Swede Levov but rather a novel about Nathan Zuckerman imagining a novel about Swede Levov. Swede is *Zuckerman*'s counterself, and entirely his invention, one that Zuckerman himself admits is more than likely wrong: "The fact remains that getting people right is not what living is all about anyway. It's getting them wrong that is living, getting them wrong and wrong and then, on careful reconsideration, getting them wrong again."[50] Nathan himself barely knows the Swede: he watched him from afar as a high school student and only encounters him once more in adult life in 1995 when the Swede has remarried and has two sons. At that meeting, Zuckerman finds the Swede to be so bland and superficial as to be unbelievable: "It was as though he had abolished from his world everything that didn't suit him – not only deceit, violence, mockery, and ruthlessness but anything remotely coarse-grained."[51] Rather, Zuckerman learns about Merry and the bomb from *Swede's* counterself: his angry, cynical brother Jerry. Armed only with the few facts about Merry that he learns from his one conversation with Jerry, Zuckerman "dream[s] a realistic chronicle" that is entirely his own invention.[52]

In this doubled strategy, then, Merry, as Swede's antagonist and the arsonist who ushers in the novel's counterpastoral, is Zuckerman's ally; her name, in fact, invokes Jerry, who is also one of her and Zuckerman's doubles. Whereas the Swede considers his daughter's descent into political rage and violence a mystery, Jerry sees her as the embodiment of that same "indigenous American berserk." "You wanted Miss America?" Zuckerman imagines Jerry telling Swede. "Well, you've got her, with vengeance – she's your daughter!... The reality of this place is right up your kisser now. With the help of your daughter you're as deep in the shit as a man can get, the real American crazy shit, America amok!"[53] Merry also possibly provides a way for Roth to reply to Updike. Like Updike himself, Merry suffers from a stutter. Both of Updike's wives were also named Mary. In his explanation for his support for the Vietnam War, Updike singles out the young, affluent protesters as the real targets of his ire. From his perspective, the protesters were "Cambridge professors and Manhattan lawyers and their guitar-strumming children" who were "spitting on the cops who were trying to keep their property – the U.S.A. and its many amenities – intact."[54] Updike also connects his support of the war to his Christian faith: "The world is fallen," he explains, "and in a fallen world animals, men, and nations make space for themselves through a willingness to fight."[55] The solution for that fallen state for Updike is not peace, but Christian salvation.[56] Roth appears to take direct aim at Updike's late explanation not only via his ironic use of a Christian frame, but also through his overt dismissal of Christian salvation entirely. Early in her life, Merry's grandmother on her Christian mother's side surreptitiously has her baptized; Swedes' irascible, intractable father – one of many irascible, intractable fathers in Roth's corpus – argues that Merry's bout of infant colic was directly linked to the baptism. Swede goes even further and wonders, "Perhaps everything bad that *ever* happened to Merry, not excluding the *worst* thing that happened to her, had originated then and there."[57] Updike's fictional dismissal of Roth's arguments against the war by means of his Christian narrative of fall and redemption gets overturned in Roth's novel: there *is* no God, and evil is "ineradicable from human dealings."[58]

While analyzing the novel's complex metafictional narrative structure, Derek Royal observes, "Roth apparently threw his readers off track by purposefully blurring the boundaries between the 'dream' and the 'real.'"[59] This deliberate deception is part of Roth's adherence to his friend Milan Kundera's conception of the modern novel as the supremely ironic art. In *Testaments Betrayed* (1995), Kundera explains, "Irony means: none of the assertions found in a novel can be taken by itself, each of them stands in a complex and contradictory juxtaposition with other assertions, other situations, other gestures, other ideas, other events. Only a slow reading, twice and many times over, can bring out all the *ironic connections* inside a novel, without which the novel remains uncomprehended."[60] According to this model, Swede's nostalgic utopia is affirmed *and* destroyed in the novel. Although Zuckerman's cynical perspective aligns more with Jerry's than with the Swede's, Zuckerman's disappearance *into* the Swede gives the Swede's perspective authority: the narrative, as Shastok explains, "speaks in two voices."[61] As Roth himself put it in an interview he gave on the occasion of his retirement from fiction writing: "The thought of the writer is figured invisibly in the elaborate pattern – in the newly emerging constellation of imagined things – that is the architecture of the book: what Aristotle called simply 'the arrangement of the parts,' the 'matter of size and order.' The thought of the novel is embodied in the moral focus of the novel."[62] This complex formulation can be applied to all the novelists examined here. For inasmuch as their sensibilities might have been forged in a more monolithic time when the white male sensibility still asserted itself as representative, these writers maintained an enduring belief in the power of fiction to provide a specific, concrete, and complex counternarrative to the sweeping metanarratives of history, politics, and religion. As Mailer himself puts it in his foreword to *The Time of Our Time*, "Fiction, as I use the word, is a reality that does not cohere to received axes of fact but is breathed in through the swarm of our male and female movements about one another, a novelistic assumption, for we perceive the truth of a novel by way of the personality of the writer."[63]

NOTES

1 John Updike, *Rabbit Angstrom* (New York: Knopf, 1995), ix.
2 David Foster Wallace, "Certainly the End of Something Or Other, You Would Sort of Have to Think," *Consider the Lobster* (New York: Little, 2005), 51.
3 Philip Roth, *I Married a Communist* (Boston: Houghton, 1998), 223.
4 Norman Mailer, *The Time of Our Time* (New York: Random House, 1998), x.
5 Ibid., ix.
6 Ibid., xii.
7 Ibid., 294.
8 Ibid., 318.
9 Saul Bellow, *Ravelstein* (New York: Viking, 2000), 19.
10 Richard Lacayo, "You've Read About Who's Influential, But Who Has the Power?" *Time*, June 17, 1996, 83. Shadia Drury, among others, has observed that Bloom's *Closing* "is the most successful popularization and application of Strauss's ideas to America"; Shadia Drury, *Leo Strauss and the American Right* (New York: St. Martin's, 1997), 111.

11 Bellow, *Ravelstein*, 10.
12 Ibid., 10, 15.
13 Ibid., 136.
14 Ibid., 124.
15 Ibid., 179.
16 Ibid.
17 Adam Phillips, "*Ravelstein* by Saul Bellow", *Raritan* 20.2 (2000): 9.
18 John Uhr, "The Rage Over *Ravelstein*," *Philosophy and Literature* 24.2 (2000): 454.
19 Roth, *Communist*, 223.
20 John Updike, *Conversations with John Updike*, ed. James Plath (Jackson, MS: University Press of Mississippi, 1994), 50.
21 Stacey Olster, "A Sort of Helplessly 50s Guy," *The Cambridge Companion to John Updike*, ed. Stacey Olster (Cambridge: Cambridge University Press, 2006), 2.
22 John Updike, "Why Rabbit Had to Go," *New York Times Book Review*, August 5, 1990, 24.
23 John Updike, *In the Beauty of the Lilies* (New York: Knopf, 1996), 5.
24 Ibid., 4; James Schiff, *John Updike Revisited* (New York: Twayne, 1998), 145.
25 John Updike, "Pigeon Feathers," *Pigeon Feathers* (New York: Knopf, 1962), 119.
26 Updike, *Lilies*, 5. David and Clarence also draw similar conclusions about the repercussions of a godless universe. As David explains to his mother, "Don't you see . . . if when we die there's nothing, all your sun and fields and whatnot are all, ah, *horror?* It's just an ocean of horror" (*Pigeon Feathers* 137–138). Meanwhile Clarence reasons that "[w]ithout Biblical blessing the physical universe became sheerly horrible and disgusting. All fleshy acts became vile, rather than merely some" (*Lilies* 7).
27 Updike, *Lilies*, 79.
28 Ibid., 104–105.
29 Ibid., 105.
30 Schiff, *Revisited*, 145.
31 Updike, *Lilies*, 243.
32 Ibid., 145.
33 Ibid., 149.
34 John Updike, *Self-Consciousness* (New York: Knopf, 1989), xi; Peter Bailey, *Rabbit (Un)redeemed: The Drama of Belief in John Updike's Fiction* (Madison, WI: Fairleigh Dickinson University Press, 2006), 22.
35 Michael Wood, "The Trouble with Swede Levov," *New York Times Book Review*, April 20, 1997, 8.
36 Charles McGrath, "Zuckerman's Alter Brain," *New York Times*, May 7, 2000, 8.
37 Ibid., 10.
38 Claudia Roth Pierpont, *Roth Unbound: A Writer and His Books* (New York: Farrar, 2013), 270.
39 Updike, *Self-Consciousness*, 126–127.
40 Pierpont, *Roth Unbound*, 185.

41 Wallace, "Westward the Course of Empire Takes Its Way," *Girl with Curious Hair* (New York: Norton, 1989), 332.
42 Updike, "Recruiting Raw Nerves," *More Matter* (New York: Knopf, 1999), 291; Pierpont, *Roth Unbound*, 184–185.
43 David Horowitz, "In Praise of William Jefferson Clinton," Salon.com (12 January, 1998), http://www.salon.com/1998/01/12/nc_12horo?
44 Mark Schechner, *Up Society's Ass, Copper: Rereading Philip Roth* (Madison, WI: University of Wisconsin Press, 2003), 158–159.
45 Ibid., 159.
46 Philip Roth, *American Pastoral* (New York: Houghton, 1997), 20, 179.
47 Ibid., 61.
48 Ibid.
49 Ibid., 86.
50 Ibid., 35.
51 Ibid., 36.
52 Ibid., 89.
53 Ibid., 277.
54 Updike, *Self-Consciousness*, 120.
55 Ibid., 130.
56 Similarly, Rabbit argues that "you have to fight a war now and then to show you're willing, and it doesn't matter where it is," a remark that follows his interior assertion that "America is beyond power, it acts as in a dream, as a face of God. Wherever America is, there is freedom, and wherever America is not, madness rules with chains"; John Updike, *Rabbit Redux* (New York: Knopf, 1971), 47–48.
57 Roth, *American Pastoral*, 390.
58 Ibid., 81.
59 Derek Parker Royal, "Pastoral Dreams and National Identity in *American Pastoral* and *I Married a Communist*," in *Philip Roth: New Perspectives on an American Author*, ed. Derek Parker Royal (Westport, CT: Praeger, 2005), 199.
60 Milan Kundera, *Testaments Betrayed* (New York: Harper, 1995), 203.
61 Debra Shostak, *Philip Roth – Countertexts, Counterlives* (Columbia, SC: University of South Carolina Press, 2004), 4.
62 Philip Roth, "My Life as a Writer," interview with Daniel Sandstrom, *New York Times Book Review*, March 2, 2014, BR14.
63 Mailer, *Time of Our Time*, xi.

CHAPTER 4

Violence

Sean Grattan

With the entrenchment of neoliberal social and economic policies, the 1990s saw an increasing constriction of possibilities for engagement in public spheres. Those on the edges of the public sphere were increasingly targeted by a proliferation of violent metaphors mobilized around perceived social ills: the wars on drugs, homelessness, and poverty. These metaphors hid a very real crystallization of violence around these issues as the various wars against social issues turned into wars against the people caught up in drugs, homelessness, or poverty. In 1993, for example, the former mayor of New York City, Rudy Giuliani, implemented a draconian regime of quality of life laws designed to clean up the city (mostly for businesses) by stringently prosecuting charges like minor drug possession or loitering. These laws predominately targeted people of color, the poor, and LGBTQ people. Giuliani's crusade to clean up the city is just one example of the battle for who has access to public spaces in the United States. Moreover, the systemic disenfranchisement of people of color, women, LGBTQ communities, and the poor underscore a nervousness around the hegemonic role of white masculinity amidst changing national demographics. This essay seeks to examine the intersections between violence, belonging, and publics in the United States during the 1990s, and to also trace the fleeting moments within representations of violence that hint at refiguring forms of belonging in a beleaguered public sphere.

Los Angeles Riots: A Search for American Character

New York City was by no means singular in the collusion between the winnowing of public space, the police, and neoliberal narratives of economic privatization. The decade was still young when the 1991 Rodney King beating created an iconic visual for the stark differences between practices of policing in the United States. In many ways, the Los Angeles riots are the definitive event of the 1990s because they encapsulate various changing attitudes around the flash points of gender, race, sexuality, immigration, and class. On April 29th, 1992, the jury returned a not guilty verdict for Stacey Coon, Laurence Powell, Timothy Wind, and Theodore Briseno on all but one count. Almost immediately decried as a travesty of justice, Los Angeles braced for unrest. From April 29th to May 4th, the city burned. The *New York Times* reported 58 deaths, 2,383 injuries, 12,111 arrests, 7,000 fire responses, and 3,100 damaged businesses in the largest uprising of its kind since the 1965 Watts riot.

The 1992 uprising did not spring out of thin air; it emerged, in part, on the back of the intensification of neoliberal privatization, which often most directly affected US cities. Urban theorist Mike Davis has extensively tracked the history of urban precarity in Los Angeles. In "Who Killed LA? A Political Autopsy," he describes the Los Angeles riots as a "volcano of Black rage and Latino alienation" that had very little lasting impression on the political dialogue occurring around the 1992 US presidential election. For Davis, the silence surrounding the Los Angeles riots and the lack of substantive financial assistance demonstrates a concrete war on urban centers. What aid that did come into being arrived inextricably linked with welfare cuts, gang-task forces, crime bills, and enterprise zones that aggressively sought to criminalize poverty and link the welfare state with the police state.[1] Along with the criminalization of the poor, the federal response to the Los Angeles riots was "radical privatization" that "paved the way for hardpressed cities to sell of $220 billion worth of federally-financed public works."[2] The financial decimation of urban centers was a bipartisan effort to eliminate revenue sharing that turned on a narrative of responsibility – both fiscal and personal – that saw the urban centers – read as black and immigrant – shouldering the blame for recession, unemployment, and a generalized sense of decline. In turn, these policies "also subsidized white flight and metropolitan resegregation."[3] The neoliberal imagination around race was propped up through the footage of Reginald Denny being pulled from his truck on the corner of Normandie and Florence and beaten with a brick by Damian Williams.

Anna Deveare Smith's remarkable one-woman show, *Twilight: Los Angeles, 1992*, explicitly demonstrates the traumatic wound of the Los Angeles uprising. Deveare Smith's play is a series of interviews about the Los Angeles riots with people ranging from Los Angeles Police Chief Daryl Gates, an anonymous juror, gang members, shop owners, Cornel West, and community leaders. There is an accretionary effect in the testimonies, as multiple witnesses refer back to Watts, distrust of the police, failed economic and social policies, and a generalized feeling of disconnection with overarching narratives of the American dream and its concomitant economic and social stability. By telling a multivocal version of the riots, Deveare Smith articulates both the scale of the event, but also the forms of care, solidarity, and hope that were not part of the national narrative. One example of this difference is the recasting of the truce between the rival gangs the Bloods and the Crips as a utopian possibility for resisting police brutality along with the financial violence imposed on Los Angeles by federal and state government policies. Moreover, the oscillation between governmental officials, gang leaders, business owners, and jurors demonstrates the far-reaching vertiginous tendrils of the riots. For instance, the voice of Owen Smet, a police officer and former gun range manager, remarks on the increased business after the riots, saying, "people are looking for an opportunity to defend themselves."[4] This is about a feeling in the city – a feeling that reflects the undercurrent of dread gripping the nation more generally.

Min Hyoung Song also points to an explosive increase in immigration into Los Angeles in the 1990s – a trend mirrored in the rest of the United States – that brought into relief "alien invasion, the misery of poor urban blacks, the declining fortunes of a white middle class," or what he calls the "triptych sign of societal changes causing the nation to experience a decline."[5] I situate this triptych as not just a central cause of the Los Angeles riots, but also as the organizing factor of much of the obsession with violence in the 90s. The conflagration of Los Angeles, splashed across newspapers and television, were symptomatic of the obsession with violence, but also the competing feelings of dread, angst, and ennui that gripped much of the decade. In *The Queen of America Goes to Washington City* (1997), Lauren Berlant similarly points to a nervousness surrounding the place of an imaginary white bourgeois mainstream culture seemingly threatened by increased immigration. Reading a series of *Time* magazine special issues on immigration in the United States, Berlant describes another triptych:

> Three specific and self-contradictory worries dominate: the fear that immigrants, legal and illegal, absorb more resources than they produce, thus diverting the assets of national culture from legal citizens; the fear that immigrants, legal and illegal, are better capitalists than natal citizens, and thus extract more wealth and political prerogative than they by birthright should; and the fear that cities, once centers of cultural and economic capital, are becoming unlivable, as spatial boundaries between communities of the very poor, workers, and affluent residents have developed in a way that threatens the security of rich people and the authority of the "family."[6]

Berlant's description of the fears surrounding immigration is rooted in not only physical spatial boundaries between people, but also the erection and destruction of ideological spatial boundaries as well. In the later 1993 issue of *Time*, the "Changing Face of America" becomes post-racial and relies on a myth of a polyglot and post-national image of the immigrant; "this global scene is economic and linguistic, it has no narrative of identity."[7] As Berlant notes, the shift away from discourses of identity enacts an erasure of multiple identities, and, instead, attempts to subsume those identities into a safe, homogenous American identity. On the one hand, this shift signals a dramatic attempt to produce an empty but inclusive narrative of a cohesive and coherent American identity, while on the other hand the photograph of a multiracial woman as signifying the face of America dredges up the fears and insecurities surrounding the social place of white men. Thus a large proportion of narratives of violence in the 1990s are predicated on porous boundaries and the fear surrounding the bleed between these spaces.

The divide between the city and the suburb, which can be read precisely as nervousness around the continued hegemony of heterosexual white men, is further instantiated by the decision to move the Rodney King trial out of Los Angeles and into the suburbs. The trial's move from Los Angeles to Simi Valley not only separates the officers from the social realities of Los Angeles, but also puts them "miles away from what many residents of the epicenter of the riots, South Central LA, would call a war between residents and and police officers."[8] Of course, Smith's multivocal and documentary realist *Twilight* is only one way of approaching the chaos of 1992 Los Angeles. Reactions were not confined to the years around 1992, but spread outward, to deeply inform texts as different as Octavia Butler's *Parable of the Sower* (1993), Karen Tei Yamashita's *Tropic of Orange* (1997), and Toni Morrison's *Paradise* (1997). In *Parables of the Sower*, Butler describes a post-apocalyptic Los Angeles that mirrors the burned out blocks of South Central Los Angeles. There is a slight safety held out by living in walled-in neighborhoods, but the first glimpse outside the neighborhood wall strikes a tone that follows the rest of Lauren Olamina's journey:

> A lot of our ride was along one neighborhood wall after another; some a block long, some two blocks, some five...Up toward the hills there were walled estates – one big house and a lot of shacky little dependencies where the servants lived. We didn't pass anything like that today. In fact we passed a couple of neighborhoods so poor that their walls were made up of

unmortared rocks, chunks of concrete, and trash. Then there were the pitiful, unwalled residential areas. A lot of the houses were trashed – burned, vandalized, infested with drunks or druggies or squatted in by homeless families with their filthy, gaunt, half-naked children.[9]

The ubiquity of walls in Lauren's Los Angeles signal a postapocalyptic setting where walls became necessary for protection – what was once a cordoning off of the haves and have-nots has become a gradient of destruction where everyone has suffered from the collapse of a stable public. Ironically enough, in the years following the celebration of the fall of the Berlin Wall, there was a rush to enclose space in the United States, to erect walls separating residents from undesirable elements. The focus on the safety of the walled city resembles another futuristic Los Angeles text, Neal Stephenson's *Snow Crash* (1992). In *Snow Crash* the walled communities are sponsored by transnational corporations, but the sense of security comes through the exclusion of outside – read here as minority, poor, or immigrant – which mirrors the destroyed Los Angeles of *Parable of the Sower*. In many ways, *Parable of the Sower* is what happens after the collapse of the walled neighborhoods of *Snow Crash*. Both, however, mark the nervy relationship between teeming underclasses and gated suburban Los Angeles communities. Lauren is an African-American empath whose empathy sets her apart from everyone because feeling pain in a postapocalyptic violent landscape is not only uncomfortable, but dangerous. Like the all-women's convent in Morrison's *Paradise*, her empathy points to an alternate version of belonging that resists privatized neoliberal subjectivity. Empathy and connection, though terrifying in a burnt-out hellscape, also allow an openness to potential forms of belonging that illuminate connections rather than dissolution between people.

The movement through and between gated communities, along certain blocks and intersections, which figure deep socioeconomic divisions in Los Angeles, are also clearly central to Karen Tei Yamashita's *Tropic of Orange*. In one of the novel's superlative set pieces, Manzanar Murakami stands above the massively traffic-snarled freeway and "conducts" traffic like a symphony. The scale of Murakami's interventions is certainly different than Buzzworm, an African-American man seemingly at the heart of all activities at the level of the Los Angeles street. These multiple scalar views, which are also represented by television news executive Emi, mirror the difference between the reportage of the Los Angeles riots – often in helicopters – and the individual voices highlighted by Deveare Smith in *Twilight*. While forms of violence abound in *Tropic of*

Orange – ranging from the economic depredations of North American Free Trade Act to organ harvesting – what is really striking about Yamashita's text is her method of representing the weaving together of transnational capital and the capital represented in bodies themselves. It is perhaps in this moment of explosive resistance to transnational capitalism, encapsulated by the Mexican wrestler fighting against NAFTA, which shows another instance of the movement toward utopian possibility that Phillip Wegner identifies at the tailend of the 1990s.[10]

Toni Morrison's *Paradise* moves away from Los Angeles as the setting for racialized violence, tying that violence intrinsically to the history of the United States. As a multi-temporal text that stretches from the nineteenth century to the novel's present of 1976, *Paradise*, perhaps more than any other text from the 1990s, clearly addresses the intersection between violence, race, and the American dream as constitutive of the American sociopolitical landscape. *Paradise* famously begins: "They shoot the white girl first," before embarking on a narrative in which the identity of that woman remains occluded.[11] Responding to insistent questions on *The Oprah Winfrey Show* about which woman is the white woman, Morrison responds: "When you know [the women's] race what do you know? You don't know anything."[12] Morrison's admonishment to her readers suggests, partially, that she is attempting to navigate murky waters around ingrained racisms, violence, and identity, but also that she understands the centrality of raced and gendered violence in the United States. The men have come, after all, to attack the convent because they have seen a long history of violence and exclusion: "from Haven, a dreamtown in Oklahoma Territory, to Haven, a ghosttown in Oklahoma State. Freedmen who stood tall in 1889 dropped to their knees in 1934 and were stomach-crawling by 1948."[13] *Paradise* insists on thinking multiple differences and identities simultaneously; it insists on pondering the heft of arguments about identity, citizenship, and belonging. Which of these marginalized bodies matter, and how might they matter differently? If one way of understanding the 1990s is as a traumatic reappraisal and reworking of earlier American history, then the repetitions of violence, the haunting of both the all-black town of Ruby and the women-led convent reinforces a nonlinear and profoundly felt temporality where violence saturates the landscape. But *Paradise* also asserts a search for a richer, more fecund, and nurturing affective space. Jennifer Wagner-Lawlor argues, for instance, that in *Paradise* "the community is imagined through symbols of its desire and through the revisions of its dominant narratives."[14] Insofar as the community searches for these revisions, Morrison critiques traumatic repetitions without difference; here, rewriting marks a reparative relationship to the past where the new social formations of the convent gesture toward the possibility of an America less gripped by racist and sexist national fantasies.

Fear of a Black Planet

One connective thread running through narratives of 1990s violence is an overwhelming fear of difference, and, crucially, an overwhelming discussion of the dissolution of white, straight, male hegemony. In 1991, in an attempt to attend to a more complicated narrative of oppression, Kimberlé Crenshaw coined the phrase "intersectionality" to describe multiple overlapping forms of oppression that operate simultaneously.[15] In other words, the intersections between gender, race, sexuality, and class all inform modes of oppression and, conversely, privilege. In *Paradise*, Morrison illustrates these layered oppressions through the violent tension between the African-American men of Ruby and the women in the convent. Moreover, the deeply patriarchal structure of Ruby itself indicates the subordinate place of the women living within the town. There was a backlash to a nuanced conception of multiple simultaneous identities, however, which took the form of a supposedly embattled white male population that saw its supposed dwindling influence as a direct result of the creeping threat represented by anti-racist, feminist, and anti-homophobic discourses. The 1990s masculinist fantasies *American Psycho* (1991) and *Fight Club* (1996) perhaps most clearly illustrate insecurities surrounding the place of white masculinity in the United States in the 1990s. In his 2012 afterword to *American Psycho*, Ellis draws a clear connection in his mind between the two texts: "I had everything a young man could possibly want to be 'happy' and yet I wasn't. I think *Fight Club* is about this, too – this idea that men are sold a bill of goods about what they have to be in order to feel good about themselves, or feel important."[16] For Ellis, both texts feature disaffected (primarily white) young men whose lives, despite their privilege, have failed to be fulfilling or satisfying. Against the backdrop of the shifting racial and gender makeup of the United States and the subsequent troubling of normative social structures, the insecurities of these disaffected young men take the form of violent acts of self-affirmation.

Fight Club situates itself within a supposed void of men being unable to relate to one another – an antidote to a cottage industry of self-help books. The framing device of Palahniuk's novel is an emotional and dissociative break that leaves the narrator pinballing between his "real name" and the anarchic Tyler Durden.[17] The narrator first meets Durden when he was exhausted from travel and work: "Every time I boarded a plane, I wanted the plane to crash, I envied people dying of cancer. I hated my life. I was tired and bored with my furniture, and I couldn't see any way to change things."[18] The invention of Durden is a "way out" of his "tiny life," free from the materialism that he had previously attempted to fill the boredom of late capitalism.[19] Durden, and the fight clubs more generally, become a form of therapy to help "a generation of men raised by women."[20] The narrator quips that "most guys are at fight club because of something they're too scared to fight,"[21] and that lurking within these men is some kind of degenerative disease passed to them by women. Perhaps most obviously, but also most tellingly, the ultimate betrayal of the fight club ethos is castration; in the text, fight clubs come into being to combat the perceived feminization of everyday life, which also sees the betrayal of fight clubs as a refeminization. It is this kind of worldview that situates castration as the ultimate punishment for betraying fight club. While the misogyny of the text is apparent, the irony is equally visible as the only central woman character, Marla, is given the task of caring for, and saving, the narrator when Durden seems to have gone too far. Is this a romantic tale, or another version of affective labor performed by women for men who blame their inability to feel on women?

What kind of reparative work or traumatic associations produce the need for the fight club, or produce – for Patrick Bateman – the need to kill to feel? Forms of self-help are intrinsically linked with neoliberal capitalism, insofar as personal responsibility is foundational to both. *Fight Club* points outward – to some extent – to class dynamics and social forms albeit still in a deeply problematic manner. Ostensibly the narrator sees the fight club movement as rebelling against a status quo predicated on a developmental model that leaves young men empty and bereft of authenticity. The narrator goes on to wonder if after going to college and getting a job he really should get married – "if another woman is really the answer [he] needs."[22] The reigning logic of *Fight Club* is that real, authentic life is increasingly mediated by consumerism, which promotes a feminized false consciousness. Fight clubs shatter these barriers: you "aren't alive anywhere like you're alive at fight club."[23] The fight clubs make men feel capable and able to "handle anything," which, if we understand one overarching masculinist gender role to center on forms of capability, firmly centers the fight clubs as a means to reattain a masculinity stolen or lost by consumerist capitalist US culture. The primitivism of the fight clubs and their second incarnation as Project Mayhem disavows late capitalism as a realm of impotence, incompetence, and femininity. While there is certainly room for the argument that both texts satirize these masculinist fantasies, they simultaneously work to entrench forms of masculinity reliant on essentialist dualisms that glorify the erasure of women.

Of course, *Fight Club* the novel pales in popularity to the surprise popularity of the David Fincher directed *Fight Club* film (1999). It is hard to watch the iconic final scene with Marla and the narrator holding hands while buildings collapse around them without thinking proleptically to the attacks on September 11, 2001. However, it would be equally difficult to watch *Fight Club* without recourse to the 1995 Oklahoma City bombing. Narratives of emptiness, longing, and belonging intersect with a fear of change, perceived exclusions, and concomitant perceived waning of power. Phillip Wegner makes a similar point, claiming, "the film offers us a new kind of populist mass, one produced by the conditions of the U.S. postindustrial economy. However, as the film unfolds, the sympathetic image of a deeply alienated public becomes one of a secret underground fascist organization, one threatening to consume society in a maelstrom of violence." This maelstrom is, according to Wegner, the "political heart" of the film.[24] While he describes the inner workings of Project Mayhem as fascistic, they are perhaps more in line with the kinds of every day masculinity on display in contemporary popular culture; these violent forms of masculinity are intensified by feelings of alienation and otherness. While *Fight Club* imagines a collectivity and belonging, it is belonging that is inherently gendered and seems to lack the forms of empathy celebrated in a text such as Butler's *Parable of the Sower*. In *Parable of the Sower* empathy is terrifying, but it is terrifying because it represents the possibility of radically collapsing the possibility of othering. A science fictional empathic environment produces social structures that no longer have to look like the masculinist discourse Palahniuk tries to revivify.

Marked by extreme violence and an affectless boredom, *Fight Club* and *American Psycho* are touchstones for the "blank fiction" movement in American literature whose practitioners might also include Jay McInerney, Tama Tanowitz, Lynne Tillman, Kathy Acker, and Dennis Cooper. In texts such as Cooper's *Guide* (1997) and *Try* (1994), along with Russell Banks's *Rule of the Bone* (1995), however, the focus on the disaffected is not confined to twenty-something young urban men, but also appears in drifting precarious teenagers as both writers bring the urban violence to suburban and small town spaces. In crucial ways, therefore, Banks and Cooper resist the siren call of situating violence as purely a reaction to, or contained within, urban spaces. Moreover, both offer troubled and uncomfortable teens the space to explore their subjectivities in contradistinction to the rapidly expanding mainstream narrative of teen violence, destruction, and fear. In a text resplendent with bikers, drug dealers, and sexual predators, Banks unflinchingly explores the violence of small-town upstate New York living. Rather than buy into certain forms of hegemonic masculinity offered by upstate New York, Banks's protagonist Bone flees to Jamaica and embraces a version of Rastafarianism that is deeply uncomfortable with his own whiteness. But it is not an uncomplicated or direct embrace; Banks insistently writes Bone navigating his discomfort. When Bone first meets the Rastafarian I-Man, for instance, he introduces himself and I-Man shakes his hand "like a regular white person as to make [Bone] feel normal which it did."[25] Yet Bone is also quick to remark that the white Rastafarians he has seen at the mall overlooked central elements of Rastafarianism in an attempt to be "an American white kid worshipping the god of your parents."[26] Leaving the United States under the tutelage of I-Man, Bone begins to reconsider his life and his place in the world. The closing passages of *Rule of the Bone* indicate this shift as Bone looks at his old friend Russ staring uncomfortably across the plaza and looking "really confused and scared" and "really pathetic," and realizing that Russ "*would've* been me, if it hadn't been for Sister Rose and I-Man and everything I'd learned about myself and life from coming to love them."[27] The uncharacteristically hopeful note *Rule of the Bone* ends on signals a connection back to Wegner's suggestion of a utopian impulse operating as a secret heart of 1990s narratives.

Dennis Cooper also focuses on drifting youth who have been traumatized or abandoned. Cooper tells a story of disenfranchised, excluded, and sexually vulnerable young men living in a world bombarded by HIV/AIDS, homophobic violence, and suicide. Cooper sees the subsequent violence of his texts as a way of also reclaiming those vulnerable and precarious bodies. While both *Try* and *Guide* were written before the brutal 1998 killing of Matthew Shepard, they occupy a similar place of excluded and precarious citizenship.[28] There are, of course, undercurrents of violence produced by exclusion and silence. In *Guide*, for instance, Cooper produces a text where the lines between violent sexual fantasy and reality blur together; the melding of the two is gristly and disturbing as a metafictional narrator named Dennis quietly describes scenes of increasingly brutal dissipation that culminate in a character being dissected by a dwarf who appears to be another stand-in for Cooper. (The dwarf has a "line of specialty videos, *Terrible Tales of the Dwarf*. They've been profiled in nonporno contexts like *Artforum*, *Sight and Sound*, and the like. Their ugliness is a social critique, to some ways of thinking.")[29] Cooper mirrors the casual violence of homophobia during the AIDS crisis with the bashings and suicides of queer youth. While this might fit into the nihilistic world-view on display in *American Psycho*, violence, for Cooper, often abuts sex, longing, and also acts as the refraction of romantic love. *Guide* and *Try* both end with optimistic notes that seem incongruous given the preceding violence, degradation, and horror. But perhaps this is one way of articulating the strange place of violence in the 1990s; Banks and Cooper both dwell on abandonment and displacement in texts tonally redolent of the angst and dread of the times, but by their conclusions begin however tentatively to map the possibility of an optimistic future.

Guide and *Try*'s optimistic endings underscore a trend in one form of violence narrative that exists throughout the 90s. The tension between violence and optimism – even in *Fight Club* – suggests the utopian possibility of a better world. Most obviously present in *The Parable of the Sower*, utopian possibility also exists in the strange narrative interruption in *Try* calling for one of the main characters to stop using heroin and realize that he is loved, and that if he can love back the world might be a radically more open, caring, and wonderful place. *Guide*, too, amidst the scattered debris left after the violent destruction of the characters, ends with an optimistic call for caring. These calls for care reflect life under the duress of violence, angst, and precariousness.

If the 1990s form a kind of interregnum – a period that lies between two master-narratives of violence (the Cold War and the War on Terror) – then the inward turn of national violence seems consistent with discomfort around multiple competing stories about citizenship in the United States. These competing models of citizenship also concretely point to the tensions between forms of violence justified and perpetrated by the state and the violences of those oppressed by these very same systemic forms of exclusion. What kinds of life are supported by or excluded through violences perpetrated in the 1990s? By examining the violences – both macro and micro – that ruptured the United States, a narrative of shifting forms of belonging appears. I've focused primarily on the Los Angeles riots because they operate as a microcosm of the larger forms of violent social upheavals in the United States in the 1990s. The crashing together of neoliberal social and economic policies, rhetorics that find their affective heft in hatred of difference with the potential for utopian possibility in forms of belonging and connection wrought out of the new terrain of neoliberal violence. In hindsight, perhaps, the 1990s were a crossroads between two potential futures for the United States: a future predicated on neoliberalism, austerity, and xenophobia, and a future of global connection predicated not on privatization, but radical forms of democracy, belonging, and connectivity.

NOTES

1. Mike Davis, "Who Killed LA? A Political Autopsy," *New Left Review* I/197 (Jan-Feb 1993): 5.
2. Ibid., 8.
3. Ibid., 15.
4. Anna Deveare Smith, *Twilight: Los Angeles, 1992* (New York: Anchor, 1994), 224.
5. Min Hyoung Song, *Strange Future: Pessimism and the 1992 Los Angeles Riots* (Durham, NC: Duke University Press, 2005), 10.
6. Lauren Berlant, *The Queen of America Goes to Washington City* (Durham, NC: Duke University Press, 1997), 196–197.
7. Ibid., 206.
8. Ibid., xix.
9. Octavia Butler, *Parables Of The Sower* (New York: Warner, 1993), 8.
10. In *Between Two Deaths*, Phillip Wegner argues that the utopian possibilities contained in the 1999 Seattle WTO protests and the unexpected popularity of Michael Hardt and Antonio Negri's *Empire* illustrate a counterpoint to the popular rhetoric of the 1990s as merely angst-ridden and violent.
11. Toni Morrison, *Paradise* (New York: Knopf, 1998), 3.
12. Quoted in Timothy Aubry, "Beware the Furrow of the Middlebrow: Searching for Paradise on the *Oprah Winfrey Show*," *Modern Fiction Studies* 52.2 (Summer 2006): 361.
13. Toni Morrison, *Paradise*, 5.
14. Jennifer Wagner-Lawlor, *Postmodern Utopias and Feminist Fictions* (New York: Cambridge University Press, 2013), 137.
15. Kimberlé Crenshaw, "Mapping the Margins: Intersectionality, Identity Politics, and Violence Against Women of Color," *Stanford Law Review* 43 (1991): 1241–1300.
16. Bret Easton Ellis, *American Psycho* (London: Picador, 2015), 385.
17. Chuck Palahniuk, *Fight Club* (London: Vintage, 2006), 172.
18. Ibid.
19. Ibid., 173.
20. Ibid., 50.
21. Ibid., 54.
22. Ibid., 51.
23. Ibid.
24. Phillip E. Wegner, *Life Between Two Deaths* (Durham: Duke University Press, 2009), 12.

25 Russell Banks, *Rule of the Bone* (New York: Harper, 1995), 114.
26 Ibid., 116.
27 Ibid., 288, 289.
28 Annie Proulx's short story "Brokeback Mountain" and its more famous film adaptation by Ang Lee might also figure prominently here.
29 Dennis Cooper, *Guide* (New York: Grove, 1997), 83.

CHAPTER 5

The End of the Book . . .

David Ciccoricco

The end of books came on June 21, 1992, in the form of a newspaper headline and a misunderstanding. That date marks the publication of Robert Coover's essay, "The End of Books," in the *New York Times Book Review*. Coover was chronicling the upsurge of narrative fiction written on and for the computer screen – narratives that take the material form of nodes connected by hyperlinks in a digital network rather than paper pages bound in a printed book. It was a new literary experiment with "hypertext," which, as Coover writes on reflection over twenty years later, was at the time still "a kind of magical mystery word that had to be carefully explained on every occasion."[1] His essay was a wide-ranging treatment of the birth of literary phenomena arising in light of a new medium, and a contemplation of the death of older media in a post-industrial age and, more specifically, the apocalyptically oriented decade of the 1990s. It further expressed measured enthusiasm for the potential of digital writing technologies to shake up not only the literary scene but also the pedagogical one. On this count, his discussion goes beyond hypertext fiction to encompass large-scale, synchronous, collaborative writing environments that he famously harnessed in his undergraduate creative writing courses.[2] Furthermore, his essay expressed foresight just as much for technological obsolescence as it did for techno-futurism, and he presaged how that dilemma would weigh down on the field with each new hardware upgrade and software update.

Needless to say, many readers were struck by, if not stuck intractably, on the provocative title. The problem with it was the fact that his title was not really *his* – or at least not his idea. Though it might not be common knowledge, it is in fact common practice for editors, not writers, to provide the headlines on newspaper articles. As Coover recalls, in working with then editor Rebecca Sinclair, his original title was something along the lines of "Hypertext Fictions," which of course would have evoked (at best) magic, mystery, and confusion. "[Sinclair] or one of her staff," he explains, "surprised me by changing it to 'The End of Books' without consulting me.

I might not have objected,... though an alarmist manifesto was not my intent, or even my belief."[3] Another key factor (mis)shaped the essay's popular reception. There was a tendency to conflate its author with either "hypertext's champions" or the "would-be executioners" of the novel to whom he refers throughout. In order to maintain a critical distance from certain key players, especially those extremists in the mix, Coover employed passive constructions (*"you will often hear it said that* the print medium is a doomed and outdated technology") and conditional extrapolations ("*which would mean that*... the novel, too, as we know it, has come to its end").[4] But readers, many responding to the piece through letters to the editor, often glossed over that gesture of critical distance, perhaps not too surprisingly given the popular press venue.[5] After all, academics can be quite adept at noncommittalness, and often for good reason, as they trace the contours of a particular debate before aligning with one side or the other, seeing if there are actually two (or more) lucid positions to assay in the first place.[6] For the same reasons, it was also not surprising that the essay, as Leah Price notes, effectively "launched a thousand eulogies for the book as we *knew* it"[7]; triggered impassioned defenses for the book as we *know* it, prizing – among other things – its operability in bathtubs, defenses complemented by borderline decorous dismissals of the "dreary and pointless" hypertext fictions thought to portend its demise[8]; and, finally, somehow all at once, the essay also "galvanized electronic literature fans around the world."[9]

The debate as a whole evinces a larger disconnect between populist critical journalism on the one hand and academic cultural theory on the other. Nonetheless, the essay sets up a fundamental incongruity that was bound to get the hackles up on the common body of the mainstream: after all, when has a literary experiment in one medium ever spelled the end of that medium?[10] There are simply more and much greater (commercial and techno-social) forces at work in a medium's demise. Media tend to lose dominance, recede to the fringes of an ever-shifting media ecology or, at worst, rise to the fore of a museum exhibit; genres, by contrast, tend to get reinvented and refashioned in new media. Thus, in the aftermath of Coover's essay and amid the hypertext zeitgeist more broadly, the category of "book" all too easily collapsed into that of "novel," which all too easily collapsed conventional narrative practice with everything that might challenge, undermine, or innovate it. Either way, the notion that the future of literary fiction would be full of hypertexts as far as the eye could see – which is to say necessarily *multilinear* or *multimedia* narratives – was a plainly misguided one with few identifiable adherents. What was irrefutable, however, was that we entered a decade that would arguably be the last one where we could take our relationship with the book for granted. The rise of a networked digital culture marked a radical, albeit productive, rupture in the book's epistemology. That is, digital textuality irrevocably altered the way we access and regulate discourse and knowledge (*how* we know), and it dislodged our dominant reliance on that textual artifact as the privileged receptacle and guarantor of that knowledge (*what* we know).

There were, of course, direct implications for literary culture and the way we theorized storytelling in both aesthetic and everyday terms. The 1990s, thanks indeed in part to Coover and other scholars writing in the same vein, forced a deeper consideration of the materiality of the texts we produce and consume, one that was amenable to rather than detached from hermeneutic practice.[11] More specifically, it allowed us to adopt finer distinctions between the kinds of physical and material closures and constraints that delimit texts as artifacts – indeed the "ends" of books or any other narrative media – and, by contrast, those endings in stories and storytelling that are the product of narrative discourse. Furthermore, the same decade gave us a new addition to our lexicon in *hypertext* while endowing us with a more supple cultural understanding of *hypertextuality*. Theodor Nelson coined the term in the mid-1960s, and concrete technical implementations, such as Douglas Engelbart's pioneering NLS (oN-Line System), followed shortly after. The emergence of hypertext fiction in the late 1980s, moreover, no doubt marked a wider awareness and adoption of hypertext as something that transcends a purely instrumental descriptor for electronically mediated linkages in and between texts. With several decades of retrospection in hand, however, it was neither the technical nor aesthetic novelty of hypertext that offers the largest cultural and intellectual payoff. After all, hypertext fiction is by now best understood as a technically and historically contingent form of digital fiction, whereas hypertext in the generic, technical sense is so ubiquitous that it has been internalized and assimilated to the point of invisibility. Rather, what we have gained from hypertext derives from what it connotes as a mode of organizing information, a mode that is not novel itself but was perhaps latent in Western logocentrism. Indeed, it is hypertextuality (that most abstract noun) – and the quality of being hypertextual (that awkward and overwrought adjective) – that offer a new conception and a new vocabulary for how we might write and how we might think.

The literary works that emerged from the congress of narrative and database – from the hypertextual network – were unlikely but serendipitous progenies. The remainder of this chapter sees these observations about materiality and hypertextuality refracted in three works that bookend the 1990s, and which are all transitional narratives in their own way. The first is an early (effectively pre-Web) and now classic work of hypertext fiction, Stuart Moulthrop's *Victory Garden*, written in Storyspace authoring software and published by Eastgate Systems in 1991, initially on a 3.5-inch floppy disk and then on CD-ROM. The second work is one of the first major examples of digital fiction (and "Net art" as it was called) on the Web: Mark Amerika's expansive and multimodal *Grammatron*, self-published on the author's own Alt-X online publishing network in 1997. The third text is Lee Siegel's print novel *Love in a Dead Language*, published with Chicago University Press in 1999. These texts serve as exemplars not only in the context of literary-critical talk of endings but also more broadly in the context of 1990s end-times rhetoric.

Before the Web and in the War: *Victory Garden*

Billy Joel may have managed to encapsulate the second half of the American twentieth century right up until 1989 with his song "We Didn't Start the Fire." But there is a sense that if he were to go back and include the 1990s, he would not only need a longer song but also a much faster one to reflect the tempo of the digital revolution. Technological upheavals notwithstanding, there also appeared to be something to the notion that the decade, or at least the "long nineties" from 1989 to 2001, was a hyper-transitional and volatile period.[12] It clearly begins with a flourish that would condone some form of terminal rhetoric. As Brian McHale writes,

> Cumulatively, the geopolitical events of the period 1989–93, comprising not only the fall of the Wall and the dissolution of the Soviet Union and its empire, but also the bloody suppression of the democracy movement at Beijing's Tiananmen Square, the release of Nelson Mandela, and the beginning of the end of apartheid, certainly seemed to herald the end of something and the onset of something else.[13]

While "history" was supposedly coming to an end according to political scientists,[14] artists were harnessing new writing technologies and creating stories without ends – or with a multiplicity of them. One could also note that George H. W. Bush's master narrative of a New World Order had been followed up by a host of narratives that had no real order. That is not to say that these new "novels for the computer" were apolitical.[15] It was, after all, the First Gulf War (1990–1991) that Stuart Moulthrop took as the backdrop for his hypertext fiction, *Victory Garden*. His narrative network conveys the experiences of a host of characters all tied in some way to the (fictional) University of Tara located in the American Deep South. One of them, Emily Runbird, is stationed somewhere in Saudi Arabia as a military mail sorter, a role that evokes its own endtimes irony in that around the same time many of us were writing our first emails, and perhaps some of our last handwritten letters.

The materiality of the medium clearly mattered for both the author and the critics of this now classic text. The hypertextuality of *Victory Garden* enters into the play of signification on both aesthetic and political terms, and carries a cutting sociohistorical critique to boot. Critics likewise saw an affinity between structure and signification in light of the new medium. As Joseph Tabbi writes,

> The fact that one of the first, and still one of the most prominent, hypertext narratives appeared in the *same* digital medium that soldiers, commanders and journalists were employing when they conducted and simultaneously publicised the war, gives to the reading of fiction a feeling akin to the subject matter: in their own ways both operations, the narrative and the military, participate in the Command, Communications, and Control systems that characterise postmodern society generally.[16]

In a sense, the screen became the only logical venue to interrogate the hyper-mediated war of Operation Desert Storm.

While 1990s literature advances in the shadow of intense geopolitical transition, there is something about the form of digital literature that foregrounds the nature of the transition itself. Hypertext technology and its literary appropriations in particular give new meaning, as well as new attention, to transitions in a bibliographical, grammatical, and poetical sense. What Tabbi has called the "processual page" describes the transition from page to screen on a broader cultural level along with the many dynamic ways in which the digital text can enfold transitions at the level of formal aesthetics.[17] After all, when we think of transitions on the printed page we think of words or phrases that link sentences, paragraphs, and ideas. Transitional devices, as one grammar guide puts it, "link sentences and paragraphs together smoothly so that there are no abrupt jumps or breaks between ideas."[18] However, the abrupt jump, the gap, or the somewhat blind leap is central to the ethos of hypertext; network aesthetics entail a rhetoric of disorientation, reorientation, and, in turn, repetition.

Hypertext fiction provides an ideal venue for staging formal transitions in between the text of individual nodes as well as in between the titles that adorn each node, and scholars have put forth various typologies for the "poetics of the link" that attempt to codify their many literary functions, from straightforward temporal story progression or metatextual commentary, to lyrical punning and polysemantic juxtaposition.[19] The playful movement of a processual page has implications beyond the formal experiments of hyper-literary fiction; indeed, it gestures toward another transition of a conceptual nature in the way that we map the communication networks that shape our sociopolitical reality. The elusive and perhaps illusive totality of such texts augurs a shift from topography to topology, from cartographic models based on mappable space to non-Euclidean networks defined by connectivity.[20] It is, moreover, the mobility of a network that calls for more than a finely detailed map; zooming in will not reveal the meaning in/of the transition. It is our (proprioceptive) movement through and within the network – not a (visual) attempt at mastery of it from above – that allows us to negotiate both a word and a world in transition.

In the Web and Near the Future: *Grammatron*

The World Wide Web – arguably the world's first successful anarchy and certainly its biggest hypertext – made the need to negotiate networks and topologies an even more pressing task. The emergence of Tim Berners-Lee's project is dated variously between 1989 and 1991, based on his initial conception and proposal, and the launch of the first publically accessible webpages, and it became more widely available to users from 1993 with the release of the first Web browser software. Several years later, and after the euphoric and utopian revelry of artists and intellectuals on the Web had been joined by others who were equally excited about commodifying it, came Mark Amerika's *Grammatron* (1997). It was the first major Web-based work of digital fiction, among the first of such works to incorporate sound and image, and one that takes on the challenge of how an individual artist, "forever drawn to eternal ideas of truth and beauty," operates "in the fast-paced media economy of information capitalism."[21]

The vehicle for Amerika's exploration of the digital terra is Abe Golam, a "legendary info-shaman, cracker of the sorcerer-code and creator of Grammatron," as readers are told in the opening passage of the multilinear narrative network.[22] The Grammatron, we are further told, is a writing machine, but Golam also postures as "the Grammatron," and through it he "was known for being a genderless prognosticator of electronic riffs spreading itself throughout the electrosphere."[23] The fact that Golam's own materiality is never made totally clear (he is described at one point as a "hypermedia construct")[24] helps flesh out the text's allusion to the golem in Jewish mythology, whereby an anthropomorphic being is fashioned from inanimate matter and mystically brought to life. Golam's love interest in the story is a computer programming prodigy named Cynthia Kitchen, and he spends much energy and emotion trying to locate her, both for his own lustful purposes and for the greater good, so that his sacred programming script does not fall into the hands of the corporates.[25] The narrative opens with Golam already worn out and well past his prime, "every speck of creative ore long since excavated from his burnt-out brain, wondering how he was going to survive in the electrosphere he had once called home."[26]

Though set in an indeterminate near future world, the opening scene of a spent info-shaman stagnating before a screen speaks to the historical moment of Amerika's America. Unlike the military genesis of its technical infrastructure of the Internet, the Web began as an academic intellectual tool. Artists of all kinds (writers, visual artists, installation artists) seized upon the platform early on in what might be seen as a second major impulse after that of the scientific community around Berners-Lee. Commerce, however, would drive a third impulse on the heels of the creative one, changing the face of the Web irrevocably (arguably we can delineate a fourth major impulse that belongs to "the people" in the form of social media). Indeed, if the Web was still its infancy, it already looked set to have a heavily monetized adolescence. In *Grammatron*, Cynthia Kitchen, fully cognizant of the commercial threat to their creative vision, warns Abe, "All of that talk about the necessity of creating cooperative adventures with other anarcho-nomads floating the cybersea, it's just a bunch of shit now Abe, Prague-23 is nothing but In-Tell's contribution to the vaporstream, all they want is to take all of our ideas and convert them into their sick paracurrencies of money, power, control..."[27]

Given that sex sells, especially when you are selling sex, the commerce of pornography unsurprisingly played an inescapable part in the Web's mid-1990s transformation. Abe too is inundated in his near future but conspicuously parallel predicament: as he "stared blankly at the screen, another marketing message broke through... and distracted him from his thought." The distraction takes the form of a crudely stilted animated GIF image depicting female buttocks. That the flashing text accompanying the image implores its viewer to *"call!"* – rather than *click!* – only underscores the strange transitional nature of the cultural moment.[28] As Amerika himself explains, "Although the narrative [of *Grammatron*] has often been cited in the context of avant-pop art firmly rooted in the rival tradition of experimental literature, in many ways the actual story being told is that of the coming reign of viral marketing and how the magic of hypertext works both ways. It gives being and substance to our fantasies, but thereby makes it possible for them to be packaged and sold back to us."[29] Nonetheless, a love story remains, and not simply between Abe Golam and Cynthia Kitchen; rather, the text ultimately forges an intimate and indelible link between writing and desire – "I ask of writing," Golam puts it bluntly at one stage, "what I ask of desire."[30] It is, moreover, a certain kind of "itinerant desire" that was coming to mark our online experience more broadly.[31]

With regard to our online lives and the impact of hypertext technology, Amerika's *Grammatron* frames significant questions about how, and to what extent, our minds are shaped by our media. In fact, a theoretical companion piece to the fiction explicitly interrogates notions of "Hypertextual Consciousness" and "Digital Being."[32] Such headings not only label new ways to *theorize* the human subject in light of the digital milieu, but they also gesture toward the possibility of entirely palpable changes in our cognitive apparatus or neural architecture arising from a coevolution of human cognition and human technology – a line of inquiry one can trace through the likes of Gregory Bateson, Douglas Engelbart, Walter Ong, Bernard Stiegler, and N. Katherine Hayles.[33] Like the mythical golem itself, which is endowed with life yet without any ability to think or act for itself, such machinic texts and the cyborg textuality they entail further foreground issues of control that would come into even sharper focus in the critical posthumanist discourse of the twenty-first century. All in all, if the development of a new hypertextual consciousness is ultimately up for debate, the fact that works such as Amerika's made us more conscious of hypertextuality is beyond doubt.

At the same time, as our minds continue on their coevolutionary course, there is something about the rhetoric of *Grammatron* that traps it somewhere in between the edgy cyberpunk or sci-fi worlds of the late twentieth century on the one hand and, on the other, a kind of turbo-charged cyberdialect meets hypertext theory-on-steroids discourse of that present 1990s moment. In a very real sense, we are still engaged in a "teleportation of narrative consciousness into the electrosphere"[34] – and indeed some kind of hypertextual consciousness – in terms of the ontogenic adaptations we are witnessing in our cognitive repertoires of attention and memory. But no one would call it that on their Facebook page, Twitter feed, or latest scholarly monograph on narrative in digital culture; more specifically, few would think to call it that now. Even though hypertext, furthermore, is today everywhere on our screens, the word itself would be largely unrecognizable, unmagical, and at best somewhat clumsy if it appeared on one.

After the Web and Long Before It: *Love in a Dead Language*

The sense that some of the language of new media had perhaps already run its course is made manifest in a novel that came at the end of the decade, which takes as its topic a "dead" language of a much older variety. Published in 1999 (and set in 1997–1998), Lee Siegel's *Love in a Dead Language* is (ostensibly) a translation of Vātsyāyana's ancient Sanskrit Kāmasūtra by Professor and Indologist Leopold Roth, with extended commentary by Roth, and edited with footnoted annotations by his sole graduate student and literary executor Anang Saighal. In addition to a translation of an ancient manual for the erotic arts, the novel is a love story, albeit a rather farcical one, between Professor Roth and one of his undergraduate students, Lalita Gupta. She is an Indian-American with no cultural connection to her parent's homeland who nonetheless comes to be a living symbol for Roth's every Indian fantasy and fetish. The novel is, moreover, a murder mystery (unfortunately for Roth, as readers learn at the start).

The narrative frames a clash of cultures, not just Eastern and Western, or even high versus low (indeed, at times, squalid and scandalous), but also print versus digital. The mouthpiece of celebratory cyber-rhetoric in the novel is N.V. Sundaralingam, an Indian national living in California. There he is the director of Seedy-ROM-Antics, a multimedia company interested in Roth's scholarly expertise for help in "developing software for a CD-ROM version of the famous Indian erotic text . . ."[35] Echoing the emancipatory bombast of the field's early theoretical fervor, Sundaralingam, in a formal letter to Roth, writes, "Let me suggest some of the ways in which you might begin thinking non-linearly about this (ad)venture, some of the ways in which the new technology will let all of us understand a discourse more metaholistically by providing us with a new, multidimensional access to it, by transforming what was confined as text into a liberated hypertext."[36] The parody is peppered with not-so-subtle evocations of George Landow's "(w)reader" and "lexia" and Espen Aarseth's "ergodic" cybertextuality in its suggestion that the Kāmasūtra was essentially an incunabular hypertext itself, foreshadowing the "floating networked windoids, the units (comprised of scriptons and textons) that comprise an ergologically dynamic hypertext."[37] He urges Roth to "[t]hink interactive, if not hyperinteractive (not to mention interhyperactive)," and signs off his letter with what is at least a hyperactive flourish: "If you are interested in this exciting, and I believe lucrative, enterprise, please contact me by telephone, mail, or E-mail on the Internet (cdromporn@multisex.net) at your earliest convenience. Cybernetically yours, N.V. Sundaralingam."[38]

If Siegel was in some sense compelled to craft a parodic riposte to the rise of hypertext and digital fiction, then the same phenomenon has perhaps compelled him to craft a novel conscious of its own materiality, hypertextuality, and embeddedness. The association of the Kāmasūtra to a protohypertext is one particularly strong iteration of such influence, one that Roth agrees with: "[s]ince the Kamasutra did not exist in Vatsyayana's mind as a linear text, but rather as a ganglionic mass of interconnected images, sounds, memories, perceptions, and ideas, we are, through the power of a new technology, redeeming the text from a dead language, bringing it back to life, electrifying it."[39] Here, of course, the observation transcends parody given that, as any Web search for "learning Sanskrit online" will attest, the Web has undoubtedly breathed new life into obscure languages and cultures (just as it paradoxically contributes to displacing them). There is also, however, a broader recognition of digital culture's influence on the thematic and formal framework of the text, one reflected overtly in the book jacket's promotional blurb that invites readers to "[f]ollow numerous victims and celebrants of romantic love on their hypertextual voyage… of folly and lust." Sundaralingam identifies the ancient Indian palm leaves that originally "bound" the Kāmasūtra with the "lexia" that are the discursive units of digitally networked texts.[40] But beyond that, digital culture's foregrounding of materiality is likely to have played some part in both shaping the book (we must turn it upside down at times or read text in a mirror) and coloring it (Roth composes one section in two different colors, the traditional Indian dyes of kumkum and kohl).

The media ecology of the 1990s reshaped not just Siegel's novel but also the novel as artifact (it is worth remembering that his novel precedes that *locus classicus* of hypertextuality in print, *House of Leaves*).[41] The influence of digital media and literary production, however, is mutual and multidirectional. For one of the sacred text's better known sections on categories of sexual union, Roth forgoes critical commentary and instead adopts the form of a board game. As Anang Saighal explains in his footnotes, "Essentially an Adaptation of Book Two, the game incorporates each chapter into some aspect of play, thus providing a way of playing rather than reading the book (concomitant with Roth's notion of hermeneutics as a ludic activity)."[42] Moving beyond the distinction of reading and playing mobilized here, the board game shifts focus from the finality of winning outcomes to the pleasures of the movement in between them – from the end-game of positions to the artful game of transitions that tether them together.[43] Even though, as the instructions indicate, the "first player to move all three of his or her pawns up the chakras and into the *Kamaloka* wins the perpetual pleasure of eternal erotic Love," this literal "Game of Love" is clearly more about the "transient pleasures of this world" that comprise the main activity of gameplay.[44] In addition, the growing mainstream predominance of game culture more generally endows Siegel's long-standing ludic interrogations with new force. Granted, rampantly indulgent embeddedness, footnoting, and literary games of all kinds are by no means new to books or, for that matter, narrative fiction in print. Nevertheless, *Love in a Dead Language* affirms that digital environments of the 1990s gave us a new critical vocabulary and a conceptual bridge with which to traverse continuity across media, making us more supple consumers of traditional literary media in turn.

Although the sexual connotations distilled from the Sanskrit *kāma* tend to prevail in the popular (Western) imagination, the term in the Hindu tradition is more encompassing, taking in the physical gratifications of sex, the emotional fulfillments of love, and the sensual experiences of aesthetic enjoyment. It is only a short conceptual and etymological step from *desire* in its diverse forms to the pleasures of language and the written word. Indeed, it is the term *sutra*, signifying a "thread" or "string," and in particular that which connects discursive elements, that ties together the text of the Kāmasūtra and evokes the wider connotations of *text* (from the Latin, *texere*, "to weave"). A number of the players in Siegel's novel suggest the same. For instance, in a reminiscence about his wife Sophia, Roth recalls:

> [A] young man and woman, students full of amatory hopes, talking about love as it is constructed by convention and intellect, imagination and inspiration in literary texts. They agreed that love was a function of language, the hypostatized foundation of an aesthetic sentiment, and that that accounted for it being so seemingly different at different times and different places, despite the intractable universality and uniformity of the sexuality that it abstracts and disembodies.[45]

Or, as Anang Saighal more bluntly observes, following an excursus on the ineffable difference between male and female orgasm and the failure of language and literary endeavor on this count, "writing about love and sex is not so much writing about love or sex as it is, and cannot escape being, writing about writing."[46] In fact, the same semantic web that interconnects sexuality and textuality would encourage readers to see something inescapably "hypertextual" about Roth's own climactic description of sexual union: " . . . there were no fixed centers, no edges either, no ends nor boundaries. All lines vanished into the erotic landscape of an exitless maze, with beginnings, middles, and ends no longer part of the immediate display of love."[47]

All in all, Moulthrop's *Victory Garden* offers a present-tense meditation on the 1990s, Amerika's *Grammatron* peers into its near future, and Siegel's *Love in a Dead Language*, albeit anchored in the same decade, excavates two thousand years of ancient literary history. The three texts take us from the pre-Web hype of digital textuality through the dotcom boom to arrive at a print novel that cannot help its own remediation in light of digital culture. Nonetheless, they are all also meditations on materiality and hypertextuality – each in their own way transitional texts that reflect on their own transience. Their stories may all grow out of a millennial decade mired in talk of endings. But much more than an apocalyptic fixation over the fate of the book, they each tap into our deepest (itinerant) desires and exhibit an enduring love affair with storytelling in its most elusive and elastic forms.

NOTES

1 Email interview conducted with Robert Coover on October 27, 2015. Excerpts reproduced with permission by the author.
2 The "Hypertext Hotel" at Brown University was an offshoot of the sprawling and entirely text-based "multi-user dungeons" (also domains/discourses/dimensions) known as MUDs.
3 Email interview, 2015.
4 Robert Coover, "End of Books," *New York Times Book Review*, June 21, 1992, 1.
5 J. E. Edwards, for instance wrote "Robert Coover and all others who predict hypertext's eventual outdoing of linear forms of written communication should be loaded onto a rocket and shot to the moon with limited supplies of oxygen and Tang." *New York Times*, August 2, 1992, 27, http://www.nytimes.com/1992/08/02/books/l-the-end-of-books-699992.html.
6 Thomas Swiss surveys this response in "Reviewing the Reviewers of Literary Hypertexts," *Electronic Book Review*, December 30, 1998, http://www.electronicbookreview.com/thread/electropoetics/corrective.
7 Leah Price, "Dead Again," *New York Times Book Review*, August 10, 2012, http://www.nytimes.com/2012/08/12/books/review/the-death-of-the-book-through-the-ages.html?_r=0, (emphasis added).
8 Of the many dismissive letters to the editor, Laura Miller's "www.claptrap.com" is the most vitriolic and the most cited (*New York Times*, March 15, 1998, https://www.nytimes.com/books/98/03/15/bookend/bookend.html). As Thomas Swiss writes, "few essays crystallize as nicely as does Miller's a set of opposing ideological and aesthetic relations as they are being played out on an emerging literary practice" ("Reviewing the Reviewers of Literary Hypertexts").

9. The text appears in the biographical details for Robert Coover on the Electronic Literature Organization (ELO) site (http://eliterature.org/people/).
10. I have elsewhere said that "hypertext fiction" may have been better framed as an innovative literary practice sustained by a small but dedicated group of (primarily academic) artists and theorists, albeit one utilizing a writing technology that was revolutionizing reading and writing practices on a more mundane plane. It instead found itself cast into a competition that it could not win and in which it did not belong: that of usurping over 500 years of literary tradition in print and "liberating" the narrative line. See "Digital Fiction: Networked Narratives," in *The Routledge Companion to Experimental Literature*, eds. Joe Bray, Alison Gibbons, and Brian McHale (London: Routledge 2012), 470.
11. For a foundational essay on digital materiality and some of the misguided assumptions underpinning it, see Matthew Kirschenbaum, "Materiality and Matter and Stuff: What Electronic Texts Are Made Of," *Electronic Book Review*, October 1, 2001, http://www.electronicbookreview.com/thread/electropoetics/sited.
12. The phrase is Phillip Wegner's, cited in Brian McHale, *The Cambridge Introduction to Postmodernism* (Cambridge: Cambridge University Press, 2015), 124.
13. McHale, *Postmodernism*, 123.
14. Francis Fukuyama famously claimed that with the collapse of the Soviet Union and fall of the Berlin Wall, the Western ideal of economic liberalism and the capitalist democratic system has reached its apotheosis as the final form of world government. See *The End of History and the Last Man* (London: Penguin, 1992).
15. Robert Coover, "Hyperfiction: Novels for the Computer," *New York Times Book Review*, August 29, 1993.
16. Joseph Tabbi, "1991, The Web," in *The Edinburgh Companion to Twentieth-Century Literatures in English*, eds. Brian McHale and Randall Stevenson (Edinburgh: Edinburgh University Press, 2006), 257.
17. Joseph Tabbi, "The Processual Page: Materiality and Consciousness in Print and Hypertext," *The Journal of New Media and Culture (NMEDIAC)* 2.2 (2003), http://www.ibiblio.org/nmediac/fall2003/.
18. See "Transitional Devices," Purdue Online Writing Lab (OWL), https://owl.english.purdue.edu/owl/resource/574/02/.
19. See, for example, Jeff Parker, "A Poetics of the Link," *Electronic Book Review*, September 1, 2001, http://www.altx.com/ebr/ebr12/park/park.htm.
20. A detailed discussion of the implications of topography and topology for digital textuality appears in Chapter 2 of my *Reading Network Fiction* (Tuscaloosa: University of Alabama Press, 2007), 44–71.
21. Mark Amerika, "Digital Bop Poetics," in *Network Art: Practices and Positions*, ed. Tom Corby (London: Routledge, 2006), 133.
22. Mark Amerika, *Grammatron* (Alt-X Online Network, 1997), http://www.grammatron.com/gtron1.0/Abe_Golam_907.html.
23. Ibid., http://www.grammatron.com/gtronbeta/Genderless_818.html.
24. Ibid., http://www.grammatron.com/gtron1.0/blood_871.html.

25 That Cynthia Kitchen is a computer programmer should not necessarily give readers any hope that she is a commanding female tech guru of the late twentieth century or some kind of Ada Lovelace (re)incarnate, which is to say a straightforward, empowered female character. Rather, Abe Golam meets her as "the delivery-chick from Nuts & Bearings, the local cyborganic simu-store that he ordered his groceries from" (http://www.grammatron.com/gtron1.0/nervous_051.html). As she explains to him upon introduction, she is also a "preprogrammed sex-machine Made in the USA," and she eagerly asks what kind of role she might play in his "GRAMMATRON movie" (http://www.grammatron.com/gtron1.0/mtv_050.html). She is invited in, hands him the bag of groceries, and proceeds to remove her work uniform (http://www.grammatron.com/gtron1.0/seductive_048.html).
26 Ibid., http://www.grammatron.com/gtron1.0/Abe_Golam_907.html.
27 Ibid, http://www.grammatron.com/gtron1.0/Thing_763.html.
28 Ibid., http://www.grammatron.com/gtron1.0/message_682.html.
29 "Digital Bop Poetics," 133.
30 Amerika, http://www.grammatron.com/gtron1.0/a52.html.
31 "[H]ypertextual discourse solicits iteration and involvement. While this is certainly a property of all narrative fiction, one can argue that hypertextual writing seduces narrative over or away from a certain Line, thus into a space where the sanctioned repetitions of conventional narrative explode or expand, no longer at the command of *logos* or form, but driven instead by *nomos* or itinerant desire." Stuart Moulthrop, "No War Machine," in *Reading Matters: Narrative in the New Media Ecology*, eds. Joseph Tabbi and Michael Wutz (Ithaca, NY: Cornell University Press, 1992), 273.
32 Amerika, http://www.grammatron.com/htc1.0/.
33 See Thierry Bardini, *Bootstrapping: Douglas Engelbart, Coevolution, and the Origins of Personal Computing* (Stanford, CA: Stanford University Press, 2000); Walter Ong, *Orality and Literacy: the Technologizing of the Word* (London: Methuen, 1982); Bernard Stiegler, *Technics and Time* (Stanford, CA: Stanford University Press, 1998); and N. Katherine Hayles, *How We Think: Digital Media and Contemporary Technogenesis* (Chicago: University of Chicago Press, 2012).
34 Amerika, http://www.grammatron.com/htc1.0/.
35 Lee Siegel, *Love in a Dead Language* (Chicago: University of Chicago Press, 1999), 146.
36 Ibid., 148.
37 See George P. Landow, *Hypertext 2.0* (Baltimore, M.D.: Johns Hopkins University Press, 1997), and Espen J. Aarseth, *Cybertext: Perspectives on Ergodic Literature* (Baltimore, M.D.: Johns Hopkins University Press, 1997).
38 Siegel, 147, 150.
39 Ibid., 152.
40 Ibid., 147.
41 Mark Z. Danielewski, *House of Leaves* (New York: Pantheon Books, 2000).
42 Siegel, 92–93.

43 There is a productive parallel to certain yogic styles, such as *vinyasa*, that entail the synchronization of breathing and movement and place emphasis on the *transitions* between poses. The same observation points to an analogous shift in focus from location to connection, or topographical mapping to topological (and proprioceptive) movement.
44 The board game appears on eight pages that are numbered but unpaginated, inserted between pp. 92–93. The quoted material can be found on the eighth page depicting the board game.
45 Ibid., 170.
46 Ibid., 100.
47 Ibid., 229.

CHAPTER 6

The End of Postmodernism

Ralph Clare

Appearing at the start of the millennium, Percival Everett's *Erasure* (2001) features Monk Ellison, a writer who is questioning his one-time embrace of postmodern aesthetics and who raises the ire of "innovative" writer and fellow member of the *Nouveau Roman* Society after delivering a conference paper, *F/V*, part parody of and part homage to Roland Barthes's *S/Z*. Becoming belligerent, the writer proclaims to Ellison that postmodernists did not "have time to finish what we set out to accomplish" because any art which "opposes or rejects established systems of creation... has to remain unfinished."[1] His unsuccessful attempt to punch Ellison lands him in an azalea bush. Suffice it to say that the blow delivered at the 1991 Stuttgart conference on "The End of Postmodernism," which included such literary luminaries as John Barth, William Gass, and Raymond Federman, was of a different variety. That such a conference dared to ask its esteemed speakers whether postmodernism was over and done with, thereby suggesting it was, encompassed a telling moment – one in which, as *Erasure* has it, literary postmodernism appeared to have reached an end that by its own theoretical premise it could never reach. Added to this was a new generation of writers who were consciously trying to break with the literary postmodernism they had been raised on, often critiquing its supposed aesthetic and philosophical weaknesses, as David Foster Wallace did in his 1993 essay "E Unibus Pluram: Television and U.S. Fiction," in which he claimed that postmodern metafiction had run its critical course and been co-opted by mainstream media and the market. Literary critics, following suit, began to distinguish these younger writers from the former generation by asking what might be emerging after postmodernism.[2] For many, literary postmodernism had indeed reached an end point.

It is tempting to propose that 1989 marked the beginning of postmodernism's end. Samuel Beckett, one of its grandfathers, died that year, as did Donald Barthelme. Most famously, of course, it is the year the Soviet

Union collapsed, a year Frances Fukuyama famously pronounced initiated the "end of history," arguing that state-centered economies had failed for good and that liberal humanism and capitalism had won the day. While Fukuyama's claim remains objectively debatable, the sense that something had ended was subjectively lived and felt by a rudderless Generation X that remained cynical regarding this professed victory during a decade that served as a kind of caesura between the so-called end of utopian ideology and the rise of the tech-driven New Economy. In contrast, and despite the critique of literary postmodernism's narcissism and textual game playing, the irreverence of texts such as John Barth's *Giles Goat-Boy* (1966), Robert Coover's *The Public Burning* (1977), and Thomas Pynchon's *Gravity's Rainbow* (1973) thrived off the kinds of functioning, if faltering, Cold War–era grand narratives that their own meta-narratives questioned. In short, not only could it be argued that postmodernism had become a codified style by the 1990s – in both the highest artistic circles and the lowest consumer discount stores – it could also be said that postmodernism as a means of upsetting the establishment, whether literary or political, no longer made the same kind of sense that it did in decades prior.

Whether they accepted postmodernism's ending or not, the early postmodernists had nevertheless begun to reflect upon the value of their art and their place in literary history that suddenly seemed, unaccountably to those in the supposed vanguard, to be passing them by. Such a passing is heralded by Barthelme's posthumously published *The King* (1990), which features a historically displaced King Arthur who, surrounded by his Round Table and court on the eve of World War II, realizes that his chivalric values are outdated, worries about his future obituary, and rewrites Merlin's prophecy of his demise to assure longevity and victory in war. Even the genre-blurring *Federman A-XXX: Recyclopedia* (1998), an edited, page-bound, hypertext-style biography of Raymond Federman that is equally a biography of literary postmodernism and poststructuralist theory, feels very much like a playful obituary for both the author and the postmodern surfiction he had long championed. In both texts, the concern with aging, legacy, and (re)writing a literary-historical (con)text might serve as an allegory for the position that many first-generation postmodern writers found themselves in during the 1990s.

During this decade, John Barth, Kurt Vonnegut, David Markson, William Gass, and William Gaddis all produced novels that feature a writer reflecting upon his writing, that consider the nature of time and aging, and that continue to practice some form of self-reflexive fiction. However, while many of these works could be considered the most aesthetically self-conscious examples of each author's oeuvre, they are, remarkably, the most explicitly autobiographical as well. In the 1990s, then, first-generation postmodernists would answer the long time complaint of critics that postmodern literature was only concerned with textual and narcissistic game playing. At a time when self-conscious fiction was no longer in vogue, these writers responded by emphasizing the ways in which their worlds were woven into text as much as text was woven into their worlds. Collectively, the result was a number of novels that anchor self-reflexivity in an array of direct and indirect autobiographical techniques and strategies. Reflecting upon their own mortality and the fast receding promise of literary immortality, these writers would self-consciously return to an autobiographical body of memories, desires, and concerns that would help to revive a body of work that appeared to be a terminal case. All told, the 1990s would come to signal if not the actual death of postmodernism, then its virtual transformation into a kind of posthumous postmodernism.

Out through the In Door

John Barth's *Once Upon a Time: A Floating Opera* (1994) comprises the single most self-involved evaluation of the literary life and potential critical death of one of postmodernism's greatest American writers. The book, Barth claims, is a "memoir bottled in a novel" and thus "not the story of my life, but... *a* story thereof."[3] While Barth sometimes cameos in his works as a character, he is the sole protagonist of *Once Upon a Time*, wherein he is drawn from a sailing expedition with his wife into a "fictitious literal voyage" (384) similar to the night-sea journeys and narrative labyrinths experienced by so many of his characters. Typical to his vision of postmodern textuality in which word stands in for world, Barth submits his own lifehistory to language, becoming a fictionalized version of himself, writing "*a* story of my life, by no means *the*" (8–9).

Structured like an opera, *Once Upon a Time*'s true impetus is not to sketch Barth's biography – much of which appears in his *Friday* essays or in *Lost in the Funhouse* (1968) – but to jumpstart his present state of complacency and to avoid what appear to be inevitable endings – death and the end of his career. Barth begins the Overture by proclaiming the century to be "gone" and accounts "for the restless air of this overture" (17) by pointing to what he calls the "close-outs" of history, from "the Cold War thawed, [and] Germany reunited" to "the new Persian Gulf crisis" that will "midwife a new world order or... abort it" (11). But if history is supposedly at a standstill, so is Barth, who finds himself in a mid-life-writing-crisis and stuck in "a terminal but far from interminable holding pattern" (59). Such concerns with physical mortality join with those of literary immortality when Barth peruses his latest notebook, remarking that the "blank space after 1991 – looks disagreeably grave-like" (10) and when he mentions the deaths of fellow postmodernists Italo Calvino, Barthelme (14), and Beckett (20), as well as the general decline of postmodern literature's stock, the "slippage in our muse's credit rating" (121). Even Barth's infamous declaration about the cultural necessity to resuscitate literature becomes a personal lament about suffering the "empty interval between imagination's exhaustion and replenishment" (12). Worst of all, he fears that *Once Upon a Time* will be his "Last Book" (382), which would essentially mean his death because although "[o]ur lives are *not* stories, . . . we may make stories of them" (169), and since life is meaningless, we must "make or find meaning in the form of *stories*" (170).

If Barth's postmodern solution to perceived narrative ends had been to turn them back upon themselves, then the way out of his own predicament would mean turning one version of his life story against its projected ending. Barth thus recycles his own postmodern method and extends it into new "nonfictional" territory. The result is at once the most straightforwardly autobiographical of Barth's fictional works, but also one of the most elusive as well, for Barth's life story plays out in a "fractal funhouse" (226) that mixes fact and fiction; contains numerous suspended passages, sudden time leaps, and meta-commentaries on different narrative temporalities; and insists by the book's end that life escapes narrative. This funhouse serves as a kind of textual time machine – not one bent on a Proustian recapturing of time, but one attempting to thwart its logic and twist it back upon itself. Barth's plan involves setting "the action of this narrative not in 'real' time but in an imagined future that the present will presently overtake, and further . . . to conceive as its plot vehicle a voyage out of the time of its imagining and writing into the time imagined and written" (127). The obvious paradox that one can escape real time through the creation and manipulation of narrative time is as complicated and suspect as one of Zeno's, a favorite of Barth's. Further, the story, or "[t]ime's funhouse" (57), is often a dizzying and confusing place, even for Barth himself (180–181), and the reader may feel trapped in a vortex. Yet, for Barth, the inescapability of the funhouse-time-paradox is not cause for despair, but the means of salvation. As he puts it, echoing his moral from *Chimera* (1972), "[n]o adversary, this labyrinth, but a resplendent arabesque, a chaos most artfully structured. Not the . . . hazard-path to some treasure, but the treasure itself" (324).

It is for this reason that the book's operatic structure is never properly concluded – it contains an abbreviated Act Three (which would contain the last two decades of Barth's life) and a two page Episong. Thwarting narrative closure, Barth has planted a water-message from the (narrative) past containing the two decades of his life that he will not recount, creating a kind of narrative time loop that protects Barth and his wife from ever revealing or reaching their narrative ends. The fat lady cannot sing, the show must go on, and it will never be curtains for Barth. In keeping with Zeno's paradox of the tortoise that Achilles can never catch, the closer we seem get to the present time of Barth's telling (to the "real" Barth himself or to the end of the story), the less is actually concluded, for "the point must come . . . when the writing present overtakes the written present and leaves it behind. I anticipate at that point something like a narrative Doppler-shift" (20). Barth thus goes to great lengths to conceal elements of his real life, suggesting that language may weave *a* world but not *the* world, challenging the misconception that postmodernists see *the* world as simply text.

Barth, in response to the perceived end of postmodernism, actually doubles down on his metafictional funhouse method. Whether this is Barth's slimy retreat into the protection of a familiar conch shell narrative, or more proof of his virtuosity in adding another elegant spiral to an endlessly elaborate structure depends upon one's view of postmodernism in the first place. Taking the long view of Barth's career, however, *Once Upon a Time* marks a moment of crisis in the 1990s that Barth would ultimately overcome by self-consciously dramatizing it via the very postmodern tactics that many considered to be all used up.

Of Tomes and Tombstones

William Kohler, the middle-aged history professor and protagonist of William Gass's *The Tunnel* (1995), is the embittered foil to the self-satisfied Barth, but the cynical Kohler is equally concerned with the fate of his work and the legacy of his academic career. When Kohler, who is unsuccessfully attempting to write a preface to his latest book, wonders at the novel's beginning, "[a]m I postponing the end because endings are my only interest?"[4] one might ask the same question of Gass himself, who famously spent thirty years writing the book he considered would be his most important.[5]

Gass's work-in-progress would span the entirety of that other work-in-progress, postmodernism itself, and embody many of its virtues and vices, ironically arriving in time to make it fittingly both a postmodern tome and a tombstone for postmodernism.

Gass has long argued for the postmodern axiom that fiction creates a world of its own and is in no way referential to a "real world," for "[t]here are no events but words in fiction."[6] *The Tunnel* takes this notion to its extreme as it addresses the problem of historical representation in that Kohler's book, *Guilt and Innocence in Hitler's Germany*, appears to be an attempt to exonerate the Nazis of blame for their actions since "neither guilt nor innocence are ontological elements in history; they are merely ideological factors to which a skillful propaganda can seem to lend causal force" (13). Indeed, the novel is not actually about the Holocaust or political fascism, but about the power of fiction and the "fascism of the heart" (366). Thus, from the postmodernist point of view, Gass's work can be seen as the high point of what self-conscious literary language and form can achieve in fiction, but from another it can be viewed as the most egregious example of postmodernism's self-involved formalism in which reality is trumped by text, and the horrors of history itself are reduced to nothing but the play and effects of figurative language.

The postmodern form of *The Tunnel* is evident in its shuttling between order and chaos. The novel is without plot yet is structured via twelve arbitrary "Phillipics," which are Kohler's rants mixed with reminiscences. Kohler's rambling takes on visual and spatial dimensions too, as the novel contains drawings, comics, limericks, concrete poetry, puzzles, and even ink-smudged pages. Such experimental textual play is classically postmodern and can be found in Gass's own *Willie Masters' Lonesome Wife* (1966) and in various works by Federman, Ronald Sukenick, and B. S. Johnson. Thus, though it is carefully structured, Kohler's twisted personal narrative feels as though it is spontaneously and randomly emerging on the page.

However, *The Tunnel* contains a tacit critique of postmodernism as well. Much like the actual tunnel Kohler is digging in his basement, all of his textual and formal play functions as an avoidance tactic. To be sure, Kohler's tunnel is the antithesis of Barth's funhouse for it is haunted, a place of despair from out of which he shapes "this prison of my life in language" (3). Although Kohler digs up his past and recreates it through literary language – which is often as beautiful and lyrical as it can be crass and pedantic – he also intentionally revises and distorts it. He is shifty regarding his involvement in Kristallnacht as a student in Germany, and it is often unclear whether his colleagues, with whom he argues about historiography, are real. It is as if Gass were suggesting that Kohler is a "bad" postmodernist, a cynical relativist deconstructing truth as a way of denying its existence entirely. For there is no reason to believe that Kohler, a narrator reliable mainly for his bitterness, has actually written *Guilt and Innocence*; his preface may well be only the endless deferral of the book that he cannot write, a preface that becomes *The Tunnel* itself, which is the real meditation on guilt and innocence and comprises Gass's meta-commentary on the potential misreading and abuse of postmodern theory.

The Tunnel, then, self-consciously puts postmodernism itself on trial around the very time when it would be critically condemned. Considering the novel's ability to critique its own vision, it is also perhaps no surprise that *The Tunnel*, like Barth's *Once Upon A Time* and other 1990s postmodern novels, contains a good deal of autobiographical content, however refracted. Gass would use much of his own childhood and family history when creating Kohler's brutal Depression-era youth, creating some of the most powerful passages in the novel.[7] Despite Gass's own claim regarding the non-referential fictional world, then, the fragments of a real world still nestle deeply in the figures of his words and can cut and draw real blood, accordingly.

The Last of Some Things

Whereas Gass's thirty-years-war with his magnum opus would end in victorious publication, the thirty-plus-year struggle of his longtime friend William Gaddis with both a Civil War play, *Once at Antietam*, and a history of the player piano would end in more of a truce. In lieu of their publications, Gaddis would recycle these would-be failures and incorporate them into his final two novels, *A Frolic of His Own* (1994) and *Agapē Agape* (2002), respectively. Gaddis, then, would do what so many of his colleagues were doing in the 1990s: self-consciously dramatize the aging writers' dilemma, thereby producing not only his most metafictional works to date but his most autobiographical as well.

A Frolic's meeting of metafiction and biography occurs in Oscar Crease, an aging junior college instructor/writer who is suing a film director for stealing the idea for a Civil War blockbuster from his unproduced play *Once at Antietam*. Crease's play is actually Gaddis's real-life unfinished one, and several of its scenes are reproduced in the novel, along with several legal opinions, a transcript of a deposition, letters, and newspaper headlines. Gaddis is able, then, to "fold" his play into "Crease," who sits at the novel's center, whether in his Long Island home or in a hospital bed, amidst a dizzying swirl of legal documents and official visitors, which is formally reproduced by the novel's frantic pace. Moreover, the play motif highlights – perhaps even more so than does *J R* (1975) and *Carpenter's Gothic* (1985) – the linguistic construction of characters that Gaddis's dialogue-driven novels always suggest. *A Frolic* solidifies the Yoknapatawpha-like metafictional element in Gaddis's Long Island novels, as Christina mentions the fate of Liz Booth, the protagonist of Gaddis's *Carpenter's Gothic*, and several other characters too.

Thus, even as literary postmodernism was ending, Gaddis would write his most explicitly meta-textual novel that ponders whether, as one of the legal decisions puts it, "'reality may not exist at all except in the words in which it presents itself.'"[8] Like Gass, Gaddis is fascinated by language's world ordering and world destroying potential, but also by the fact that language is a system that gives rise to and underpins all social systems. *A Frolic*'s main theme centers on the differences between justice and law and the abuses of a legal system that, as Oscar puts it, "that's all it is, language" (284). The danger is that if "every profession protects itself with a language of its own" (284), then each becomes much like one character's critique of art theory as merely the "self referential confrontation of language with language and thereby, in reducing language itself to theory, rendering it a mere plaything" (34–35). Gaddis thus takes up the critique of postmodern language play, but turns it toward America's institutions instead. Regardless of Oscar's defense of his play's artistic integrity, his play can only "speak" as potential evidence in a copyright lawsuit because money is "the only language they understand" (422). Gaddis's suggestion in the deposition transcript that literature is a language premised on sharing and developing ideas, not creating them for private profit, provides a different communicative model than that of the capitalist system, but it is not one that holds much sway in this world.

Gaddis's most explicit coming to grips with endings, however, comes in the novella *Agapē Agape*, which was prepared in manuscript before Gaddis's death in 1998, though it was not published until 2002.[9] Gaddis, suffering from ill health in the late 1990s, returned to writing his monumental history of the player piano, yet instead fictionalized this last attempt in *Agapē Agape*. Much like Edward Bast's opera that ends up a simple cello suite in *J R*, Gaddis's vast history would shrink to a final, concentrated novella.

The protagonist of the novella, who delivers a long rant directly to the reader, is the most autobiographically raw of any of Gaddis's characters. Like Gaddis, he is a terminally ill writer trying to get his documents (thus his life) in order, since "we don't know how much time is left and I have to work on the, to finish this work of mine while I . . . get this property divided up and the business worries that go with it."[10] The narrator is also concerned with his literary legacy, that he gets his ideas "written down before my work is distorted misunderstood turned into a cartoon" (28). To that end, the narrator's real desire, as is Gaddis's, is to finish his history of the player piano, which exists in a welter of notes, clippings, articles, and various papers that he tries to put into a coherent narrative. Gaddis's familiar theme of the struggle of order against chaos is here more personal and urgent than ever.

As in Barth's *Once Upon a Time*, the writer's body of work is synonymous with his physical body, the skin of which is like "dry old parchment" (11). But if it is true that "[g]etting old your only refuge is your work" (19), then the textual tornado that envelops the narrator both sustains him and threatens him. Failure to arrange the "whole trash heap over the floor go down and I'd be part of the trash heap" (72) is thus the narrator's failure too because his work has always been "about the collapse of everything" (28). A specific part of that "collapse" in the 1990s that Gaddis is responding to is changing literary tastes. The narrator grouses over the "[f]act that I'm forgotten that I'm left on the shelf with the dead white guys in the academic curriculum" (48). The physical body thus collapses with the forgotten body of work. As women writers and the multicultural novel began to fulfill the pluralistic, non-hegemonic promise of postmodernism in different ways, even Gaddis realized that high literary postmodernism was finished. Yet, despairing though it is at times, the carefully orchestrated chaos of *Agapē Agape* is Gaddis's most self-revealing example of his artistic process and an assertion that a better self can be created in the face of inevitable failure.

Around the Block and Back Again

While the 1990s novels of Barth, Gass, and Gaddis extended their commitments to a postmodern aesthetic, it could be argued David Markson's *Reader's Block* (1996) is his most radical postmodern novel, though it arrived at a time when postmodernism was at an end. *Wittgenstein's Mistress* (1988), Markson's most critically lauded novel, represents the formal breakthrough in his work that would come to characterize the late style of his writing – as *Reader's Block* puts it, a "[n]onlinear . . . Discontinuous . . . Collage-like . . . assemblage"[11] or "[a] novel of intellectual reference and allusion, so to speak minus the novel" (61, 137). *Reader's Block*, however, could be said to take the modernist Eliot-like aesthetic of *Wittgenstein's Mistress* and make it more properly postmodern. Yet it too features an aging author obsessed with endings and self-consciously reflecting on the value of his life's writing.

Although *Reader's Block* runs on the most metafictional of premises – it is about a writer writing about a writer writing – its bare-boned, allegorical characters, Reader and Protagonist, are partly autobiographical. Similar to many a Beckett narrator who creates a series of fictional selves to flee, find, or maintain a self through storytelling, the narrator of *Reader's Block* invents Reader, the "main" character, who spends the novel wondering how to create Protagonist. All three characters are practically one and the same, however, for at times "Reader is essentially the I" (10) and must decide "[h]ow much of Reader's own circumstances or past [to] give Protagonist" (12). Haunting this novel "of no describable genre" (140) or "poem of sorts" (166), then, is the consideration that the narrator/Reader is "in some peculiar way thinking of an autobiography" (137, 41). In this sense, *Reader's Block* is "a seminonfictional semifiction" (140). As Markson once stated in an interview, "How much of myself is in there? It's all me."[12]

Despite certain ambiguities, a general picture of Reader/Protagonist emerges as an aging, lonely man, who is either without family or estranged from his children, has suffered or is suffering from cancer, and who once had a literary career that is all but forgotten – in short, he is the familiar figure of the aging author in 1990s postmodern fiction. All told, we are offered the barest of plots, in which Reader is staying either at a beach or near an old cemetery and where he watches a mysterious woman who reminds him of his own failed romantic relationships (60, 73, 186); and we learn only the skeletal detail of his life, including an inventory of mementos, such as a baseball "hit foul by Ted Williams at Yankee Stadium" (60), a portrait of Dante (50), and a human skull (55). Not surprisingly, Reader's thoughts are often morbid, as when he wonders, "*[d]id it ever, once, enter even Protagonist's bleakest conjecturings that he would finish out his life alone?*" (188). Reader, true to his name, even wonders what book will be "the last he ever read" (181).

But the transformation of autobiography through postmodern metafiction that pointedly occurs in 1990's postmodern novels is put to different ends in Markson. Barth, Gass, and Gaddis employ autobiography to flesh out character, provide backstory and setting, or for thick, realist description. Where they add, Markson subtracts. If Reader, like Protagonist, "has come to this place because he had no life back there at all" (9) – "back there" being the space of pre-narrative non-being, the outside of (the) text – then, by extension, so has the narrator and Markson himself. The self in Markson is a kind of fiction intricately tied up with the act of reading, of connecting with other texts, and this self comes into being through language. To be sure, the linguistic self is a motif in many a postmodern text, but rarely is it treated as if so much is at stake. Intertextuality in Markson is not simply a formalist game of texts at play with each other, but a portrait of how the self is informed by, and in intimate dialogue with, those texts as well.

Thus, Markson's minimalist autobiography is incomplete without joining the biography of art and literature itself, which *Reader's Block* offers in a way. The biographical and anecdotal fragments, for instance, become a kind of protagonist too. The fear, much like in Gaddis's *Agapē Agape*, is that all of these fragments have been consigned to the "[w]astebasket" (the novel's last word) of history, yet in constructing his allusive mosaic-novels Markson delays the very ending of culture and history that he fears. For *Reader's Block*, as its title suggests, is concerned with overcoming (Reader's) writer's block. As such, the novel succeeded wildly, for it is the first book in what could be considered a tetralogy along with *Vanishing Point* (2001), *This is Not a Novel* (2004), and *The Last Novel* (2007). Markson, much like Barth, turned a possible ending into a new beginning by metafictionally considering to what ends he could put "the ending."

Time after Time

Unlike Barth, Gass, Gaddis, and Markson, Kurt Vonnegut's works had, as early as his third novel *Mother Night* (1961), incorporated autobiographical elements, and not in a veiled way but directly so. Like Barth, Vonnegut sometimes appears in his novels, such as in *Slaughterhouse-Five* (1969) and *Breakfast of Champions* (1973), yet he also began a number of his novels with an autobiographical preface that helped to create the "character" of Vonnegut that so many readers would grow to know and love. Although the postmodern author was supposedly dead (merely an author function or an ever playfully shifting signifier), Vonnegut managed to flesh himself out in a way that appealed to readers. Nevertheless, even Vonnegut's professed final novel *Timequake* (1997), like other 1990s postmodern novels, displays an overt concern with aging, literary legacy, and is, by far, Vonnegut's most metafictional and autobiographical novel.

Timequake is a novel about writing, repetition, and failure. Its premise, a postmodern twist on Nietzsche's notion of "eternal recurrence," is that in 2001 the world plummets back in time ten years, and everyone is forced to act exactly as they did over the ensuing ten year span while being unable to change or stop what occurred. When time and free will finally return to the world, science-fiction writer Kilgore Trout (Vonnegut's long-time "alter ego"[13]) attempts to awaken the world from its funk. Despite, or perhaps because of this premise, the novel contains almost no actual plot or action. Instead it repeats or recycles two of Vonnegut's familiar themes and his most famous character, Trout, and puts Vonnegut center stage. Further, the novel is constructed via a loose collage of short autobiographical pieces, family history, political commentary – much of which Vonnegut has written about before – as well as literary and artistic references, historical anecdotes, jokes, poems, and numerous stories by Kilgore Trout. The mix of these fragments and sparse plot gestures to Markson's work (Vonnegut mentions Markson's *Reader's Block* [40]), and the fact that time seems to "stand still" as Vonnegut reviews his past recalls Barth's manipulation of time in his fictional funhouses.

Vonnegut's metafictional temporal play is a formal feature of the novel as well. In a move similar to Gaddis's inclusion of his "failed" texts into novels about writers who are failing to write them, Vonnegut picks apart the failed draft of *Timequake*, which he refers to as *Timequake One*, in order to write *Timequake Two*, or the very novel that we are reading. Once again, the postmodern novel shows itself capable of turning perceived endings against themselves. In fact, for Vonnegut such failure is necessary to write the novel in the "first" place. *Timequake Two*, for instance, is not merely a newer draft of *Timequake One* but "a stew made from its best parts mixed with thoughts and experiences during the past seven months" (xii), and Vonnegut usually begins a story in the narrative by attributing it to *Timequake One*. Thus, *Timequake* is as much about *Timequake One* as anything, and *Timequake Two* ironically ends up being the "first" and "original" novel predating its "earlier" incarnation, to which it ironically gives the title *One*.

Vonnegut's ability to rework the old into something new, however, does not quell his concerns about the death of literature and literacy itself. Though he defends the fact that Trout, like himself, "created *caricatures* rather than characters. His animus against so-called *mainstream literature*, moreover, wasn't peculiar to him. It was generic among writers of science fiction" (63), he still fears that the Internet is making books irrelevant (157). One of Trout's stories tells of the Booboolings, who are so enamored of television that "[t]hey would look at the printed page or a painting and wonder how anybody could have gotten his or her rocks off looking at things that simple and dead" (18). In postmodernism's heyday, *Slaughterhouse-Five*'s Billy Pilgrim tellingly interrupts a radio broadcast about "whether the novel was dead or not,"[14] but roughly thirty years later Vonnegut truly worries over the possibility.

Ultimately, Vonnegut bids goodbye to his fictional world, much like William Butler Yeats does in "The Circus Animals' Desertion," as he caps his novel-writing pen for good. Metafictional to the last, Vonnegut stages "a clambake on the beach at Xanadu" for his fictional characters and real-life friends (199). However, if Yeats's circus ends with a realization of "the foul rag and bone shop of the heart," the usually melancholy Vonnegut models his big-top finale after "the last scene of *8 1/2*" (Federico Fellini's meta-film about a director struggling to make his ninth film), in which the movie set is revealed and the all of the film's characters dance in a circle together (199). Similarly, in *Timequake* Vonnegut chooses to finish his career in a celebration of the intricate play of life and art and to accept the ending of the performance as an apotheosis of sorts.

After Words

What the critical afterlife of literary postmodernism will be after its few remaining originators pass on is an open question. After the canon wars, the end of the "linguistic turn" in literary studies, and the rise of post-postmodern literature, the presence of first-generation postmodern literature, despite its initially strong institutional ties, has largely waned inside the academy. Outside the academy, the story is essentially the same. With the exception of the bestselling Vonnegut, the *Library of America* series, a kind of barometer of popular canonized authors, has yet to admit a well-known postmodernist novelist, such as Barth, Coover, or Pynchon, into its ranks, whereas this generation's more realist-based contemporaries, such as Philip Roth, John Updike, and Saul Bellow, have all received multiple volumes.

Despite this trend, however, postmodernists have continued to write and to publish. Since 1990, for example, Barth and Coover have produced works on a fairly regular basis, and even the once sporadic outputs of Pynchon and Gass have nearly doubled that of their early careers. In an act of literary audacity, in 2014 Robert Coover would publish *The Brunist Day of Wrath*, the sequel to *The Origin of the Brunists* (1966), arriving nearly a half-century after its predecessor. Once again, an apparent ending became grounds for a postmodern beginning, suggesting that perhaps the postmodernists have been playing posthumous all along.

For Al Greenberg

NOTES

1 Percival Everett, *Erasure* (New York: Hyperion, 2001), 36–37.
2 See Ziegler ("The End of Postmodernism"), Harris ("PoMo's Wake"), McLaughlin ("Post-Postmodern Discontent" and "Post-Postmodernism"), Andrew Hoberek ("After Postmodernism), and especially the introduction to Stephen Burn's *Jonathan Franzen at the End of Postmodernism* (2008).
3 John Barth, *Once Upon A Time: A Floating Opera* (New York: Little, 1994), Program Note. Further references are parenthetical.
4 William H. Gass, *The Tunnel* (New York: Harper, 1995), 15. Further references are parenthetical.
5 "William H. Gass," Interview by Carole Spearin McCauley, *The New Fiction: Interviews with Innovative Writers*, ed. Joe David Bellamy (Urbana: University of Illinois Press, 1974), 42.
6 William H. Gass, *Fiction and the Figures of Life* (Boston: Nonpareil, 1979), 30.
7 Heide Ziegler, *Introduction to The End of Postmodernism: New Directions, Proceedings of the First Stuttgart Seminar in Cultural Studies, Aug. 1991*, ed. Heide Ziegler (Stuttgart: Verglag, 1993), 17.
8 William Gaddis, *A Frolic of His Own* (New York: Poseidon-Simon, 1994), 30. Further references are parenthetical.
9 Joseph Tabbi, *Afterword to Agapē Agape* by William Gaddis (New York: Viking, 2001), 102.
10 William Gaddis. *Agapē Agape* (New York: Viking, 2001), 1. Further references are parenthetical.
11 David Markson, *Reader's Block* (Normal, IL: Dalkey Archive, 1996), 14. Further references are parenthetical.
12 Quoted in Francoise Palleau-Papin, *This is Not a Tragedy: The Works of David Markson* (Normal, IL: Dalkey Archive, 2011), xxvi.
13 Kurt Vonnegut, *Timequake* (New York: Putnam, 1997), xiii. Further references are parenthetical.
14 Kurt Vonnegut, *Slaughterhouse-Five: Or, The Children's Crusade* (New York: Dial, 2009 [1969]), 263.

PART II
Forms

CHAPTER 7

Encyclopedic Fictions

Stephen J. Burn

"The prognosis for the nineties is not encouraging... we should not expect any large, overarching books"
— Frederick R. Karl, "Where are We?" (1992)[1]

The story that the 1990s told itself through its early and middle years was the story of a national literature's decline. Yet while the exact angle of that downward arc depended on how the narrative was framed, what these accounts shared was the sense that an epochal shift was taking place, and that it marked the end of the kind of "large, overarching" encyclopedic narrative that had become a signature form of both institutionalized modernism and postmodernism. We might see Don DeLillo's *Underworld* or Gass's *The Tunnel*, but a new generation of writers would no longer work on such ambitious scales, this argument ran, because of seismic realignments in American literary culture. For Sven Birkerts in 1994, this decline in American letters was heralded by the approach of "the electronic millennium,"[2] as the "vestigial order" of print culture gave way to new digital horizons (119). In this weightless, distributed world, where "lateral vistas of information... stretch endlessly in every direction" (75), the habits of concentrated attention and reflection that sustain serious literary fiction would soon be exiled to the outer darkness. For John Aldridge, assessing the scene two years earlier, the problem was instead the institutional machinery that produced and regulated literary fiction in the United States. The efflorescence of Creative Writing programs, Aldridge contended, had attained the status of an "assembly line" that dominated the contemporary field, punctually turning out interchangeable books for which the encyclopedic novel was not a viable model. Yet despite tracing divergent etiologies, both diagnosed a communal dwindling of large-scale literary ambition amongst younger writers. Birkerts succinctly crystalized this failure in his claim that "no one thinks any longer about writing the Great American Novel" (207).[3]

At greater length, Aldridge lamented the end of the "great tradition of technical innovation and experiment that, from Joyce... Pynchon, Gaddis, and DeLillo, produced the... novel of rich intellectual complexity... that embodied the ambitious view that literary works can and should become artistic microcosms of a whole society or the modern world."[4]

At the start of the decade there were certainly other reasons why the encyclopedic project might seem to have run its course. After all, philosophers such as Alasdair MacIntyre had begun the 1990s by decisively relegating the encyclopedia to a now defunct, nineteenth-century order of knowledge.[5] But Aldridge's and Birkerts's insistence on retaining the encyclopedic narrative as the standard to measure new works precisely roots these critics in the decade's renewed interest in establishing the form's contours. While earlier pioneering critics of the form had framed the encyclopedic narrative's significance in terms of its critical neglect,[6] there is an unusual concentration of attempts to define its dimensions (or curate its memory) in the 1990s.[7] Despite divergent obsessions and terminology, these definitions overlap in their sense that such works (1) self-consciously gather and deploy an unusual range of knowledge; (2) develop intricate, multifocus plot structures that swell the book beyond the mainstream novel's conventional horizons; and (3) condense a range of literary styles into a single volume. In the hands of different critics, these loose parallels might be pressed to probe epistemological questions (LeClair and Clark), to excavate homologies with earlier forms (the revival of degenerative satire [Weisenburger], or of the epic [Moretti]), or be put in dialogue with emerging studies of biological self-organization (Strecker, House). But regardless of focus, the shared taxonomy often came with a shared history, as the form was canonized around certain literary historical flashpoints that reveal clusters of encyclopedic works in the 1920s and 1970s. Despite Aldridge and Birkerts's concerns, the nineties are arguably a comparable historical flashpoint, with the encyclopedic fiction not simply proliferating across the decade but also developing both new structures and more diverse cultural resonance. Such developments are more visible with the benefits of two decade's distance, though Tom LeClair did much to define the scope of the 1990s encyclopedic narrative and the centrality of the two younger writers who have become most synonymous with it in an essay published in the middle of the decade: "The Prodigious Fiction of Richard Powers, William Vollmann, and David Foster Wallace" (1996).

Identifying two key 1990s novels – Powers's *The Gold Bug Variations* (1991) and Wallace's *Infinite Jest* (1996) – alongside Vollmann's earlier *You Bright and Risen Angels* (1987) – as evidence of an emerging post-Pynchon generation, LeClair's pioneering article argued that *The Gold Bug Variations* and *Infinite Jest* were united by the following six fundamental similarities: a tendency to write "explicitly about information"; an unusual "fluency with technical or mathematical languages"; a preference for biology and the life sciences over concepts such as entropy; a fascination with "young, precocious characters"; a commitment to "supplement the digital mode of print with ... analogue representations such as diagrams and drawings"; and an overarching aesthetic predicated on artistic excess that deforms generic expectations.[8] To this persuasive list, with its emphasis on each book's scientific freight, we might add a series of structural and technical isomorphisms.

In terms of narrative design, both books begin at or near the end of scrambled plot lines that are relayed in temporally disparate installments. These nonlinear structures speak both to a relatively traditional reliance on delayed revelations to keep readers turning pages, but also to the significance of legacy to each writer: these opening sequences are built upon a kind of informational incompleteness that requires the reader's immersion in the narrative past to understand the opening episodes' present. Wallace's and Powers's use of such plot structures are not sequestered from the decade's millennial shading – the point of the Christian millennium is, after all, to make of the present moment an endtime that revisits and catalogues past sins – yet, more specifically, the past that each book excavates sets up a two-tiered narrative structure that splits along generational lines. These structures juxtapose a sequence of younger characters with the previous generation, especially focusing upon a literal or symbolic father figure (James Incandenza for Wallace, Stuart Ressler for Powers). Such tiered architecture prefigures the next decade's revival of the three-generation family saga (Franzen's *The Corrections*, Eugenides's *Middlesex*, Egan's *A Visit from the Goon Squad*), but also advertises the extent to which these works unfold their original designs by rehearsing the pattern of a key literary ancestor (James Joyce for Wallace, Poe – albeit via Bach – for Powers).

At the level of the paragraph, the encyclopedic dimension of both Wallace's and Powers's fiction has been persuasively linked by Paul Dawson to different modes of omniscient narration,[9] yet it is also true that speech is unusually central for both writers. In obvious ways, Wallace's fiction is disproportionately tilted toward stretches of apparently unmediated dialogue, and the very absence of the narrator in such exchanges strategically obscures the speaker's identity until contextual details and diction reveal that information:

"Can I ask you how it is being in that thing?"
"Thing?"
"You *know*. Don't play *dumb* and *embarrass* me."
"A wheelchair is a thing which: you prefer it or do not prefer . . ."
"I can't believe I'm *drinking*. There's all these people in the house they're always worried they're going to *drink*. I'm in there for *drugs*."[10]

On one level this technique is part of the novel's imitative form, paralleling AA protocol regarding consistent anonymity. But the book as a whole also unwinds an overarching investigation into the question of where voices come from that mirrors such small-scale instances of this technique, both through the presence of a wraith who has to make use of "somebody's like internal brain-voice if it wanted to try to communicate" (831), and in the book's more general exploration of why Hal is unable to communicate in the opening scene. In less overt fashion, *Gold Bug* probes parallel issues: the reader is similarly forced to question where words come from when – at the book's end – Jan and Todd reveal that they have collaboratively authored earlier parts of the novel; Powers even includes communication from beyond the grave, when one year after Ressler's death, Jan triggers a message he has left for her within an ATM so that he appears to be alive "lodged inside [a] circuit."[11]

Finally, in a decade shaped by globalizing energies, these books are surprisingly static, building their intellectual expansiveness upon a predominantly binary geography: Arizona and Boston for Wallace, the Midwest and Boston for Powers.[12] In this last respect, in particular, Vollmann's nineties work is distinct from Wallace's and Powers's, and it's significant that LeClair has to reach back to the mid-1980s for a Vollmann novel that matches *Gold Bug* and *Infinite Jest* – *You Bright and Risen Angels* (1987) – and that he notes that data is no longer a textual obsession in Vollmann's 1990s fiction, but is palpable only in submerged form, "implicit in the detailed research necessary to write these books."[13] Driven to narrativize his "longing to devour the horizons of this world,"[14] Vollmann's nineties projects substitute the encyclopedia's map of eclectic intellectual fields for expansive models that map space (cartography in his palindromic *The Atlas* [1996]) or time (history in his *Seven Dreams* series). To some extent, *The Gold Bug Variations* and *Infinite Jest* set the standard for their generation's engagement with the encyclopedic novel, and – in the wake of LeClair's article – have justly received extensive scholarly attention. Yet even as Vollmann's career pursues an alternate direction in the decade, Powers's and Wallace's ambitious masterworks do not stand alone as examples of youthful encyclopedic fictions, and rather than recovering familiar ground[15] it is worth thinking beyond their example to get a richer sense of the form's evolution in the 1990s. Across the decade, the white, male axis that had dominated the genre and its attendant criticism began to weaken, while the form's privileged position as the exemplary *literary fiction* was also opened up by encyclopedic works in long form poetry (A. R. Ammons's *Garbage* [1993]), and by novels such as Neal Stephenson's *Cryptonomicon* (1999) that were typically catalogued as genre fiction. Mapping this decadal breadth yields a more complicated picture of the encyclopedic form's mutations, even as it points to the wider resonance of the formal, intellectual, and technical parallels that Powers's and Wallace's works demonstrate.

One way to approach the varied shape and style of encyclopedic fiction in the 1990s is to track the way it splinters into two distinct strands as it reaches the confluence of millennial energies and anxieties that drove Birkerts's study. One strand (exemplified by *Gold Bug* and *Infinite Jest*) responds to reports of the printed book's final hours by creating what we might call a *novelistic encyclopedia*, reliant on a layering aesthetic that overloads the text with bookish and novelistic devices: expansive diegetic narration of the kind Dawson describes, extreme stylistic variation (ranging from the imitation of specialist discourse to the inclusion of poems), end- or footnotes, chapter or episode titles, diagrams, and so on. The intensive strategies of such works approach an encyclopedic fullness that belongs in a genealogy stretching back through Barth, DeLillo, and Pynchon to such European ancestors as James Joyce and Laurence Sterne. The second strand more closely follows the emerging network culture where "vistas of information . . . stretch endlessly in every direction." Here an aesthetic of layering gives way to one of stripping away, which produces a shadowy inversion of the first volume, a kind of *skeletal encyclopedia*, whose intellectual range is predicated on little or no stylistic variation, the removal of narratorial armature, and the emptying out of novelistic devices to present a starkly isolated voice or sequence of voices. Representative examples include Carole Maso's *AVA* (1993), Evan Dara's *The Lost Scrapbook* (1995), and David Markson's *Reader's Block* (1996).

Considered spatially, the first encyclopedic form stresses the horizontal connections of ordinary narrative design, pushing the reader forward through the plot's vectors despite the nonlinear arrangement of episodes; the second form's networked design mostly replaces this horizontal movement with a vertical stacking of fragments; emphasizing the functional equivalence of each fragment more than the incremental progress achieved by reaching the end of a plot, this architecture typically achieves its narrative ends through the accretive process of variation on a theme.

Perhaps because its experimental structure often eliminates the comforting ballast provided in traditional novels by one or more central personalities, the skeletal encyclopedia is the most overlooked of the decade's two encyclopedic forms. The low critical profile of Evan Dara's masterpiece, *The Lost Scrapbook*, which was published in the middle of the decade, offers a representative case of this comparative neglect.[16] Although Franzen identified Dara in the *New Yorker* as one of his "classmates in the Neo-Furrowed-Browist school of American fiction,"[17] because critics rarely discuss his work at length, the subtlety and philosophical reach of his innovative narration, as well as his novel's exemplary deployment of skeletal encyclopedic structures, have been largely ignored. In the novel's virtuosic opening, however, Dara simultaneously introduces this sparse technique, negotiates his relationship to literary convention, and outlines the novel's philosophic freight:

> – I am, yes; certainly;
> – So how about medicine . . . ?
> – Listen to me: Yes; I am; *absolutely* . . .
> – Or law – ?
> – Of course;
> – Then forestry; does that – ?
> – Immeasurably;
> – And – ?
> – Profoundly . . .
> – Or – ?
> – *Passionately* – !
>
> along with marine acoustics and quantum biography and psychogeology, not to mention their respective subdisciplines; but what I am *not* interested in, Ms. Clipboard – or Mr. Canker or Mrs. Murmur or Call-me-Carol, *all* of you – is your questions . . . it's a bizarre enterprise, this deciding what "to be": mostly it feels like negotiating what *not* to be.[18]

In obvious ways, the passage's account of a speaker apparently facing a career counselor presents a narrative threshold of the kind familiar from any number of traditional novels. Yet while this might be a coming-of-age threshold in many narratives, leading us forward into a plot sequence where one particular career path leads to some future event, what is significant about Dara's opening is its refusal of the threshold, and of progression in favor of a static, additive process in which branching options that are never taken accumulate.[19] Instead, the conventional narrative situation is sliced open and plot decays into catalogue – significantly (given the book's encyclopedic range) into a catalogue of disciplines and "subdisciplines."

As the novel continues, this incomplete opening situation is simply replaced by an additional (and equally fragmentary) episode as the book accumulates and runs together partial stories in what Jeremy Green calls a "war on discrete and sealed particles of meaning" that is reflected in the book's grammatical preference for ellipses, dashes, and semicolons over the closure of periods.[20] This proliferation of voices makes the novel what LeClair calls "a multi-track oral history,"[21] and for good reason, LeClair, Patrick O'Donnell, and Green identify Dara's stark rendering of speech as indebted to "the fiction of William Gaddis."[22] Yet, as this opening passage makes clear, Dara's approach to speech is distinct from Gaddis's in several ways. Gaddis's dialogue runs in real time in specific locations, and what is said is, at times, less important than what is happening around the speech act: characters' lines, as Moore observes, are "often truncated, with constant interruptions by other characters – and by telephones, televisions, and radios."[23] Even when characters do not listen to each other, exchange – between characters, between character and narrative world – is vital to the reader's experience of Gaddis's dialogue because the text itself masquerades as a raw transcript of multiple speakers. As even a cursory flick through a Dara novel reveals, his fiction relies much less frequently on actual exchanges between speakers, and in place of Gaddis's clipped lines of rapid-fire conversation, Dara more often provides longer paragraphs of individual speeches. In this respect, the novel's opening eleven lines of short, incomplete statements, are not characteristic of the book as a whole, inasmuch as they initially *appear* to be a transcript of an actual exchange. Yet this is only an apparent conversation: as the ensuing long paragraph makes clear, there is no career counselor present, but rather an imagined composite figure ("Ms. Clipboard – or Mr. Canker or Mrs. Murmur or Call-me-Carol, *all* of you"), conjured to provide the occasion for the opening character's private speech. Put simply, then, Gaddis wrote novels of dialogue; Dara writes novels of speech. The former, as Joseph Tabbi observed, sees "the author's function [replaced] altogether by a recorder"[24] and the text (for all its metaleptic leaps) as self-contained transcript; the latter, by contrast, always evokes an implied audience, a specific recipient for the speech's message who is not present within the text.

Abstracted from the kind of contingent detail that typically anchors and explains novelistic speech, Dara's mysterious succession of monologues echoes and extends the fascination with where voices come from that runs through *The Gold Bug Variations* and *Infinite Jest*. But it also enables and underpins Dara's encyclopedic project: because the book's additive process depends upon bringing in a sequence of characters to talk from a particular perspective without necessarily linking or justifying those speeches in relation to a pre-existing plot pattern, Dara can rapidly establish the novel's intellectual plenitude. Much of the opening 300 pages, in fact, seem to be devoted to accumulating analogies for the novel's own processes that also expand the book's spectrum of cognitive concerns. Moving from Sergei Eisenstein's montage techniques, through psychology's Rorschach tests, M. C. Escher's "inlacings and refractions" (10), Beethoven's obsessive variations, Bronislaw Malinowski's anthropology, and even neuroscience's vision of "crosslinked neural networks" (180), the rapid succession of intellectual frames encourage the reader to constantly reformulate her understanding of the book, and set it next to increasingly large non-literary contexts. The skeletal encyclopedia's techniques for condensing intellectual range in this fashion underlines why length or word count – which would make encyclopedic fictions indistinguishable from bloated beach novels – is the crudest, and at times most misleading, index for conceptualizing the form.[25] Nevertheless, *The Lost Scrapbook*'s proliferation of information, and the kaleidoscopic shifts between different fields, can seem overwhelming until they are retrospectively fitted into the book's looping architecture. As LeClair notes, the novel is effectively split into two halves: the second half (beginning on page 327) establishes the nearest thing the novel offers to an overarching plot – a tale documenting chemical pollution in Isaura, a Missouri town. The voices in the book's first 300 pages are, then, reframed as "refugees, literal and figurative, from Isaura,"[26] but because Dara's structure reverses cause and effect, the relation between these two parts only becomes clear when the reader takes the novel's self-description as a "Möbius culture" literally (191), and bends back from the end to the start.

This inverted timeline parallels the way *Gold Bug* and *Infinite Jest* begin at the end, and links the novel's encyclopedic accumulation of data to a shared diagnostic interest in causes. It also encourages the reader to reexamine the truncated opening line in terms of the novel's closing eco-tale. While both Virginia Woolf and Gaddis had begun novels in mid-conversation, Dara's novel begins mid-phrase in a fashion that lays the groundwork for the book's later ecological disturbances. As we have seen, the opening sequence is not true dialogue, but a solitary speaker's meditation on existence. The first words – "I am" – which are established "certainly" and "absolutely," seem, then, to be the second half of the "first principle" – "so certain and so evident" – of the philosophy that Descartes (having similarly withdrawn from the world) erected over the void of absolute doubt: "I think, therefore I am."[27] That the phrase is itself cut in half reflects the book's single explicit reference to Descartes as a member of the philosophical "slice-'n'-dice cartel," whose rationality works "by dividing, by reducing" (276). This reductive process is not only formally opposed by the book's additive narrative procedures, but also by its composite vision of a network of voices bound together "in a living exchange" (321). By beginning the book (if not the chronology) with Descartes, Dara roots the later eco-disaster in the Cartesian "slice-'n'-dice" philosophy that isolated the individual (who could only be certain of themselves) from the rest of humanity, and from responsibility toward a doubtful external world that was now rife for exploitation. Merging Descartes with corporate capitalism, the book's encyclopedic vision is a reconstructive one whose aggregate of voices attempts to prove the inverted *cogito* that Dara will offer in his next novel: "I think, therefore *you* are."[28]

Dara's community of voices has few obvious counterparts in contemporary US fiction – perhaps the much fuller focalized narration of Robert Coover's *John's Wife* (1996) is the closest analogue – but its broader narrative mechanisms are echoed in the decade's other skeletal encyclopedias. Albeit late in his career, David Markson employed a similar approach in his spectacular final quartet of novels, beginning with *Reader's Block* (1996). Like Dara, Markson begins with a traditional plot situation (a meeting on a street) that rapidly decays into static qualifications that primarily serve as a loose framework for an encyclopedic accumulation of fragments from literary and artistic history:

> Someone nodded hello to me on the street yesterday.
> To me, or to him?
> Someone nodded hello to Reader on the street yesterday.
> Church bells were already ringing, to announce the Armistice in November 1918 when word reached Wilfred Owen's family that he had been killed in battle one week before.
> Picasso made Gertrude Stein sit more than eighty times for her portrait.
> And then painted out the head and redid it three months later without having seen her again.[29]

Slim yet expansive, the book thus becomes "a novel of intellectual reference and allusion... minus much of the novel" (61), with the reader forced to either supply the thin "connective tissue"[30] between the juxtaposed fragments (art and absence join the Owen and Picasso anecdotes) or to map connections across the book: we wait 30 pages, for instance, for the next instalment of Picasso's portrait ("when told that Gertrude Stein did not look like her portrait: / Never mind. She will" [40]); 139 more pages for an elaboration on Owen's death (he was "attempting to cross an enemy-held canal, when he was machine-gunned" [179]). Beyond such links, *Reader's Block*'s static voice works like Dara's to create coherence by accumulating multiple variations on a fixed series of themes, principally (as Peter Dempsey notes) "anecdotes ... about the difficulties of the imaginative life" and anti-Semitism.[31]

Carole Maso's *AVA* (1993) restores a more coherent plot as it similarly gathers sparse fragments into a sequence that (the novel tells us) "let[s] silence have its share and allow[s] for a fuller meditative field than is possible in linear narrative or analysis."[32] Yet, in the context of the decade's skeletal encyclopedia, *AVA* is most significant in the ways that, even as it accumulates fragments and thematises the "strict alphabetical order of encyclopedic dictionaries" (139), it resists and challenges a data-gathering impulse ("Why try again to make the familiar catalogue from which something escapes" [24]) that it codes as fundamentally masculine. In this sense, Maso's book promotes alternative structures – notably invoking numerology (the book is fascinated by threes)[33] and cosmology (stars, planets, and the Zodiac recur) – and in her essay "Rupture, Verge, and Precipice," *AVA*'s skeletal design is explicitly opposed to the fuller encyclopedic form of the encyclopedic authors who came to prominence in the 1990s:

> Wish: That straight white males consider the impulse to cover the entire world with their words, fill up every page, every surface, everywhere. Thousand-page novels, tens and tens of vollmanns – I mean volumes. Not to own or colonize or dominate anymore.[34]

In the hands of varied writers, then, the skeletal encyclopedia might be spliced with the eco-thriller (Dara), with art history (Markson), or bent toward the creation of "feminine shapes"[35] (Maso). But the decade's other strand of encyclopedic fiction was equally vibrant, and while Maso merges works that "fill up every page" with both white, male writers and colonial domination, that position more accurately reflects the decade's critical construction of the encyclopedic genre (whose horizons were typically limited to a white-male axis) than the decade's literary production itself. In its most geopolitically expansive forms, the novelistic encyclopedia not only used its scale and stylistic range to probe the aftermath of colonial domination (Lee Siegel's superb *Love in a Dead Language* [1999] and Bob Shacochis's *Swimming in the Volcano* [1993]), but also began to move beyond "straight white males'" near-exclusive hold on the form. Released at decade's end after a long struggle with various publishers, Helen DeWitt's *The Last Samurai* (2000) exemplifies not just this broadening, but also one of the key ways that the novelistic encyclopedia embeds its diverse specialist knowledge.

DeWitt has noted that, in terms of its compositional history, *The Last Samurai* belongs "in the cohort of *Infinite Jest*,"[36] but it also overlaps with Wallace's and Powers's books in terms of its innovative form and diverse knowledge. Like *Gold Bug* and *Infinite Jest*, DeWitt's novelistic encyclopedia has a genealogical structure, which she signals in the novel's first words ("My father's father"),[37] and that primarily exists to contrast the Newman family's two younger generations. The novel begins with a short history of the two preceding generations in America's "motelland" (24), before switching to Sibylla Newman's first-person account of her research on ancient cultures at Oxford, her work with publishers, and her efforts to raise Ludo, her gifted son. Ludo – who is, like Stuart Ressler or Hal Incandenza, one of LeClair's "young, precocious characters" – eventually usurps Sibylla's narrative primacy, and he relates the bulk of the novel until its last pages. Laid out in this way, *The Last Samurai* appears more linear and more conventional than its male counterparts, but the genealogical pattern is simply the framework for a much more complicated narrative design. On one level, this design comments on male writers' obsession with narrating how "fathers impact sons"[38] by satirizing the search for a father figure through multiplication: after Sibylla refuses to reveal Ludo's father's identity – and then after Ludo finds his real father, and finds him unsuitable – Ludo embarks on five separate quests in which he declares a famous figure from a different field to be his father, and sets out to confront him with this news. Part parodic commentary, this process generates a sequence of parallel, micro-*bildungsroman* that are woven over the top of the Newman family's linear story, and that, in turn, generate and contain the novel's intellectual breadth. Taking *bildung* literally, the novel becomes a series of nested stories of education, starting with a polyglot linguistic history (instigated by Sibylla's advanced research at Oxford and her unorthodox decision to teach four-year-old Ludo to read *The Odyssey* in Greek), and then rapidly switching between astronomy, international diplomacy, and so on, as Ludo excavates the intellectual growth of each potential father and his subfield. Because Sibylla (following Yo Yo Ma's education), believes that any topic can be mastered by reducing it to the repetitive process of learning one subtask per day, the novel's approach to education is echoed in its geography, which becomes even more static than in comparable books, as Sibylla and Ludo spend their days riding London's Circle Line in endless loops.

This embedded structure exemplifies one of the ways the novelistic encyclopedia conveys its intellectual breadth in the 1990s, though what differs between writers is the relative distance between academic institutions and the nested bildungsroman. In *Gold Bug*, for instance, Powers (like DeWitt) establishes considerable distance, as he sets a central character to undertake "the Jan O'Deigh Continuing Education Project" (124): an autodidactic endeavor whose episodes punctuates the novel with mini-essays conveying the specialist biological knowledge that Powers needs the reader to understand. Perhaps because (as Mark McGurl has argued) Wallace was a "highly reflexive inhabitant of... educational institutions,"[39] *Infinite Jest* (like Siegel's *Love in a Dead Language*) typically shortens that distance, at times even recording its broader knowledge not simply in stories of institutionalized education, but in the institution's exemplary instrument for measuring educational growth: the essay or chapter. Thus the book's imagined geopolitics are relayed through long stretches of an essay on Canadian terrorism (1055–62n304), and the book's futuristic take on physics (491–503) ostensibly reprint "Ch. 16, 'The Awakening of My Interest in Annular Systems'" (1034n208). Unlike the skeletal encyclopedia's vertically stacked fragments of diverse knowledge, this embedded structure depends on the way the *bildungsroman*'s horizontal narrative of growth intersects with different educational institutions.

In *The Last Samurai*, the polyphonic vision implied by DeWitt's multiplying stories of education is reflected, on a page-by-page basis, in the novel's unstable treatment of narrative voice. Like Dara, Powers, and Wallace, DeWitt teases the reader with the question of where voices come from not only by varying the way she renders dialogue, but also through subtle typological shifts that mark distinctions between passages that would otherwise appear to be continuous summary by the same narrator (on the same page, for instance, DeWitt's narrator relays the same sentence in two different forms: "And he said OK"/ "& he said OK" [114]). If such shifts suggest that the narrative voice may be less homogenous than it appears – or that there may be more than one narrator – such suspicions gain traction from passages where DeWitt superimposes narration of one scene over another so the reader must jump backwards and forwards across paragraphs to restore continuity:

> the fact is that a clever man so seldom needs to think
> What's a syllabary?
> A syllabary is a set of phonetic symbols each representing a syllable
> he gets out of the habit.
> What's a syllable? (35)

The book offers a sequence of explanations for refusing the stable, single narrative world that fiction typically depends upon: on one level, this is a formal attempt to represent simultaneity, comparable to Woolf's parentheses in *To the Lighthouse* (1927); on another level, and in the context of the book's fascination with music, the technique parallels the novel's description of African drumming, where "two competing rhythms [are] played simultaneously" (164).[40] Yet such overlapping narrative layers are also enmeshed deeper in the novel's mind, and reflect a dynamic obsession with branching possibilities that shapes the book's sentences. DeWitt's treatment of Sibylla's sentences, in particular, often resist closure in favor of an open-ended dash:

> I was tempted to stay where I was, and if only –
> I won't think that. I don't mean that, but if only – (26)

Even where dashes are omitted, the novel's sentences often stall in comparable ways on the refrain *what if*, which appears seventeen times in the book. Sometimes the phrase substitutes for a period at the end of an incomplete sentence ("rub it back & forth and what if" [181]); elsewhere it feeds into larger reflections on recording technologies, as when Yamamoto tells Ludo, "When you play a piece of music there are so many different ways you could play it . . . When you buy a CD you get one answer the question. You never get the what if" (525). Style, here, is a vector of thematic content not in the sense that the parallel *bildungsroman* and what-if structure suggest an either/or choice, but rather that the book's overlapping techniques parallel extrapolations from many worlds theory that describe the state of a microscopic system not as "a set of alternatives . . . but a genuine overlapping combination of possible realities."[41] Just as quantum realities "overlap and interfere with each other," so DeWitt's narration layers as many as four different simultaneous "realities" in a single scene, jostling for the reader's attention,[42] or seems to narrate from different positions in consecutive scenes.

Sibylla adds a dark twist to this analogy when she merges the quantum universe with quotidian life in a passage (just before Ludo's narrative world displaces her own) where she likens seeing her image on a TV screen to "glimpses into possible worlds, worlds where the sun rises and the trains run without you. There are pushchairs to be pushed but not by you, bad memories to be dodged but not by you" (117). To think of "possible worlds" in terms of being both alive and dead evokes the condition of the "'live-dead' cat"[43] in Erwin Schrödinger's famous thought experiment, but it also resonates in subtle ways through Sibylla's narration. While Sibylla clearly interacts with other characters in the book, at times she casts doubt on her status by reflecting that she "would come back from the grave" to possess a particular book (22). At the level of literary allusion, her position is similarly qualified as she takes her name from the Cumaean Sibyl who both marks the threshold to the underworld in Virgil's *Aeneid*, and was chosen by T. S. Eliot to front his poetic catalogue of characters who are "neither / living nor dead."[44] On one level, then, this is Schrödinger's cat filtered through classical sources, and we can see the book's layered and unstable construction unfolding according to a quantum conceit; on another level, it parallels the voices from beyond the grave that provide climactic moments in *Infinite Jest* and *Gold Bug*. In different ways, each of these books works through the specialized voices of different disciplines, yet cannot suppress a metaphysical yearning for narration that transgresses the boundaries of lived experience.

An intricately structured and densely textured novel whose expertise courses through language, music, and mathematics, *The Last Samurai* – like *The Lost Scrapbook*, *Love in a Dead Language*, *Swimming in the Volcano*, *AVA*, and *Reader's Block* – demonstrates the continuing vitality of an encyclopedic tradition across the decade even as such texts have attracted little attention from scholars. The prevailing critical tendency to focus on only a small group of nineties encyclopedists has obscured the way that the white male hold on the form begins to weaken across the decade, opening the way for works such as Colson Whitehead's *John Henry Days* (2001) and Marisha Pessl's *Special Topics in Calamity Physics* (2006). Pessl's extravagant novel, in particular, exemplifies the novelistic encyclopedia's bookish form and emphasis on education, and that fulsome strand of encyclopedic fiction is amply represented in the new century by Mark Z. Danielewski's *House of Leaves* (2000), Sergio De La Pava's *A Naked Singularity* (2008), Reif Larsen's *I am Radar* (2015), and Jim Gauer's *Novel Explosives* (2016). The skeletal encyclopedia continues, too, in Dara's *The Easy Chain* (2008), Evan Lavender Smith's *From Old Notebooks* (2010), and (less obviously) in the looping repetitions of Lynne Tillman's single-voiced *American Genius* (2006). While it was understandable that Birkerts and Aldridge, both writing in proleptic mode at decade's start, might have doubts,[45] it is clear from a twenty-first century perspective that the canon of nineties encyclopedic fictions has been too small for too long.

NOTES

1 Karl, "Where are We?" *ANQ* 5.4 (1992): 201–202.
2 Sven Birkerts, *The Gutenberg Elegies: The Fate of Reading in an Electronic Age* (London: Faber, 1994), 117. Further references are parenthetical.

3 That this claim might be read in light of the encyclopedic novel is confirmed by Lawrence Buell, who argues that one particularly twentieth-century form of the Great American novel narrative emphasizes "sprawling performances of encyclopedic scope with multiple agendas from the ethnographic to the metaphysical" (Buell, *The Dream of the Great American Novel* [Cambridge, MA: Belknap, 2014], 349).
4 John Aldridge, *Talents and Technicians: Literary Chic and the New Assembly-Line Fiction* (New York: Scribners, 1992), 33.
5 MacIntyre's *Three Rival Versions of Moral Enquiry* (London: Duckworth, 1990), argues that the encyclopedia is inextricably linked to a model of unitary liberal rationalism that no longer matches modern epistemologies.
6 Edward Mendelson could argue in 1976 that the form "has not yet been fully recognized," "Encyclopedic Narrative: from Dante to Pynchon," *MLN* 91.6 (1976): 1267.
7 This urge, manifest in both the decade's novelists and critics, would include such representative examples as (on the brink of the decade) Tom LeClair's *The Art of Excess* (Urbana: University of Illinois Press, 1989); Hilary Clark's *The Fictional Encyclopedia* (New York: Garland, 1990); John Barth's discussion of "maximalism," ("It's a Long Story" [*Harper's* July 1990, 71–78]); Steven Weisenburger's "Enclopedic Satires" (*Fables of Subversion* [Athens: University of Georgia Press, 1995]); Franco Moretti's *Modern Epic* (New York: Verso, 1996); Ilan Stavans's "The Brick Novel," *Art and Anger* (New York: Palgrave, 1996); Trey Strecker's "Ecologies of Knowledge" (*Review of Contemporary Fiction* 28.3 [1998]: 67–71); and Richard House's "The Encyclopedia Complex: Contemporary Narratives of Information," *SubStance* 92 (2000): 25–46. A similar impulse is notable beyond studies of twentieth-century fiction, in such works as Giuseppe Mazzotta's *Dante's Vision and the Circle of Knowledge* (Princeton, NJ: Princeton University Press, 1993).
8 LeClair, "The Prodigious Fiction of Richard Powers, William Vollmann, and David Foster Wallace." *Critique* 38 (1996): 12–37.
9 Paul Dawson classifies Powers use of a "social commentator" narrator, whose "'omniscience' operates in the hyperbolic sense of displaying polymathic knowledge"; Wallace, by contrast, relies for Dawson on a "pyrotechnic narrator," who asserts "control over events being narrated through a "flourishing and expansive narrative voice." Dawson, *The Return of the Omniscient Narrator: Authorship and Authority in Twenty-First Century Fiction* (Columbus: Ohio State University Press, 2013), 22, 111.
10 Wallace, *Infinite Jest* (Boston: Little, 1997), 774. Further references are parenthetical.
11 *The Gold Bug Variations*, 631.
12 While precursor encyclopedic fictions – Gaddis's *The Recognitions*, Pynchon's *Gravity's Rainbow* – circle the globe, Wallace is frequently accused (not always fairly) of parochialism, and even *Infinite Jest*'s major international conflict hinges on a never-glimpsed Canada; Powers's other novels – notably *Plowing the Dark* and *Generosity* – are more attuned to global power currents,

and Caren Irr classifies him as a "moderate globalist" (*Toward the Geopolitical Novel* [New York: Columbia University Press, 2014], 18).
13 LeClair, Ibid. 14.
14 Vollmann, *The Atlas* (New York: Viking, 1996), 265.
15 Wallace's novels have been read in light of both the tradition of the encyclopedic novel and their use of "junk text" by David Letzler, in "Encyclopedic Novels and the Cruft of Fiction," *Studies in the Novel* 44 (2012): 308. The best account of the way Powers codes disparate information into *Gold Bug* remains Jay Labinger's excellent essay, "Encoding an Infinite Message," *Configurations* 3 (1995): 79–93.
16 With the exception of Jeremy Green's detailed and pioneering discussion of the novel in *Late Postmodernism* (New York: Palgrave, 2005), and Patrick O'Donnell's lively account of the novel's encyclopedic dimension in *The American Novel Now* (Malden, MA: Blackwell, 2010), scholars have made only incidental references to *The Lost Scrapbook*: in the earliest critical reference to the novel, for instance, Charles B. Harris identifies Dara as one of a younger "generation of postmodern writers" who are "even more socially conscious" than their ancestors ("At Play in the Fields of Formal Thinking," *Musing the Mosaic: Approaches to Ronald Sukenik*, ed. Matthew Roberson [Albany: SUNY Press, 2003] 59); John Blair Gamber's *Positive Pollutions and Cultural Toxins* (Lincoln: University of Nebraska Press, 2012) identifies Dara's novel as part of a sequence of antiurban narratives from the 1990s that deal "with issues of waste and toxicity" (195n27); Steven Moore notes in the conclusion to the expanded edition of his *William Gaddis* (New York: Bloomsbury, 2015) that Dara denies being influenced by *J R* (213).
17 "FC2" *New Yorker* 18 March 1996, 116.
18 Dara, *The Lost Scrapbook* (Normal, IL: FC2, 1995), 6. Further references are parenthetical.
19 Dara underlines this static quality by interrupting the opening scene with a sequence of signs all of which indicate truncated journeys: "YIELD" (9), "TOW-AWAY ZONE" (12), "KEEP DOOR CLOSED" (15).
20 *Late Postmodernism*, 191. Green astutely notes that "the novel's sole period appears before the very last word of the book."
21 LeClair, "Voices from an American Nightmare" *Washington Post Book World*, June 9, 1996, 11.
22 O'Donnell, Ibid., 197. In reviewing Dara's second novel, LeClair also noted that Dara disclaimed Gaddis's influence.
23 Moore, *William Gaddis*, 76.
24 Tabbi, "The Technology of Quotation: William Gaddis's *J R* and Contemporary Media" *Mosaic* 28.4 (1995): 144.
25 Understandably, many accounts *do* see length as a defining feature. Stefan Ercolino, for instance, presumably following Moretti's offhand comment that the modern epic is "very long" (4), maintains that "encyclopedism" cannot fully function "in a restricted space" (*The Maximalist Novel* [New York: Bloomsbury, 2014], 21).

26 LeClair, "Voices", 11.
27 René Descartes, *Discourse on Method and the Meditations*, trans. F.E. Sutcliffe (Harmondsworth: Penguin, 1968), 53–54. In this respect, the putative career counselor's otherwise inexplicable jumbling together of medicine, law, and forestry as potential career paths make sense: Descartes trained as a lawyer, devoted much of his career to medical research, and described his philosophical position as resembling that of a traveller "astray in some forest" (46).
28 Dara, *The Easy Chain* (New York: Aurora, 2008), 170.
29 Markson, *Reader's Block* (Normal, IL: Dalkey, 1996), 9. Further references are parenthetical.
30 Moore, "This is Not a Review" *American Book Review* 37.4 (2016): 17.
31 Dempsey, "Novelist of Shreds and Patches: The Fiction of David Markson," *Hollins Critic* 42.4 (2005): 10.
32 Maso, *AVA* (Normal, IL: Dalkey, 1993), 184. Further references are parenthetical.
33 In addition to the book's trisection of morning, afternoon, and night, Ava has three husbands, her name has three letters, she is 39, and so on.
34 Maso, *Break Every Rule* (Washington, DC: Counterpoint, 2000), 171.
35 Ibid., 178.
36 Quoted in Christian Lorentzen, "Publishing Can Break Your Heart," *New York* July 11, 2016, http://www.vulture.com/2016/07/helen-dewitt-last-samurai-new-edition.html.
37 DeWitt, *The Last Samurai* (Toronto: Knopf, 2000), 3. Further references are parenthetical.
38 Wallace, ibid., 32.
39 McGurl, "The Institution of Nothing," *Boundary 2* 41.3 (2014): 30.
40 A full consideration of music's relevance to the 1990s encyclopedic fiction is beyond the scope of this essay, but musical analogies (especially including variations) recur in Dara, DeWitt, and Powers.
41 Paul Davies, *Other Worlds* (London: Penguin, 1980), 129.
42 DeWitt, ibid. On pages 26–28, for instance, DeWitt simultaneously recounts a job offer, a conversation with Ludo, her reflections on Ludo's upbringing, and a summary of a scene in *Seven Samurai*.
43 Davies, Ibid., 131.
44 Eliot, *The Waste Land*, ed. Michael North (New York: Norton, 2001), 6.
45 Writing in the proleptic mode always offers a second chance, and it is important to note that two years after *Gutenberg*, Birkerts at least qualified his position, noting that he "had not thought enough about how" technological disruptions to our sense of time and history create a "a whole new category of need – one which the novel is wonderfully suited to meet." (Birkerts, "Second Thoughts," *Review of Contemporary Fiction* 16.1 [1996]: 9).

CHAPTER 8

Historical Fiction

John N. Duvall

The 1990s saw a remarkable number of major American novelists, both postmodernists and latter-day realists, publish fiction with historical content. In the same decade, theory and literary criticism frequently turned to the novel to discuss the relationship between history and postmodernity. The terms of this debate were set at the end of the previous decade largely by Linda Hutcheon and Fredric Jameson. In *A Poetics of Postmodernism* (1988) and *The Politics of Postmodernism* (1989), Hutcheon takes exception to Jameson's original 1984 articulation of his thesis about the way in which a degraded historicism pervades postmodernism, which therefore cannot provide an oppositional aesthetic but only serve as the cultural logic of multinational capitalism. For Hutcheon, however, postmodernist fiction functions as historiographic metafiction and ultimately allows for an implicated critique of the order of things.

Jameson's and Hutcheon's competing positions, although they would significantly impact literary criticism's approach to historical novels throughout the 1990s, were based on readings of novels published, by and large, in the 1970s. As she defines her concept of historiographic metafiction, Hutcheon turns to Robert Coover's *The Public Burning* (1977) and E. L. Doctorow's *The Book of Daniel* (1971), two novels that reimagine the trial and execution of the Rosenbergs. Novels such as these, Hutcheon argues, "do not rewrite, refashion, or expropriate history merely to satisfy either some game-playing or some totalizing impulse"; rather "they juxtapose what we think we know of the past (from official archival sources and personal memory) with an alternate representation that foregrounds the postmodern questioning of the nature of historical knowledge. Which *facts* make it into history? And *whose* facts?"[1] Hutcheon's choice of these two novels points toward both what has made her concept historiographic metafiction both so appealing and problematic. Coover's style is antimimetic and ludic in the extreme. The novel imagines then–Vice President Richard M. Nixon narrating alternating chapters as he tries to figure out how he can be the next incarnation of Uncle Sam (the US president) and attempts to resist his growing erotic interest in Ethel Rosenberg; ultimately, the novel depicts the Rosenberg execution occurring in Times Square, an event triggering a mass orgy. Doctorow's treatment of the same material, however, is at base realist, despite his use of a self-conscious narrator, the convicted spies' son, Daniel. Doctorow renames the Rosenbergs the Isaacsons, but Daniel's attempt to burrow into the archive about his parents' execution reveals in the end the limits of the historian's ability to know the past. In sum, Coover may use the right names, but there's not much history in *The Public Burning*; Doctorow may change the names, but one leaves *The Book of Daniel* with a clear sense of the historical shift from the Old to the New Left. If books as different as Coover's and Doctorow's can both be labeled historiographic metafiction, then the term may have some political relevance (as a set of texts with left-leaning tendencies), but certainly cannot identify a coherent postmodern narrative poetics.

In 1991 Jameson in turn responds to Hutcheon in his *Postmodernism, Or, The Cultural Logic of Late Capitalism*, specifically denying any efficacy to contemporary metahistorical fiction, so that even Doctorow's is but another instance of the crisis of historicity such that his fiction "remains the most peculiar and stunning monument to the aesthetic situation engendered by the disappearance of the historical referent. The historical novel can no longer set out to represent the historical past; it can only 'represent' our ideas and stereotypes about that past (which thereby at once becomes 'pop history')."[2]

What disturbs the Marxist theoretician Jameson (our inability any longer to think historically, which would allow us to cognitively map the present – or, in plainer language, to come to class consciousness), however, is precisely what the neocon political scientist Francis Fukuyama tells us not to worry about. In his 1989 essay "The End of History?" (subsequently developed into his 1992 book *The End of History and the Last Man*), Fukuyama argues that the fall of Communism signals "an unabashed victory of economic and political liberalism" (3).[3] Wishing to reclaim the Hegelian dialectic from Marx, Fukuyama posits "the end of history as such: that is the end point of mankind's ideological evolution and the universalization of Western liberal democracy as the final form of human government" (4). For Fukuyama, liberal democracy, not communism, is the last stage in the dialectic of history. Major events may happen, but no new form of social organization will ever arise. In other words, humanity had reached its final and most satisfying form of social organization in (neo)liberal democracy.

This intellectual climate suggests why American novelists repeatedly turned to historical fiction during the 1990s. History (whether its promise, its failure, or its irrelevance) was, quite simply, a key cultural issue. From our historical distance now of over a quarter of a century, Hutcheon's historicizing metafiction, Jameson's crisis of historicity, and Fukuyama's end of history all can be read in part as responses to late–Cold War conditions that lead to the fall of the Berlin Wall in November 1989 and ultimately the dissolution of the Soviet Union by the end of 1991. All of the authors who wrote historical novels in the 1990s lived most of their adult lives during the time of the powerful Us–Them binary that was the United States versus the USSR. This legacy includes the local hot war of Vietnam and the cultural and economic imperialism that accompanied the US effort to contain the threat of communism. While much good critical work has been done that focuses on the historical periods that 1990s historical novels represent, such work often overlooks the obvious historical context of the time that these novels were written – the last decade of the twentieth century, when it looked as though the American Century would soon open onto the American Millennium in the twenty-first century. Read historically, the historical novel of the 1990s serves as a reflection on the post–Cold War status of American exceptionalism, on what it means, in other words, for the United States to have come out on top as the world's last remaining superpower (a fantasy that will dissipate most dramatically on September 11, 2001).[4] Many of these novels are critical of the emerging neoliberal order of capitalism or remind us of America's failure during the Cold War to adequately address the problem of race and the legacy of slavery.

I will first explore the two most overt and massive reflections on the Cold War, Norman Mailer's 1168-page *Harlot's Ghost* (1991) and Don DeLillo's 827-page *Underworld* (1997). Taken together they recapitulate both the utility and the limitations of historiographic metafiction as they focus our attention explicitly on the Us–Them relationship of the United States and the Soviet Union. I then turn to Thomas Pynchon's *Mason & Dixon* (1997), Toni Morrison's *Paradise* (1997), and Charles Johnson's *Middle Passage* (1990). Unlike Mailer and DeLillo, Pynchon, Morrison, and Johnson treat the post–Cold War condition at the remove of allegory; they consider the personal and political consequences of different Us–Them binaries that uncannily double that of the United States–USSR; at the same time, they (like DeLillo) depict spiritual mystery (whether ludic or magic realist) to think about the way forward in post–Cold War America. The final section turns to novels by two realist writers – Madison Smartt Bell's *All Souls' Rising* (1995) and Philip Roth's *The Human Stain* (2000) – that fall outside of the conversation about postmodernism but that, like their postmodern counterparts, take stock of matters such as slavery and racism that come into clearer focus following the end of the Cold War.

The Cold War Metafictionalized: Mailer and DeLillo

In their treatment of the Cold War, Mailer and DeLillo both blur the boundary between history and fiction, mixing fictional characters with actual historical figures and events. Both imagine such historical events as the Cuban Missile Crisis and the assassination of President John F. Kennedy. Performances by the comedian Lenny Bruce appear in both novels. Despite these superficial similarities, the two novels depict the paranoia of the Cold War very differently. In a sense, Mailer plays Doctorow to DeLillo's Coover. In other words, like Hutcheon's foundational authors for her concept of historiographic metafiction, Mailer is more the realist; DeLillo, the ludic postmodernist (certainly in his novel's prologue and epilogue).

Although replete with metafictional elements, *Harlot's Ghost* (similar to Doctorow's *The Book of Daniel*) is largely an exercise in mimesis. In the fictional present of December 1983 to March 1984 that frames the novel, CIA operative Herrick (Harry) Hubbard travels to Moscow in order to find his paraplegic mentor, a high-ranking CIA agent, Hugh Montague (Harlot), who Harry believes has faked his death to conceal his true identity as a long-time Soviet mole in the Agency. Harry takes with him microfilm of his long memoir about his experiences in the CIA with him to read and then destroy before it falls into the wrong hands. The bulk of the novel, then, is Harry's memoir, told in large part in epistolary fashion.

Practically all of the agents in Mailer's novel are either homosexual, consider themselves to be heterosexual but have had homosexual experiences, or have repressed homosexual desires. Infidelity is a major trope in the novel. To successfully have an extramarital affair seems to be the sign that one has what it takes to be good secret agent. But such infidelity is a double-edged sword. At the beginning of the novel, Harry is having an affair but is certain that his wife, Kittredge, loves him. But Harry had an affair with Kittredge (who is also a CIA agent) while she was still married to Montague. He returns home to discover that Kittredge is leaving him for a rival in the Agency who once homosexually propositioned Harry. All of the adultery in the novel serves as a trope for Harry's relation to the spies he handles because he can never be sure (as is the case with spouses in the novel) whether their intercourse (verbal or sexual) is for him alone. Harry himself is serially unfaithful to his various bosses in his assignments around the world. He routinely betrays their top-secret confidences either to Kittredge or Montague.

Harlot's Ghost thematizes the central argument that Timothy Melley has made in *The Covert Sphere*. For Melley, following World War II, the profound growth of top-secret agencies means that "foreign policy matters" have been "sequestered from the public sphere" and have fundamentally altered the shape of American democracy.[5] The public sphere of informed democratic debate has been replaced by the covert sphere that operates by disinformation, plausible deniability, and covert action, all of which has fueled the rise of postmodernism. In whatever form (film, television, or novels), "fiction is one of the few discourses in which the secret work of the state may be disclosed to citizens."[6] Paranoid postmodern fiction, then, is one logical response to a world in which we know that we don't know what the American government is doing in our names, and so fiction ironically becomes the only way the vast majority of Americans can ever begin to understand the duplicity and disinformation created by US secret agencies.

Mailer's Harlot is particularly contemptuous of the public sphere. Harry is in Berlin when the United States has succeeded in tapping into a Soviet cable line, an operation that provides intelligence that the Soviets' military is not as strong as had been suspected. But Harlot tells Harry, "Nonetheless, we keep pushing for an enormous defense buildup. Because, Harry, once we decide the Soviet is militarily incapable of large military attacks, the American people will go soft on Communism.... So we don't encourage news about all-out slovenliness in the Russian military machine."[7] The tap is soon discovered, and Harry suspects that Harlot may have had a hand in tipping off the Russians. US foreign policy in Mailer's world happens not through Congress and the president, but rather by happenstance, through the various plots to secure CIA jurisdiction over the FBI and infighting between and among various top officials in the CIA who hope to replace Allen Dulles when he retires as Director of the Agency.

If the epistemology of the closet and adultery are Mailer's central tropes for the affect of the Cold War period, DeLillo makes waste – whether nuclear or that of consumer society – his central figure in *Underworld*. The prologue to the novel, "The Triumph of Death," immediately signals a difference between Mailer's primarily mimetic presentation and DeLillo's more ludic approach. *Underworld* opens at what is one of the most iconic baseball game ever played: the third and deciding game of a playoff for the 1951 National League pennant between perennial rivals – the Brooklyn Dodgers and the New York Giants. In "The Power of History," an essay that appeared on the eve of *Underworld*'s publication, DeLillo reflects on a massive historical irony. The very day, October 3, 1951, that Bobby Thomson hits his game-winning home run for the Giants, the United States learns that the Soviet Union has nuclear capability. If this day is remembered, however, it is for its significance to the history of baseball, not that of the Cold War.

DeLillo imagines the game from various angles of vision, that of (1) Russ Hodges, the radio voice of the Giants; (2) Jackie Gleason, Frank Sinatra, Toots Shore, and J. Edgar Hoover who all sit together in Leo Durocher's box seats; and (3) an African-American teenager, Cotter Martin, and Bill Waterson, a white middle-aged architect, who watch the game together in the left-field seats. Hodge's perspective adds a metafictional element inasmuch as Russ recalls how he broadcast Washington Senators games, even though he was not present; he created a sense of verisimilitude for his audience by inventing details of what was happening on the field and in the stands while merely reading the bare facts of the games as they came in over the wire. DeLillo, of course, plays precisely this role in fleshing out the details of this famous baseball game from long ago. While DeLillo deploys Gleason and Sinatra for laughs, this perspective becomes significant when an FBI agent approaches Hoover during the postgame celebration to inform him of the Soviet nuclear test. In the shower of paper that fans toss, Hoover happens to catch a *Life* magazine reproduction of Bruegel's *The Triumph of Death*, and sees in the Flemish painter's nightmarish vision a harbinger of nuclear apocalypse. But the outfield perspective is ultimately the most central to the novel as a whole since it is Cotter who retrieves the ball Thomson hits. The apparent camaraderie of two Giant's fans turns ugly when Cotter refuses to sell the ball to Bill, who becomes increasingly more belligerent in his attempt to procure the souvenir. Ultimately the supposed pastoral of baseball cannot mask underlying racial tensions, a fact marked by the way that the novel subsequently represents Cotter's sister, Rosie, at a 1964 civil rights march attempting to help a man being beaten by a cop with a billy club (which of course suggests a miniature baseball bat).

The baseball itself in any other context would be waste, a used baseball that, if not for the fact that it were the ball Thomson hit, would quite literally be relegated to the trash heap. But instead the ball becomes a valuable commodity, one that increases with value each time it passes from one collector of sports memorabilia to another. One of the plot devices DeLillo uses is to trace the ownership of the baseball to Nick Shay, who works in waste management.

Waste, of course, is what remains from consumption, and *Underworld* posits that the United States won the Cold War not so much through the government policy of the containment of communism, but rather through its ability to have both a strong military and a robust consumer society. The Soviets may have been able to match America's nuclear tonnage, but not its consumerism. The hidden costs of American consumer culture are observable in a national identity shaped by the Cold War's master Us-Them binary – the United States versus the USSR. At the same time, DeLillo's novel considers what happens when this stable ground of belief is removed with the fall of communism. The Cold War effectively masked the nature of the political economy, but when the Cold War ends, nothing can mask the rapaciousness of multinational capital. The threat of nuclear apocalypse may have receded, but *Underworld* suggests, with little to contain capitalism's saturation of global markets, an environmental apocalypse looms.

The epilogue of *Underworld*, "Das Kapital," takes Nick to post–Cold War Kazakhstan where an entrepreneurial neoliberalism is embodied by Viktor Maltsev, who plans to monetize Russia's old nuclear arsenal by using controlled underground nuclear explosions to vaporize hazardous waste (including nuclear waste) from the West. Viktor also takes Nick to Semipalatinsk and the Museum of Misshapens to show him specimens of preserved fetuses, the result of mothers who lived downwind of aboveground nuclear test sites. *Underworld*'s epilogue underscores one of the novel's central concerns – the hidden environmental costs of the US victory over the Soviet Union.

At the same time, however, the epilogue allows DeLillo, a lapsed Catholic, to do what he so often does: namely, introduce the possibility of spiritual mystery into the postmodern. After a Hispanic girl has been raped and murdered in the Bronx, people gather before a billboard to witness what they take to be her superimposed image appear at night whenever a subway train's lights shine through the advertisement. The skeptical Sister Alma Edgar (one of Nick's former teachers) goes to investigate the phenomenon and becomes a true believer. But in the wake of growing crowds, the billboard is papered over with the message "Space Available."[8] When the possibility of the miraculous has been erased, Sister Edgar dies; however, she does not go to heaven but rather to cyberspace where she becomes linked to her germaphobic male double, J. Edgar Hoover. DeLillo's more ludic form of historiographic metafiction is consistent with other metahistorical novels that do not directly represent the Cold War.

Allegorical History: Pynchon, Morrison, and Johnson

In *Mason & Dixon* Pynchon writes about the Enlightenment values that inform the construction of America. Jameson may have argued for the importance of cognitive mapping, but Pynchon literalizes the importance of mapping. This narrative of a pre–Revolutionary War America is told in the early days of the new republic, shortly after Charles Mason's death in November 1786. That Pynchon's novel can be read as a commentary on contemporary America is signaled early in the opening chapter: "This Christmastide of 1786, with the War settl'd and the Nation bickering itself into Fragments, wounds bodily and ghostly, go aching on, not ev'ry one commemorated, – nor, too often, even recounted."[9] *Mason & Dixon*, then, with its postwar setting published just a few years into the post–Cold War period recounts the paranoid struggles of various institutions with possible secret political agendas (from the Royal Society and the East India Company to the Jesuits) competing for the soul of an America yet to be born. In a sense, the novel maps Cold War paranoia onto colonial America, suggesting that this earlier historical period had its own cold war prior to the eruption of the Revolutionary War.

Pynchon's is doubtless the most ludic of all historical novels from the 1990s. While its style mimics the spelling conventions (and at times the tone) of an eighteenth-century novel, *Mason & Dixon* abounds with all manner of anachronistic references that disrupt our sense of verisimilitude and point to contemporary America. The story of the collaboration between the astronomer Charles Mason and the surveyor Jeremiah Dixon is narrated by the fictional Rev. Wicks Cherrycoke to his nieces and nephews. The fictional Cherrycoke accompanied the famous pair during their earlier assignment observing the Transit of Venus in Cape Town and was also a member of the surveying team's party as they set their American boundary line. Pynchon's naming his narrator for a product that Coca-Cola introduced in 1985 (nearly the bicentennial of Mason's death), along with his allusion to such twentieth-century pop culture as *Star Trek* and Daffy Duck suggests the extent to which the author signals to readers that they should think about the present as much as the past when engaging *Mason & Dixon*.

Following the end of the US–USSR conflict, Mason and Dixon themselves are a study in overcoming binary oppositions: Mason is melancholic; Dixon, jovial. Mason drinks wine and tea; Dixon prefers beer or whiskey and coffee. Despite their different personalities, they forge a friendship that lasts the rest of their lives, an optimistic note that Pynchon sounds about the possibility of the reconciliation of differences in the post–Cold War period. But this element of hope is tempered by the effects of the boundary line that Mason and Dixon draw between Pennsylvania and Maryland. Cut through frontier, wilderness, and Indian land, the border is the enclosure movement writ large, its absolute straightness made possible by Enlightenment science. But the boundary line is also for that reason an insult to nature. On the one hand, it follows no terrain, such as river, valley, or hill that previously would have marked different ownership. On the other hand, human nature is insulted by the boundaries demarcating free Pennsylvania from slave-holding Maryland, thus encoding – even before the establishment of the United States – the impetus for the geo-political divisions that would erupt in the American Civil War.

The irony is that these men are ignorant of the future of violence they inscribe upon the land, for Mason and Dixon are personally appalled by slavery when they encounter it – first in South Africa, and later in America. As Cherrycoke notes:

> Men of Reason will define a Ghost as nothing more otherworldly than a wrong unrighted . . . But here is a Collective Ghost of more than household Scale, – the Wrongs committed Daily against the Slaves, petty and grave ones alike, going unrecorded, charm'd invisible to history, invisible yet possessing Mass, and Velocity, able not only to rattle Chains but to break them as well.[10]

In this regard, Pynchon's novel (like Morrison's, Johnson's, and Bell's) functions to bring to light what the archive of official history has failed to record.

Against their embodiment of Enlightenment principles, Mason and Dixon constantly encounter marvels, mystery, and magic, such as a talking dog and an automaton duck that has acquired the ability to love. The surveying of the line indeed ends when Mason and Dixon encounter a party of Indians who inform them that they may not cross the mystical Warrior's Path. The Indians, however, take Mason and Dixon across this path to show the white men a land of giant vegetables. In such encounters, Pynchon (as he has done throughout his career) reminds of us of everything that a technocratic rationality suppresses.

Like Pynchon's novel, Morrison's *Paradise* uses an equally freighted time present of American history – 1976, the US Bicentennial – to comment on the post–Cold War period and the myth of American exceptionalism. Ostensibly a historical account of the Exodusters migration to the West, *Paradise* imagines the Us–Them binary of an all-black town – Ruby, Oklahoma – and the nearby Convent, which has developed into a collection of wounded and traumatized women who band together in an attempt to heal their personal traumas. In coded form, then, Morrison uses this opposition to think about the fate of exceptional community, the City on the Hill. The utopian dream of Ruby as the creation of a more perfect union is immediately challenged in the opening chapter, which exposes this black community's contradictions when a group of townsmen brutally murder the women of the Convent.

The attack, while it develops Morrison's recurring explorations of the limitations of a black patriarchal and materialistic family and/or community that cannot understand the spiritual difference of female-centered community, also eerily comments on what had been a key fantasy of American's Cold War stance toward the otherness of the Soviet Union. As Donald Pease notes, "The cold war state fantasy of American exceptionalism allowed U.S. citizens to experience their national community as coherently regulated through the disavowal of its inherent transgressions required to counteract the Soviet threat."[11] Ruby, it turns out, instantiates the security state. Founded by World War II veterans, Ruby stands as these men's attempt to preserve the spirit of their original all-black town, Haven, founded by dark-skinned former slaves who migrated to Oklahoma. For the Morgan brothers, descendants of the leader of the band of former slaves, their town is a utopia worth protecting, a place where there is no jail and no one dies in the town proper, not since their sister, Ruby – for whom the town is named.

Like Pynchon and DeLillo, Morrison infuses her historical fiction with spiritual mystery. The founding of Haven is almost biblical with former slaves wandering in the wilderness until they begin following a mysterious stranger who suddenly disappears at the site of what becomes their new town. More significantly, what readers thought they knew about the attack on the Convent is rewritten in the penultimate chapter not as a slaughter of the women but the women's heroic battle against the attacking men. The women may be killed, but when Roger Best drives his hearse out to the Convent to pick up the bodies, there is nothing to recover; the bodies have all disappeared. Rev. Richard Misner and Anna Flood go to investigate what they take to be a secular mystery, but encounter spiritual mystery instead. Standing outside the Convent, "they saw it. Or sensed it, rather, for there was nothing to see. A door, she said later. 'No, a window,' he said, laughing." The laugher is necessary "to avoid reliving the shiver... [W]hat would happen if you entered? What would be on the other side? What on earth would it be? What on earth?"[12] This door or window stages what follows: we encounter the murdered women embodied again meeting and making peace with (or chastising) family members who have been the source of their traumas. On the novel's final page, Morrison leaves history behind entirely for the mythic as a young woman rests with the divine figure of Piedade on an ocean shore.

As for the town of Ruby, Morrison implies a better future now that the dream of an exceptional, morally superior community has exploded. One of the Morgan brothers, Deacon, has taken responsibility for his violence and the town will now enter history: death will return to the community and the outside world, with all its problems and complications, will come to a people who can no longer claim to be innocent victims.

Charles Johnson's *Middle Passage*, which tells of shipboard slave revolt in 1830, also signals its allegorical treatment of the historical through its clear homage to the fiction of Herman Melville, particularly *Moby-Dick* (1851) and "Benito Cereno" (1855), the later of which similarly recounts a different maritime slave revolt of 1799. Like Melville, Johnson uses the past to comment on his present. Faced with debts and a marriage he wants to avoid, Rutherford Calhoun, a freed slave, stows away on the *Republic*, captained by the philosophical madman, Ebenezer Falcon. The *Republic* is, of course, a figure for the republic that is the United States, and on the voyage to the Gulf of Guinea and the slave factory at Bangalang, Calhoun is surprised to learn that "the *Republic* was physically unstable ... perpetually flying apart and reforming ... In a word, she was, from stem to stern, a process."[13] Far from being a unified set of timeless values pertaining to life, liberty, and the pursuit of happiness, the United States is at sea amidst the conflicting desires of politics and capitalism. In this way, *Middle Passage* questions the ascendency of the new neoliberal order championed by Fukuyama.

Assigned to work without pay as the cook's assistant, Calhoun is dismayed to learn that part of the *Republic*'s return cargo consists of forty slaves from the fictional Allmuseri tribe – Africans with reputed magical powers. But not only does Falcon take the Allmuseri, he also boxes up their god, another manifestation of postmodern writers' interest in spiritual mystery. In a clear rewriting of Melville's black cabin boy, Pip, who goes mad in *Moby-Dick*, Johnson depicts the white cabin boy, Tommy, who is driven to madness when he is lowered by a rope to describe to the other sailors what is contained in the mysterious box. *Middle Passage* also implies that the Allmuseri god is responsible for the severe storm that cripples the *Republic* as it tries to return to New Orleans. Members of the crew, fearing that the captain is mad, plan a mutiny. Calhoun, in all of this, is a conduit of information, a double agent of sorts, privy to the mutineer's plans, informant to captain, yet also – because he is black – alerted by the Allmuseri about the impending revolt.

After the slaves revolt, Calhoun is sent by the Allmuseri to convince Falcon to help them plan a route back to Africa. In his meeting with the captain, Calhoun learns that Falcon is not the power he had seemed to be. When Calhoun tries to tell the captain that the Africans now own the *Republic*, Falcon responds:

> "They're wrong... She wasn't *our* ship from the start, Mr. Calhoun. Every plank and piece of canvas on the *Republic*, and any cargo she's carrying, from clew to earring – including that creature below [the Allmuseri god] – belongs to the three blokes who outfitted her in New Orleans and pay our wages. See, someone has to pay the *bill*. I'm captain 'cause I know how to bow and scrape and kiss rich arses to raise money for this run... [A]nd they'd just as soon see us drown, if I sail home empty-handed, as hear me report their fixed capital seized control of this brig and swung her back to Bangalang."[14]

Hearing this, Calhoun realizes that Falcon "was no freer than the Africans," which resonates with Ishmael's question in the opening chapter of *Moby-Dick* when he describes the relation of the worker to the capitalist: "Who ain't a slave?"[15]

Similar to Morrison's *Paradise*, Johnson's novel does not attribute all African American ills to whites but shows the implicating force of capitalist exploitation extends beyond one race. The true villain of the novel turns out not to be Captain Falcon, but rather a mixed-race Creole, Philippe (Papa) Zeringue, who owns one-third of the *Republic*. Seduced by the promise of having his capital outlay tripled by investing in a slave ship, Papa has no moral qualms about what he has done. Like DeLillo, Pynchon, and Morrison, Johnson uses the form of the historical novel to question the assumed good of the neoliberal order of the 1990s by presenting us with a clear instance in which the deregulation of capital does not necessarily result in more liberty, as Fukuyama argued was the case.

Realism and Racial Histories: Bell and Roth

Another novel that might logically be spoken of in relation to Morrison's and Johnson's is Madison Smartt Bell's *All Souls' Rising*, an account of the rise and fall of Toussaint-Louverture, a former slave who became the leader of the slave revolt in Haiti during the 1790s. As such, the novel is yet another reminder that the legacy of slavery's trauma, on both its victims and perpetrators, was coming into sharper focus in the aftermath of the Cold War when the narrative of American exceptionalism, so necessary to maintain during the decades-long struggle with the Soviet Other, could no longer mask the contradictions of America's Enlightenment origins. Like postmodern historiographic metafiction, Bell's novel mixes fictional and historical characters; however, the metafictional impulse in *All Souls' Rising* is negligible. With a preface that reads like a history book, as well as its appendices (the "Chronology of Historical Events" and a dictionary of French names and slang), Bell never nods to the reader that what he has written is a fictional construct, but rather seems to announce "this is the way it really was," and hence there is simply no historiographic reflection. This element, which one finds in Morrison's historical trilogy of *Beloved* (1987), *Jazz* (1992), and *Paradise*, is something that *All Souls' Rising* could use, a narratorial reflexivity that might remind the readers of their voyeuristic implication in the violence depicted. Bell, it seems, wants to outdo Morrison's *Beloved* in presenting the sexualized violence of slavery, so much so that many moments in his novel seem to devolve into torture porn. The opening of Chapter 1 establishes this element when Dr. Hebert, a central white character newly arrived in Haiti, approaches a plantation and sees a still barely living black woman slave nailed to a pole:

> Pulling against the vertex of the nail her pectoral musculature had lifted her breasts, which were taut, with large aureoles, nipples distended. Although her weight must have pulled her diaphragm tight, the skin around her abdomen hung comparatively slack. At her pudenda appeared a membranous extrusion from which Doctor Hebert averted his eye. Her feet were transfixed one over the other by the same sort of homemade nail as held her hands.[16]

This extended description of the woman's dying moments and the doctor's registering the beauty of her head continues for another paragraph. As shocking as the description of the dying woman, the fact is that Hebert continues on to the planter's house but says nothing to the planter about what he has seen. After dinner, he accompanies the planter back to the pole. The woman has died and Hebert, who had recognized that the woman's body showed that she had recently given birth, learns that she had been executed because she had murdered her child (almost certainly fathered by the planter) the moment it was born.

This opening moment is but the first of the novel's numerous instances of graphic violence – whites raping blacks, blacks raping and murdering whites, blacks raping mulattoes, whites eviscerating blacks, blacks eviscerating whites, and so on.

Despite its explicit violence, *All Souls' Rising* does remind the reader that the New World treatment of slaves, whether in French Haiti or America,

Historical Fiction 137

created the long nightmare of racial strife that was still part of the United States in the 1990s, to say nothing of today. The Cold War may have ended, but the video that captured the brutal beating of Rodney King by Los Angles police and the subsequent 1992 riots that ensued when the officers were acquitted of state charges illustrate that Bell's nightmare is one that we have yet to awaken from, and recalls William Faulkner's famous statement that "The past is never dead. It's not even past."[17]

I would like to conclude by turning to Philip Roth's *The Human Stain* (2000). This novel, along with *American Pastoral* (1997) and *I Married a Communist* (1998), constitutes the author's American trilogy, which explores the post–World War II history of Newark, New Jersey. All three novels explicitly participate in the millennial reflection on America's Cold War legacy: the first takes up protests against the Vietnam War and racial unrest in the 1960s; the second, 1950s Red Scare and blacklisting of actors and writers with suspected communist sympathies. But it is *The Human Stain*, written in 1999, that stands as the last passing novel of the twentieth century. In the politically correct environment of Athena College, classics professor Coleman Silk resigns in the wake of a charge that he used the word "spooks" in a racially insensitive manner to identify African-American students. Although from the context the charge is false – Silk was simply questioning whether these students on his roster who he had never met and had never attended his class were material beings – the larger irony is that light-skinned Silk himself is African-American. He cannot use his perfect defense ("But I'm black, too.") because to do so would be to admit that his entire life had been a lie. After serving in World War II, Silk returns home, goes to NYU, and decides to pass as Jewish in order to escape what he felt to be the "tyranny of the we" that he had sensed in his first prewar college experience at Howard University where he discovered that he could only be seen as another Negro.[18] Silk's decision to pass illustrates the extent to which he believes in the American Dream of the self-made individual who is "free to be whatever he wants" and at the same time reveals that such exceptionalist thinking about personal freedom is ultimately fantasy.[19] In a sense, Roth's novel returns us to this chapter's starting point, *Harlot's Ghost*. Roth, like Mailer, eschews the spiritual mystery favored by DeLillo, Pynchon, Morrison, and Johnson for secular mystery. If Harry wants to learn if Harlot is really a double agent, Roth's Nathan Zukerman is trying to solve a crime the police do not acknowledge even exists: Were Silk and his lover Faunia murdered by her ex-husband, the violent Vietnam veteran Les Farley? Silk, like Mailer's CIA agents, leads a closeted double life, which reminds one of the difference between Roth's passing novel and earlier passing novels by African-Americans. Texts like James Weldon Johnson's *Autobiography of the Ex-Coloured Man* (1912) or Nella Larsen's *Passing* (1929) speak to the racism blacks faced in those novels' contemporary moments.

At the same time that Roth reminds us that the post–Cold War decade of the 1990s still carries the scar of unresolved racial conflict, his novel also explores another hidden cost of the US Cold War victory – the shattered lives of Vietnam veterans suffering from post-traumatic stress disorder. Vietnam veterans are, of course, also Cold War veterans inasmuch as Vietnam staged a local hot war in compliance with the US strategy of the global containment of communism.[20] Les Farley may be a murderer, but Roth does not deny the character his humanity.

Whether focusing either on the twentieth century or on more distant colonial histories, American novelists of the 1990s repeatedly craft narratives that seem to track along the lines of Coover's and Doctorow's historical fiction of the 1970s; however, these later novels assert their difference from their forebears by attempting to think through and beyond polarized worlds of Us and Them. While individually taking up such issues as the erosion of the public sphere, the degradation of the environment, the effects of slavery, and the ascendency of neoliberalism, these historical novels collectively shape counternarratives that might serve to usher America into the twenty-first century in a way that would lay to rest the intertwined fantasies of American exceptionalism and innocence. What these writers could not know is that early in the new millennium, a terrorist attack on US soil would reactivate these same narratives of exceptionalism and innocence, returning American politics to a new instantiation of Us and Them.

NOTES

1 Linda Hutcheon, *The Politics of Postmodernism* (London: Routledge, 1989), 71.
2 Fredric Jameson, *Postmodernism, Or, The Cultural Logic of Late Capitalism* (Durham: Duke University Press, 1991), 25.
3 Francis Fukuyama, "The End of History?" 3.
4 In *After the End of History: American Fiction in the 1990s* (Iowa City: University of Iowa Press, 2009), Samuel Cohen also argues that historical fiction in the 1990s entered the conversation "about the role of the United States in the world after the Cold War" (27), though without my emphases on the critique of exceptionalism, neoliberalism, and racial progress.
5 Timothy Melley, *The Covert Sphere: Secrecy, Fiction, and the National Security State* (Ithaca: Cornell University Press, 2012), 4.
6 Melley, 6.
7 Norman Mailer, *Harlot's Ghost* (New York: Ballantine, 1991), 355.
8 Don DeLillo, *Underworld* (New York: Scribner, 1997), 824.

9 Thomas Pynchon, *Mason & Dixon* (New York: Holt, 1997), 6.
10 *Mason & Dixon*, 68.
11 Donald E. Pease, *The New American Exceptionalism* (Minneapolis: University of Minnesota Press, 2009), 8.
12 Toni Morrison, *Paradise* (New York: Knopf, 1998), 305.
13 Charles Johnson, *Middle Passage* (New York: Scribner, 1990), 36–37.
14 Johnson, 147.
15 Herman Melville, *Moby-Dick* [1851] (New York: Norton, 2002), 21.
16 Madison Smartt Bell, *All Souls' Rising* (New York, Penguin, 1995), 11.
17 William Faulkner, *Requiem for a Nun* [1951] (New York: Vintage, 1994), 73.
18 Philip Roth, *The Human Stain* (New York: Vintage, 2001), 108.
19 Roth, 109.
20 Another realist historical novel that might also be used to assess the trauma of Vietnam veterans is Charles Frasier's *Cold Mountain* (1997). Although set near the end of the Civil War, the novel has been taken as a coded commentary on Vietnam. See Amy J. Elias, *Sublime Desire History and Post-1960s Fiction* (Baltimore: Johns Hopkins University Press, 2001), 17.

CHAPTER 9

Lyrical Thinking in Poetry of the 1990s

Thomas Gardner

When you think about American poetry of the 1990s as a whole, you see not just a collection of brilliant, individual attempts to use language in new and more deeply expressive ways, but a sustained investigation of the powers and possibilities of the lyric itself. The previous decade had seemed to insist on a sharp division between writers committed to voice and song as central to the dream of revelatory self-expression and those, loosely connected with what came to be called Language writing, suspicious of those same terms and goals. (Think, for example, of how different from each other books such as Louise Glück's voice-centered *Descending Figure* and Lyn Hejinian's language-centered *My Life*, both published in 1980, seemed at the time.) The 1990s, in contrast, moved beyond this opposition and asked about the cross-fertilization of these approaches. Roger Gilbert notes that "the nineties saw a decided softening of the boundaries between competing poetic modes," a coming together especially clear in the work of a "new generation of poets for whom such divisions seemed counterproductive."[1] Stephen Burt describes poets coming of age in this period as trying to "split the difference between a poetry of descriptive realism on the one hand, and, on the other, a neo-avant-garde" focus on language itself.[2] In almost every case, it was a renewed focus on the lyric's unique way of unfolding or inhabiting the very edge of what can be brought into language that brought together expression and experimentation, the two seemingly opposed emphases of the previous decade. Today, most poets and critics would agree with Elizabeth Willis, in an article subtitled "Thoughts on the Late Lyric," that in "its privileging of sound over meaning; its difference in time signature; its divergence from mimesis," the lyric now "overlaps with, rather than opposes, the aesthetics of 'language' or 'post-language' writing."[3] This reopening of lyric possibilities had its roots in the 1990s.

As Robert von Hallberg points out, the lyric is a form driven by desire: "One thinks in a poem not so much *of* a truth as *toward* something unpossessed – maybe lost, like Eurydice, or never fully attained, like Beatrice."[4]

The lyric is "driven by an intensity of conception" ever outward, he writes, its music "an evocation of the edge of what one comprehends."[5] It leads us into spaces where, straightforward narrative and propositional logics having been put aside, new forms of articulation flourish. As the poet Susan Howe writes, we see in the lyric writers "pulling representation from the irrational dimension love and knowledge must reach."[6] What lyrical or musical thinking does, von Hallberg adds, is "summon into being patterns of thought that are unsatisfactorily accounted for in disciplined prose, . . . link[ing] words and phrases in ways that do not depend on concepts or propositions."[7] Using nonpropositional, musical patterns of thinking drawn from Dickinson and other major figures in the history of the lyric but brought into visibility by contemporary experimental, language-centered writers, many of the most interesting writers of the decade dedicated themselves to mapping consciousness in new ways. In particular, as I will argue here, we see in the work of the writers I examine attempts "to articulate those moments when meaning is slipping away," making a powerful new music out of bewilderment itself.[8]

Let's begin with a summing up. When Charles Wright published his third of three trilogies, *Negative Blue: Selected Later Poems*, in 2000, collecting three books written in the 1990s, he added a seven-poem sequence entitled "North American Bear" (1999) in which he powerfully reflected on his work of that decade. It reads as a coming to terms with the lyric. Each of its poems, at various points in the year and in various weathers, charts what Wright calls our "sidereal jones" – our addictive fixation on the stars and what they represent.[9] Like so much of Wright's work, the poems are brief takes, sidelong glances prompted by the moon and breeze and the stars themselves at what we might call the lyric impulse. They are poems about thinking, about how inwardness lifts itself into speech. These inner constellations, he writes, "blurred star chart[s] in the black light," are little more than stitched together patches of memory, eaten away by time and then erased by death. Yet the night sky seems to tell us that we are not alone in our impulse to shape and preserve: "We live our lives like stars, unconstellated stars, just next to / Great form and great structure, / ungathered, uncalled upon."[10]

Gazing at the stars, then, Wright sees something like the lyric impulse itself, emblazoned across the heavens, impossibly out of reach but not out of sight. "Programmed, unalterable," the stars seem to gesture toward "an order beyond form," even as they testify that such an order is "not there." ("Not here, either," he adds.)[11] The stars, he knows, are "random word strings" and yet there is something crucial they call us to:

> What is it about the stars we can't shake?
> What pulse, what tide drop
> Pulls us like vertigo upward, what
> Height–like reversal urges us toward their clear deeps?
> Tonight, for instance,
> Something is turning behind my eyes,
> something unwept, something unnameable,
> Spinning its line out.[12]

That upward vertigo, I would suggest, is what the lyric in the 1990s pulls us toward. It is where the lyric wants to make a home – in bewilderment or what Wright calls "insolub[ility]."

The crucial thing Wright lets us see, as he looks back on his work of the 1990s, is the deep attraction of vertigo. His poems draw us into the deep doubt that drives the lyric. He doesn't try to add anything up there, and yet he insists on the power and beauty of the work doubt opens up:

> The country we live in's illegible, impossible of access.
> We climb, like our deepest selves, out of it forever.
> Upward, we think, but who knows.
> Are those lights stars or the flametips of hell?
> Who knows. We dig in and climb back up.
> Wind shear and sleight-of-hand, hard cards, we keep on climbing.[13]

Wright brilliantly describes lyric thinking in the 1990s. In poem after poem, he brings us to the point of vertigo, lets us feel the rush of possibilities alive there, and then returns us to the earth and groundedness, prepared to launch out again soon. Whether one might attempt to do more there is a question other writers of the decade pursue, as we will see. But Wright's more than thirty-year acknowledgement of the lyric's call is an important place to begin.

Another brilliant investigation of the lyric situation is Louise Glück's book-length sequence *The Wild Iris* (1992). It too is an elegiac unfolding of limits, exploring the "irrational dimension love and knowledge must reach" by, quite literally, analyzing voice itself, the medium by which we reach out and in. The poem is set in a garden. Plants speak, a human gardener speaks, and God speaks. If we step back and take in each of these voices in turn, we can see Glück mapping the limits within which intense expression comes alive.

The flowers speak to the gardener, to those of us with human voices. Their voices are, of course, unheard. They describe what it's like to move from one realm to another, noting in passing our fierce drive to make sense of the world through speaking: "It is terrible to survive / as consciousness / buried in dark earth. / Then it was over: that which you fear, being / a soul and unable / to speak, ending abruptly, the stiff earth / bending a little."[14] They are deeply aware of what it's like to awaken into voice – "remembering / after so long how to open again / in the cold light / of earliest spring" – yet not at all committed to speech's solitary nature: "Not I, you idiot, not self, but we, we – waves / of sky blue like / a critique of heaven."[15] To the flowers, we seem absolutely mistaken in thinking we die. Their life is cyclical, continual, and they see that, in our emphasis on single consciousness and in our yearning for another world, we are "neither here nor there," lost and to be pitied, bewildered. The flowers are rooted, communal, single-voiced. Humans, by contrast, are never one thing and thus never wholly present.

God focuses too on our drive toward individuality. His voice also is unheard. In breaking from him – "You wanted to be born; I let you be born" – we gained the ability to express ourselves – "all brilliance, all vivacity" – but at a cost.[16] We lost any sense that our voices were heard beyond ourselves. God's response, after the separation was complete, became only a "persistent echoing / in all sounds that means good-bye, good-bye –." Expression then becomes a sounding of our in-betweenness, a marking out of the limits of a world which "begins and ends in stillness – / which *begins* and *ends*."[17] We "were not intended to be unique" but were allowed to move that way "because you required / life separate from me."[18] In Glück's dark reading of the lyric, then, our speech simply sounds the depths of our isolation. God says:

> My great happiness
> is the sound your voice makes
> calling to me even in despair; my sorrow
> that I cannot answer you
> in speech you accept as mine.[19]

From the human point of view, essentially echoing the comments of God and the flowers, speech is reaching out into a great void, a space where no one seems to listen. We say to God: "I cannot love / what I can't conceive, and you disclose / virtually nothing."[20] Of course, we do not know that we are being watched and listened to, and if there is any hope that someone or something hears, it is framed, much as in Charles Wright, as a sort of nostalgic exercise, a desperate attempt to make something out of nothingness: "why would you wound me, why would you want me / desolate in the end, unless you wanted me so starved for hope / I would refuse to see that finally / nothing was left to me, and would believe instead / in the end *you* were left to me."[21]

Like Wright, then, Glück explores the limits of speech, anatomizing the power and wounded sources of its drives, but refusing to claim any sense of stability or rest or arrival for all its wanderings. When Glück's speaker *does* attempt lyric speech on her own, amidst those clashing voices, the poems are deliberately muted, almost gagged. They use phrases such as "baring the heart" or "acquir[ing] souls" knowingly, as if they had quotation marks around them, the speaker stepping back and examining the very terms she works with. The poems express dreams and then shake them off. They yearn, at times, to be free of expression's demands: "I wanted to stay as I was / . . . prior to flowering, . . . /before the appearance of the gift, / before possession."[22] Much like Wright, Glück brilliantly opens up the lyric's bewildered limits, ruthlessly and even mockingly marking the edges of what it can confidently claim, and then pausing – as if there could be no going on from there.

There may not be, but a number of other poets in the 1990s thought very hard about new ways of moving forward into the spaces Glück and Wright describe, as we can see in a number of the strongest poems from this period, all deeply engaged with what an embrace of language's bewilderment sets free. My first example is Robert Hass's poem "Dragonflies Mating" from *Sun Under Wood* (1996).[23] The poem is set in "early morning heat, / first day in the mountains," the poet thinking of creation stories told by Native Americans who "lived here before us" and "also loved these high mountain meadows on summer mornings." Thinking almost idly about one of those stories, the poet is surprised by two thoughts – two memories really: his own creation stories. He thinks first of "stories about sick Indians" associated with St. Raphael's parish, originally a hospital, where he had been a student. Sister Marietta in that school would have told him those stories of the priests who had brought "influenza and syphilis and the coughing disease" with them to California and almost emptied the state of its native inhabitants, a darkly ironic creation story: "They meant so well, she said, and such a terrible thing / came here with their love." That story is immediately crossed with the poet's memory of basketball practice at school and never knowing if his mother would show up, "well into one of those weeks of drinking she disappeared into," bringing with her love another sort of terrible thing – humiliation, terror, uncertainty, bewilderment. What he remembers is standing at the free throw line and seeing her in the entryway looking for him. "I'd bounce the ball," he says, and:

>   study the orange rim as if it were,
> which it was, the true level of the world, the one sure thing
> the power in my hands could summon. I'd bounce the ball
> once more, feel the grain of the leather in my fingertips and shoot.
> It was a perfect thing; it was almost like killing her.

This is really quite extraordinary. The poet remembers both the humiliation and bewilderment her wounding love would cast him into and the very textures and rhythms by which he would launch himself into that blank and try to control it. That launching was an essentially lyric action, a made thing – the arc of the ball perfect and sure. But it was more than that, his memory reminds him. He was killing *her* in that act, controlling the terror by erasing it through an act of imagination.

To remember all that now, on this early mountain morning, is to feel both the drive to perfect and control and touch and make beautiful, and the fear and bewilderment that are the sources of those drives. It is to find oneself both establishing and undercutting the lyric's way of making sense of the world. It is to be thrown into the same state of vertigo that Wright and Glück draw us toward.

Having spelled out that flash of insight about his own creation, the poet turns to his actual subject: the dragonflies "mating in the unopened crown of a Shasta daisy / just outside your door." They "seem to be transferring the cosmos into each other / by attaching at the tail, holding utterly still, and quivering intently," he notes, reaching out toward nature's "one sure thing" with all the precision he can manage. He thinks that "they mate and are done with mating. / They don't carry all this half-mated longing up out of childhood / and then go looking for it everywhere," as he is doing now, taking note of his own hunger for something perfect and still and level and satisfying. "They don't go through life dizzy or groggy with their hunger, / kill with it, smear it on everything," as he had as a child, "killing" his mother out of a need for perfection and stability. Here, I suspect, we see a step beyond Glück and Wright, for the poet continues on, speaking into that uncertainty. Not possessed by this half-mated longing, the dragonflies, he notes, never feel what he does now, as a swallow dips down to the surface of the pond and "marries" for a moment its reflection in the reflected sky, "and the heart goes out to the end of the rope / it has been throwing into abyss after abyss, and a singing shimmers / from every color the morning has risen into." Knowing what he knows, the poet nonetheless throws his heart toward the abyss or bewilderment he is surrounded by and just for a moment *meets something there* – a singing shimmering back to him from every color of creation.

What is striking is seeing the poet take the risk, aware that this same desire has killed and smeared, aware of the impossible longing it grows from and of his own reluctance to take that risk of reaching out again. Counting the cost but taking the shot, he hears creation's very song responding. He has entered into the lyric's wound, acknowledging its history and failures and limits, and discovering within those charged limits a new way of singing. He has made a new sort of lyric out of his own self-chastening, employing the language that has passed through that scrutiny with a kind of sudden abandonment.

In her poems of the 1990s, Jorie Graham walks us into that same charged lyric space, but even more deliberately than Hass. Where he seems to casually talk himself into that confrontative self-undoing, sifting through and unfolding thoughts and second thoughts, Graham quite deliberately cuts her way down to the live issues, paring bone from sinew, as one poem puts it, "cutting, unfastening" her own language's mastery until its deepest secrets are exposed. "Fission" from *Region of Unlikeness* (1991) is an excellent example.[24] It's a conventional poem, in a way – an account of hearing the news that Kennedy was shot. The poet remembers being in a movie theater in Rome. Kubrick's *Lolita* was being shown, and just at the moment Lolita famously lowers her heart-shaped shades and glances up and out and into the auditorium, the theater's electric lights are turned on, the sound is cut, and the movie is whited out but continues – "I watch the light from our real place / suck the arm of the screen-building light into itself / until the gesture of the magic forearm frays / and the story up there grays, pales." A man rushes to the front of the theater calling for everyone's attention; he is referring to Kennedy, of course, but we are also being called to attend to the eroding or undoing of the lyric situation itself, its beautiful story up on the screen. The man screams, the theater's skylight is opened, and the story on the screen is whited-out "one layer further / till it's just a smoldering of whites / where she sits up, . . . / . . . vague stutterings of / light with motion in them, bits of moving zeros / in the infinite virtuality of light, / some *likeness* in it but not particulate, / a grave of possible shapes called *likeness*." This is where the lyric, in the hands of the most engaged writers of the decade, often seeks to go – the moment when its ways of moving forward come undone and come alive. What are we to make of this space, each of these poets we have been examining asks. What are we to *do* there?

The poem shifts position, as if the poet needed to gather herself, to step back a moment and think about that undone space, whether to go further in or not. She steps back from both Lolita and her youthful self in order to wrestle with the issues of desire and forward motion suddenly alive in the poem: "There is a way she lay down on the lawn / to begin with," "a way to not yet be wanted," before plot and speed and desire and wanting. In reimagining the scene, Graham locates its issues within herself by means of a long, exploratory sentence: "Where the three lights merged: / where the image licked my small body from the front / . . . where the electric lights took up the back and sides, / . . . where the long thin arm of day came in from the top / to touch my head, / . . . where they flared up around my body unable to / merge into each other / over my likeness / . . . where they kiss and brood . . . / . . . *there* / the immobilism sets in, / the being-in-place more alive than the being." The poet feels that charged sense of being unable to move now, as she writes. It is the lyric's edge, the charged, aroused space where *likeness* flares and falters in the presence of something it can't take fully in. Just as Hass found the drive to hold and fondle and shoot undone and brought newly back into play by his acknowledgment of the fear and uncertainty he was trying to wipe away with the gesture, so Graham is almost overcome by the tug of war between the coming undone of history and story and forwardness and a still-present need to separate and choose and distinguish: "*choice* the thing that wrecks the sensuous here the glorious here – / that wrecks the beauty." Her real power as a poet is the way she lets us feel both the cost and the inevitability of moving forward, separating "the layers of the real" and the wrappings of light. She holds us there, as if coming to know that point is what the lyric's skepticism about its ways of moving has always been about: "Don't move, don't / wreck the shroud, don't move –." But she holds us there only to build the tension and cost, not to stay there permanently. This is the place Hass moved into when he saw what the drive to perfect or connect or fling his heart out led to, the place from which he risked the lyric gesture anyway. Graham moves forward as well, but she does something new with lyric by slowing that moment of acknowledgment down so that one can feel its full weight, experiencing what desire and desire's undoing look like there. For Hass and Graham, then, the lyric does indeed become a way back into life, not through using language transparently, but through opening up and experiencing the limits and costs enfolded in its ways of making meaning.

In *The Master Letters* (1995), Lucie Brock-Broido unfolds the lyric's self-undoing by building out from a situation sketched in Emily Dickinson's work: the relationship suggested by three draft letters addressed to a Master found in Dickinson's papers after her death. We don't know who Dickinson was writing to or even if the letters were ever sent, but the situation – reaching out toward a figure who may never hear or respond – brilliantly encapsulates the lyric's charged use of language on the edge of what can be known or conceptualized.

The strongest poem of the book, "I Don't Know Who It Is, That Sings, nor Did I, Would I Tell," is addressed to *Master* and signed *Your, L*, linking both poets in a single encounter with the unknown.[25] The poem is framed with transformations of two lines from Dickinson's Master Letters: a reply to his puzzlement about poems she had apparently sent him ("You asked me what my flowers said – then they were disobedient – I gave them messages") and a plea for him to come to her ("Could you come to New England – would you come to Amherst – Would you like to come – Master?").[26] These become, in Brock-Broido, accounts of entering into a stammering blank terror, shared almost inadvertently with a lover:

> You say I have Misenveloped & sent you something Else. In the middle of it all, my mind went blank, all the red notes of terror, blinking. Please to tell me – have I unsettled you by this?
>
> . . .
>
> Suddenly, I am stammering in the face of Probability. I thought when the sparse trees began descent, that you would come to me. There is the thunder now; it gives the world a rampant tinge.

Within this frame, drawing from another set of Dickinson letters written spring through fall 1858, Brock-Broido enters into and explores the space opened up by the stutter.[27] She quotes four sentences from these letters. They all grapple with mystery, from unseen insects choiring from the darkness ("I don't know who it is that sings"), to the question of who gathers us in once time mows us down ("I wonder how long we shall wonder, how early we shall know"), to the fear of losing something precious to the unpredictable sweep of death ("Where shall I hide my things?"). The fourth sentence, Dickinson's partially tongue-in-cheek response to a sermon about our lack of standing before a holy God, captures Brock-Broido's response to stammering terror of not knowing: *"What a privilege it is to be so insignificant!"* Acknowledging one's insignificance becomes a way of entering into what remains incomprehensible and yet full of possibility. Indeed, weaving her own situation around these Dickinson sentences, Brock-Broido discovers within their lyrical stammer the charged limits of articulation that Dickinson called "Possibility – a fairer house than prose:"

> He has, after all, an ancient soul; he is unbent by Possibility as he walks sturdy in the rain, steady as a metronome's pendulum keeping – Time. No slicker. No hazard, no hood. If I lose him I will be insignificant. *What a privilege it is to be so insignificant.*

Losing the *he* referred to here would usher the poet into the very storms of Possibility, or lack of significance, that she acknowledges throughout the poem by turning aside from claims about her language's originality. It would prepare her to enter into, in the lyric's stammer, what she calls "*Bliss* – [something] *unnatural.*" Her (natural) voice quieted, she would enter into a space where, as Hass suggested and the title of this poem confirms, a new sort of singing might be encountered, carried out without words or logic or identifying markers.

The late C. D. Wright's book-length poem *Just Whistle: A Valentine* (1993), enters this lyric situation in a more physical way. A woman is awakened by a lover's words – "I wish you wouldn't wear your panties to bed" – and suddenly comes alive, wounded by his "closed words" but "enlivened" somehow by his breach of decorum, his "solecistic remark about the panties, which the body had not really noticed so used was the body to the cloth, the plight of their facticity, the elastic in the legs and waist not being felt, the discoloration having blended them perfectly with the flesh."[28] The nontransparent language here, sliding between different registers, is deliberate. The woman gets out of bed, his words having created an "unmistakable run in the heretofore seamless nights," "a definite rupture in the zone in which they interpenetrated with decreasing frequency almost without knowing it."[29] Not removing the panties, she walks to the kitchen and sits, thinking of her body, "the crumbling, hacky, runny body, the stiff, fitful body, the dumb, anachronistic body."[30] Shocked into wakefulness, she gradually embraces the freedom of her body's own more open language, responding to the charges against it: "The body is a suspect / in the offense of crow" (desire, sexuality, materiality, difference) with a statement of rights.[31] "Let the record show," she writes, and proceeds to defend the body against claims made against it throughout history, working through its wounds, its mouths, its "howling os," its fears and dreams and limits. What does it want? It wants life, she concludes, with all its risks: "To meet another body, coming through the haulm. Swinging its plums freely. Awhistling."[32] With that, the speaker returns to bed, separate, embodied, alive, and aroused, taking her lover in: "The pitch of the body unbent / risen on an elbow its abundant bushes / its hills of goldenrod and especially in a circle at the center / sickle senna in brilliant darkness a fresh apron / in extraordinary regeneration."[33]

What's fascinating about the poem is its language – abstract, distant from any thoughts of transparency, but also deeply private. It is sometimes stiff and distant and clinical, but it repeatedly rises into a charged, almost unwordably intimate exchange, a language of gaps and silence and lyric beauty. The poem's wide linguistic range is deliberate, and one realizes that Wright, in telling a story of the body's embrace and celebration of its own materiality, has also been exploring that same story within the realm of language. This is the lyric's task, as she understands it. We pull away from and then gradually embrace the thickness of the poem's language – its flows, its stubborn thereness, its bewilderment – until, like the speaker and her lover, we nod in agreement: "Is it. Is it. / it is. it is. / an object of worship. / graven. / an object of contempt. / craven."[34] Here, then, is another imagining of what the lyric brings to life in its unfolding of language's limits: its material body, its wreckage and "distended folds," its "deadening pedagogy" and "healing beat." Wright makes a new music out of this "insignificance," what the poem calls "a whistling," or we have been calling the lyric's new song. It arises out of embracing the body, celebrating the fact that its speech is not transparent but thick, rich, balky, and exuberant.

Rae Armantrout's "A Pulse" from *Made to Seem* (1995) is, like much of her work, a poem made out of discrete fragments drawn from various linguistic registers but all speaking into the same situation – what we've been calling bewilderment or silence, the edge of comprehension.[35] Like the other poems we have been examining, this piece reaches into the silence where comprehension comes to a halt, searching for what it calls "a pulse" or a sign of life. The first fragment establishes the situation in almost narrative terms, pointing to an attempt to "Find the place / in silence / that is a person // or like a person / or like not / needing a person." Imagine a loved one growing wordless over time, so deeply changed that one hovers between responding to her as a person and not. How does one find a place in that silence? How does one take it in, find its pulse? These are the lyric concerns each of our poets has considered, although here the language is abrupt, seemingly yanked into visibility from some other linguistic situation. The second fragment describes a person after a heart attack filling her apartment "with designer accents – / piece by piece." The connection between the fragments, I think, is the act of marking or accenting. The apartment after the heart attack seems so different that the woman feels a need to draw it back into visibility. In the third section, the poet notices a similar sort of activity in the way someone perhaps marketing a nursing home continually readjusts and renames that uncertain space – "a bed" becoming "an abiding" and the time spent there being described as "close to *lastly* / but nicer." We might call this a kind of "separation anxiety" "as next / tears itself off," she remarks in the fourth section. How to mark and acknowledge this edge? That is what each of these fragments, in language not lyric in itself but lyric in its employment, explores. The fifth section envisions the act of marking as a hospital calendar's turn to nostalgia: it "shows the sun going down / on an old-time, / round, lime-green / diner." Returning, in memory, to such a moment is yet another way of making something out of bewilderment: "Just a quick trip back / to mark the spot / where things stop / looking familiar."

Finding the place, filling its sudden empty reaches, shifting language toward something nicer, making a quick trip back to where the familiar first gave way – all of these reactions to "next tearing itself off" from next attempt to draw some sort of language, however worn and clichéd, out of bewilderment. They are all acts of location, newly resonant and visible to the poet as she muses over the slipping away of a loved one. To label the lyric "separation anxiety" is to be both critical of the more hackneyed forms it takes and deeply sympathetic to what drives it. It is to make a record of placelessness out of an open-eyed, lovingly critical gathering of the language we throw at it. It is to see the lyric as a marking, not an abiding.

In an essay written in 1999, "Imagining the Unimagined Writer," the African-American experimentalist Harryette Mullen wrote that she was "more interested in working with language per se than in developing or maintaining my own particular voice or style," a claim that many of the writers I have been examining would share.[36] Four of the four-line stanzas of her book-length *Muse & Drudge* offer a concluding comment about how much work can be done by the attending to the ways of thinking embedded in the lyric's own materials. Much like Graham focusing on choice or Armantrout on finding a place, Mullen interrogates the "material" she works with even as she uses it:

> why these blues come from us
> threadbare material soils
> the original colored
> pregnant with heavenly spirit[37]

Drawing from the blues tradition and its "original," "threadbare" embodying of "spirit," Mullen slows her singing down in these lines, thinking lyrically by piecing together different strips of language into rhyming, resonating, four-line blocks of memory – what she calls string quilts or kente strips:

> stop running from the gift
> slow down to catch up with it
> knots mend the string quilt
> of kente stripped when kin split

Such an act of thinking, such a music, she suggests in another stanza on that page, is an act of protest, not unlike burning a flag "in a public place." It calls attention to "the cost of free expression" by taking back the material the poet works with from exploitative "cover" versions, not unlike what C.D. Wright sought to do with the body. It releases original energy, freeing language and sound to obey its own logic and go its own way:

> white covers of black material
> dense fabric that obeys its own logic
> shadows pieced together tears and all
> unfurling sheets of bluish music

"Why these blues?" Mullen asks. Because music – sheets of bluish music, the body's Os, the tearing shroud of beauty, the faint pulse of life against nothingness – is what all of these poets seek to discover and record. It's what poets of the decade have found at the edge of expression. Political, focused on the body, wounded, self-aware, filled with mourning and yet "pregnant with heavenly spirit" (Mullen), each of these writers is both privileged to be "insignificant" and filled with "Bliss" (Brock-Broido). Slowing the poem down and focusing the imagination on the materials it works with, as each of the poets I examine does, is a legacy from earlier generations of experimental poets, transformed into a deeply expressive cries of the heart. A blues, an offering, a protest, and a prayer – such a poetry, in the words of Mullen, produces a linguistic conflagration in which, out of the lyric's apparent collapse, "smoke rose to offer a blessing." "Stop running from the gift," writes Mullen in words all of these poets would share. The limits of speech are where a new articulation of consciousness begins.

NOTES

1 Roger Gilbert, "Awash with Angels: The Religious Turn in Nineties Poetry," *Contemporary Literature* 42 (2001): 245.
2 Stephen Burt, *Close Calls with Nonsense* (Saint Paul: Graywolf, 2009), 355.
3 Elizabeth Willis, "The Arena in the Garden: Some Thoughts on the Late Lyric," in *Telling it Slant: Avant-Garde Poetics of the 1990s*, ed. Mark Wallace and Stevens Marks (Tuscaloosa: Univ. of Alabama Press, 2002), 228.
4 Robert von Hallberg, *Lyric Powers* (Chicago: University of Chicago Press, 2008), 125.
5 Ibid., 128, 232.
6 Susan Howe, *The Birth-Mark: Unsettling the Wilderness in American Literary History* (Hanover: Wesleyan University Press, 1993), 83.
7 von Hallberg, *Lyric Powers*, 227–228.

8 Juliana Spahr, "Introduction," to *American Women Poets in the 21st Century: Where Lyric Meets Language*, ed. Claudia Rankine and Juliana Spahr (Middletown: Wesleyan University Press, 2000), 2.
9 Charles Wright, "North American Bear," in *Negative Blue: Selected Later Poems* (New York: Farrar, 2000), 201.
10 Ibid., 193.
11 Ibid., 194.
12 Ibid., 196–197.
13 Ibid., 199.
14 Louise Glück, *The Wild Iris* (Hopewell: Ecco, 1992), 1.
15 Ibid., 6, 14.
16 Ibid., 10.
17 Ibid., 15.
18 Ibid., 34, 45.
19 Ibid., 57.
20 Ibid., 12.
21 ibid., 52.
22 Ibid., 33.
23 Robert Hass, "Dragonflies Mating," in *Sun Under Wood* (Hopewell: Ecco, 1996), 6–11.
24 Jorie Graham, "Fission," in *Region of Unlikeness* (New York: Ecco, 1991), 3–8.
25 Lucie Brock-Broido, *The Master Letters* (New York: Knopf, 1997), 62.
26 *The Letters of Emily Dickinson*, ed. Thomas H. Johnson (Cambridge: Harvard University Press, 1958), letters 187, 233.
27 Ibid., letters 190–195.
28 C.D. Wright, *Just Whistle: A Valentine* (Berkeley: Kelsey St. Press, 1993), 7, 10.
29 Ibid., 11.
30 Ibid., 11.
31 Ibid., 26.
32 Ibid., 20.
33 Ibid., 47.
34 Ibid., 43.
35 Rae Armantrout, "A Pulse," in *Veil: New and Selected Poems* (Middletown: Wesleyan University Press, 2001), 73–74.
36 Harryette Mullen, "Imagining the Unimagined Reader," in *American Women Poets*, 404.
37 Harryette Mullen, *Muse & Drudge* (Philadelphia: Singing Horse, 1995), 32.

CHAPTER 10

Story Cycles

Paul March-Russell

In 2001, James Nagel observed that "never has the genre of the short-story cycle been used with greater force or variety than in the American fiction of the 1980s and 1990s, when it became the genre of choice for emerging writers from a variety of ethnic and economic backgrounds."[1] More recently, Jeff Birkenstein has also acknowledged the importance of ethnic diversity for an understanding of the resurgence of the short story cycle in the last quarter of the century – he quotes J. Gerald Kennedy on the need to represent "characters living on two sides of the hyphen" – but sees this as part of a changing representation of the idea of community over the last hundred years.[2] In building upon these observations, this chapter does not propose to revisit the definitional debates that surround the short story cycle or the other synonyms that have been suggested for the genre: short story sequence, composite novel, short story novel.[3] Instead, it focuses on what the genre achieved in the 1990s via a series of recurring tropes, such as history, memory, community, race, and sexuality, at the same time as a post–WW2 consensus on the meaning of these concepts declined, in part, because of developments such as multiculturalism. As Birkenstein argues, in his comparative analysis of Sherwood Anderson's *Winesburg, Ohio* (1919) and Kelly Cherry's *The Society of Friends* (1999), the short story cycle lends writers both a tradition to work in and a flexibility to work with, where neither generic nor social convention are static but are contingent upon historical change. In that sense, the flourishing of the story-cycle during the 1990s is symptomatic of other attempts within the literature of the period to negotiate its immediate predecessors and to encourage what Jeffrey Eugenides called "new language . . . from human voices, not just new theories."[4]

Nevertheless, despite the understandable celebrations of the genre's cultural reach to be found amongst short story critics such as Birkenstein, Nagel and others, its re-emergence during the decade also reflected tensions within the literary marketplace. Whilst on the one hand, the eclipse of high postmodernism and the absorption of its tropes into mainstream culture suggested the demise of experimentalism, on the other hand, the prospects for hypertext and a revolution in print and digital media suggested a large-scale renovation of the publishing industry and the novel form (see Chapter 5). The short story cycle, given its roots in a residual oral tradition, could be seen as one way of reenergizing and keeping alive the novel form in a decade of uncertainty about its future direction, let alone its survival into the new millennium. The marketing of themed collections of short stories as novels was a further means by which the novel could be legitimated despite doubts over its sustained existence. At the same time, whilst small independent bookstores were under attack from the aggressive practices of chains such as Borders, the bookshop could also be legitimated as a venue for cultural consumption through the heavy promotion of novels (even if, in practice, they were actually short story cycles). The maintenance of these outlets and the visibility of such promotions provided opportunities for writers, often graduates of creative writing programs trained in the construction of short stories, to publish cycles that were marketed as novels. Although the practice of publishing, selling, and reviewing themed collections as if they were novels has frequently been criticized as a categorical error,[5] a more pragmatic response would be to say that it enables writers to be published and promoted whilst maintaining the industry's illusion that there is such a thing as a (quote, unquote) novel. Sustaining this illusion would reap benefits for the short story cycle in the twenty-first century, for example, in the popular and critical successes of such books as Jonathan Franzen's *The Corrections* (2001) and Jennifer Egan's *A Visit from the Goon Squad* (2010). Short story cycles of the 1990s therefore exemplify a publishing industry in a state of transition. To explore this transitional phase I examine the work of six authors in relation to three respective themes – trauma, history, and sexuality: Tim O'Brien and Robert Olen Butler; Louise Erdrich and Sherman Alexie; and A. M. Homes and David Foster Wallace.

Memories of Vietnam

The title story of *The Things They Carried* (1990), Tim O'Brien's fictionalised account of the platoon with whom he fought during the Vietnam War, first appeared in 1986, one year after his third novel, *The Nuclear Age*. As Mark Heberle notes, "the shorter stories took on a life of their own" so that O'Brien's fourth novel (*In the Lake of the Woods*) did not appear until 1994.[6] O'Brien's compulsive need to keep working on both the content and structure of his collection at the expense of, what might be termed, the proper business of novel writing seems to confirm Heberle's description of O'Brien as "a trauma artist": his writing intertwined with his uncontrolled and repeated obsession with the primal scene of horror.

Yet, insofar as O'Brien is a writer of trauma, he particularly contributes to the contemporaneous acceptance of trauma as a conceptual tool.[7] For Roger Luckhurst, following the science historian Bruno Latour, such concepts are better described as "knots" that entangle often competing cultural discourses, in this instance, a postmodern ethic of the unrepresentable, a deconstructive concern with aporia, and a psychoanalytic emphasis upon repetition.[8] In repeatedly returning to the same events from multiple perspectives, O'Brien not only mimics the melancholic behaviour of the traumatized subject but also, in terms of textual effect, produces further ways of viewing and articulating the same material. It is in that latter sense that O'Brien's use of trauma complements Latour's conceptual understanding of the knot since, in disentangling the narrative, the reader constructs further discourses, further ways of seeing and saying the same events. Trauma, then, in O'Brien's fiction is not simply a melancholic condition that silences speech, but rather a strategy that serves to articulate the impossibility of voicing the unrepresentable.

Central to this process is O'Brien's discussion in the story "Good Form" of the relative merits of "story-truth" and "happening-truth."[9] The latter, as Stefania Ciocia relates, "makes a claim to literalness, factuality and objectivity" whilst the former tries "to salvage, and then communicate, the exact intensity of the original impact of the narrated events on those who experienced them."[10] In this latter sense, then, O'Brien's writing not only veers to what Nathaniel Hawthorne termed "the truth of the human heart" but, in rooting itself within the aesthetic legacy of the American Renaissance, also resists what O'Brien has disparaged as the frivolous excesses of postmodernism.[11] Yet, in seeking to contextualize O'Brien's use of trauma within an overriding commitment to storytelling,[12] Ciocia omits that the ethical turn in O'Brien's fiction is itself a consequence of how trauma has been conceived as a procedural strategy in his fiction. Such a strategy is clear, for example, in the emphases upon witnessing and representation as embodied by the meta-commentary to "How to Tell a True War Story." The use of trauma as a storytelling principle not only resists narrative closure – as O'Brien's narrator informs the reader, "You can tell a true war story by the way it never seems to end"[13] – but it also produces critical interpretations that, far from explicating O'Brien's motivations, can only result in a tentative reading of the text.

O'Brien's successful contribution to the revival of the short story cycle is, arguably, due to the capacity of his writing to produce multiple and possibly conflicting readings. By contrast, the sub-genre has traditionally been thought of as a self-sufficient structure, circling around a central theme, location, or protagonist before looping back upon itself. The attempts of more recent critics, such as Robert Luscher, to open-out this enclosed unity by describing the cycle as a linear sequence that (paradoxically) constructs "a network of associations that binds the stories together and lends them cumulative thematic impact" glosses over the deliberate non-linearity and multiple meanings of texts such as *The Things They Carried*.[14] Instead, the concentric structure of the short story cycle lends itself to the kinds of knotted experience that O'Brien is attempting to articulate, during which the stories not only shift in points of view but also in time and space, and oscillate between history – publically received accounts of the war – and memory – the subjective perceptions of the protagonists, both then and now. The stories not only return to the same events, but also generate a feedback loop of extra data, which in turn creates additional layers of interference in terms of what can be communicated to the reader. "There is no clarity. Everything swirls," the character Mitchell Sanders observes.[15] But this "great ghastly fog" of war not only expresses the perception of the fighting man but also the frustrated desire of the reader, specifically a US reader of the early 1990s, to render the meaning of the war transparent. It is this traumatic relationship between the reader and the text, this entanglement, which contributed to its success.

By contrast, in Robert Olen Butler's *A Good Scent from a Strange Mountain* (1992), the trauma is off-stage but nevertheless pervades the memories and experiences of the immigrant Vietnamese community in Louisiana. In many respects, the collection is a more traditional short story cycle than *The Things They Carried*, since it is bound by theme and location, and this, allied to its multicultural characters, may have contributed to its Pulitzer Prize award in 1993. Whereas O'Brien foregrounds the tensions between, and within, history and memory, Butler presents his characters in the muted realism typified by the immediate legacy of Raymond Carver. This formal and stylistic tendency in Butler's collection lends both dignity and respect to his treatment of the Vietnamese but it also marks the limits of what Butler, as a white North American, can know about the migrant experience. In much the same way as O'Brien has been accused of machismo and misogyny, Butler has been criticised for "cultural ventriloquism."[16] Yet, just as O'Brien's fiction can be read as a perilous negotiation of these tendencies, so Butler grounds his characters within the setting of Louisiana and the tensions faced by first-generation settlers; a move that, like O'Brien's affinity for Hawthorne, places his fiction within the patterns of migration and assimilation that have characterised American history.

The collection can also be positioned in terms of an ethical turn and, more broadly speaking, the hauntological discourse that pervaded the Humanities during the 1990s, a mix of Derridean deconstruction, post-Freudian psychoanalysis, and the melancholic legacy of neo-Marxists such as Walter Benjamin, in which official versions of history remain haunted by the unsublimated memories of spectral presences. Following Benjamin, the memories of Butler's dislocated Vietnamese remain at the level of raw experience (*Erfahrung*), unprocessed into a sense-making narrative (*Erlebnis*).[17] This disjuncture, which some critics have read as indicative of Butler's postmodernism, can instead be seen as symptomatic of the negotiations around the subject of realism that characterised American fiction of the 1980s and 1990s in the wake of the postmodern literature of exhaustion.[18] What gives it nuance is Butler's attempt to migrate between an American-styled literature of lowered expectations, and memories, histories, and folklore that are Oriental in origin. Examples include the character of Thâp, the Vietnamese villager turned spy who commits suicide in the opening story, and whose tragedy is recalled by a former army translator; the historical figure of Ho Chi Minh reimagined by a dying man on his deathbed in the title story; and the succubus who devours a Vietnamese major in "A Ghost Story." The hallucinatory or fantastical elements in the latter stories are given credence by Butler's seemingly realist style and his use of classic storytelling devices, such as the "shabby Oriental man, a little frayed at the collar and cuffs" who tells his fellow bus passenger the story of the succubus.[19] This fantasy aspect is also reinforced by the folkloric structures and supernatural motifs that surface in other stories in the collection (for example "Fairy Tale," "Mid-Autumn," and "In the Clearing") and which, as with late Carver stories such as "Blackbird Pie" (1988), unsettle their otherwise realistic frameworks. Unlike the work of his near contemporaries, however, the discordant tonal registers of Butler's fiction suggest the irresolution of a Vietnamese cultural identity into its new American setting. As Ted, or rather Thiệu, comments in the story "Crickets," he is drawn to "the flat bayou land of Louisiana" because it reminds him of the Mekong Delta.[20] The projection of the Vietnamese landscape onto that of Louisiana not only indicates Ted/Thiêu's cultural displacement, but also his melancholic and traumatic fixations on the past, a cyclical effect complemented by the narrative resources of the short story cycle.

Native American Histories

This sense of an unresolved or hybrid identity is given memorable expression in Louise Erdrich's *Love Medicine* (first published in 1984). Set in and around a fictional reservation in North Dakota, the book describes the interlaced histories of Ojibwa, mixed-blood, and European-American families over a fifty-year period. Although subtitled and marketed as a novel, seven of the original fourteen chapters were published as short stories and, as Hertha Sweet Wong observes, were scarcely revised for the book.[21] The remaining chapters, edited as customary with Erdrich's husband Michael Dorris, followed the same episodic structure.

In 1993, Erdrich revisited the text with the apparent intention of fitting it better into the quartet of novels that also included *The Beet Queen* (1986), *Tracks* (1988), and *The Bingo Palace* (1994). As Sarah Bennett notes, Erdrich's revisions ranged from the relatively minor to resolving loose ends within the original text, to introducing characters and altering the development of those already present, to clarifying and correcting details so that they (mostly) accord with the other works in the saga.[22] The question, then, is the extent to which these changes not only brought *Love Medicine* into line with the overarching structure of her novel sequence, but also rendered it less a short story cycle and more a fully integrated novel with a continuous narrative? At the same time, however, Erdrich complicated this apparent opposition between novel and short story cycle by expanding one of the chapters, "The Beads," and by interspersing four new chapters through the course of the narrative. Whilst these additions created bridges between *Love Medicine* and *Tracks*, as well as setting up *The Bingo Palace* as the next part in the sequence, they also reemphasized the original text's episodic form. Although "The Island," for example, complements earlier chapters by offering Lulu's perspective as the third party in a love triangle that also involves Nector and Marie, the shift in point of view strengthens the original text's fragmented and multi-perspectival structure.

Wong, finding neither Luscher's short story sequence nor the composite novel of influential Native American texts such as Leslie Marmon Silko's *Storyteller* (1981) adequate to describing *Love Medicine*'s form, positions the text in terms of an oral tradition that emphasizes narrative expansion and recursion, including the embedding of stories within stories.[23] Such a move, although acknowledging the reservation's traumatising effects upon the indigenous population, nevertheless distances the book from Butler's and O'Brien's uses of trauma by positing these narrative strategies as the residual folk culture's archetypes. Yet, instead of regarding the tensions and distortions upon the narrative as symptomatic of a history that, *pace* Fredric Jameson, hurts,[24] it is possible to read them as an inoculation against such a history, in particular by suggesting that – despite it all – community, rather than individual alienation, is what endures.

We might then reverse how critics viewed Erdrich's deletions, additions, and expansions both at the time of the reedited volume and in subsequent years. Instead of seeing these changes as attempts to calibrate *Love Medicine*'s form and content within the other texts' overarching framework, we could value them for the way in which they complicate that structure. Instead of dismissing Erdrich's description of Eli, for example, as Rushes Bear's "youngest son" as an error introduced by reediting,[25] we could respond to how it productively affects the rest of the series. There are now two versions of the same genealogy, one in which Eli is the youngest, the other where his brother, Nector, is younger. Although this paradox may offend Western-centric views of narrative time, in which memory and genealogy operate according to a rectilineal sense of historical progression, it nonetheless accords with the cyclical and simultaneous experience of time to be found within Native American cosmologies. This affinity not only breaks open the historical continuum in ways that appear similar to O'Brien's traumatized narratives, but it is also grounded within a folklore that offsets the modishness of postmodern thought. Erdrich, then, expands upon the narrative structure of the family saga by subjecting it to her own cultural heritage's belief systems.

Sherman Alexie approaches the same dichotomy of modish, postmodern re-readings of historical narrative versus traditional indigenous beliefs in cyclical experience, but in an even more playful way. Published in the same year as Erdrich's revised *Love Medicine*, Alexie's *The Lone Ranger and Tonto Fistfight in Heaven* prefigures his novel, *Reservation Blues* (1995) by introducing the Spokane Indian Reservation and the characters Thomas Builds-the-Fire, Victor Joseph, and Junior Polatkin. Despite these links, however, there is no clear sense that Alexie saw the story cycle as a try-out for the novel; as he more pragmatically put it in interview, "I had a two-book deal with Atlantic Monthly Press."[26] (The novel eventually appeared with Warner Books.) Instead, the story cycle should be read in terms of its play with mythic and historical representations of the Native American peoples.

As Birkenstein comments, the collection is underwritten by the characters' conflicting "desire to remain on the reservation and to leave it," a paradox that results in "the stasis of indecision."[27] This uncertainty associates the protagonists with the characters of other, pioneering short story cycles such as Anderson's *Winesburg, Ohio* and James Joyce's *Dubliners* (1914). Unlike his modernist predecessors, however, the indecisiveness of Alexie's characters is racially circumscribed, so that their doubts as to where they should belong is symptomatic of a struggle between what the reservation represents – the surviving remnants of a Native American culture brutally suppressed by European settlers – and what departure embodies – a vicarious hope of freedom but, more likely, economic and social marginalisation within a dominant white, Anglo-Saxon, Protestant culture.

Two quotations capture the limited parameters within which Alexie's characters operate. First, there is the epigram interpolated into the fragmentary story: "Imagining the Reservation": "Survival = Anger × Imagination. Imagination is the only weapon on the reservation."[28] Second, there is the question posed in the same story by Victor: "How can we imagine a new language when the language of the enemy keeps our dismembered tongues tied to his belt?"[29] If language and communication have been so viciously silenced, then what hope is there for imagination to be articulated? This dilemma underwrites the Kafkaesque tale, "The Trial of Thomas Builds-the-Fire," in which Thomas, the storyteller, after nearly twenty years of silence, is arrested for making "small noises," "syllables that contained more emotion and meaning than entire sentences constructed by the BIA."[30] Responding to this story, Elizabeth Archuleta argues that Thomas' storytelling in court "introduces a horizontal system of justice" that confounds both the hierarchies of the court system and the restrictions upon what can be counted as evidence.[31] Despite the absurd denouement, in which Thomas is sentenced to two concurrent life-terms for retelling the story of a nineteenth-century Native American who killed a pair of soldiers, he not only rediscovers the power of storytelling but, as the courtroom erupts "into motion and emotion,"[32] also reconnects with his community. Indeed, when Thomas is persuaded by the other convicts in the prison van to tell a story, Alexie's tale hints at the opposition between storytelling and political authority that critics such as Michael Hanne regard as vital to the workings of fiction.[33] As if to confirm this point, Thomas's grandson, who finds that "the younger people on the reservation had no time for stories," becomes a hotel worker before meeting a (presumably) grisly end, drunk and alone.[34]

The construction of Alexie's text, though, works against such a downbeat conclusion. As the final report in "The Trial of Thomas Builds-the-Fire" indicates, where Thomas is "transported away from this story and into the next,"[35] his confinement could be read as nothing but a metafictional exercise. Yet, as with the postmodern elements that occur in Erdrich's and O'Brien's narrative strategies, these techniques are motivated by a moral anger at a history that is both traumatic and unrepresentable. Alexie's use of such devices draws not only upon the same elements of folklore as utilized by Erdrich but also upon the greater self-reflexivity to be found in the short story cycle as opposed to the realist novel. More than this however, Alexie not only questions the authority and demarcations of the judicial system, distinctions between what is just and unjust, legal and illegal, admissible and inadmissible, he also contests how literary fiction is organized and, in particular, the author's arbitrary powers of selection such as moving one character from one story to the next. The author is no more objective than Thomas's judge: the decentring of his/her position paves the way for the blending of myth, history, folklore, and popular – principally televisual – culture to be seen in Alexie's text.

Medicated Selves

A. M. Homes's story cycle, *The Safety of Objects* (1990), is one of the examples used by David Foster Wallace in his essay-cum-manifesto, "E Unibus Pluram" (1993), to describe what he terms "Image-Fiction," in which "the transient received myths of popular culture" are utilised "as a *world* in which to imagine fictions about 'real,' albeit pop-mediated, characters."[36] As part of his wider thesis, this loose subgenre of texts not only mines televisual culture as a source of inspiration but also that the irony, which Wallace sees as integral to TV's production and consumption, negates fiction's efforts to transfigure that material into something which might revolutionize either medium (see Chapter 13).

Whether this description is true of Homes's collection is another matter. *The Safety of Objects* can instead be viewed as part of the hyperrealism that characterised the work of Carver and his contemporaries, such as Richard Ford and Tobias Wolff, a kind of modest postmodernism that nevertheless realistically explored its characters through their relationship to such simulacra as television, shopping malls, and commercial brands, as well as suburban towns such as Homes's fictional setting in Westchester County, New York. In this respect, Homes's work is representative of how this strategy of accommodating postmodern elements within an otherwise realistic framework became a familiar trope in other North American fiction of the period (for example, in the stories of Douglas Coupland, Rick Moody, or Lorrie Moore). At the same time, the more shocking aspects of Homes's cycle – the preoccupations with sex, death, drugs, and madness – echo the darker tendencies of the so-called dirty realism of the 1980s; for example, in T. Coraghessan Boyle's "Greasy Lake" (1982). In that sense, then,

Homes's collection represents a working through of several of the *leitmotifs* that had characterized American short fiction of the 1980s in addition to the influence of the televisual culture that Wallace pinpoints. As with Carver's focus upon the lives of blue-collar workers, however, it is also possible to see Homes's work fitting into a tradition that harks again to Anderson's *Winesburg, Ohio*: the concentration upon psychologically or emotionally divided individuals alienated from one another within an otherwise claustrophobic small-town environment. Within that context, Homes's cycle fits with a number of dissident fictions both in print and on television – David Lynch and Mark Frost's *Twin Peaks* aired for the first time in the same year – that invert the sentimental stereotype of small-town America.

Nonetheless, what gives the cycle its contemporaneity, and what extends the focus of Homes's debut novel *Jack* (1989), is its preoccupation with childhood and adolescence. In this respect, the collection shares affinities with such works as Denis Johnson's short story cycle *Jesus' Son* (1992) and Jeffrey Eugenides's novel *The Virgin Suicides* (1993), in that the texts can be seen as responding to Neil Postman's influential jeremiad *The Disappearance of Childhood* (1982). For Postman, childhood is a relatively recent social development formed symptomatically from the divisive effect of print culture upon the "adult" and the "child." Contemporary media though, and here Postman is thinking specifically of television, erases this distinction and inducts children prematurely into adult concerns: "for they not only promote the unseating of childhood through their form and context but reflect its decline in their content."[37] So, in stories such as "Chunky in Heat," "A Real Doll," and "Yours Truly," Homes's adolescents explore their sexual desires often through media-saturated fantasies and commercial products: most notably, in "A Real Doll" where the narrator forms a perverse sexual relationship with his sister's Barbie. At the same time, the supposedly grown-up protagonists of stories such as "Adults Alone" and "Jim Train" regress into juvenile behaviour – arguing, uncleanliness, petty drug-taking, or silly pranks (urinating on the office plants).

More insightfully, however, Homes suggests that this conduct is symptomatic of how childhood – and, indeed, adulthood – have been socially constructed and perceived. In "Looking for Johnny," for example, Erol's kidnapper eventually lets him go because "[y]ou're not the kid I thought you'd be."[38] The kidnapper takes no responsibility for Erol's inability to measure up to the ideal of a boy who excels at sports, fishing, and craftwork, and instead Erol blames himself: "I ran until I didn't know the names of the people in the houses around me. I ran through backyards until I stopped hearing Rayenne's voice calling Error."[39] Similarly, in "A Real

Doll," the narrator's desire for Barbie is in part motivated by his incomprehension at how his sister treats her:

> "Why do you let her do this to you?"
> "Jennifer owns me," Barbie moaned.
> Jennifer owns me, she said, so easily and with pleasure. I was totally jealous.[40]

In seeing his sister only as a rival for Barbie's affections, the narrator fails to understand both the complex love-hate relationship between little girls and their dolls, and his own heteronormative thinking about gender and sexuality: after masturbating into Ken's body, he asks himself whether a "decision about my future life as queerbait had to be made?"[41] Homes's young protagonists are subject as much to the already internalized cultural meanings of childhood as they are to their remediation via the influence of televisual culture.

Arguably, the same set of anxieties surrounding childhood's construction, perception, and understanding underwrites Wallace's exploration of (primarily) male sexuality in *Brief Interviews with Hideous Men* (1999). "Forever Overhead," the first of the longer stories in the collection placed after two preliminary sketches and significantly before the first set of "Brief Interviews," focuses on a thirteen-year-old boy's birthday as he prepares to dive into the local public swimming pool. Uncharacteristically for Wallace's fiction, the allegorical meaning of the story is as transparent as the water below: the dive is an initiation, a "chance for people to recognize that important things are happening to you."[42] As the protagonist dwells upon his sexual development, and observes his parents and the pride they feel for him, the "girl-women ... curved like instruments or fruit," and the pool as "a system of movement,"[43] he is temporarily lost in self-consciousness like many of Wallace's other characters. In a more experimental move, the story narrates the individual's self-division in the second-person: the protagonist is both the subject and object of the narration. This liminal space is finally breached once he becomes aware of time's inexorable movement. "Now that there is time you don't have time," and the boy takes the (both literal and metaphorical) plunge: "Step into the skin and disappear."[44] The dive may represent the passage from innocence into experience, from self-consciousness into bodily sensation, but in the context of Wallace's usage of the story cycle, it also represents a descent into the confusion of sexual behaviour that pervades the collection: the next voice that the reader hears is from a man who spontaneously shouts, "Victory for the Forces of Democratic Freedom!" at the moment of ejaculation.[45]

Four sets of "Brief Interviews" punctuate the collection and act as a framing device for the book's investigation into misogyny and male sexuality. As Wallace notes, these sections describe "events that are being related to an interlocutor, and in fact a hostile one, so that there is a blur between how much of the stuff is involuntary and how much is the rhetoric of the presentation."[46] In other words, the interviews – like other stories in the collection – feature a tension between self-conscious performance and unconscious slips where something authentic in the character's discourse may be glimpsed. One such slip that recurs during the collection is that of a woman's comparison to a toilet as an object into which the man can evacuate himself, a degrading misogynistic image in which the woman is portrayed as a void to be filled by the man's sexual excess. Such imagery, suggesting in psychoanalytic terms a primal wound, gap, or tear that underscores the illusory wholeness of male sexuality, is justified by men such as interviewee #48 who are equally well-versed in psychoanalytic and poststructural theory: "whether I might... tie them up, is describable, at least in part, in the phrase of Marchesani and Van Slyke's theory of masochistic symbolism, as *proposing a contractual scenario.*"[47] In this instance, however, an ironic distance is discernible between Wallace's reading in such theories (of which Marchesani and Van Slyke are a fictional parody) and their manipulation by his male characters for the sake of their own self-justification.

Wallace is less successful, however, in portraying female sexuality except as contingent upon the mythical primacy of the phallus (the illusional status of which is integral to the suggestively titled story "Signifying Nothing"). In "Adult World (I)," for example, the young wife worries that in her own sexual satisfaction "she had selfishly forgotten about his thingie and might have been too hard on it."[48] Her increasingly obsessive attempts to satisfy her husband are written off in "Adult World (II)" as a series of clichés – akin to an early Philip Roth short story – by Wallace's presentation of the sequel as a series of working notes to the author. Although Wallace is merciless in his analysis of male sexual psychology, his investigation into female desire marks (at least here) the limit of his imagination. Instead, as in the narcissism and quick-fix solutions of "The Depressed Person," whose self-absorption bores her own therapist into committing suicide, Wallace's real target is the dual melancholic and self-congratulatory moves of postmodern metafiction that he lampoons in "Octet." Such tactics may mean that even genuine honesty may be dismissed as someone who "goes around at the party and goes up to strangers and *asks* them whether they like him or not."[49] The stranglehold of metafiction is therefore not unlike the social protocol of the opening sketch "anxious . . . to preserve good relations at all times."[50]

While Nagel and Birkenstein were right to identify the short story cycle as a forum for exploring multicultural identities and experience, the work of these six authors also reveals that the subgenre did vital work in this period by attempting to move literary fiction beyond the paradigms of postmodernism and to engage with concepts such as memory, history, culture, and identity that the latter had appeared to erase. In that respect, it also helped to revitalize the resources of the novel within the changing market conditions of the 1990s.

NOTES

1. James Nagel, *The Contemporary American Short-Story Cycle: The Ethnic Resonance of Genre* (Baton Rouge: Louisiana State University Press, 2001), 17.
2. Jeff Birkenstein, "Should I Stay or Should I Go?": American Restlessness and the Short-Story Cycle," in *A Companion to the American Short Story*, ed. Alfred Bendixen and James Nagel (Malden MA: Wiley-Blackwell, 2010), 483.
3. Some of the key texts within this critical debate include Forrest L. Ingram, *Representative Short Story Cycles of the Twentieth Century* (The Hague: Mouton, 1971); Susan Garl and Mann, *The Short Story Cycle* (Westport CT: Greenwood, 1989); J. Gerald Kennedy, ed. *Modern American Short Story Sequences: Composite Fictions and Fictive Communities* (Cambridge: Cambridge University Press, 1995); Maggie Dunn and Ann Morris, *The Composite Novel: The Short Story Cycle in Transition* (New York: Twayne, 1995); and George R. Clay, "Structuring the Short-Story Novel," *Writer's Chronicle* 31.3 (1998): 23–31. See also Robert M. Luscher's overview, "The American Short-Story Cycle: Out from the Novel's Shadow," in *A Companion to the American Novel*, ed. Alfred Bendixen (Malden, MA: Wiley-Blackwell, 2015), 359–372.
4. Jeffrey Eugenides, interview with Jonathan Safran Foer (2002), in *BOMB: The Author Interviews*, ed. Betsy Susler (New York: Soho Press, 2014), 141.
5. See, for example, Nagel on the original publication of *Love Medicine*, 18–20.
6. Mark A. Heberle, *A Trauma Artist: Tim O'Brien and the Fiction of Vietnam* (Iowa City: University of Iowa Press, 2001), 177.
7. In the influential work of trauma theorists, for example, such as Cathy Caruth, *Unclaimed Experience: Trauma, Narrative, and History* (Baltimore: Johns Hopkins University Press, 1996) and Shoshana Felman and Dori Laub, *Testimony: Crises of Witnessing in Literature, Psychoanalysis, and History* (New York: Routledge, 1992).
8. Roger Luckhurst, *The Trauma Question* (London: Routledge, 2008), 5–10.
9. Tim O'Brien, *The Things They Carried* (London: Flamingo, 1991), 179.
10. Stefania Ciocia, *Vietnam and Beyond: Tim O'Brien and the Power of Storytelling* (Liverpool: Liverpool University Press, 2012), 4–5.
11. See also Ciocia, 3; 218.

12 Contrast, for example, Ciocia's reading of the story "In the Field" with Brian Jarvis' analysis of the same story, "Skating on a Shit Field: Tim O'Brien and the Topography of Trauma," in *American Fiction of the 1990s: Reflections of History and Culture*, ed. Jay Prosser (London: Routledge, 2008), 134–147.
13 O'Brien, 73.
14 Luscher, "The Short Story Sequence: An Open Book," in *Short Story Theory at a Crossroads*, ed. Susan Lohafer and Jo Ellyn Clary (Baton Rouge: Louisiana State University Press, 1989), 149.
15 O'Brien, 78.
16 Quoted by Susan Lohafer, "Between Story and Essay: Micro-Markers of Storyness," in *Liminality and the Short Story: Boundary Crossings in American, Canadian, and British Writing*, ed. Jochen Achilles and Ina Bergmann (New York: Routledge, 2015), 112.
17 Walter Benjamin, "On Some Motifs in Baudelaire" (1939), in *Illuminations*, ed. Hannah Arendt, trans. Harry Zohn, 2nd edn (London: Fontana, 1992), 159.
18 Contrast, for example, Michael Orlofsky, "Historiografiction: The Fictionalization of History in the Short Story," in *The Postmodern Short Story: Forms and Issues*, ed. Farhat Iftekharrudin et al. (Westport CT: Praeger, 2003), 58–60 with Paul March-Russell, *The Short Story: An Introduction* (Edinburgh: Edinburgh University Press, 2009), 235–245.
19 Robert Olen Butler, *A Good Scent from a Strange Mountain* (New York: Grove, 2001), 111.
20 Butler, 60.
21 Hertha D. Sweet Wong, "Louise Erdrich's *Love Medicine*: Narrative Communities and the Short Story Cycle," in *Love Medicine: A Casebook*, ed. Hertha D. Sweet Wong (Oxford: Oxford University Press, 2000), 85–86.
22 Sarah Bennett, "Review of *Love Medicine: New and Expanded Version*," *Studies in American Indian Literature* Series 2, 7.1 (1995): 112–115.
23 Wong, 87–89.
24 Fredric Jameson, *The Political Unconscious: Narrative as a Socially Symbolic Act* (Ithaca: Cornell University Press), 102.
25 Louise Erdrich, *Love Medicine* (New York: Holt, 1993), 101.
26 Quoted in Daniel Grassian, *Understanding Sherman Alexie* (Columbia SC: University of South Carolina Press, 2005), 78.
27 Birkenstein, 489.
28 Sherman Alexie, *The Lone Ranger and Tonto Fistfight in Heaven* (London: Vintage, 1997), 150.
29 Alexie, 152.
30 Alexie, 94.
31 Elizabeth Archuleta, "'An Extreme Need to Tell the Truth': Silence and Language in Sherman Alexie's 'The Trial of Thomas Builds-the-Fire,'" in *Sherman Alexie: A Collection of Critical Essays*, ed. Jeff Berglund and Jan Roush (Salt Lake City: University of Utah Press, 2010), 57.
32 Alexie, 99.

33 Michael Hanne, *The Power of the Story: Fiction and Political Change* (Providence RI: Berghahn, 1994).
34 Alexie, 135.
35 Alexie, 103.
36 David Foster Wallace, *A Supposedly Fun Thing I'll Never Do Again* (Boston: Little, 1997), 50.
37 Neil Postman, *The Disappearance of Childhood*, 2nd ed. (New York: Vintage, 1994), 120.
38 A. M. Homes, *The Safety of Objects* (London: Viking, 1991), 54.
39 Homes, 55.
40 Homes, 170.
41 Homes, 169.
42 Wallace, *Brief Interviews with Hideous Men*, 2nd ed. (London: Abacus, 2001), 4.
43 Wallace, 6–7.
44 Wallace, 12–13.
45 Wallace, 14.
46 Quoted in Mark Shechner, "Behind the Watchful Eyes of Author David Foster Wallace" (2000), in *Conversations with David Foster Wallace*, ed. Stephen J. Burn (Jackson: University Press of Mississippi, 2012), 107.
47 Wallace, *Brief Interviews*, 88.
48 Wallace, 137.
49 Wallace, 134.
50 Wallace, 0.

CHAPTER 11

Materiality in the Late Age of Print
Mary K. Holland

Long before *The Blair Witch Project* sparked the *cinéma vérité* trend that has occupied film for nearly twenty years, writer William Gibson collaborated with artist Dennis Ashbaugh and publisher Kevin Begos, Jr., to produce art as found testimonial object. Published in 1992, the "deluxe" edition of *Agrippa (a book of the dead)* appears to be an unearthed, fire-scarred black box, containing a shrouded, partially burned manuscript bearing photographic and linguistic representations of DNA sequences – and a floppy disk. When run, the program on the disk generated a 300-line semi-autobiographical poem based on photographs held in Gibson's father's old album; upon completion, the poem disappeared via self-encryption. Likewise, the ink on the manuscript pages was designed to fade over time. Thus *Agrippa* simultaneously enacts our enduring faith in art as stand-in for the elusive past and material witness to reality, and our late twentieth-century anxiety that technology will make art, its testimony, and perhaps the material world disappear.

Once inalienable and invisible, textual materiality becomes, in a digital age against which it must redefine if not defend itself, a literary aspect demanding consideration by authors and readers alike. Though variously exploited by earlier writers (such as Laurence Sterne's white and black pages, or William Blake's etchings) and a key component of the metafiction explosion in early postmodernism, materiality in literature at the end of the American twentieth century differs from these earlier appearances in quantity and quality. What amounted to an interesting but exceptional smattering of materially experimental texts in the late 1960s and early 1970s became an increasingly common feature of 1990s American writing in increasingly diverse texts: men and women, prose and poetry, short story, novel, art book, and memoir, even children's books began to experiment with the physical qualities of language and of printed text. These many and varied experiments produced equally varied ways of paying attention to textual materiality in the 1990s, which can be organized into two main types:

texts that recognize the physicality of the medium that contains language, pointing to and often distorting the material aspects of the traditional print book; and those that emphasize the visual and physical properties of language on the page and its ways of acting materially in the world or materializing the world in language.

The first type draws attention to the physical properties of printed texts as works of art, as things in the world, rather than allowing literature to become synonymous with transparent textuality. In the wake of Barthes's death of the work and the birth of the all-encompassing text, such books instantiate acts of language and of reading, reminding us of our own embodiment as we interact with books in time and space. Such physically assertive literature thus accomplishes what Susan Sontag called for in reaction to the dawning age of interpretation, replacing a "hermeneutics of art" with an "erotics of art."[1]

The second type of materiality is conscious of layout, space, and the shapes of letters, viewing language as marks in and on the world. Consider the murderous view of language in Don DeLillo's *The Names*, when anthropologist Owen reminds us that "character" comes from the Greek for "pointed stake" and cultists kill people according to their initials,[2] or Walter Benn Michaels's book-length rejection of the "identity politics" he sees as inherent in reading "the shape of the signifier" as meaningful[3]: literature that asserts meaning in the physical properties of language implies its ability to impact the embodied world in visceral and contentious ways. In the anti-humanist context in which subjectivity is socially inscribed on the body, such literature reminds us of the threat to the individual posed by systems of language and ideology.

Materiality in literature, then, especially at the height of theory, the tail end of high postmodern literature and the beginning of critical and creative debates about where literature should go next, is more than another kind of formal play or rejection of literary status quo. It participates in the period's debates about the abilities and dangers of language not just to mean but to impact the real world, and posits new textual responses to those debates. It also demonstrates literary reactions to the rapid transformation, from mechanical to digital, of the means of production, communication, and dissemination of information, art, and entertainment in America.

Material and Digital

The rapid development of electronic literature in the 1990s provides one clear motivation for this new investment in the physicality of language and text. Whether trying to keep pace, or simply adapting the possibilities for literature afforded by this new medium, print literature of this decade increasingly incorporates the openness, multiplicity, and interactivity in genre and structure developed by electronic lit. Meanwhile, evolving printing technology also enabled print literature to emulate electronic literature's innovations by manipulating the physical aspects of texts – incorporating images, carving out space and depth through typesetting, linking and layering texts and characters through mixed fonts and colors. Yet at the same time, texts began reacting to and even resisting the influence of electronic literature, separating themselves from it rather than embracing it by emphasizing the materiality of their print medium – drawing attention to the colors, textures, even shapes that pages and bindings can take – and of language itself. Often texts did both, as N. Katherine Hayles points out,[4] making this simultaneous absorption of and resistance to innovations brought about by literature's movement into the electronic realm a defining characteristic of materiality in literature of the 1990s.

The generic and structural innovations of some texts clearly and consciously mimic those of new media. Carole Maso, for example, first considered publishing *AVA* (1993) as an electronic hypertext, and even in print it creates a kind of hypertextual movement between repeated and related fragments.[5] Mark Danielewski actually did originally publish most of *House of Leaves* online in 1999, about a year before publishing the entire text in 2000. His is the print novel perhaps most often and adamantly compared to hypertext, its four levels of authorship (Zampanó, Johnny Truant, Pelafina, and The Editors) creating a Möbius-strip structure that can only emerge when the narrators are read as integrally interdependent, the reader jumping from one to the other and back again; its refusal to authorize one author or reading while linking its narrative to real-world people and encounters results in the kind of boundary-free text of multiple realities that we associate today with electronic literature. But even these texts remain firmly grounded in print structure and physical form. *AVA* counterbalances its fragmentation and hypertextual linking with an otherwise Aristotelian structure that gathers its nonlinear mental wanderings into three sections completing a single day: "morning," "afternoon," and "night." Danielewski similarly stresses that he conceived of the book only as print, rejecting offers to buy its rights for film, and composed it using solely mechanical means.[6] That the book focuses on a series of multiply mediated films, and that Danielewski was himself a filmmaker, further emphasizes how thoroughly he rejected the electronic media he understood, worked in, and considered using for this book, in favor of print.

Other texts of the decade feature characteristic structural and formal innovations of electronic literature, suggesting shared influence, without expressing interest in or awareness of new media. Perhaps the most prominent example of an innovating author who remained for the most part uninvolved with electronic media is David Foster Wallace, who neither wrote for electronic media nor heavily used the Internet before his death in 2008.[7] Yet his innovations in print narrative resemble electronic ones: his *Infinite Jest* (1996) uses endnotes to create nonlinear reading and a sense of networked information, and relies on a structure defined not just by significant narrative gaps (the meeting between Don Gately and Hal; the climactic events between the tournament and the chronologically final scene of the novel), but by its failure to contain the entirety of the narrative while signaling an entirety which the reader can build with its parts, requiring the kind of interaction and multiple encounters that characterize electronic literature.[8] Likewise, Wallace's intrusion into copyright notices (as in *Jest* and *Consider the Lobster*) enacts e-lit's multiplication and blurring of authorial layers in the manner of *House of Leaves*, while "Host's" flowcharted typesetting reorganizes the page into hypertext. Similarly Lee Siegel, whose *Love in a Dead Language* (1996) is in many ways a precursor to the hypertextual *House of Leaves*, has expressed faith in the fate of the book in an electronic age,[9] but not interest in making his books in any way electronic.

But not all writers, or readers, share Siegel's confidence in the print book. One consequence of the rise of electronic media and the print book's increasing adoption of its characteristics is the development of what has become an ongoing anxiety about "the death of the book" that is often associated with Robert Coover's 1992 essay "The End of Books." But while Coover went on to become a pioneering e-lit publisher and critic, founding Electronic Literature Organization with Scott Rettberg and Jeff Ballowe in 1999, books simply went on, as more recent commentators on the "death of the book" anxiety acknowledge. Many books that persist as print in an increasingly digital world do so quite self-consciously, invoking the presence and possibilities of the digital while foregrounding their own refusal to play along. Such books cultivate what Jessica Pressman calls an "aesthetic of bookishness," which she defines as a practice of "exploit[ing] the power of the print page in ways that draw attention to the book as a multimedia format, one informed by and connected to digital technologies." In addition to revealing its inherent multimedia possibilities, such a text "take[s] itself seriously as a material object."[10] Certainly *House of Leaves*, coupling its structural hypertextuality and thematic celebration of mediation with a formal insistence on print, is the decade's best example of such a text. But many other books, like *Jest*, do not place their materiality against the context of books' digitization. These insistently material texts of the period exhibit not an "aesthetic of bookishness" – the term itself privileging abstraction over substance, book*like*ness over book itself – but rather keen awareness and clever enlistment of the powers already given to the book by its ability to organize language and its status as a physical object. This constantly renewed vitality of the ancient powers of print thus contributes, along with a new "aesthetic of bookishness," to the book's survival alongside the development of digital textuality, while also connecting literary materiality of the 1990s to earlier anti-Realist experiments that had not yet imagined electronic vistas.

Books and/as Bodies

Richard Federman's *Double or Nothing* provides insight into the complex roots and intentions of emphatically material literature in the 1990s. Published originally as a typescript in 1971, during that early postmodern flourishing of materialist texts, Federman's novel was revived in 1992, as e-lit took off and the book was declared terminal. Presumably, it benefitted from the growing interest in visual and structural narrative experiments being conducted in electronic literature, and from publishing advances that made reissuing the novel more feasible. Federman had originally typed the novel from handwritten notes as a single five-hundred-page sentence. Out of this linguistic material he painstakingly sculpted the final novel, which depicts through concrete and pictographic language a writer's obsessive, digressive, and displaced – via multiple layers of invented narrators – attempts to write a story. A "novel of performance," the text is less finished narrative than artifact of the character-narrator's experience of trying and failing to write.[11] The book's affinity with and influence on other experimental fiction of the decade and beyond are evident, as will become clear below. But ironically, the very changes in publishing that brought *Double or Nothing* back to print and spread its influence also destroyed design aspects that best communicated the novel's material meaning. Word-processed and digitally rendered in 1992, the book quietly became a product of the digital, its fonts regularized and spaces standardized, no longer a record of the individually inscribed mark on the page or artifact of the embodied experience – not just the narrator's but those of Federman himself – that hammered the marks over time. This translation of the text from mechanically to digitally produced points out what is lost in the transformation from mechanical to digital art, to ways in which books in the digital age, for all the new realms of representation available to them, are inherently distanced from the material realm that used to produce and hold them, and at least for now holds the bodies that read them.

But Federman's novel also points out how much is gained, not just from digital production and electronic media, but from how these changes in media and production enlarge our sense of what any text can be. Quite contrary to the open-ended nonlinearity of books such as *House* that exhibit an "aesthetic of bookishness," or a kind of digital envy, *Double or Nothing* emphatically confines itself to the closure that it sees as inherent in print. Deep into this unorthodox literary experiment, which eschews all recognizable elements of traditional realism, lies an argument that because every novel is "always a question of expressing, of translating something which is already there," and because "all fictitious work forms a block [in which] nothing can be taken away from it nor can a single word be changed," every novel, no matter how anti-Realistic, reproduces the tight economy of Realism. The printed text, in its unalterable inscription, constitutes for Federman "a discourse fixed once and for all," which naturalizes each of its elements according to its rules, however scattered and strange.[12] In the context of digital literature, in which text is never fixed, finished, or "already there," such assumptions about the inherent closure and limitations of what fiction can be or how it can be read become laughable. Here is the revelation of materially experimental print reproduced in a digital age: it exposes the ways in which not only texts written in a mechanical age but even our ideas about materiality, language, and the possibilities for literature can never be the same after the advent of the digital. Realism's logic of closure and formalism's logic of unity cannot survive unscathed the invasion of digital tools, production, and culture. But neither can the signifying capacities of print.

Perhaps in compensation for this loss by print, even texts of the 1990s that show affinity for the workings of e-lit also exhibit, and force readers to experience, intense awareness of the material existence of both reader and text. *Jest*, while hypertextually sending us back and forth between main narrative and nearly a hundred pages of endnotes, also locates us firmly in the physical world: flipping through 1,079 pages is nothing like clicking on a line of blue text. *Love in a Dead Language* exacerbates the aggravation by forcing us to turn the book backwards and upside down in order to read the "Wives and Mistresses/Mistresses and Wives" chapters, the latter of which runs on the backs of the pages of the former; elsewhere the novel quotes an entire stanza of poetry printed backward.[13] In so doing Siegel materializes two of the novel's key thematic notions: that the arrangement of printed text is inherently hierarchical, should be unfixed and multiple, but really can't be ("Wives" always wind up coming first), and that all written language contains the potential, if not the largely unrecognized realization, of puzzles, secrets, and unseen meaning if only we could look differently at it, which printed text makes rather cumbersome to do (few readers are going to leave their comfortable chairs to find a mirror). Like Wallace, Siegel makes us aware of the effort and reward of looking awry, as well as of the body that is part of every act of reading, every act of reading an embodied translation.

Several steps down a road put on the map by the entirely linguistic *Pale Fire* (1962), Siegel's novel adds to the combination of text and commentary (in this case, the translated *Kamasutra* and Roth's interpretation of it) another set of annotations informed by a different set of commentaries, some of whose parts are rendered by copies of other texts – newspaper clippings, board games, essays, letters, ads, photos – slipped in to the main manuscript (the translation of and commentary on the *Kamasutra*). This novel is thus not simply one narrative distorting another to exponentially increase the ways of reading the whole. Rather, it also materializes the poststructural insight that all texts are remixes of other texts, revised in the late age of print into the proposition that all books are constructed of other books. The novel's scrapbook-like composition both relies on and belies texts' ability as artifacts of the real world to fulfill our desire for something true. In a terminal act of materialization, Roth is killed near the end of the novel by the word whose manifestation had been his life's pursuit – he is hit in the head by a Sanskrit-English dictionary, opened to *kama*, or "love."[14] At that point, his narrative is taken over – invaded, usurped, and colonized – by documents that stand in for his death and for the culmination of his work, chosen and placed by others whose commentaries fix their implications. The reassembled pieces of a torn-up love letter[15] and the six reinserted pages of Roth's journal,[16] all of which had been crumpled and discarded by Roth, act both as "real-world" artifacts, communicating piercing truths about suffering – we can imagine the tearing and crumpling, whose effects are visible in the documents – and, inserted by others into the text, as betrayals not only of Roth but of the book he had meant to complete.[17]

House of Leaves repeats *Love*'s material breakdown of the structural hierarchy of academic writing – reorganizing space on the page – by allowing Johnny Truant's commentary, like Anang's, to break out of the footnotes and occupy the main text in all of Chapter XXI. But *House*'s materialization of textual power, and of the power of text to become material, goes farther than this and farther than *Love*'s: for Johnny, our most present narrator in *House*, the process of piecing together the book left in a shamble of incomplete pieces by Zampanó *is* a translation of text into body: first when the papers he's working on become a "body" or "a child," then when he becomes the beastly body/belly that houses the book and its first author, and finally when he is reborn in his final story as the baby who can let go, the baby whose brain is as undifferentiated and incomplete as the substance of this book.[18] Meanwhile, as Johnny thematically materializes the book, the book materializes on the page the impact of its narrators and even of its own story: just as we can read the check mark on page 97 as a materialization of Pelafina's power to inscribe on Zampanó's narrative,[19] we can read the visual concretizing of the house in the "Labyrinth" chapter and of Navidson's actions in Chapter XX as the *book's* embodiment of its own thematic content through words on the page.

Also like *Love*, *House* is a book made of many documents – including letters, poems, newspaper clippings, photos, and drawings – and is aware of the importance of things, and of documents' and texts' abilities to act, like things, on the world. The frontispiece that greets us is a collage of things that motivate, measure, or document the action of the book (compass, measuring tape, drugs, bullet, blood), alerting us from the start that language and texts – acts of representation – yield consequences for the real world, the one in which we are reading. Before we open the book, it warns us of this connection, the front cover half an inch shorter than the rest of the book, so that even when closed the things of the book and the horrors they represent spill out at us, as if crossing the threshold from text to world. The shortened cover also implies that the book can't contain itself, so that, with its blueprint of the house and its endless stairs, it makes the book seem to embody in physical form the central physical and philosophical dilemma of the house: it's bigger on the inside. Thus *House of Leaves* may be about the incommensurability of language and the real world, and the necessity of electronic remediation to recuperate identity and meaning in that world.[20] But it also asserts, through insistent thematic and visual materiality and use of physical form to embody the linguistic and existential dilemmas of the text, that the material world remains the site where we can best investigate those dilemmas. Like the theories of social construction of subjectivity that define the academic 1990s, *House* demonstrates that however abstract these dilemmas of identity, language, and knowledge are, they are always written on the body.

Materializing (with) Language

Almost a decade and a half before twenty-first century print literature became redefined as fundamentally reacting to electronic, Carole Maso read the impact of e-lit differently, as an opportunity to discover in print literature "a new respect for the mark on the page" and reawaken our "love for the physical, for the sensual world." Maso's novel *The Art Lover* (1990) seeks to preserve a connection between the truths of the material world and language by explicitly asking how to "love not things that are certain, but simply things in themselves"[21] – unstripped of their ambiguity by fixed representation – and how to capture that love in art. Peppering her attempts to capture truth in art are examples of how we fail because of elaborate theories, like her father's modernist use of art to distance us from pain, or, worse, our ancient desire to use not just art but our own visions of the world to distance ourselves from reality and its suffering. One recurring example of the dangers of (modernist) art is the repetition of "I saw the figure five in gold" by various characters in conversation. Their ironic deployment of the line traces a vast distance from the embodied experience the words describe, appropriating Demuth's 1949 painting *I Saw the Figure Five in Gold*, itself an ekphrasis of William Carlos Williams's poem "The Great Figure" (1922) – which Williams claims in his autobiography was inspired by his own vivid experience in New York City.

The novel also critiques the ways we convert the material world itself into art. Pictorial and linguistic images of constellations recur, in "Sky Watch" clippings cut from the main narrator's life and in momentous imagery she supplies for her characters, alerting us to our human habit of arranging the world to suit our needs for meaning and order: we make pictures out of suns, co-opting entire galaxies to soothe ourselves. This is the annihilation of the real that the narrator wants to avoid in her art: "I've got to feel flesh, bone, hair, earth, somehow in words. The urgency of flesh, bone, hair. The thousand demands of blood."[22] As she searches for a mode of art that will preserve the real, she notes methods of translating and preserving visual, aural, and tactile experience – sign language, grave rubbings, recordings of lovemaking – and of fusing the material into art: Van Gogh's thick pigment transferring height onto canvas.[23] Ultimately, Maso solves the problem of art's intimacy with the real by breaking into her novel to tell the truth behind the novel's embedded stories, the story of the death of her dear friend Gary Falk from AIDS.[24] Though a metafictive solution – a product of abstract textual elements like generic form and point of view – Maso's self-referentiality ultimately forces the reader to re-read the novel as doing exactly what Maso aspired to do in her essay, as recording her own "marks on the page," the result of her "desire to put the body on the pages of a book."[25]

Perhaps even thornier than the problem of how to use art to connect to the real world, or to materialize through abstraction, is the question of what "the real" is, and how it can relate to language at all. This linguistic dilemma has long been taken up by the Language poets, whose attention to language as material – as the stuff that poems are made of – and only problematically related to reality grew out of modernist convictions and practices like Gertrude Stein's, persisting into the twenty-first century and experiencing renewed vigor in the late 1980s and early 1990s. Poems of the 1990s by Charles Bernstein, former editor of the journal $L = A = N = G = U = A = G = E$ and prominent Language poet, poke tenaciously at this disjunction between language and reality, as if with enough persistence the distance between word and thing could finally be fathomed. Whereas one poem in *Rough Trades* (1991) declares that "Only / the imaginary is real," another claims "Only the real is real." Then in *My Way: Speeches and Poems* (1999), "This line refuses reality," while two years later, in *Let's Just Say*, a self-reflexive poem declares "It's/ real."[26] What is real for Bernstein? Primarily language, whose materiality – how it occupies space on the page, how it sounds in our heads or ears – is what makes it mean, *is* its reality, not its capacity to express: words are "Fundament be-/ yond relation."[27] Similarly, "This Line" (1999) uses irony to illustrate that the poem exists apart from every reading we impose on it: "This line/ is only about itself./ This line has no meaning,"[28] but the versified denial of meaning is a poem, and its denial is its meaning. Likewise, "Of Time and the Line" (1991) insubstantiates the literal poetic line – if there is such a thing – by cataloging all the useful "lines" it is not (hem-, picket-, blood-, comic, geometric), then pointing out the "line's" irrelevance even to poetry, which has become linelessly prosaic. Yet this sequence of lines, too, forms a poem, as does the page that declares only "*THIS POEM INTENTIONALLY LEFT BLANK.*"[29] These poems use form to materialize meaning, building the thing itself – the poem on the page – out of the articulation of its denial.

Bernstein intensifies this technique in "The Lives of the Toll Takers" (1994), whose erratic textual layout looks at times like that of *Double or Nothing*, at times like *House of Leaves*, and yet is really the opposite of concrete. Rather than arranging words on the page to mimic visually the idea or action being represented, Bernstein uses placement, word division, and punctuation to force us to see and hear the language on the pages. Punning jokes like "ther / e's / no crime like presentiment" suggest that revelation lies waiting in well-worn phrases just a few letters down the line (of the poem, of signification) – like a poetic invocation of *Pale Fire*'s word golf. Increasingly irksome linebreaks become their own joke when they make a pretentious assertion about irony and idealism even more difficult to follow, rendering the specious as spacious, and full of hot air (155–157). Interestingly, while many of the poems of Joan Retallack's 1998 *How To Do Things with Words* suggest the combinatory possibilities of the digital – for example, the seemingly random reappearance of words and phrases through the columns of "Shakespeare Was a Woman" – more often the poems, like Berstein's, delineate subjection to the confines of the page. In "Here's Looking at You Francis Bacon," words lie trapped in boxes, while in "ditto Marchel Duchamp? ditto ditto Gertrude Stein?" words form a box that stands in for the "*memento mori,*" a stubbornly fixed *Agrippa*. In rendering content via format in these ways, what such poems do best of all is force us to see each word involved, at times even every letter and punctuation mark, not only revealing the materializing power of poetry but transforming it into letters fixed in time and space, marks on the page.

The multiple fonts of Bernstein's "Mao Tse Tung Wore Khakis" (2000), which seems to collect a series of written statements from various media and voices, make the poem another kind of artifact, not of documents but of words that preserve their original inscriptions. Each differently formatted statement is another kind of hyperlink, a connection to a past articulation *in print*. This is one of many materializing techniques that William H. Gass enlists in his mammoth book *The Tunnel* (1995), whose concretized and versified language demonstrates its devotion to poetry long before the narrator-author declares himself, in the end, a frustrated poet. The novel uses textual effects to materialize the memories out of which its narrator, Kohler, attempts to build a present self (while materializing his own attempt by digging a tunnel in his basement). As in *Love*, some material effects function artifactually, as traces of its narrator's embodied experience, such as the smudged and crumpled page, partially obscured by a garbage-bag label, on which he recounts the painful end of an affair.[30] More often, Gass, like Federman, Siegel, and Danielewski, employs textual layout to concretize past experience in language, as when he represents "Mad Meg" as an empty center delineated by words that signify the people his Baudrillardian view of history could not touch.[31] In direct opposition to Meg's theory, Kohler also employs language, much like Federman's narrator, to eliminate the distance between word and thing, scattering "pow!" and "pop pop pop" across pages to make present the violence of a World War II battle and of Kristalnacht; elsewhere, page numbers become stenciled numerals that recall Holocaust markings on trains. Equally materially present for him are poignant memories from his childhood, like "Olio di Oliva" on a grocer's window, which marks his unspoiled sense of freedom and pleasure as a child.[32] These words and numbers, recorded in the fonts in which Kohler experienced them in the world, operate, as in Bernstein's poem, not as arbitrary signs pointing somewhere else but as materializations of the actual things – signs as things – that populated his formative experience.

Not surprisingly for Gass, who argued that, "the sentence confers reality upon certain relations,"[33] these hundreds of pages of materializations of and through language culminate in the narrator's realization that the problem of fiction is the problem of form. All forms, whether history, narrative, limerick, or even language itself, distort and demean, while also allowing us to carve meaning out of the deluge of language, as Kohler digs a tunnel to make a space in the Real. Ultimately, Kohler recognizes poetry, with its rules and structures, as the most materializing medium since it "created a permanent and universal present like a frieze of stone, and was therefore what any one of us might see and feel who followed its lines and felt its forms."[34] It's hard to find Kohler's discovery redemptive; after all, he's not in the end a poet. Or if he is, he's an entirely secret one, as his gargantuan record of carving self out of language remains hidden in the pages of the history book whose introduction he never writes. Such a solipsistic view of language as unable to communicate beyond the self is so typical of the late postmodern period that we can read literary materiality as employed by Maso, Bernstein, and Gass as registering or resisting this earlier postmodern/poststructural disconnection between language and world, and recognizing the limits and possibilities of our attempts to materialize meaning and self in language.

Materiality into the Twenty-First Century

The first decade or so of the early twenty-first century has produced even more materially attentive texts than did the same period at the end of the twentieth, suggesting that writers' interest in using the book's physical form to manifest the real world it witnesses and critiques – often in the context of technology that threatens to eclipse it – continues and intensifies. Creative typesetting and use of images like those in Gass, Federman, and Danielewski shape Salvador Plascencia's *The People of Paper* (2005) and Steve Hall's *The Raw Shark Texts* (2007); Danielewski's visual construction of narrative multiplicity in *House* seems even to have entered nonfiction, as evident in *The Lifespan of a Fact* (John D'Agata and Jim Fingal, 2012).

Materiality in the Late Age of Print

Steve Tomasula's work smartly complicates earlier creations of text as artifact of experience: his *VAS: An Opera in Flatland* (2004) documents the vast cultural evidence amassed by its narrator as he struggles to decide what the limits of science's dominion over the body should be, while echoing *House of Leaves*'s equation of book and body through covers that evoke flesh and blood. Similarly, Debra Di Blasi's *The Jiri Chronicles and Other Stories* (2007) crafts a biting feminist critique by blending Lee Siegel's reliance on fake documents in *Love in a Dead Language* with Tomasula's enlistment of artifacts from reality.

Recent experiments go beyond innovations in layout and design, reproducing in three-dimensional and tactile ways the book as found object and personal witness, materially fragmented and unfinished. Most seriously archival to date is J. J. Abrams and Doug Dorst's *S.* (2013), which comprises a library book and its annotations by two readers, along with documents including postcards, maps, letters, notes, and even a code-breaking device tucked in among the pages. All of these pieces are required to construct the narratives of the mysterious "S." and of the readers' love story. The book materializes the chaotic state in which Anang and Johnny Truant found the sources that became *Love in a Dead Language* and *House of Leaves*, just as reading it becomes an embodiment of the editors' experiences converting the first texts into the second.

This widespread drive to manifest reading and writing strategies materially means that physically, books have never been weirder, nor has formal oddity ever been so mainstream. Jonathan Safran Foer, for example, whose 2D uses of metafiction, image, and textual layout have made him one of our most popular contemporary experimental writers, created the 3-D *Tree of Codes* (2010), whose conversion of an existing novel into his own novel via die-cut gaps is more sculptural than legible. That novel's logical end in turn is the totally illegible literary sculpture, a type of art book so popular that Barnes and Noble sold several versions (the pages of *Sense and Sensibility* folded to form "love," as one example) during the 2014 holiday season. But the print book that is probably the most materially daring is one that will never be sold by Barnes and Noble, or anyone else. Since 2003, Shelley Jackson has been choosing volunteers to become "words" in her short story "Skin," which will only ever be read in its entirety by those who have tattooed its words, as assigned by Jackson, on their bodies. The ultimate equation of body and word, Jackson's *Ineradicable Stain* project materializes language, unifies reader and text, and disperses the text to mutate continuously in space, while shackling it to time. It is a culmination of the meeting of materialized language with the fluidity of e-lit, which is no surprise from the author whose *Patchwork Girl* (1995) defines electronic literature's first phase.[35] Jackson's work – still being published by tattoo parlors everywhere – demonstrates dramatically what print literature of the 1990s had already discovered: how radically changes in production alter textual form and meaning, and how the body – textual and human – remains the site for registering and reading those changes.

Works like Foer's, Jackson's, and Barnes and Noble's also demonstrate how the persistence of hypermaterial texts in the increasingly digital twenty-first century does not simply question the "lateness" of print in the 1990s. In their emphasis on physical form at the expense of traditional readability, these texts also question the signifying capacity of print that self-conscious materiality aimed to demonstrate in the 1990s, and thus can seem to exhibit not a defiant "aesthetic of bookishness" but rather an aesthetic of the dead book. Meanwhile, theories of "electracy,"[36] or methods for reading electronic texts, emphasize the role played by materiality – of code, of language, of the embodied and temporal experience of reading electronic literature – in making digital texts meaningful, continuing the tradition begun by Hayles in her 1999 *How We Became Posthuman*. In this context, today's insistently and often awkwardly physical texts repeat rather than resolve the anxiety about the status of the print book as historical artifact that *Agrippa* expressed so well in the 1990s. At the same time, they remind us that materiality in the "late age" of print[37] is not a singular experimental foray, but rather part of long-standing evolutions of literary technique and technology – both of which have the power to materialize meaning or make it disappear.

NOTES

1 Susan Sontag, *Against Interpretation and Other Essays* (New York: Picador, 2001), 14.
2 Don DeLillo, *The Names* (New York: Vintage, 1982), 10.
3 Walter Benn Michaels, *The Shape of the Signifier* (Princeton, NJ: Princeton University Press, 2004), 18.
4 N. Katherine Hayles, *Electronic Literature: New Horizons for the Literary* (South Bend, IN: University of Notre Dame Press, 2008), 162.
5 Stephen J. Burn, "The End of Postmodernism," in *American Fiction in the 1990s: Reflections on History and Culture*, ed. Jay Prosser (London: Routledge, 2008), 228.
6 Hayles, *Writing Machines* (Cambridge: MIT Press, 2002), 126.
7 Little, Brown did publish "Up, Simba" electronically in 2000.

8 For Wallace's descriptions of *Jest*'s structure, see Burn's *Conversations with David Foster Wallace* (Oxford: University of Mississippi Press, 2012), 57 and 72.
9 Burn, "Anatomizing the Language of Love: An Interview with Lee Siegel," *electronic book review* (28 September 2006).
10 Jessica Pressman, "The Aesthetic of Bookishness in Twenty-First Century Literature," *Michigan Quarterly Review* 48.4 (2009): 465, 467.
11 Serpil Oppermann, "Raymond Federman's *Double or Nothing*: A Prolegomena to a Postmodern Production Aesthetics," *American Studies International* 35.3 (1997).
12 Raymond Federman, *Double or Nothing* (Boulder, CO: FC2, 1998), np.
13 Siegel, *Love*, 54.
14 Ibid., 325.
15 Ibid., 334.
16 Ibid., 237–238.
17 One year later, Richard Grossman made the same point about texts colonizing texts in *The Book of Lazarus*, a scrapbook of photos and documents that witness the deaths of the drugged-out members of the "People's Liberation Brigade" (Normal, IL: FC2, 1997). But the original scrapbook is co-opted by one of its descendants, who alters it by adding her own explanatory narrative. The book she has produced is then altered by the addition of her death date on the "tombstone" that opens the final book: her life is the price for seeing the book to print, a conversion of body to language. For both Grossman and Siegel, manifesting language, rather than solving the problems of language, runs the risk of altering or dematerializing body – the body of the text or of the human – a metaphor for the power struggles inherent in every act of writing.
18 Mark Z. Danielewski, *House of Leaves* (New York: Pantheon, 2000), 326, 338, 518.
19 Hayles, *Writing Machines*, 129.
20 Ibid., 114.
21 Carole Maso, "Rupture, Verge, and Precipice; Precipice, Verge, and Hurt Not," *Review of Contemporary Fiction* 16.1 (1996), 63; Maso, *The Art Lover* (New York: New Directions, 1990), 150.
22 Ibid., 73.
23 Ibid., 34, 71, 97, 234.
24 Charles Harris, "The Dead Fathers: The Rejection of Modernist Distance in *The Art Lover*," *Review of Contemporary Fiction* 17.3 (1997).
25 Maso, "Rupture," 71.
26 Charles Bernstein, *All the Whiskey in Heaven* (New York: Farrar, 2010), 144, 145, 233, 258.
27 Ibid., 144.
28 Ibid., 8–10.
29 Ibid., 245.
30 William H. Gass, *The Tunnel* (Dalkey Archive, 1995), 174.

31 Ibid., 8.
32 Ibid., 48–49, 308, 331–332; 31, 33; 61.
33 Gass, "Philosophy and the Form of Fiction," in *Fiction and the Figures of Life* (Boston: Nonpareil, 1979), 14.
34 Gass, *The Tunnel*, 642.
35 Hayles, *Electronic Literature*, 7.
36 George Ulmer introduced this term in *Teletheory: Grammatology in the Age of Video* (New York: Routledge, 1989).
37 Ted Striphas coined this term, already with irony, in his book *The Late Age of Print: Everyday Book Culture from Consumerism to Control* (New York: University of Columbia Press, 2009), which demonstrates the ongoing impact of printed books.

CHAPTER 12

Manifestos

Rachel Greenwald Smith

The odd condition of fiction manifestos in the 1990s is at its most pronounced in a 1996 special volume of the *Review of Contemporary Fiction*, edited by David Foster Wallace. The volume consists of defining statements by a number of the period's most influential fiction writers, and while none are explicitly manifestos, in their interest in forecasting the future of literature and positioning their own work within that future, they aspire to many of the same rhetorical aims as traditional manifestos do. In his editor's introduction to the volume, Wallace expresses skepticism toward the very enterprise of writers writing about writing. "Nobody knows where anything important is going, really," he reflects, "and the deeper the stake a writer has in something, I think, the less reliable a diagnostician or forecaster she's going to be."[1] So why read these essays? "A couple ... are kind of inspiring,"[2] Wallace allows, but "not one of them is 'right' in any argumentative or predictive sense." This statement, pushed to its logical conclusion, could mean that authors would do best to withdraw from the project of imagining the future of writing and merely do what they do best: write. Yet, Wallace does make a small allowance for some meaning behind the endeavor. Having denounced all of the essays in his volume as failures in advance, he writes, "But I think this is OK. I myself ended up reading these essays more like diary entries than anything else – the only real object of revelation is the writers themselves."[3] This, for Wallace, is analogous to what he sees when acquaintances discuss religion: "though these heartfelt utterances present themselves as assuasive or argumentative, what they really are are – truly, deeply – *expressive* – expressive of a self's heart's special tangle."[4]

This might be a perfectly fine reason for Wallace to find a collection of essays on the future of literature interesting, but it falls skew of what most scholars agree art manifestos should accomplish. A manifesto, according to Martin Puchner, is a means of "declaring a new departure, of setting one ism against the next, and of laying claim to the future at the expense of the past."[5] This definition runs in accord with the traditional view that the specific form of the art manifesto is strongly associated with the presence of a self-styled avant-garde, which, for Puchner, "presumes some unified historical axis along which humanity moves, some being ahead and some being behind," such that "a new movement's claim to fame [resides] not in its intrinsic qualities but in the mere fact of its being new."[6] In other words, a manifesto is explicitly *not* expressive in aim; it is, by turns, performative, projective, and prophetic – it aims not to unveil the secret self but to call into being and announce a new and changed world.

So Wallace's insistence on reading these essays as primarily vessels of individual expression begs the question: What is the role of personal expression in the art manifesto form? Further, can the art manifesto be a vessel for personal expression without ceasing, in some important way, to be a manifesto? In what follows, I will argue that this question is an implicit preoccupation of many of the major nonfiction statements made by fiction writers in the 1990s, including two collected in Wallace's volume that I will explore in greater depth, Jonathan Franzen's "I'll Be Doing More of Same" and Carole Maso's "Rupture, Verge, and Precipice: Precipice, Verge, and Hurt Not," as well as in Wallace's own statement of purpose, "E Unibus Pluram," (1993) and Franzen's longer lament for the future of literature, "Perchance to Dream" (1996). As it turns out, Wallace's interpretation is not as much of an intuitive stretch as it might seem. Many 1990s fiction manifestos – all of those examined here, with the important exception of Maso's, in fact – invoke the primacy of self-expression explicitly and defensively. In these manifestos and others, personal expression becomes a means of fighting against the imposition of popular culture upon the literary sphere (as in Wallace and Franzen); as a means to theorizing what will be lost as digital publication replaces print (as in Sven Birkert's book-length argument, *The Gutenberg Elegies* (1994) and Peter Dimock's "Literature as Lyrical Politics" [1996]); and as a significant priority of literature that rejects the programmatic expectations of twentieth century avant-garde movements (as in Rebecca Wolff's manifesto justifying the intervention of the influential literary journal *Fence* [1998]). So the stakes of the question become much more than whether or not Wallace's reading is tenable. They become, rather, whether or not there is a qualitative shift in statements by writers in the 1990s away from the kind of prophetic pronouncements we might associate with the tradition of twentieth-century avant-garde manifestos, and if there is such a shift, what that shift means for literature's self-understanding at the turn of the millennium.

Wallace's introduction neglects to mention the likely reason that he was chosen to edit the issue in the first place: the breadth and ambition of his own attempt to envision the future of fiction published in the *RCF* three years earlier. The essay, "E Unibus Pluram: Television and U.S. Fiction," examines the appropriation of ironic self-reference, once the hallmark of high postmodernist fiction, by popular television shows. The essay argues "that irony and ridicule ... are agents of a great despair and stasis in U.S. culture" and that while it is true that "pop-conscious postmodern fiction ... [makes] a real attempt to transfigure a world of and for appearance, mass appeal, and television," it is also the case that "TV ... has become able to capture and neutralize any attempt to change or even protest the attitudes of passive unease and cynicism TV requires of Audience in order to be ... viable."[7] Television, in this view, has neutralized the tools of critique that were seen as most useful to artists in the 1970s and 1980s, leaving the 1990s cultural producer to make a choice between simple capitulation to the world as it is and engaging in an empty form of criticism that, given its appearance in the worst of popular culture, looks again very much like complicity.

This central conundrum – the notion that the old ways of challenging the status quo have become thoroughly appropriated by the status quo – both make the project of writing a manifesto for the future of writing urgent (because the present seems so impossible) and makes writing such a manifesto in the traditional vein impossible. This latter point is particularly acute because, for Wallace, the force that has been most thoroughly neutralized by TV is the very force of rebelliousness itself. "Here's the stumper for the 1990s U.S. fictionalist," he writes, "How to rebel against TV's aesthetic of rebellion?"[8] Up through the 1960s, the manifesto was the go-to form that radical political and aesthetic movements could use to position themselves within a longer history of rebellion. The manifesto's key formal features – the collective first-person plural pronoun "we," the list of demands, the retelling of history from the point of view of the oppressed, the call to action and prophecy for a changed future – all both invoked and reflected a modern subject who could self-understand herself as both essentially included in a universal category ("the human," "the citizen," etc.) and as excluded from that category as a result of the injustices of history.[9] As Janet Lyon puts it,

> Where the universal subject is, there the manifesto shall be; for since the mid-seventeeth century the manifesto has acted out both an affirmation of and a challenge to universalism. On the one hand, the manifesto always displayed – indeed, performed – its indebtedness to the political developments of modernity that made possible the ideal of citizenship ... On the other hand, the genre's whole raison d'etre was to critique the uneven implementations of universalism.[10]

The universalism that was so essential to the manifesto form, however, received a major hit in the 1970s and 1980s from the rise of poststructuralism. Suddenly it seemed that the humanist ideal of universal citizenship could be seen as a symptom of injustice – of Eurocentrism, of knee-jerk secularism, of Enlightenment rationalism, of the long history of nationalism – rather than injustice being a mere function of its "uneven implementation" or, as Jurgen Habermas would have it, modernity's "incomplete project."[11] At this point, the manifesto begins to be a genre on the wane, particularly in the arts – but in politics too. The moment of the long 1960s persists through the 1970s in the form with pockets of continued vibrancy, particularly in feminism and poetry, but the manifestos of the 1980s get very strange: the bloated, ranting Unabomber Manifesto, the brief, first-person Hacker Manifesto, and the turn to more straightforward academic prose that accompanies the tail end of Language Poetry's high moment of the 1970s. By the time Wallace publishes "E Unibus Pluram" in 1993, the notion of appealing to a universal subject, a "we" with any expansiveness, seems laughably anachronistic. For this reason, even calling "E Unibus Pluram" and the various statements in Wallace's issue of *RCF* "manifestos" is undoubtedly a stretch. Most are written in the first-person singular, not the collectivist first-person plural of the traditional manifesto. Few issue demands directly – they lack the telltale numbered lists that, for many, most clearly signal that a piece of writing is a manifesto. Yet these are the closest pieces of writing to manifestos that we have from fiction writers of this period. Observing something similar in domain of poetry, Mark Wallace writes of his statement "Toward a Free Multiplicity of Form" (1996) that insofar as his "'manifesto' here is *not* a manifesto promoting a literary form or genre," the work "does not exhibit the characteristics of the twentieth-century manifesto."[12] He continues with an ambivalence to the form typical of the period, "if my argument here is to a certain extent a manifesto, it is one that points out that the quickest road to Rome might be to go someplace else entirely."[13]

Returning to David Foster Wallace's conundrum: "How to rebel against TV's aesthetic of rebellion?" We can see that this is a problem not only for the fictionalist, but also for the would-be manifesto-writer. Except that the specific form of rebellion that Wallace sees as impossible – ironic self-reference – was primarily a fiction-writer's form of rebellion. It simply isn't the case that in 1993 there was no way to rebel anymore anywhere – history would show that rebellion could take a range of forms in the 1990s and beyond: the tactical solidarity actions of the Seattle WTO protests, the terrorism of Al Qaeda, the anarcho-syndicalism of the European left, the spontaneous mass actions of the Arab Spring and Occupy, the radical electoral upheavals of the Tea Party. But it was the case that fiction writing had confronted what appeared to be a limit to the provisional solution to the critique of the universal subject it had found in the form of ironic self-reference. Fiction needed something entirely new: hence the manifesto. But it needed something new in a cultural context that forbade universal proclamations: hence, the inability to write a manifesto.

So we might agree with Wallace when he suggests that the paradox he traces could, in fact, have an escape route for someone who isn't as bound by his generation's orthodoxies. In a final paragraph – one that has become one of the defining statements on fiction of the turn-of-the-twentieth century – he writes:

> Entirely possible that my plangent cries about the impossibility of rebelling against an aura that promotes and attenuates all rebellion says more about my residency inside that aura, my own lack of vision, than it does about any exhaustion of U.S. fiction's possibilities. The next real literary "rebels" in this country might well emerge as some weird bunch of "anti-rebels," born oglers who dare to back away from ironic watching, who have the childish gall to endorse single-entendre values. Who treat old untrendy emotions in U.S. life with reverence and conviction. Who eschew self-consciousness and fatigue. These anti-rebels would be outdated, of course, before they even started. Too sincere. Clearly repressed. Backward, quaint, naïve, anachronistic. Maybe that'll be the point, why they'll be the next real rebels.... The new rebels might be the ones willing to risk the yawn, the rolled eyes, the cool smile, the nudged ribs, the parody of gifted ironists, the "How banal." Accusations of sentimentality, melodrama. Credulity... Who knows. Today's most engaged young fiction does seem like some kind of line's end's end. I guess that means we all get to draw our own conclusions. Have to. Are you immensely pleased.[14]

I quote this passage at length because it is often excerpted in such a way that allows it to be used as a direct invocation of fiction's future – as a call for the emergence of this new group of literary rebels, or as an effort at prophecy that turns out to be right when weighed against the return to realism that occurs in the early 2000s. Look at most works of scholarship on contemporary literature (including some of my own) and you'll see this quotation start with "the next real literary 'rebels'" and end with the sentence that begins "willingness to be suckered..." Wallace's own self-reference, in other words, tends to be excised for the sake of brevity and clarity. But this self-reference is crucial context for two reasons. First, it's a layering of his point in the essay: he can't think outside self-reference, and he can't write outside of it either. Pushing this point further, the final sentence of the paragraph and of the essay as a whole is a reference to the "Most Photographed Barn in America" scene in Don DeLillo's *White Noise*, which he engages with at length earlier in the essay. Murray Jay Siskind, DeLillo's caricature of a self-satisfied postmodernist, revels in the layers of self-watching in the scene and, reporting on them as a good cultural critic, seems "immensely pleased with himself." Here, Wallace casts both the reader and himself as Murray figures, prone to finding pleasure in the saddest of postmodern *mise-en-abymes*.[15]

But more crucially, Wallace's positioning of himself as inescapably stuck in the trap he describes emphasizes his lack of ability to imagine his way out. In this context, the section most of us quote when we want to say what Wallace thought would happen to fiction next – the whole "next literary rebels" bit – is a performance of how impossible it is for Wallace to think his way out of the fix he, and all of us, are in, rather than an earnest prediction of the future. These rebels "might well" emerge as those willing to risk single-entendre principles. "Who knows." Your guess is as good as mine, Wallace tells us. The possibility he offers, the anti-rebel possibility, seems as right as any other, when one's fundamental position is one of not being able to see any possibility for rebellion at all. For that reason, what seems like an offhand caveat at the end of the essay, "I guess that means we all get to draw our own conclusions," might actually be the point of this final paragraph. If there's no way out of ironic self-reference and ironic self-reference is the lifeblood of a destructive cultural dominant, then any effort to imagine one's way out of that conundrum is likely to just be a matter of one's own individual impulse, taste, or whim.[16]

In "I'll Be Doing More of Same" – the essay in the volume that Wallace thinks is "very, very close to being right" – Jonathan Franzen addresses similar concerns, albeit on a slightly more conservative register. Early in the piece he writes: "It's hard to resist nostalgia for a general audience that expected some entertainment for the money it spent on books; hard not to prefer a system in which wage-earners subsidized good authors for dubious reasons to a system in which tenured professors subsidize dubious authors for good reasons."[17] Here Franzen expresses a clear preference for the bad-old days of "general audience" over the "good-old-days" of postmodernist experimentalism. Echoing Wallace's concern about the lack of teeth that postmodernism has by the late twentieth century, he argues, "when the avant-garde is all that remains – when the rebels who kept the establishment honest are themselves enshrined as the establishment – we're left without an opposition."[18] The argument is slightly different –

here it is the academic "enshrinement" of postmodernism rather than its appropriation into popular culture that makes it no longer oppositional – but the takeaway is the same: the general audience (read: universal subject) is dead, postmodernism is toothless, so the enterprise of fiction seems like it is at a dead end. Franzen's narrative of why the general audience no longer exists does differ from Wallace's insofar as it blames the dissolution less on the rise of post-structrualism and more on the rise of identity politics, or as he calls it, "the new tribalism."[19] His essay also lacks the self-awareness of its own embeddedness in a self-aware dominant. Franzen comes off less like a character stuck in a Don DeLillo novel and more like someone's cranky great-uncle, pissed off that the world has left him behind and fearful that the youngs will crash the car of literary history into a telephone pole. "When times get really, really awful, you retrench"; he explains, "you reexamine old content in new contexts; you try to preserve; you seem obsolete... The day comes when the truly subversive literature is in some measure conservative."[20] This second-person voice is, of course, a thinly veiled first-person singular, as is revealed in the more clearly autobiographical longer version of this argument published in *Harpers* under the title "Perchance to Dream" (1996). In this piece, Franzen tells a story that sounds much more like Wallace's: a story of being stuck feeling as if he should be writing postmodern novels and being unable to write them to his satisfaction. Whereas in the *RCF* essay Franzen appeals to "content and context" as "vectors of the new," in "Perchance to Dream" the solution is more specific and autobiographical. Having been paralyzed by the difficulty of engaging with the social world of the early 1990s in all of its complexities, Franzen resolves to try to forget about that "grim duty" and simply go about "peopling and arranging my own little alternate world."[21] "I'm amazed, now," he writes, "that I'd trusted myself so little for so long, that I'd felt such a crushing imperative to engage explicitly with all the forces impinging on the pleasure of reading and writing."[22] The answer for Franzen, in other words, is not entirely unlike Wallace's answer: knowing the future of literature is impossible. What you can know, however, is yourself. The result is that the manifesto becomes autobiography – either explicitly, as in "Perchance to Dream" or implicitly, as in "E Unibus Pluram." Given the prevalence of this conclusion, it is easy enough to see why Wallace would read all attempts to imagine the future of writing as (mere) self-expression.

But there is a strange exception to this trend in 1990s fiction writing-about-writing, and it happens to be another essay included in Wallace's volume of the *RCF*: Carole Maso's "Rupture, Verge, and Precipice: Precipice, Verge, and Hurt Not." It's worth noting from the start that Maso's position in relation to 1990s literary culture is substantively different from Wallace's and Franzen's for two reasons: first, she is a woman; second, her work is largely published by independent presses and her writing is often grouped with the more marginal "experimentalists" of her day. I point out these differences because Maso sees them as important; indeed, they are at the core of the polarized vision of her manifesto, which makes conscious use of two distinct pronouns: "you" and "I." The piece begins:

> You are afraid. You are afraid, as usual, that the novel is dying. You think you know what a novel is: it's the kind you write. You fear you are dying.
> You wonder where the hero went.
> You wonder how things could have gotten so out of hand.
> You ask where is one sympathetic, believable character?
> You ask where is the plot?
> You wonder where on earth is the conflict? The resolution? The dénouement?
> You imagine yourself to be the holder of some last truth. You imagine yourself to be in some sinking, noble, gilt-covered cradle of civilization.
> You romanticize your fin de siècle, imbuing it with meaning, overtones, implications.
> You are still worried about TV.[23]

Sound like anyone we know? Because the piece was written in spring of 1995 (Maso provides us with exact dates at the end of the piece – more on that later), we can be certain that she had not read either of Franzen's pieces, at least in published form. But it is likely that she read "E Unibus Pluram," and given the consistency of the "oh no, literature is dying, what will we do?" lament of the majority of the essays in the special issue her essay appears in, she was undoubtedly aware of this discourse as the dominant narrative of her time. This "you," which, it becomes clear as the piece continues, is clearly meant to stand in for the literary hegemons of the day – the mostly male, mostly white writers of what she calls "middlebrow" writing works that nevertheless position themselves as high literature. This "you" is countered with an "I" that appears at the bottom of page two:

> But I, for one, am on to you. Your taste for blood, your love of competition, your need to feel endangered, beleaguered, superior. Your need to reiterate, to reassert your power, your privilege, because it erodes.
>   Let's face it, you're panicked.[24]

In Maso's manifesto, the notion that literature is under threat is a symptom of the destabilizing of the exceptional position of cultural elites, a destabilizing that she sees as ultimately good, not only politically, but aesthetically. In a passage that reads as if it is a direct address to Franzen's call to "preserve," to create fiction that is "in some measure conservative," Maso writes: "You can't see a place for yourself in it and it frightens you. You dig in your heels as a result. Spend all your considerable intelligence and energy conserving, preserving, holding court, posturing, tenaciously holding on, now as you munch your last green leaves, yum."[25] Maso's manifesto, then, accurately reflects a primary division between two camps in mid-1990s fiction. The future that Franzen and Wallace see as a threat to the very enterprise of writing literature, the "I" of the text sees as the opposite: "the future is all the people who've ever been kept out, singing."[26]

But what might look like a clear-cut manifesto at last, with its polarizing discourse and pronouns, its intentionally inflammatory rhetoric, its call to action ("Wish: That we be open-minded and generous. That we fear not."[27]) turns out to have more in common with Franzen and Wallace, rhetorically speaking, than we might at first think. Ultimately Maso, too, pushes back against the rigid we/them structure of the traditional manifesto. While the I/you structure of "Rupture" seems like a mere replication of the we/them, Maso's chosen pronoun pair functions very differently. Casting the manifesto's opposition as "you" is a welcoming gesture, as harsh as the descriptions of the "you" are in the text. Maso emphasizes this in a few moments of self-reflection in the text of the manifesto itself. Fairly early in the text she writes, "I'm getting a little tired of this 'you' and 'I.' Still I am learning a few new things about you – and about me."[28] Later: "I am getting a little tired of this you-and-I bit. But it tells me one important thing: *that I do not want it to have to be this way.* I do not believe it has to continue this way – you over there alternately blustery and cowering, me over here, defensive, angry."[29] Here, the oppositional party in the manifesto is not called upon, as it is in the traditional manifesto form, as a shared enemy to consolidate the revolutionary "we." Rather, it is cast as one of two parties in a lovers' quarrel, with the implied hope that there may be a place for reconciliation.

Indeed, Maso comments on this in a reflection that appears immediately after the text of the manifesto. Dated "25 April 1995 / Germantown, New York," six weeks prior to the date of the manifesto, which is signed "1 June 1995," the reflection is framed with thoughts about spring. It begins, "A walk around the loop and I notice the bloodroot has begun to bloom. A bluebird, two bluebirds! . . . The world begins again. In this vision. In the words *bloodroot* and *bluebird*."[30] Spring is cast as a time of environmental and creative rebirth. The reflection also invokes personal autobiography, as Maso describes the difficulty of making a decision about where to teach in the fall and her feelings about the overdue essay she owes the *RCF*. In the final lines of the reflection she writes:

> What I wonder most is if there is a way, whether there might be a way in this whole wide world, to forgive them. Something for the sake of my own work, my own life I need to do – have needed to do for a long time. Perhaps in my essay I will make an attempt, the first movement toward some sort of reconciliation, at any rate. If it's possible. To set up the drama that might make it possible.
> This breakable heart.
> April. How poised everything seems. How wonderfully ready. And I, too, trembling – and on the verge . . . [31]

Casting this description back on the manifesto, the work starts to look less like an attempt to do away with the opposition, and more like a "drama" that might make reconciliation possible. More play than program, the manifesto sets up two personae and lets them talk. The result is, given their pronounced differences in position, divisive, but, according to Maso in her reflection, that's not the point. The point is for Maso to embody both of these personae and through that embodiment be reborn in the spirit of the spring during which she writes.

Crucially, for Maso, as for Wallace and Franzen, the manifesto is a form of autobiography. But whereas Wallace and Franzen start with an attempt to address a social phenomenon and end up with personal expression as the only reliable answer, Maso begins with autobiography, but does so as a way of situating her perspective. For this reason, it isn't a coincidence that the initial descriptions in her reflection are environmental ("Today I saw three enormous turtles sunning themselves on the pond," she muses early in the piece).[32] She begins with where and when she is writing from ("25 April 1995 / Germantown, New York"), before describing her personal impulses and emotions. Out of that position, we get a social intervention in the form of the manifesto. Reversing the temporal order between the manifesto and the reflection allows the manifesto to be presented as primary – and indeed it should be, its intervention is the point – but dating the reflection exposes the situatedness of the self who performs the "you and I" of the manifesto. This is the precise opposite of Franzen and Wallace, who end up situating themselves as expressive individuals only once they reach the dead-end of a social polemic. For Franzen and Wallace, the existence of the expressive individual becomes the solution to a social problem, rather than the site out of which a social address emerges – as it is for Maso.

This distinction is critical, because it refigures the relationship between irony, earnestness, and expression. For Wallace, irony is a trap that can only be answered with an earnest form of self-expression, a form of writing that is almost impossible given the prevailing mood of ironic self-reference in popular media and the metafictional dominant in literary fiction. For Maso, on the other hand, the privileged vessel for self-expression is a theatrical version of the self. The "I" of the manifesto is an explicitly performed "I," a character in the drama she stages with the "you." In turn, she is able to write something that looks more like a manifesto than most of the other fiction writers of her period can muster. This is because self-expression is not figured as a place to end up, but as an impulse that can be harnessed to get somewhere else; it's used as a vehicle for changing the world, not as a reason to stop trying. In other words, whereas Wallace sees an incompatibility between a given manifesto being "'right' in [an] argumentative or predictive sense" (as the essays in his volume ostensibly aim to be) and "diary entries," (as they ultimately end up being), Maso demonstrates that what looks very much like a diary entry ("25 April 1995 / Germantown, New York") can be the ground from which a serious argumentative and predictive work might emerge.

What does this mean for an assessment of literature's self-understanding in the 1990s? If the literary manifesto reemerges as an expressive form in the decade, it might look at first as if the future-oriented impulse of the avant-garde has been definitively eclipsed in favor of a more conservative, inward-looking tendency. It would be easy enough to line that turn up with the renewed interest in psychological realism that builds over the course of the decade and sees its fulfillment at the turn of the twenty-first century. But as Maso's piece suggests, there is more than one valence to the notion of self-expression as a form of reflecting on the future of literature because there is more than one definition of self-expression. Self-expression can be the private, individual musings of a specific person. This is the way Franzen and, with a few more caveats, Wallace see it. But self-expression can also be a performance: the theatrical posing of a given self as a way of channeling language's expressive properties. This is the way Maso imagines it, and the difference between the two is significant.

In this context, we might see the 1990s not only as the moment when the fiction writing manifesto was diluted into a personal form, but also as a moment when the fiction manifesto joined a range of other manifestos in envisioning how a period that seemed to signal the end of revolutionary possibilities could be imagined to be a moment not of capitulation, but of creative destruction. Maso would then make less sense in the company of Franzen and Wallace and more sense in the company of Kathleen Hanna, frontwoman of the punk band Bikini Kill. In the Riot Grrrl manifesto (1991), Hanna writes, "we must take over the means of production in order to create our own moanings."[33] Replacing "meanings" with "moanings" here could easily be read as a personalization of politics, ceding the ground of political debate in favor of a celebration of affective expression. But like Maso, Hanna sees these "moanings" not as instances of individual expression, but as socially meaningful "BECAUSE," as she explains it later in the manifesto, "I believe with my wholeheartmindbody that girls constitute a revolutionary soul force that can, and will change the world for real."[34] Or we might think of the Queer Nation manifesto (1990), which responds militantly to straight culture's lack of response to the threat of AIDS in terms that also rely upon a theatrical use of first-person expressive language, as when the anonymous authors declare, "Remember there is so, so little time. And I want to be a lover of each and every one of you."[35]

I want to be a lover of each and every one of you. Wholeheartmindbody. Revolutionary soul force. Moanings. All the people who have been left out, singing. These are not individualistic "expressions of a heart's special tangle," but calls to collective action. They may not aspire to being "right in any argumentative or predictive sense," but they do envision a radically different future. For Puchner, the distinction between the desire to anchor art in an objective discourse on the one hand and the use of theatricality to address the shifting terrain of artistic practice on the other defines the distinction between the modernist and the avant-gardist. He writes, "While modernism . . . sought to exorcise theatricality so that a true and pure art might be preserved, the avant-garde embraced this threat to art and therefore sought to theatricalize art in order to thoroughly change, deform, and even destroy it."[36] In this formulation, Wallace and Franzen, by seeing an objective argument about the future of literature as impossible and self-expression as the only remedy, are failed modernists. Maso, along with Hanna, the authors of The Queer Nation manifesto, and others, on the other hand, in embracing theatricality as a means to merging self-expression and argument, demonstrate the continued relevance of the avant-garde at the very moment of its supposed demise.

NOTES

1 David Foster Wallace, "Quo Vadis – Introduction," *Review of Contemporary Fiction* 16:1 (1996), 8.
2 Ibid., 7.
3 Ibid., 8.

4 Ibid.
5 Martin Puchner, *Poetry of the Revolution: Marx, Manifestos, and the Avant-Gardes* (Princeton, NJ: Princeton University Press, 2006), 70–71.
6 Ibid., 77.
7 David Foster Wallace, "E Unibus Pluram: Television and U.S. Fiction," *Review of Contemporary Fiction* 13:2 (1993): 171.
8 Ibid., 184.
9 I borrow the broad contours of this history and definition from Lyon's excellent work in Chapter 1 of *Manifestoes: Provocations of the Modern* (Ithaca, NY: Cornell University Press, 1999).
10 Lyon, 32.
11 Jurgen Habermas, "Modernity – An Incomplete Project," in *The Anti-Aesthetic: Essays on Postmodern Culture*, ed. Hal Foster (New York: New, 2002): 3–15.
12 Mark Wallace, "Toward a Free Multiplicity of Form," in *Telling it Slant: Avant-Garde Poetics of the 1990s*, ed. Mark Wallace and Steven Marks (Tuscaloosa: University of Alabama Press, 2002), 201–202.
13 Ibid., 202.
14 Wallace, "E Unibus Pluram," 193.
15 Wallace's negotiation of irony and sincerity throughout his work is highly fraught and widely debated in scholarship. See Lee Konstantinou, "No Bull: David Foster Wallace and Post-Ironic Belief," *The Legacy of David Foster Wallace*, ed. Samuel Cohen and Lee Konstantinou (Iowa City: University of Iowa Press), 2012: 83–112 and Adam Kely, "David Foster Wallace and the New Sincerity in American Fiction," *Consider David Foster Wallace: Critical Essays*, ed. David Hering (Los Angeles: Sideshow Media Group, 2010): 131–146.
16 The political quietism that stems from such a posture is, as Ryan Brooks argues, a result of "[Wallace's] tacit acceptance of the premise that capitalism's problems can be addressed at the level of personal values and relationships." In "Conflict Before Compromise: A Response to Rachel Greenwald Smith," *The Account* 4 (2015).
17 Jonathan Franzen, "I'll Be Doing More of Same," *Review of Contemporary Fiction* 16:1 (1996): 34.
18 Ibid., 36.
19 Ibid., 35.
20 Ibid., 38.
21 Jonathan Franzen, "Perchance to Dream: In the Age of Images, a Reason to Write Novels," *Harper's Magazine*, April 1996, 54.
22 Ibid.
23 Carole Maso, "Rupture, Verge, and Precipice: Precipice, Verge, and Hurt Not," *Review of Contemporary Fiction* 16:1 (1996): 54.
24 Ibid., 55.
25 Ibid., 58.
26 Ibid., 60.
27 Ibid., 68.
28 Ibid., 58.

29 Ibid., 69. Italics in original.
30 Ibid., 75.
31 Ibid.
32 Ibid.
33 Kathleen Hanna, "Riot Grrrl Manifesto," *One War Art*, http://onewarart.org/riot_grrrl_manifesto.htm.
34 Ibid.
35 Act Up, "The Queer Nation Manifesto," *History is a Weapon*, http://www.historyisaweapon.com/defcon1/queernation.html.
36 Puchner, 88.

CHAPTER 13

Revisionary Strategies
Christian Moraru

When Pia Pera rewrote Vladimir Nabokov's *Lolita* in her 1995 *Diario di Lo*, the Italian writer challenged her audience to read her book both alongside and against its "tutor" text. According to its author, *Lo's Diary* sought to give a "transformative" response to the "challenge" Nabokov himself issued in the 1955 masterpiece, and it can be argued that the rewrite largely succeeded. For Pera's work is at once re-creative and creative. While Nabokov's fans cannot miss the reiterative vector of her *re*telling, they should keep an eye out for the revisionary thrust of the italicized suffix too, that is, for the story Pera declines to restore as well as for that which rewriting deliberately un-tells, counter-tells, and overall "transforms" so as to render the rewrite at once original and critical of the original. Of course, in play here and throughout postmodernism is a new, counterintuitive but polemical concept of originality, one that, in its most aggressively appropriative cases, derives novelty from explicit and programmatic reworking of past works. It is the overt aggression, the allegedly ethical and legal impropriety of in-your-face appropriation rather than its creative thrust that, as Ralph Blumenthal informs us, led the Nabokov estate to accuse Pera of "aesthetic and literary vampirism"[1] and "fil[e] suit to block [the release of the English translation of the] retold *Lolita*."[2] The "legal battle over copyright infringement and the limits of artistic borrowing" resulted in Farrar, Straus & Giroux cancelling the publication of *Lo's Diary*.[3] The fact that *Lolita* itself "vampirizes" Edgar Allan Poe or that Kurt Vonnegut (*Slapstick*), Gilbert Sorrentino (*Mulligan Stew*), and Steven Millhauser (*Edwin Mullhouse: The Life and Death of an American Writer, 1943–1954*) had already recycled Nabokov made little difference to the American publisher. Not to mention that Pera follows in the age-old tradition of writing as appropriation of extant writings. "Long before Shakespeare," Blumenthal specifies, "writers appropriated each other's historical themes, plots and characters, refashioning them into new works."[4] However, while listing certain "flagrant" instances of modern rewriting, Blumenthal does not wonder if its

199

expanding presence in American bookstores and courts is culturally symptomatic of the 1990s in the United States and possibly in the world at large.[5] He is not asking what draws fiction authors to this literary-cultural formation after the Cold War, nor is he curious about how rewrites adjust to this new moment in US and world history.

In raising such questions here, it bears noting, first, that both the Nabokovian "prototype" and its transatlantic rejoinder instantiate the intertextual recreation so typical of literature since modernism. Of course, whether Joycean, Nabokovian, or of a later sort, "stollentelling" – to recall, as David Cowart urges us, a *locus classicus* in *Finnegans Wake* – has a longer history behind it.[6] As Matei Calinescu observes in his overview of the subject, "[t]hat rewriting ... is a relatively new and fashionable term for a number of very old techniques of literary composition need not be argued ... It will suffice to remind ourselves of just some major concepts of traditional poetics ... [T]hey include imitation, parody, burlesque, transposition, pastiche, adaptation, and even translation. Critical commentary, including description, summary, and selected quotations from a primary text, also falls under this heading." But Calinescu also rightly allows that "modern (modernist, postmodernist) modes of rewriting add some new twists to older kinds of textual transformations: a certain playful, hide-and-seek type of indirection, a tongue-in-cheek seriousness, an often respectful and even honorific irony, and an overall tendency toward oblique and even secret or quasi-secret textual reference."[7]

It is rewriting as a whole, though, that, in postmodernism – and in the late postmodernism of the 1990s more than in previous decades – becomes a literary and cultural "dominant" as a steadily swelling cohort of writers rewrite in order to write their books. Also, the stylistic arsenal of rewriting during this time is pressed into the service of oppositional politics more emphatically than ever before. That is, as a formal tactic, rewriting is subordinated to a socio-literary revisionary strategy or, as Marcel Cornis-Pope insists, to a more complex, "cultural rewriting."[8] Elsewhere, I have described this rewriting as "extensive." Rewriting is intensive, I have proposed, insofar as the rewritten text's avatar retells its ancestor in painstaking detail, oftentimes by means of recognizable narrative parallels, analogies, and other pointedly isomorphic configurations of plot, character, setting, theme, and so on; and rewriting is extensive in that what gets revisited is not just an earlier literary work but also older, sometimes ingrown representations of nationhood, gender, race, ethnicity, sexuality, and so forth. These are deep-seated in that emblematic text and have left their imprint on US history and the American literary canon, on Herman Melville,

Henry David Thoreau, Nathaniel Hawthorne, Walt Whitman, Louisa May Alcott, Poe, and other American classics now subject to reworking by entire postmodern genres ranging from cartoons, mashups, and avant-pop "graftings" such as Mark Leyner's "heinous revisions," Raymond Federman's "playgiarisms," or Kathy Acker's literary "piracy," to more full-blown reprises.[9]

More notably yet, 1990s fictional rewriting seems to rely on a certain pattern of form and theme. Formally, "intensive" appropriations, sequels, and interpolations of the "apocryphal," permutational, re-textualizing, and "re-lettering" kind are vehicles of choice for an extensive or cultural rewriting that becomes increasingly cross-cultural on a global scale. The intertextual exchanges and, most revealingly, the geographical imagination of US authors overlap less and less with the domestic archive and territory. No happenstance, this discrepancy bears witness to a widening, epoch-defining asymmetry and is part of a revisionary project that distinguishes both late postmodernism and, as I have suggested, the slow transition out of the postmodern paradigm.[10] Alongside literary critics, historians, sociologists, political scientists, global studies specialists, and other humanists, the decade's American "rewriters" suspect that, as Arjun Appadurai claims in one of the most observant scholarly books of the time, "[n]ation-states, for all their important differences . . . make sense only as part of a system." "[E]ven when seen as a system of differences," the "system," Appadurai adds, "appear poorly equipped to deal with the interlinked diasporas of people and images that mark the here and now." "Nation-states," the critic concludes, may be "units in a complex interactive system," but it is unlikely that they will manage or think it through effectively.[11]

Wrapping and dramatizing our globalizing planet in something that might be dubbed – à la Appadurai's "globalscapes" – "storyscape," the world-embracing fictional imagination of the 1990s both comes on the heels of this surging interactivity and takes upon itself to handle it conceptually and affectively.[12] Undergirded by this "worlded" imaginary of nomadic myths, stories, plot structures, and motifs, post–Cold War era cross-cultural rewriting literally and thematically operates transnationally: on one side, it effectively rewrites across national traditions and territories; on the other side, it thematizes this textual de- and trans-territorialization by taking up inherited, territory-bound constructions and enactments of nation, national affiliation, and the like. The other identity components in which revisionary rewriting has been interested do not fall by the wayside, but the problematics of nationhood demonstrably take center stage, as a testimony to rewriting's cross- and supranational plays after 1989. Rewriting still obtains intra-culturally, but, generally speaking, it amplifies textually and contextually into a narrative ecology or "narratosphere" subsuming and linking up national domains and the interactions inside their cultural environments. Progressively and emphatically intercultural in a transnational and even planetary sense, the rewrites stemming from this symbolic commerce take, as we shall see momentarily, postmodern revisionism to another level, of more conspicuously and capaciously geocultural significance, thus opening up new spaces across, beyond, above, and sometimes against the nations' centripetal pull. Attesting to the post-Berlin Wall dynamic, velocity, and topology of global transactions, to the sped-up mobility of people, commodities, texts, ideas, and data, in brief, to the quintessential "interconnectedness" of the late twentieth-century "world system," as Immanuel Wallerstein would say, the world order of stories that coalesces in the 1990s goes to show that this system is not only economic but also literary – textual and *inter*textual.

Inside this system, the position occupied by *Lolita* is twice relevant. For one thing, the novel is a major text in the late-modern Western canon. For another, the book and its rewriting legacy cast light on a certain progression, on the global integration and growth of the system. If Pera's "Italian Lolita," coming along as it does within the Euro-North American continuum, still offers a largely intra-cultural reply to Nabokov, Lee Siegel's 1999 novel *Love in a Dead Language* provides a saliently inter- or cross-cultural response. Where Pera employs the diary technique to let Lo's voice be heard in a fashion reminding one of gender-oriented and feminist rewrites by Jean Rhys, Maryse Condé, and Sena Jeter Naslund, Siegel turns to the complex trope of narrative "travel" and translation to unfold an ampler, more ambitious, and inherently cosmopolitan panorama of stories, cultural and erotic affinities, compatibilities, conversions, and traffickings – a vision attuned to our time's global-scale, cross-national developments.

Both in his scholarship and fiction, Siegel shows how discourse works as a potent agent of communication and exchange that sets up a revisionary dialogue between Western and Eastern traditions through world literary flows and narrative "vagrancy." His books pursue the role stories hold in the fostering of cultural languages that cut across idioms, locations, and political-economic systems. Not unlike Mircea Eliade, another historian of religions who resorted to fiction to flesh out scenarios of intercultural encounters, Siegel suspects that "stories unify the world," as he puts it in his 1995 novel *City of Dreadful Night*. "Real stories have no end," his character Brahm Kathuwala assures his audience. "None of the storyteller's stories," he goes on, has a beginning or an end – the story he has just told is but an interlude in a larger story... Though the weaver of tales often stops with *but that's another story*, there are no other stories, no separate, discreet tales. There are no borders... All of the stories, each one having limited versions, each with infinite recensions, are interlocked and interlinked episodes of a greater, amorphous epic, and each contains the whole in a mysterious, unexplainable way... Every story is embedded in the middle of this great, circular epic. There's no way out of it.[13]

In Siegel's fictionally oversaturated world, stories, plots, motifs, characters, and images journey across the planet and make it one narrative continuum in the process. They cover the world so tightly that "there's no way out of it" (Siegel, 1995, 50). They travel the world but not necessarily "well" (as we say of certain wines), for they themselves *transmigrate*: they move around, and, as they do so, they change as they are exported to unwonted locations faster and more profoundly than ever. Thus, *City of Dreadful Night* places Dracula in India and redoes Bram Stoker's work by detailing the "influence" of "Bra[h]m Stokerji" on Indian narratives of vampires, ghosts, ghouls, and ogres, while Siegel's best book to date, the 1999 novel *Love in a Dead Language*, incorporates the *Kamasutra* and, in a sense, resettles it in the United States, while rewriting and relocating to India *Lolita* and elements of Philip Roth's *The Professor of Desire* and *Operation Shylock*. In Siegel's transtextual and transcultural imaginary, Western stories and their characters turn up in Eastern garments and vice versa, swathing the world in "spirals of recursion."[14] Thus, Lolita is renamed Lalita (Gupta); one Leopold Roth, a Sanskrit scholar, does the "Humbert Humbert in India" routine; and the *Kamasutra* provides, funnily enough, the erotic ideal to which Nabokovian fantasies fail to measure up.

Despite its thick cultural-intertextual fabric, *Love in a Dead Language*'s plot is deceivingly simple because, to adapt the classical distinction between *inventio* and *dispositio*, Siegel does not quite "invent." Or, if you prefer, he does invent – he is amazingly inventive and creative, truth be told – but he does not "originate" his story. He "transmigrates" it. A variety of rewriting, transmigration is his narrative and cultural recipe. In a manner that becomes increasingly typical of late twentieth-century postmodernism, he deliberately and ironically puts together an allusive, identifiable, intertextual, and transcultural plot by moving extant stories around and challenging them to make new sense in their new places and in crosspollinating conversation with those places' own narrative traditions. The reader might, for instance, discern in this plot a basic metafictional convention, namely, the text and its "double" or "metatext," in the form of a faux translation, critical "commentary" similar to Nabokov's *Pale Fire*, or both. Significantly, Siegel weaves two different formal threads into this complexly nested structure, Western and Southeast Asian, and, in this regard, he reminds one of recent international, multiethnic, and postcolonial writers who draw storytelling analogies and build narrative bridges between West and East and North and South while engaging with national identity and location: Condé, Salman Rushdie, Bharati Mukherjee, Arundhati Roy, Maxine Hong Kingston, Gish Jen, Édouard Glissant, Nicole Mones, or the Chinese-French novelist Dai Sijie.

These cultural-interpretive translations across spaces, languages, and cultural-political customs are foregrounded in the novel's front matter. *Love in a Dead Language* is, as its complete title announces, "a romance by Lee Siegel being the *Kamasutra* of *Guru Vatsyayana Mallanaga* as translated and interpreted by *Professor Leopold Roth* with a foreword and annotation by *Anang Saighal* following the commentary of *Pandit Pralayananga Lilaraja*." The "romance" re-romances, so to speak, Nabokov's *Lolita*: "Lalita Gupta is the reason for this text," Roth confesses in his journal (Siegel, 1999, 5). But *Love in a Dead Language* imitates structurally both *Lolita*, which is, we will remember, Humbert Humbert's memoir prefaced and edited by one John Ray, Jr., PhD, and *Pale Fire*, which uses even more substantially the Russian-doll-like ploy of text-cum-commentary-cum-commentary-on-commentary and, in Siegel, shows up in a telltale reference to "Zemblan" language. Furthermore, *Love in a Dead Language* draws on the *Kamasutra* of Vatsyayana (ca. third century AD), a real if elusive text, and on the more mysterious translation into Persian of the original Sanskrit and commentary in verse by one Pralayananga Lilaraja, a seventeenth-century scholar and poet at the court of Shah Jahan at Agra. In the Foreword, Saighal tells us that, as an editor of Roth's work, he is primarily interested in Pralayananga's gloss on the *Kamasutra*, while Roth was attracted chiefly by Pralayananga's translation, which Roth had translated in his dissertation (Siegel, 1999, xv). I could not find Pralayananga's text – *Love in a Dead Language* does feature a bibliography, but much of it has been made up, à la Jorge Luis Borges – and the fact that the name of the book's editor as well as Lalita/Lolita's is anagrammatically inserted into Pralayananga's strikes me as a serious deterrent to further efforts in this direction. However, despite its textual acrobatics, jokes, hoaxes, and plays, *Love in a Dead Language* must be taken seriously for its stylistic accomplishments, no less than for how it forces us to revisit the ways we think of ourselves, our communities, and our world. Alongside other authors of rewrites variously classified as postmodern, postcolonial, diasporic, transnational, or multiethnic, Siegel raises the issue of what Emily Apter has identified as "an emergent internationalized aesthetics."[15] But what his work reveals about our time, our world, and our places in it reaches beyond the aesthetic. Siegel may remind us of another dexterous Nabokovian, John Barth, who, in "Dunyazadiad" and elsewhere, indulges his humorous metafictional experimentalism and tackles issues of gender, culture, and power by lifting forms, settings, and characters from *The Arabian Nights*. While working with a similar blend, Siegel assembles, more insistently than Barth, a worldly discourse that forefronts, both in form and substance, the turn-of-the-millennium's global assemblages, exchanges, and mobility. Acting out late postmodernism's expanding, intertextual, and intercultural relatedness, Siegel's manifest and sophisticated rewriting reflects, and reflects on, the global age's network culture. The homology between how his narrative represents, what it represents, and the world in which it does so becomes apparent in the book's twin model of narrative and cultural interconnectedness. This model simultaneously shapes the novel's fictional world and conveys the shape of the "real" world. In a sense, then, we are talking about a narrative apparatus that has to do with stories, what they are, and how they go around. But we are also privy to their world metamorphoses, to the translation travail they undergo as their travel into the world of the other: another space, language, culture, and the whole *Weltanschauung* set into this otherness.

Thus, on the one hand, stories, authors, and narrators spread globally so that no place on earth is "safe" from them, left unclaimed by texts and representations, narrative-free. This is why globalization also emerges as a fluid yet reasonably ordered storyworld: in the very narrative enveloping, organizing, and unifying of the world, the global reveals itself, plays its makeup out. This outspread and intermingling of the rewritten and the rewrite across gaps of time, space, and cultural difference is, in a very metafictionally postmodern vein, possibly *the* topic of Siegel's works as well as their structural principle. Encapsulated by the novel and intertwined with this worldview of narrative fluidity is, on the other hand, a theory of cosmopolitan writing as twofold translation: commonly understood translation, from one idiom into another, but also cultural translation, translation as *translatio*, narrative travel and splicing up over all kinds of boundaries. The *Lolita*-as-the-new-*Kamasutra* plot enacts, and speaks to, a trans-idiomatic paradigm of "attraction," a global erotics of language and communication that seizes on both eroticism and textuality as cosmopolitan aggregates. The term "cosmopolitan," I might add, pops up frequently in the Sanskrit original reproduced in the novel and also appears in Roth's translation. The cross-cultural texture and dialogical nature of idiom and discourse and their bodily counterpart, the polyphonic language of play, desire, and pleasure, are what Siegel performs. Of course, "Lalita" means "pleasant" and "playful" in Sanskrit, but, more generally, love, being-with-the-other, is here translation and transsubstantiation of desire into pleasure and self into/as other. So are idiom, alphabet, writing, and rewriting. None is a reflection of an origin lying this or that side of the I/you, we/they, and here/there divides but entails translating from an/other text – from the text of alterity – into the vulgate of subjectivity, intimacy, and affect. Hardly lost in translation, the self "originates" in it instead, in the pleasurable rendition of the other and his or her stories. Text is texture in which the ontological and aesthetic gap between primary source and gloss closes and everything becomes commentary, fictional rather than scholarly, of originals themselves second order. De facto, the whole world order of stories is second-order, metanarrative, apocrypha.

Fairly popular with American authors of the 1990s, apocryphal rewriting is Mukherjee's main strategy in *The Holder of the World*.[16] More revisionary than *Love in a Dead Language*, the novel speaks to a pattern shaping her entire oeuvre. Critics have noticed "narrative mimicking" in earlier works such as *The Middleman and Other Stories*, *Jasmine*, and *Wife*, and the same technique could be spotted in the later novels as well as in her essay "Mimicry and Reinvention," which has been linked to Homi Bhabha's theory of mimicry as "imitative performance" that "disturbs an originary essence of identity by returning a *different* and strange image of the self."[17] The essence *The Holder of the World* sets out to disturb has been historically articulated along national, imperial, territorial, cultural-linguistic, ethnic, and gender lines. These lines, hints Mukherjee, can be best read between, and sometimes even on, the lines of such American classics as *The Scarlet Letter*, hence the reason of rewriting the romance in the 1993 novel.

Mukherjee is not the first to take on Hawthorne's masterpiece. Acker, John Updike, Samuel R. Delany, Toni Morrison, and Margaret Atwood, to name but a few, have also attempted "renarrativizations" of *The Scarlet Letter*. What sets her apart is an apocryphal retelling that extends Hawthorne's story and world across time and space, a worldly relettering of *The Scarlet Letter* that brings into view histories, cultural lineages, literary hierarchies, places, and actors (as well as actresses) the Hawthornian script concurrently illuminates and obscures. Mukherjee's revisionary strategies bring to the fore our moment's unprecedented circulation and refashioning of commodities, ideas, styles, icons, and people. In effect, at the novel's end, Beigh Masters, her protagonist and transparent alter ego, flaunts *The Scarlet Letter* as the book's "source." "We have," the character discloses, "the shipping and housing records, we have the letters and journals and the *Memoirs*, and of course we have *The Scarlet Letter*." "Who can blame Nathaniel Hawthorne for shying away from the real story of the brave Salem mother and her illegitimate daughter" (Mukherjee, 1994, 284), asks Beigh rhetorically. Making up for the predecessor's coyness, *The Holder of the World* tells the "real [i.e., apocryphal] story." Mukherjee does not pretend her book actually recovers or is somehow inspired by a possibly forgotten, heretofore unknown, or patently incomplete Hawthornian text. Nonetheless, "people and their property often get separated" (5), as Beigh remarks, and her author does not hesitate to "appropriate" what used to be Hawthorne's exclusive property and work it into a "pseudo-Hawthornian" sequel that puts back in stuff Hawthorne "left out" or "miswrote." This way, the unwritten and the otherwise textually "repressed" in Hawthorne's letter(s) return in the rewrite.

They do so with a revisionary vengeance. Its effects are, in Beigh's words, "transcultural adumbrations" (230). These bring out the geoanthropological complexity, the worldliness that, in Hawthorne, shies away from print and remains unpursued possibilities of gender, location, human connection, and plot. A Massachusetts "asset-hunter," Beigh gets hired by a "Hollywood mogul" to locate a precious stone called "The Emperor's Tear." She finds the gem embedded in the bloody history of late seventeenth-century southern India. In the search, Beigh is assisted by her Hindu boyfriend, a computer wiz who is developing a software capable of "recapturing of past reality . . . [by] absorb[ing] my manuscript and all the documents, the travelogues and computerized East India records, the lavishly illustrated *namas*, or chronicles, of the emperors of the Mughal" (280). Accessing the past by virtual-reality technology, Beigh witnesses crucial scenes of Indian history and tracks down the diamond. If *The Scarlet Letter* recuperates a founding moment in the United States' biography, the "story of [India's] Coromandel Coast" as told by *The Holder of the World* is "the story of North America turned inside out" (160). Hawthorne supplies the fictional grid for mapping out Indian lands and Indianness. Making the map and the territory compatible are shared cultural and historical experiences that trace, across oceans and continents, "the tangled lines of India and New England" (11). Hannah plays the role of the female agent connecting, like Siegel's Lalita, the newly "discovered" Extreme West, along with their stories of conquest and desire. At both ends of the British Empire, in the New England of John Hathorne, Nathaniel's ancestor, and in India alike, Hannah bumps against race-, gender-, and religion-based purist, if not always Puritan, orthodoxies. In New Salem she comes to be known as the Salem Bibi, the nonconformist white concubine of the

Devgad ruler, Raja Singh, whose child she will bear. This is, as the Hawthorne aficionados might expect, the ultimate stigma, but it is borne proudly because the *Ramayana* episode that it also alludes to provides a relief as ethical as it is intertextual. Furthermore, if *The Scarlet Letter* forces Hester Prynne to wear the infamous veil, Hannah, one of her reincarnations in *The Holder of the World*, takes up "needlework" on her own, which gives her fame and her author another opportunity to show off the novel's revisionary and apocryphal relettering. One of Hannah's embroideries plays in great detail on the "rag of scarlet cloth" Hawthorne's authorial narrator discovers in the Custom-House. As the reader will remember, the "embroidery" bearing the infamous *A* "had been twisted" around a "small roll of dingy paper ... containing many particulars respecting the life and conversation of one Hester Prynne" – the "groundwork of a tale,"[18] which tale is, as we know, the romance itself.

Rolled around Hawthorne's "roll," Mukherjee's own tale and the motif of the cloth within it retextualize Hawthorne's text, dazzlingly complicating its cultural fabric. Hannah's "little embroidery" weaves together the West and the East, what with its verses from Psalms "emblazoned" in colors "so tropical" that the "threads Hannah used had to have been brought over from a mysterious place with a musical name: Bandar Abbas, Batavia, Bimlipatam" (Mukherjee, 1994, 44). The needlepoint, which Hannah "took ... with her to England and then to India" (47), "is a pure vision" (44) in which worlds, stories, gender roles, and cultural scripts break down, recombine, and cover the world. Symbolically completing the world-embracing trajectory of her cloth and life, Hannah, now called Pearl, like Hester's daughter, returns to New England to join her outcast mother and give birth to her own daughter, also named Pearl. Back home, she finds her mother wearing her "outmoded woolens with the shameful I ... sewn in red to her sleeve" (283). But the meaning of *I* and, with it, the meanings of Mukherjee's entire cultural dictionary, are far richer than "Indian lover" (283). The "branded letters of sin" with which we often spell out our received ideas are transcribed by the novel into new words and worlds. Relettering Hawthorne's narrative letter rather than its "spirit," Mukherjee furnishes us with a whole "subversive alphabet" (54) in which "*A* is for Act ... *B* is for Boldness ... *C* is for Character ... *D* is for Dissent" (54) ... "*E* [is] for English, Extraordinary, Ethical" (127), and "Ecstasy" (54), "*F* is for Forage ... [, a]nd *I* is for ... Indian lover" and "Independence" (54).

Not the first rewriting of Alcott's *Little Women* – or *Meg, Jo, Beth and Amy* – Barbara Kingsolver's 1998 *The Poisonwood Bible* is certainly the most revisionary thus far. It "invents" its own subversive alphabet of gender, domesticity, sexuality, dissent, nation, and geopolitics through a two-pronged, apocryphal reworking that literally – and "leterally" too – scrambles the literary and cultural alphabets of the Bible and of the 1869 classic besides other world-renowned works. The central place of the precursor texts in the novel is conspicuous.[19] No less obvious is the author's sometimes sketchy understanding of US and African politics and history. Kingsolver's characters expound freely on developments in Congo and Zaire, on the overtly exploitative and covertly destabilizing presence of foreign governments in Western and Central Africa, and on other aspects of a geopolitical drama in which heroes and villains are given in advance, which makes characters such as Leah, the "amazon," both ardently committed to an ahistorical Africa and self-righteously preachy. This is ironic in a book whose targets include Leah's father, Nathan Price, an Ahab-like Georgia preacher, but also, and more broadly, American missionarism, Christianity, their institutions and texts, and even more broadly the United States' self-assigned mission in post–Belgian Congo, Africa, and the world. Put otherwise, Kingsolver's painting of the "big picture," an undertaking more and more tempting for US authors after 1989, is rather awkward. More convincing is what she does inside the picture, at the micro level of the African everyday on which the lives of the displaced Prices undergo a plethora of transformations and rearrangements.

Instrumental to capturing these changes are the technique and cultural-political motif of the palindrome.[20] An extreme, more pugnacious variety of Siegel's anagrams, the palindrome is a "counter-writing" tool, a relettering that rereads and rewrites backwards. It does so in a general sense, turning sequences of culture, mores, and discourse on their head, but also literally. The two procedures work as the two arms of the same "criticist" scissors. Wielding it, Kingsolver reads policies, documents, and representations against their grain, upsetting their rhetorical order by showing how their real-life upshots run counter to their purported or advertised meanings. But, through Leah's twin sister, Adah, whose name itself is a phonetic palindrome, the author also inverts the arrangements of letters in words, names, and texts, in a symbolic attempt to reverse, block, and otherwise derail the original's denotations. Thus, largely speaking, all of Kingsolver's intertexts are sometimes under Emily Dickinson's tutelage, palindromically reordered or at least "anagrammatically" repositioned, from John Bunyan's *Pilgrim's Progress* (which, for the Prices, regresses to disaster), Joseph Conrad's *Heart of Darkness*, David Livingstone's famous travelogue, and Alcott's book to the Bible. To enforce the patriarchal strictures encapsulated by *Little Women*'s domesticity discourse and, by extension, to reinforce a certain definition of American power in the home and in the world, Nathan punishes his daughters by "giving" them the "Verse"; that is, by forcing them to recite or copy biblical lines. But Leah, Adah, and, arguably, all the Price women learn to piggyback on the Verse's inherent reversibility (*versus* comes from Lat. *vertere*, to "turn [back]") and give the verse back to him and to its sacred source. Eventually, Nathan himself "g[e]ts the Verse – the ultimate verse – as he perishes in the depth of the jungle.[21]

Especially in the Adah chapters, the novel abounds with intentional misprints, anagrams, paronomasias, palindromes, and cognate linguistic plays. These both perform and allegorize the fate of Euro-American scripts, languages, spirituality, and economic-political designs in Africa as the intermeshing of worlds intensifies, rather than subsiding, under postcolonialism. The puns about the Bible, including palindromes such as Adah's "enema" for the "Amen" in her father's sermons, these sermons' (mis)translations into Kikongo by Anatole, Leah's Congolese husband, or by Nathan himself, and the syncretic adulterations of Christianity on African soil give rise to an other to the Bible and its religious routines. There is, accordingly, an anti-canonical, apocryphal dimension to women's anti-patriarchal and anti-(neo)colonialist dissent in Kingsolver. Her book retextualizes and dilates a "master" text of North-Atlantic culture so as to add new, less orthodox chapters to the Bible, as well as to the world's collective narrative.

Further expanding this narrative, Chang-rae Lee's 1995 novel *Native Speaker* pivots from the missionary version of the "Americans abroad" theme to late-twentieth-century immigration and the "new Americans" within.[22] In Lee's book, the transatlantic scenario acquires transpacific and, indeed, global proportions while Richard Wright (*Native Son*), Ralph Ellison (*Invisible Man*), and, most prominently, Whitman replace Melville as the hub of the book's intertextual economy. As in *The Holder of the World*, Paul Auster's *The New York Trilogy*, Maxine Hong Kingston's *Tripmaster Monkey* and *The Fifth Book of Peace*, or Michael Cunningham's *Specimen Days*, Whitman here is a symbolic figure. Lee summons it for revisionary purposes, as he will again in novels like *A Gesture Life* and *Aloft*. For him, Whitman speaks across time of and to an America that risks coming short of the national dream of inclusiveness.[23] Remaking himself into a turn-of-the-millennium Whitman, Lee both draws from the Whitmanesque generous vision and revisits it for an America that may deem itself "postethnic" and "postnative," but still entertains exclusionary fantasies of nativism.

Excerpted from Whitman's poem "The Sleepers," the novel's motto places Lee's work squarely under the patronage of the American classic from the outset: "I turn but do not extricate myself, / Confused, a past-reading, another, / but with darkness yet" (Lee, 1995, xi). The conversation with Whitman goes on with the telltale scene featuring Korean-American Henry, the protagonist, and his wife, Lelia, among the "sleepers" in an El Paso park (Lee, 1995, 12), continues with the image of the "slumber bound," sinking swimmer in the "Peanut Butter Shelley" lines reproduced later in the novel (233), and otherwise runs through the entire novel at several levels. From a plot standpoint, for example, it is noteworthy that "[t]he spectacle from which Whitman turns [in his poem] is a shipwreck."[24] More exactly, the drowning of the hyperbolic "beautiful gigantic swimmer" in "The Sleepers"'s third section becomes a shipwreck in the next. Lee incorporates this incident into his book explicitly and allusively. Toward the novel's end, he references the 1993 wreck of *Golden Venture*, a freighter that sank in the New York harbor (1995, 246–247, 327). The ship was smuggling hundreds of Chinese, some of whom drowned while the rest were rescued but only to be imprisoned and eventually deported. Critics have noted the media impact of this intensely publicized catastrophe, which the news networks spun as a legal and national security event indicative of the assault on America by undocumented Asians.[25] But this reading of the *Golden Venture* affair, along with the mainstream reading of the overall Asian-American venture into full-fledged Americanness, is precisely what Lee displaces with Whitman's help. In this light – the light Whitman casts on *Native Speaker* – it is highly relevant that "The Sleepers" does not simply mourn the drowned. The poem is also an obituary that, albeit posthumously, finds a place for the world's dead in the America of which they failed to make a home. Analogously, Henry makes himself at home as his voice and face modulate alternate modalities of being, sounding, and looking like an American, while his author makes room for himself in the history of American literature by rewriting its celebrated masterpieces. At the same time, Lee joins Siegel, Mukherjee, Kingsolver, and other writers from the United States and other traditions, in building up the narrative world system. Formed and reformed by extensive and intensive rewriting, the system is driven by a revisionism and haunted by a geography that reaches in the 1990s, as Wai Chee Dimock aptly stresses, across deeper and deeper spaces and times. Granted, after 1989, the well-known, cultural critique–propelled protocols of revisionary rewriting have not come to a halt, and their classical foci – race, gender, ethnicity, nationality, and so on – have not disappeared either. But the world system itself has changed and, with it, the geocultural stage on which these protocols play out. This stage now is, more and more, the world as a whole. It is against this backdrop of "worldedness" and in close relation to it that American writers of the last century's final decade deploy their revisionary strategies.

NOTES

1. Ralph Blumenthal, "Disputed *Lolita* Spinoff Is Dropped by Publisher," *New York Times*, November 7, 1998, B7.
2. Ralph Blumenthal, "Nabokov Son Files Suit to Block a Retold *Lolita*," *New York Times*, October 10, 1998, B9.
3. *Lo's Diary* came out in 1999 from a small press, Foxrock, in Ann Goldstein's translation.
4. Blumenthal, "Nabokov Son Files Suit to Block a Retold *Lolita*."
5. Alice Randall's *The Wind Done Gone*, a 2001 rewriting of Margaret Mitchell's 1936 highly popular novel *Gone with the Wind*, faced legal challenges similar to Pera's *Lo's Diary*.
6. David Cowart, *Literary Symbiosis: The Reconfigured Text in Twentieth-Century Writing* (Athens: University of Georgia Press), 2–26.
7. Matei Calinescu, "3. 2. 1. Rewriting," in *International Postmodernism: Theory and Practice*, ed. Hans Bertens and Douwe Fokkema (Amsterdam: John Benjamins, 1997), 243–248.
8. Marcel Cornis-Pope, *Narrative Innovation and Cultural Rewriting in the Cold War Era and After* (New York: Palgrave, 2001).
9. Christian Moraru, *Rewriting: Postmodern Narrative and Cultural Critique in the Age of Cloning* (Albany: SUNY Press, 2001), 23–27. Also see my articles on "Postmodern Rewrites" and "Narrative Versions" in *Routledge Encyclopedia of Narrative Theory*, ed. David Herman, Manfred Jahn, and Marie-Laure Ryan (London: Routledge, 2004), 385–386 and 460–461. On "postmortem postmodernism," I refer the reader to Laura Savu's *Postmortem Postmodernists: The Afterlife of the Author in Recent Narrative* (Teaneck, NJ: Fairleigh Dickinson University Press, 2009). Also, for contemporary and postmodern rewritings of American classics, I only mention here my book *Rewriting* and Betina Entzminger's *Contemporary Reconfigurations of American Literary Classics: The Origin and Evolution of American Stories* (New York: Routledge, 2013).
10. Christian Moraru, *Cosmodernism: American Narrative, Late Globalization, and the New Cultural Imaginary* (Ann Arbor: University of Michigan Press, 2011), especially 307–316.
11. Arjun Appadurai, *Modernity at Large: Cultural Dimensions of Globalization* (Minneapolis: University of Minnesota Press, 1996), 19.
12. On the imagination, stories, and "the global cultural order," see Appadurai, *Modernity at Large*, 53.
13. Lee Siegel, *City of Dreadful Night: A Tale of Horror and the Macabre in India* (Chicago: University of Chicago Press, 1995), 49–50.

14 Stephen J. Burn, "The End of Postmodernism: American Fiction at the Millennium," in *American Fiction of the 1990s*, ed. Jay Prosser (Routledge: London, 2008), 226.
15 Emily Apter, "On Translation in a Global Market," *Public Culture* 13.1 (2001): 1.
16 Bharati Mukherjee, *The Holder of the World* (New York: Random House, 1994).
17 Gail Ching-Liang Low, "In a Free State: Post-Colonialisms and Postmodernism in Bharati Mukherjee's Fiction," *Women: A Cultural Review* 4.1 (Spring 1993): 13.
18 Nathaniel Hawthorne, *The Scarlet Letter* (New York: Library of America, 1990), 31–33.
19 Entzminger dwells on these issues in *Contemporary Reconfigurations of American Literary Classics*, 89–97.
20 I am aware of only a short note on this subject, Jeff Grant's "Poisonwood Palindromes," in *World Ways: The Journal of Recreational Linguistics* 38.1 (February 2005): 75.
21 Barbara Kingsolver, *The Poisonwood Bible* (New York: HarperCollins, 1998), 487.
22 Chang-rae Lee, *Native Speaker* (New York: Riverhead, 1995).
23 "Through his narrative," Liam Corley remarks in his article "'Just Another Ethnic Pol': Literary Citizenship in Chang-rae Lee's Native Speaker," "Lee revises Whitman's heritage of representative Americanness to include the immigrant experience as central" (*Studies in the Literary Imagination* 37.1 [Spring 2004]: 74).
24 Corley, "'Just Another Ethnic Pol,'" 74.
25 Corley, "'Just Another Ethnic Pol,'" 62–63.

PART III
Interconnectivity

CHAPTER 14

Borders and Mixed-Race Fictions
Aliki Varvogli

In Richard Powers's novel *Orfeo* (2014), avant-garde composer Peter Els is commissioned in late 1989 to write an opera for the 1993 season. He considers storylines involving the fall of the Berlin Wall or Causescu, but settles instead on a historical event: the 1535 siege of Münster. By the time the opera is finished, events have overtaken Els' imagination:

> He has needed forty months to deliver 170 minutes of music. During those years, the war that has lasted since his childhood comes to an end. The evil empire crumbles into a dozen-plus countries. All the world's data weaves together into a web. In the desert on the far side of the planet, Els's country goes to war, made godlike by technology. The apocalypse of smart bombs and computer screens would all have made for dazzling opera if Els hadn't already been busy with one – an opera as strange to the present as the present has become to him.[1]

Writing with the benefit of hindsight, Powers correctly identifies the early 1990s as a time of rapid change, political turmoil, and fears of an apocalyptic future, intensified as the decade drew closer to its conclusion, bringing with it fears of the "millennium bug," or "Y2K," that would supposedly cause computers to malfunction and civilization as we know it to collapse. The decade that ended in fear had barely started in the hopeful glow of the end of the Cold War when Iraq invaded Kuwait, an event that led to the Persian Gulf War. Images of optimistic young people smashing the Berlin Wall were soon replaced by terrifying ones of gas masks, burning oil wells, and environmental catastrophe. Over in Europe, maps were being redrawn as Yugoslavia descended into a bloody civil war, bringing questions about how borders create national coherence, but also mask ethnic, racial and religious conflict. Meanwhile, the very concept of the physicality of the world around us started to be questioned as the use of technology spread and the concept of "cyberspace" entered popular consciousness. Hotmail launched in 1996, and a year later Google registered its domain name. Soon, the "new

217

world order" that George H. W. Bush had announced at the beginning of the decade was supplemented by a new concept of (hyper-)reality, opening up endless possibilities for democracy, freedom, and of course capitalist gain. George H. W. Bush made his famous "new world order" speech in March 1991, announcing the end of the Gulf War and heralding an era that would see the end of "barbed wire and concrete block."[2] Sadly, events proved him wrong. The "dotcom bubble" burst in 2000, dashing hopes that technology would free us of borders and make the world a better, and richer, place. Six years later, George W. Bush revived the "barbed wire" world his father had denounced by signing the Fence Act, which authorized the building of a reinforced structure to keep illegal Mexican immigrants out of the United States.

The 1990s are therefore rightly viewed as a time of transition from old to new world orders; a time when walls, fences, and boundaries collapsed, and technology and media began to alter our perception of reality. While the world was busy rearranging itself and falling into new patterns of power and of geographical boundaries, the United States was also busy reassessing its place in the world. Scholars of American literature and culture were quick to understand, and respond to, the changing climate of the 1990s. 1994 saw the publication of *Cultures of United States Imperialism*, a collection of essays that broke down "the boundary between the study of foreign relations and American culture to examine imperialism as an internal process of cultural appropriation and as an external struggle over international power."[3] The same year, Carolyn Porter published a review essay in *American Literary History* in which she noted the following:

> American literature has been remapped first by African-Americanist and feminist critics and then by the flourishing scholarship on Asian-American, Native American, and Chicano literatures. These emerging fields have begun to undermine the fundamental terms by which American literary history must be comprehended and taught. Both the historical and geographical frames once dictated by the national, and nationalist, narrative of the U.S. are collapsing... because of their permeability as national boundaries, geopolitical borders are foregrounded as regions, borderlands that in turn reveal and renew cultural networks linking the Caribbean and Latin America to the North.[4]

Porter's perceptive assessment of the changes taking place in the ways American scholars thought about their country was supported by several other critics writing in the same decade. "Boundaries" and "borderlands," for example, also featured in Priscilla Wald's essay of 1998, where she considered the transnational turn in American studies and its implications.[5]

What these, and several other scholars, were responding to was the growing realization that the United States had been studied as a unit, a static nation, whereas it might be more profitable to situate its study in its interactions with the world beyond its borders. American authors, of course, had already been doing just that. 1987 saw the publication of both Toni Morrison's *Beloved* and Gloria Anzaldúa's *Borderlands/La Frontera*, two highly acclaimed books that brought the border to the foreground through their emphasis on the transatlantic slave trade and the Mexico/US border respectively. However, for most readers and scholars, it is Cormac McCarthy's fiction that epitomizes the concept of the border in the 1990s.

Cormac McCarthy's Border Trilogy – *All the Pretty Horses* (1992), *The Crossing* (1994), and *Cities of the Plain* (1998) – arrived at a time when the United States was coming to terms with this new world order. A story about "historical change and transformation,"[6] McCarthy's chronicle of a vanishing way of life caught the public imagination as well as the attention of critics. As Dianne C. Luce has argued, protagonist John Grady "rides into the sunset at the end of his novel and into 'the world to come,'" a moment of transition that in many ways exemplifies the larger trends that emerged in 1990s American writing.[7] Transition functions in the novel both literally and figuratively: John Grady crosses the border into Mexico, and (as John Blair argues) moves "from innocence to experience."[8] As well as being concerned with moments of transition, *All the Pretty Horses* opens and closes with images that emphasize reflection: "[the] candleflame and the image of the candleflame" (3) are the first words the reader encounters, while the novel ends with Grady riding into the sunset and merging with his shadow, man, horse and their shadow passing "in tandem like the shadow of a single being" (302). The emphasis on reflection nods toward the legacy of the self-reflexive fictions of literary postmodernism, making the novel itself a hybrid, border-crossing postmodern western. Stephen J. Burn has identified the 1990s as the "twilight" of American postmodernist fiction, and this novel is a good example of what that means.[9] While the book clearly owes a debt to much more experimental styles of writing, it also gains much of its appeal from a more traditional form of storytelling. Stylistically, the novel eschews speech marks, embedding the dialogue into the narrative in a way that also calls attention to borders and boundaries: the boundaries between man and environment, self and world.

In the novel's memorable final sequence, McCarthy includes a strong reference to "indians" who watch Grady with stony indifference, watching him pass "solely because he was passing. Solely because he would vanish" (301). Of course, the world of those Indians is also a vanishing one, and just as this novel ends with an image of transition and flight, so much of Native American writing of the 1990s also concerns itself with moments of transition and passing. Near the end of the decade, Paula Gunn Allen summed this up by choosing an apt title for her essay collection: *Off the Reservation: Reflections on Boundary-Busting, Border-Crossing Loose Cannons* (1999). That same year, Leslie Marmon Silko published a novel that also busted boundaries and crossed borders. *Gardens in the Dunes* tells the story of Indigo, a young girl of the Sand Lizard people who is taken in by a white couple who take her overseas, to England and Italy. Though the novel is set in the late Victorian era, there is little doubt that its thematic preoccupations stem from the time of the novel's composition. Native American literature very often uses travel, crossings, and movement as ways of attempting to situate Native American life and culture on and off the reservation, but in *Gardens* Silko sought to merge the local with the global by taking her Native American character on a grand tour. The formative experience of a cultural pilgrimage across Europe is a familiar trope in white Euro-American culture, but for a Native American author and her characters to embark on such a trip entails a crossing of boundaries both real and symbolic. When Indigo travels to England or Italy, she doesn't just cross national borders; she also steps out of the prescribed boundaries of her ethnic identity.

Of course, American fiction has always engaged with the world beyond the country's geographical borders, but the 1990s is a time when these interactions began to change the very way in which American literature was defined, taught, and understood. At the end of the decade, these changes became more widely established when the US Census of 2000 acknowledged more fully the racial and ethnic plurality of the country's citizens. The Census included a new category: "some other race." Despite the slightly derisory tone of the phrase, "some other race" sought to accommodate people for whom older, fixed categories of race seemed inflexible and irrelevant. The Census Bureau website offered the following explanation:

> "Some Other Race" includes all other responses not included in the White, Black or African American, American Indian or Alaska Native, Asian, and Native Hawaiian or Other Pacific Islander race categories described above. Respondents reporting entries such as multiracial, mixed, interracial, or a Hispanic or Latino group (for example, Mexican, Puerto Rican, Cuban, or Spanish) in response to the race question are included in this category.[10]

In addition to accepting that Americans can belong to "some other race," the 1990s also consolidated the belief that Americans might also belong to some other place. In Cristina García's *Dreaming in Cuban* (1992), Pilar Puente has a boyfriend who plays in a band called The Manicheans. The band's name draws attention to traditional interpretations of national identity as an either/or concept, but the author is keen to reject polarities, and the narrative concludes with Pilar's realization that she belongs in the United States *more than*, and not *instead of*, belonging in Cuba. García's novel sets the tone for much of the rest of the decade, where many subsequent novels and story collections not only deal with immigrant narratives, but also have their characters revisit their originating cultures, and thus gradually move the American immigrant novel away from its teleological roots. García also uses multiple narrators and a fragmented timeline to highlight the new ways in which immigration is experienced and expressed.

Natalie Friedman identifies the immigrant narratives of the late nineteenth and early twentieth centuries as the "classic tales of Americanization," and notes in them an absence of nostalgia explained by the imperatives of hard work and "the writers' inability to return to their native lands, even for a visit." She concludes that these classic narratives "suggest that the immigrant sought to assimilate and erase the past, converting wholeheartedly to an American way of life."[11] By contrast, she argues that new immigrant novels feature characters who do not "view Americanization as a definitive, totalizing act."[12] This shift is best seen in narratives from the 1990s, and it manifests itself not only on the thematic level, but also on the structural. In 1982, William Boelhower published an influential essay on immigrant autobiographical narratives. He argued that these followed recognizable structural patterns in which the immigrant journey and the process of assimilation are narrated in chronological order.[13] This type of narrative came to define the cultural and textual expression of the immigrant story in the United States, and it is this pattern that 1990s fiction challenges. In his 2006 study of immigrant narratives, David Cowart applied a Proppian analysis to the genre and highlighted narrative fragmentation as one of the "general features of immigrant fiction."[14] What Cowart did not make explicit was the crucial role that 1990s texts played in this shift from order to fragmentation. Cowart writes in his introduction that the new immigrant writing that he is concerned with starts in the 1970s. Yet, with the exception of a chapter on Kosinski and Bellow's "transitional texts"[15] from 1970–1971, nearly all the books that he discusses were published in the 1990s.

The 1990s may therefore be viewed as a crucial but perhaps unacknowledged decade in the development of immigrant narratives. However, the 1990s is also the decade that saw more immigrants arrive in the United

States than in any other decade in history, and it is a time when stories of ethnic diversity gained more commercial appeal as well as critical acclaim and scholarly interest. When George H. W. Bush signed the Immigration Act of 1990 on November 29, he made the following statement:

> Today I am pleased to sign S. 358, the 'Immigration Act of 1990' – the most comprehensive reform of our immigration laws in 66 years. This Act recognizes the fundamental importance and historic contributions of immigrants to our country. S. 358 accomplishes what this Administration sought from the outset of the immigration reform process: a complementary blending of our tradition of family reunification with increased immigration of skilled individuals to meet our economic needs.[16]

The immigration act of 1990 also brought with it the Diversity Immigrant Visa, a system that became popularly known as the DV Lottery.

It needs to be stressed that there is little *direct* correlation between the new immigrants arriving in the United States in the 1990s and the authors publishing immigrant narratives in the same period. Yet it is no coincidence that a decade that saw an unprecedented volume of migration also saw an explosion of immigrant and other border-crossing narratives. When President Bush spoke of "family reunification," and his policies championed greater diversity, he was referring literally to immigrants and their contribution to American life. At the same time, on the imaginative plain of fiction-writing, "family reunification" and "diversity" became key topics, as can be seen from several milestone publications by Asian and Caribbean immigrants. 9,775,398 immigrants arrived in the United States between 1990 and 1999. Of those, 14 percent came from Europe, 29 percent from Asia, and 53 percent from the Americas. The latter category comprises a majority of Mexicans but, as defined by the department of Homeland Security, it also includes the islands of the Caribbean.[17] Fiction of the 1990s contains some very strong examples of border-crossing narratives from those geographical groupings, and what many of them have in common is an emphasis on the family. Where George H. W. Bush wanted immigrants to come so they could create greater stability by being reunited with their family members, the literature of the period looked at the darker side of family, or explored alternative family models. The primacy of the family is a dominant cultural myth in American life, and several immigrant authors used the unhappy family as a trope for criticizing what they perceived as the failings of the American Dream.

Bharati Mukherjee's 1989 novel *Jasmine* used the heroine's unhappy experience working as a nanny for an American couple and their adopted daughter as a way of initiating the character into the realities hidden beneath the veneer of the typical, all-American family. The relationship between the nanny and her employer also carried undertones of *Jane Eyre*, thereby highlighting the significance of the author's post-colonial identity. Similarly, Jamaica Kincaid's 1990 *Lucy* followed the main character from the West Indies to North America, where she found work as an au pair. Lucy's growing awareness of the cracks in her employers' marriage unfolds alongside her own coming-to-terms with her past and her present. Early in the narrative, she recalls being made to recite William Wordsworth's "I Wandered Lonely as a Cloud"; the daffodils, alien to her Caribbean background, become a symbol of the arrogance of colonial practice in a way that is similar to Mukherjee's use of the *Jane Eyre* trope. Gish Jen's 1991 *Typical American* also questioned family models as well as telling an immigrant story. Ralph, a Chinese immigrant, is saved by his sister Theresa in America, and he sets up home with her and her roommate Helen, who becomes his wife. The members of this unusual, alternative family unit attempt to find their own place in America by defining themselves against everything they perceive as "typical American." The shaky relationship they have with their new homeland is highlighted through the recurrence of images of crumbling houses. Early in the narrative, a crack develops in the ceiling of Ralph's bedroom, covering him in white plaster dust. Later, when the family finally move out, Ralph confirms that the house could have fallen down: "'Any day,' Ralph said, patting her. And to Helen, '*Any day that corner could have fallen out . . .* ' But as it happened, the house had held, and now they were moving on."[18] The house that did not collapse is an apt image for this unusual, adaptable family, who never quite become "typical American" as their story comes to a close and Ralph realizes that "a man was as doomed here as he was in China."[19] This subversion of the traditional story of immigrant success and acceptance of a new identity is to be found in several other key texts from this decade.

Chang-rae Lee's *Native Speaker* (1995) and *A Gesture Life* (1999) are good examples of the ways in which emergent voices in American literature explore new American identities and new modes of self-expression. Both books cross generic as well as geographical borders in order to question the primacy of the American individual and the privileging of the narrative of successful assimilation. *Native Speaker* is a spy novel in which the trope of spying is used as a vehicle for exploring the immigrant's sense of in-betweenness. The narrator protagonist, Henry Park, describes his American nationality as "an accident of birth, my mother delivering me on this end of a long plane ride from Seoul."[20] This reluctant participation in

American citizenship acknowledges a shift from a static to a dynamic concept of nationhood: the symbolism of the birth at the end of a plane journey clearly underscores the importance of travel and movement rather than the fixed destination that was the goal of earlier immigrants. *A Gesture Life*, meanwhile, subverts the narrative of assimilation by ordering as a bildungsroman in reverse: the story of a life unravelling rather than coming together. Hamilton Carroll argues that the novel "tells a story quite different from the typical tale of immigration and assimilation," noting "a shift in perspective" toward "a fragmented, transnational narrative."[21] The novel ends with its protagonist, Doc Hata, leaving his American home and embarking on a journey that may be real or metaphorical. Hata imagines being away from home, "in this town or the next or one five thousand miles away,"[22] and this unmooring is read by Carroll as a call for "a renewed consideration of the conditions that produce and withhold citizenship under transnationalism."[23]

The call for renewal that Carroll sees in Chang-rae Lee can also be found elsewhere in the literature of this border-crossing decade. In 1998, Dominican-American author Julia Alvarez published a collection of essays whose title emphasized her status as an outsider arriving in the United States: *Something to Declare*. In it, she chronicled the struggle to find a voice as a bilingual author: "a way into my bicultural, bilingual experience."[24] She wrote of her own journey toward becoming an American author, but she spoke for fellow Caribbean authors who were increasingly realizing that the border crossings that took them to the United States, and the linguistic and racial borders that they themselves embodied, were now becoming the subject of fiction. Junot Díaz and Edwidge Danticat followed in Alvarez's footsteps, writing stories and novels about the experience of hybridity. In 1996, both Díaz and Danticat were selected for *Granta*'s "Best Young American Novelists" issue. They both went on to win a MacArthur "genius grant," Danticat in 2009 and Diaz in 2012. The two authors have highlighted the significance of the border in their own originating countries: they come from the island of Hispaniola, an island more commonly known by the names of its divided halves, Haiti and the Dominican Republic. Danticat and Díaz's fiction crosses and recrosses boundaries, with stories set both on the island and in the United States, and with the authors charting not only the story of migration to the United States, but also the troubled history their characters leave behind.

Like many of the books that deal with border crossing in the 1990s, Díaz's crosses generic as well as geographical borders. *Drown* is a collection of stories that almost add up to an immigrant novel. "Ysrael," the first story in the collection, introduces us to a nine-year-old narrator on summer holiday in the Dominican countryside. Away from the familiarity of the city where he grew up, he is a bored outsider, conscious already in his own childish way of his otherness. We learn that the boy's father is away working in *Nueva York*, but the father's story is only narrated in the final installment of the collection. The stories that follow "Ysrael" are set mainly in the United States, with occasional forays back to the Dominican Republic, and they encourage the reader to assume that the narrator is an older version of the same boy. David Cowart sees the story-cycle structure as one that supports the book's main thematic concerns: he describes the stories as striving, "with a lack of success at once ironic and instructive, to gather themselves into a whole."[25] Similarly, Nahem Yousaf argues that in *Drown* Díaz "refuses teleology and the burden of representation" by not telling a linear story of arrival and acculturation, and by drawing attention to the narrative's own linguistic articulation.[26] As in Cormac McCarthy's fiction, the dialogue here is rendered without quotation marks, highlighting the permeability of borders between self and other, or between reality and representation. The issue of representation is also made prominent through Díaz's use of Spanish words throughout the text. Though the book contains a glossary, many words are not included there. The experience of the non-Spanish speaking reader therefore contains an element of disempowerment that accurately reflects the linguistic struggles faced by Díaz's immigrants. Both Gloria Anzaldúa and Julia Alvarez have written of the difficulties of living in a culture where the Spanish tongue is seen as inferior, and where humiliation and corporal punishment at school are acceptable methods of promoting assimilation. Díaz adds a further twist to the practice of "code-switching" which, as Lourdes Torres points out, became prevalent in 1990s fiction.[27] Díaz's narrator occasionally highlights the difference between the language of the text and the language of the fictional characters within it. In "Edison, New Jersey," for example, the narrator tells the reader that he switches from English to Spanish while speaking to a rich man's maid, but the Spanish is absent form his narrative at that point. Later, he makes a punning joke in English, but finds himself unable to translate it to the Spanish-speaking maid, indicating that his mastery of English is now yielded as a weapon, conferring power over the weaker.

The final story in the collection gives an insight into the life of the young narrator's father. Newly arrived in the United States, he learns of the FOB store, where immigrants go to buy American-looking clothes. The acronym stands for "Fresh off the Boat," a term that is derogatory in its intent but which, if reclaimed, could easily describe the transformation of the American literary scene in the 1990s by the migrants who crossed borders and fought for a place in the great American narrative. Edwidge Danticat gained wide recognition through the 1996 issue of *Granta*, but her 1994 novel *Breath, Eyes, Memory* had already announced the arrival of a strong voice on the literary scene. Where Díaz used exaggerated macho posturing to highlight his characters' vulnerabilities, Danticat focused on the female experiences of virginity, rape, and pregnancy in order to tell a story that was both a story of immigration and a story of intergenerational trauma. Like Cristina García's fiction, Danticat's also makes use of stories of mother-daughter relationships set in domestic interiors in order to show how the wider forces of history shape individual lives. Also like García, Danticat did not conceive of immigration as a one-way teleological narrative, choosing instead to send her main characters back to Haiti, and then back to the United States again. *Krik? Krak!*, a collection of short stories, was published the year after *Breath*. With it, Danticat crossed the border back to Haiti, telling stories of poverty, unhappiness, and brutality. At the same time that this American book told stories about Haitian women, it also widened another area: that of the oral storytelling tradition, reclaimed and championed already by African-American authors. The title of the collection describes a Haitian version of call and response, where the storyteller starts with *Krik?* and the listeners respond with *Krak!*. It could be argued, then, that African-American authors paved the way for new stories to be told, expanding the ways in which American readers related to the issues of race, blackness, and the African heritage.

The success of Danticat and Díaz in the 1990s is also notable because it highlighted the continuing relevance of the short story form in American fiction. Near the end of the decade, Jhumpa Lahiri's *Interpreter of Maladies* made another significant contribution to the genre. The stories in the collection rejected the notion that ethnicity and nationality are stable concepts tied to country of residence or birth, highlighting instead the clashes that occur when people cross boundaries and find themselves in different contexts. In the collection's title story, Lahiri has her Indian-American characters visit India. Against the backdrop of their originating culture, their Americanness is thrown into relief, with their local tour guide marveling at their American ways and the insolence of their American children. In her subsequent writing, Lahiri has continued to explore the crossing and recrossing of borders as her characters move between India and the United States, while more recently the author has crossed another kind of boundary by publishing a nonfiction book directly written in Italian (*In Altre Parole*, 2015). In her *New Yorker* essay "Teach Yourself Italian," Lahiri wrote eloquently about a sense of not belonging: "I'm used to a kind of linguistic exile. My mother tongue, Bengali, is foreign in America. When you live in a country where your own language is considered foreign, you can feel a continuous sense of estrangement. You speak a secret, unknown language, lacking any correspondence to the environment."[28] Her fictional output is marked by diversity, and yet she returns to those key themes of linguistic exile and estrangement throughout, tracing the psychological effects of border crossings and other kinds of displacement. In the same essay, she wrote that every language "belongs to a specific place. It can migrate, it can spread. But usually it's tied to a geographical territory, a country."[29] This may be broadly speaking true, yet American literature derives much of its energy through an examination of how language crosses borders and seeps into new territories, with the Mexican/American border being the most notable example. T. Coraghessan Boyle and Karen Tei Yamashita use the border to think about linguistic identities, but also to highlight several key concepts that have defined the 1990s as a decade of transition and change.

The thematic concerns in T. C. Boyle's *The Tortilla Curtain* (1995) are anticipated in Mike Davis' prescient analysis of Los Angeles in *City of Quartz* (1990):

> Welcome to post-liberal Los Angeles, where the defense of luxury lifestyles is translated into a proliferation of new repressions in space and movement... this obsession with physical security systems, and, collaterally, with the architectural policing of social boundaries, has become a zeitgeist of urban restructuring, a master narrative in the emerging built environment of the 1990s.[30]

Davis outlined a world of fences, gates, and enhanced security, painting a picture of Los Angeles as a repressive urban environment that suppresses the socially excluded at the same time that it expands to swallow up its natural environment. *The Tortilla Curtain* dramatizes Davis's concerns by telling the intersecting stories of Delaney Mossbacher, a well-meaning nature writer whose views on immigration and fence-building are hardened as the narrative progresses, and Cándido Ricon and America, two illegal Mexican immigrants who hide out in the hills above Malibu and gradually realize that the American dream will elude them. The novel takes borders and boundaries as its main themes, using a multi-layered approach. In addition to the physical border that the Mexican immigrants have had to cross, there is the border separating the natural environment from the built-up areas. Delaney has chosen his home at the outskirts of the built environment so he can have easy access to the hills nearby for his nature walks.

As his community becomes increasingly fearful of wild animals and illegal Mexicans, however, they decide to build a wall that will leave the undesirables out but will also block Delaney's easy access to the natural world he so prizes. Other kinds of boundaries are also breached as the once-tolerant and open-minded Delaney succumbs to scare-mongering and learns to hate the illegal immigrants with the same hatred he once despised in his more bigoted neighbors. As Jelena Šesnić points out, the United States has been "amnesiac about its exclusionary and restrictive immigration practices,"[31] a fact that is satirized in Delaney Mossbacher's multiethnic name, set against the simplicity of the illegal immigrants' names. Appropriately for a story set in Los Angeles, the novel ends in an apocalyptic note as floods follow fire. As nature exacts its revenge, the novel extends its enquiry into relations between human and nonhuman cultures and systems, an inquiry that is also central to *Tropic of Orange*.

Šesnić highlights the connections between the two novels by arguing that "the moving tropic is just a more fantastic way of casting the real-life effects of the tortilla curtain,"[32] and her emphasis on the fantastic as another trope for rendering the reality of the border is astute. Yamashita's novel is not simply *about* globalization; it enacts, queries, and subverts the globalizing processes that it concerns itself with. At the level of genre it abolishes boundaries, taking in elements of magical realism and science fiction and weaving them seamlessly into the narrative fabric. At the level of language, Spanish is used in a non-hierarchical relationship to English, though inevitably the narrative is primarily written in English. Yamashita writes about a small cast of characters, but she places them within complex networks, emphasizing not only human interconnectedness, but also our reliance on local and global networks. Furthermore, the author writes about geographical borders in a way that highlights not only the human face of immigration, but also its attendant economic necessities. In this book, it is not only people with stories to tell who cross borders; drugs, fruit produce, human organs, and human labor are also shown in transition, thus emphasizing the interdependence of the two words across the border while also providing a microcosm for the wider process of globalization. Sue-Im Lee argues that the novel is "deeply immersed in the phenomena of globalization," but she further notes that Yamashita's criticism is not an "indictment" of "globalization per se, but a particular view of globalization – the view that globalization results in the economic, political, and cultural intimacy and shared fate of a primordialist village."[33] In *The Tortilla Curtain*, T. C. Boyle used alternating chapters to tell the stories of his main characters, thus emphasizing both their shared fate and the economic and cultural gulf that separated them. Similarly, Yamashita organizes her narrative around chapters that focus on different characters and different but overlapping storylines. The result is a novel that takes on the magical qualities of an optical illusion: a narrative where depth and surface, unity and separateness are laid out on a grid, and the reader is tasked with reconstructing or further deconstructing the different layers whilst realizing that the whole picture remains elusive. For example, one of the characters, Manzanar Murakami, can see that "*[t]here are maps and there are maps and there are maps.* The uncanny thing was that he could see all of them at once, filter some, pick them out like transparent windows and place them even delicately and consecutively in a complex grid of pattern." The layers that he sees are vertical, starting with "the very geology of the land," then the "man-made grid of civil utilities" and "the great overlays of transport".[34] Buzzworm, meanwhile, studies a map that has been torn out of Davis's *City of Quartz*. He finds the map useless because it does not include horizontal layers: "which police department covered which beats," "which schools got which kids," and so on. He concludes that "[i]f someone could put down all the layers of the real map, maybe he could get the real picture."[35] Yamashita foregrounds the unavailability of "the real picture," and Los Angeles serves her well as the setting for a story that deals with layers of meaning and layers of social and geographical space. Similarly, the novel begins with a traditional table of contents where the chapters are shown in a vertical, sequential arrangement, but there is also an alternative table of contents where the emphasis lies on spatial and temporal convergence, and where the book is shown to be organized on a horizontal axis with each main character also used as the organizing principle. The questioning of traditional concepts of a novel's use of time, space and character is well supported by the book's setting, which focuses not only on the magical, shifting tropic of cancer, but also on LA itself as a site that shifts and morphs and blends fact with fiction.

As Lee notes, "Yamashita's choice of Los Angeles as the ultimate site of confrontation speaks to the city's synecdochical role in the contemporary imagination as the epicenter of global confluence."[36] Her observation implies a connection that Rachel Adams makes explicit: the book's relationship with Thomas Pynchon's *The Crying of Lot 49*. Both narratives emphasize layers and networks, and both end in a state of suspension: Oedipa waits to hear the calling of lot 49, while Bobby is literally suspended on invisible cords which he lets go at the end of the narrative. Adams argues that the two works, published thirty years apart, "can be read together as bookends bracketing one possible beginning and end to a particular kind of US literary postmodernism."[37]

Alongside the end of American postmodernist fiction, Adams identifies the beginning of what she terms the contemporary: "Contemporary U.S. fiction takes other spatial and ideological imaginaries as its setting. It draws on a global archive of literary traditions in its search for innovative formal strategies," she argues, and frames such borrowings "in terms of the contact among people and cultures resulting from globalization."[38] If the 1990s mark the twilight of US literary postmodernism, they also mark the beginning of the contemporary: a new kind of literature for a new world order that anyone writing in the 1990s could not have predicted. Geoff Ward has argued that the American author says what "the rest of America won't admit," and writers who engaged with the border in this decade also expressed what the rest of us took longer to realize.[39] Writing border fictions in the 1990s was also writing about "the world to come."

NOTES

1. Richard Powers, *Orfeo* (New York: Norton, 2014), 273–274.
2. George Bush, "Address Before a Joint Session of the Congress on the Cessation of the Persian Gulf Conflict," http://www.presidency.ucsb.edu/ws/index.php?pid=19364&st=&st1=, 21 January 2016.
3. Amy Kaplan and Donald E. Pease (eds.), *Cultures of United States Imperialism* (Durham: Duke University Press, 1993), 676.
4. Carolyn Porter, "What We Know That We Don't Know: Remapping American Literary Studies," *American Literary History* 6.3 (1994): 468.
5. Priscilla Wald, "Minefields and Meeting Grounds: Transnational Analyses and American Studies," *American Literary History* 10.1 (1998): 199–218.
6. Stephen Tatum, *Cormac McCarthy's All the Pretty Horses: A Reader's Guide* (New York: Continuum, 2002), 36.
7. Dianne C. Luce, "The Vanishing World of Cormac McCarthy's Border Trilogy," in *A Cormac McCarthy Companion: The Border Trilogy*, ed. Edwin T. Arnold and Dianne C. Luce (Jackson: University of Mississippi Press, 2001), 163.
8. John Blair, "Mexico and the Borderlands in Cormac McCarthy's *All the Pretty Horses*," *Critique* 42.3 (2001): 301.
9. Stephen J. Burn, "The End of Postmodernism: American Fiction at the Millennium," in *American Fiction of the 1990s: Reflections of History and Culture*, ed. Jay Prosser (London and New York: Routledge, 2008), 220.

10 United States Census Bureau, http://www.census.gov/population/hispanic/about/comparison.html, 21 January 2016.
11 Natalie Friedman, "Nostalgia, Nationhood, and the New Immigrant Narrative: Gary Shteyngart's *The Russian Debutante's Handbook* and the Post-Soviet Experience," *Iowa Journal of Cultural Studies* 5 (2004): 78–79.
12 Ibid. 79.
13 William Boelhower, "The Brave New World of Immigrant Autobiography," *MELUS* 9.2 (1982): 5–23.
14 David Cowart, *Trailing Clouds: Immigrant Fiction in Contemporary America* (Ithaca, NY: Cornell University Press, 2006), 7.
15 Ibid., 13.
16 George Bush, "Statement on Signing the Immigration Act of 1990," http://www.presidency.ucsb.edu/ws/index.php?pid=19117, 21 January 2016.
17 U.S. Department of Homeland Security, https://www.dhs.gov/publication/2000-statistical-yearbook#, 21 January 2015.
18 Gish Jen, *Typical American* (London: Granta, 1991), 120.
19 Ibid., 295–296.
20 Chang-rae Lee, *Native Speaker* (London: Granta, 1995), 334–335.
21 Hamilton Carroll, "Traumatic Patriarchy: Reading Gendered Nationalisms in Chang-rae Lee's *A Gesture Life*," *Modern Fiction Studies* 51.3 (2005): 592–593.
22 Chang-rae Lee, *A Gesture Life* (New York: Riverhead, 1999), 356.
23 Carroll, 614.
24 Julia Alvarez, *Something to Declare* (Chapel Hill, NC: Algonquin, 1998), 168.
25 Cowart, 192.
26 Nahem Yousaf, "'Come Change Your Destiny, Turn Suffering into Silver and Joy': Constituting Americans," in Prosser, *American Fiction*, 35.
27 Lourdes Torres, "In the Contact Zone: Code-switching Strategies by Latino/a Writers," *MELUS* 32.1 (2007): 76.
28 Jhumpa Lahiri, "Teach Yourself Italian," *New Yorker*, December 7, 2015, http://www.newyorker.com/magazine/2015/12/07/teach-yourself-italian.
29 Ibid.
30 Mike Davis, *City of Quartz: Excavating the Future in Los Angeles* (London: Vintage, 1992), 223.
31 Jelena Šesnić, "The Concept of the US-Mexican Borderlands between the Global North and the South," *Americana e-Journal of American Studies in Hungary*, 7.1 (2011): np.
32 Ibid.
33 Sue-Im Lee, "'We Are not the World': Global Village, Universalism, and Karen Tei Yamashita's *Tropic of Orange*," *Modern Fiction Studies* 52.3 (2007): 503.
34 Karen Tei Yamashita, *Tropic of Orange* (Minneapolis, MN: Coffee House, 1997), 56–57.
35 Ibid., 81.

36 Lee, "'We Are not the World,'" 504.
37 Rachel Adams, "The Ends of America, the Ends of Postmodernism," *Twentieth-Century Literature* 53.3 (2007): 249.
38 Ibid., 268.
39 Geoff Ward, *The Writing of America: Literature and Cultural Identity from the Puritans to the Present* (Cambridge: Polity, 2002), 2.

CHAPTER 15

Globalization

Paul Giles

As time passes, the idea that American literature of the 1990s constitutes a definable period has come into clearer focus. Philip E. Wegner has identified the "long nineties" as running from the fall of the Berlin Wall in November 1989 to the sudden impact of September 11, 2001, with American attention gradually shifting from the external threat of Communism to that of radical Islam.[1] Within this framework, the 1990s represented a hiatus during which the United States entertained the idea that it had triumphed in the Cold War and that its conception of free market values enjoyed purchase over the entire globe. Francis Fukuyama's *The End of History and the Last Man* (1992), suggested "a remarkable consensus concerning the legitimacy of liberal democracy as a system of government" and "a universal evolution in the direction of capitalism," with Fukuyama proclaiming, like a proselytizer for the New Jerusalem, that "good news has come."[2] Michael Denning, who also sees 1989 as marking the end of a particular phase of history, commented on the paradox of understanding in relation to periodization a globalization impetus that was triumphantly announcing "the end of history."[3] Globalization was not of course something that originated in the twentieth century – many scholars draw attention to earlier iterations of interactive world systems – but it was a concept that enjoyed particular prominence in the new financial and technological conditions that appertained after 1980, when computers came into widespread use and world markets communicated instantaneously. The idea also came to have a particular political charge in the 1990s, with Bill Clinton making the "global" a key reference point in his 1992 election campaign, linking both the threats and the opportunities for the United States to a global landscape that was post-industrial as well as post-Communist.[4] Commercial use of the Internet also began in 1991 with the World Wide Web itself established in 1992, and the era's social theorists discussed globalization in terms of its capacity to restructure time and space, with Roland Robertson describing it as a concept that "refers to both the compression of the world and the intensification of the world as a whole," and Frances Cairncross associating it with "the Death of Distance."[5]

One aspect of this globalization process involved a shift in social and economic power from national jurisdictions to transnational corporations, with (for instance) Shell's gross national product (GNP) at this time being three times larger than Guatemala's. This new scope for economic control across an international axis reinforced the power of the United States as what Michael Hardt and Antonio Negri called a "decentered and deterritorializing" empire, one grounded not upon the occupation of land, but upon incorporating "the entire global realm" within its orbit of transnational capital and influence.[6] George H. W. Bush announced in 1991 a "New World Order" in response to the Soviet Union's demise, and, as Jay Prosser has suggested, it is possible that some of the peremptory overseas interventions by US forces in the 1990s (Iraq, Somalia, Haiti, Bosnia) served ultimately to heighten a "backlash" against US hegemony that manifested itself in subsequent attacks upon the blithe equation of American free market fundamentalism with a universal order. It is, however, important to recognize how globalization formed part of the popular imaginary in the United States during the 1990s, with global corporations such as Microsoft and Starbucks seeming to be, in Prosser's words, "everywhere and indispensable."[7] Various technological changes associated with globalization also threatened literature's institutional position, with Jeremy Green commenting on how "the *literary field* in advanced capitalism" inevitably involved a negotiation with computers, television, the commodifications of mass culture and the all-pervasive spirit of Oprah Winfrey's Book Club.[8] Masao Miyoshi's invocation in 1993 of a "Borderless World" where the nation state was left as "a nostalgic and sentimental myth" and the transnational industries of "cable TV and MTV dominate the world absolutely" was surely a hyperbolic exaggeration, but it did crystallise an emerging phenomenon whereby the increasingly permeable boundaries of national formations coincided with a tectonic shift from print to electronic media, so that the morphing of national into global narratives could be seen to overlap with an equivalent form of globalization within the realms of media production and distribution.[9] HBO's *The Sopranos*, which is now regularly cited as one of the era's most enduring works of fiction, firmly locates its plot within the New Jersey Mafia's purlieus, but it rapidly achieved global status through overseas television and DVD channels after its first series aired in 1999.

At the end of the 1980s, there were various well-publicized "Culture Wars," with Stanford University's 1989 decision to replace its first-year course "Western Culture" with the unit "Culture, Institutions, and Values" attracting national attention. Stanford was criticized by Reagan's Secretary of Education, William Bennett, for neglecting works anchored in the traditions of Western civilisation, and this controversy carried particular resonance for American literature, whose academic canon was then undergoing radical scrutiny from scholars seeking to reestablish hitherto marginalized works by women and people of color. American novels published around this time – Bharati Mukherjee's *Jasmine* (1989), Jessica Hagedorn's *Dogeaters* (1990), Julia Alvarez's *How the García Girls Lost Their Accents* (1991), as well as Sandra Cisneros's collection of short stories *Woman Hollering Creek* (1991) – implicitly intervened in these culture wars, since their female protagonists claimed equal rights within the fabric of American society. All of these fictional works retell stories of immigration and accommodation within the broad matrix of US culture, with their clear message being that American literature should be seen as a multicultural phenomenon made up of multinational strands. Mukherjee's *Jasmine* tracks its heroine's progress from the Hindu constraints of a small Indian village, where daughters were considered curses, to Elsa County, Iowa, with the central protagonist priding herself on her capacity for change. Jasmine's openness to personal "transformation" is linked explicitly to the American frontier myth: "Adventure, risk, transformation: the frontier is pushing indoors through uncaulked windows."[10] However, this susceptibility to metamorphosis is also interestingly aligned with Hindu traditions of reincarnation, and part of the book's traction derives from the various ways in which Jasmine feels herself "suspended between worlds" as she "shuttled between identities." It is clear that the superimposition of an American future upon Jasmine's Indian past creates stress in the heroine's "fragmentary" life – she talks of how "extraordinary events can jar the needle arm, jump tracks" – but it is also evident how she regards this psychological violence as a price worth paying for the benefits of personal renewal: "There are no harmless, compassionate ways to remake oneself. We murder who we were so we can rebirth ourselves in the images of dreams."[11] Mukherjee's novel has been frequently criticized for apparently eulogizing American values of mobility, and it is true that there is a seemingly heartless dimension to Jasmine's sense of her own providential place in "God's plans," something manifested in her willingness to drop her American husband Bud after he is shot and maimed.[12] Caught "between the promise of America and old-world dutifulness," the heroine turns "Jasmine the reliable caregiver" into "Jane the prowling adventurer," with the book's epigraph from James Gleick's *Chaos* – "It is a geometry of the pitted, pocked, and broken up, the twisted, tangled, and intertwined" – speaking to the fractious and "intertwined" nature of Mukherjee's immigrant landscape.[13]

Generically, one characteristic Mukherjee's novel shares with others at the turn of the 1990s is its mediation of a distant, overseas past through the voice of a female narrator who looks back at her native heritage from a position safely ensconced within the American heartland. Jessica Hagedorn's *Dogeaters* is set in the Philippines of the 1950s, and it evokes the island society's hybrid nature, where American popular culture has become all-pervasive. Hagedorn's narrator Rio luxuriates in recalling how the 1951 film *A Place in the Sun*, starring Elizabeth Taylor, was "condemned by the Archdiocese of Manila as vile and obscene."[14] She also remarks that her "philosophy of life" involves "keeping things slightly off-balance" with her father's transnational affiliations – he has "dual citizenship, dual passports, as many allegiances to as many countries as possible at any one given time" – speaking to her own narrative's multidirectional aspects. The way Hagedorn interweaves her narrator's voice with extracts from the fictional *Metro Manila Daily* and from Jean Mallat's historical work *The Philippines* (1846) lends this whole text a deliberately decentered idiom, as though its multiple fragments formally reflect the "fragmented nation" of the Philippines, "our tropical archipelago of 7100 known islands."[15] But Rio grows up to live in the United States, amid all the American popular culture she experienced as a child only by proxy, and the novel's final scenes focus on the processes of memory and the difficulties of aligning retrospective recollections with contemporary experience: "All Souls' Day, 1959. Or 1960 – why is it so difficult to recall? Why didn't I write it all down, keep diaries and journals . . . " For all the liveliness of Filipino society recollected here, it also represents "a corrupt regime – a *dictatorship*," against which the United States is positioned as a point of security.[16] Similarly the final chapter in Alvarez's *How the García Girls Lost Their Accents* focuses upon the narrator Yolanda's escape from "the dictator Trujillo" in the Dominican Republic and the flight of her family to the safe haven of the Bronx.[17] Alvarez's work is told chronologically in reverse order, starting in 1989 and then tracking back to the Dominican Republic in the 1950s, and this again foregrounds the discourse of memory, how past experiences continue to shape present perspectives. Indeed, the whole fictional narrative is structured like a therapy discourse, with Yolanda's mother continually saying she wants to forget the past even though she "remembers everything," her father "haunted" by the memory of Trujillo for the rest of his life, and her sister Carla growing up to be a "child psychologist." Alvarez emphasizes excavating the past, and how the modernity of the United States relates to a formative cultural heritage that is kept here at a distance, both spatially and temporally.

Yolanda, after immigrating to the United States, feels she "would never find someone who would understand my peculiar mix of Catholicism and agnosticism, Hispanic and American styles," but her fictional memoir inscribes precisely such a style of principled hybridity, where Dominican assumptions can be assimilated within the ever-expanding circle of US multiculturalism.[18]

In the same year that Alvarez's novel appeared, Betty Jean Craige published in *PMLA* an essay entitled "Literature in a Global Society," describing a "clash between traditionalism, manifesting itself in nationalism, and cultural holism, manifesting itself in globalism." Craige's agenda involved "appreciating the world's variety of human expression" through "promoting cultural exchange on a global scale," with her "hope" being "that eventually a widespread appreciation of diversity, which multicultural education fosters, and a desire for cooperation will supplant the intercultural competition that now predominates."[19] While this now looks very dated, its key terms, *multicultural* and *diversity*, speak aptly to political engagements and alliances current in this era. Sandra Cisneros's *Woman Hollering Creek* accommodates diversity but also self-consciously looks backwards, correlating its memories of the narrators' Hispanic pasts with a focus on life on both sides of the Mexican border. In Cisneros's case, this bilateralism also expresses itself in bilingualism, with the story "Little Miracle, Kept Promises" including letters written in Spanish as well as English. As in Alvarez, the idea of past time here takes on a recursive quality, with the narrator of "*Bien* Pretty" saying: "We have to let go of our present way of life and search for our past, remember our destinies, so to speak."[20] For Cisneros, this temporal shift takes on a reflexive dimension, with these rhetorical paradoxes ("remember our destinies") mirroring divisions in the narrator's subjectivity. Such textual instabilities, characteristic of postmodernism, epitomize ways in which linguistic difference shapes the characters' minds: in "*Bien* Pretty," the narrator suggests how the "true test of a native Spanish speaker" is when he yells "¡*Ay*!" rather than "Ouch!" when accidentally hammering his thumb.[21] By thus relating multiculturalism to a play of the sign, Cisneros accommodates postmodernism's contingent dynamic, suggesting how ethnicity is a linguistic and cultural construction rather than an essentialist form of identity.

In 1997, Slavoj Žižek aligned "multiculturalism" with "the cultural logic of multinational capitalism," one in which "Western cultural imperialism ... treats *each* local culture the way the colonizer treats colonized peoples – as 'natives' whose mores are to be carefully studied and 'respected.'" Žižek went on to describe "multiculturalism" as "a disavowed, inverted, self-referential form of racism," a "racism with a distance," and it is certainly true that, from a subsequent historical perspective, American literature of the 1990s often appears quaint in its instinctive assumption of the United States as the privileged centre to which the rest of the world appears peripheral or subordinate.[22] Though Gish Jen's *Mona in the Promised Land* (1996) takes its epigraph about change, flux, and motion from Ovid, the reiterated claim of its heroine that "Nothing's impossible" involves an extension of American utopianism, complete with its frontier spirit, into a universal mantra.[23] Mona's invocation here of America's "Promised Land" involves rejecting ethnic authenticity – "There isn't room enough in this country for everyone to be authentic all day long" – and accommodating cultural differences within the conventional template of the American "melting pot – no, mosaic – no, salad bowl," with such ethnic identification consequently being cast, according to an emollient postmodern logic, as a volitional or discretionary phenomenon. The idea, much repeated here, that because "This is America" the heroine can "be what I want" becomes a way of consolidating both the metamorphic quality of personal identity and the template of US national identity as a guarantor of individual freedom.[24] The idea that there might be ontological impediments to such capacities for transition is regarded, within the context of 1990s America, as largely outmoded.

In the 1994 book *Nations Unbound*, a team of social scientists described a situation where old distinctions between temporary migrants and permanent immigrants were falling into disrepair, with many US residents developing "networks, activities, patterns of living, and ideologies that span their home and the host society."[25] Multicultural American literature of the 1990s often reflected this pattern in the way it represented what Michael S. Laguerre called a "politics of simultaneity" rather than a "politics of succession," whereby the old country came to seem connected to the American mainland through cheap flights and new communications technologies.[26] Peggy Levitt in 2001 described what she called a "new cartography" of transnational villages, where migrants opt to participate in different societies simultaneously.[27] There is, in other words, a characteristic tension in nineties ethnic fiction between narratives that regard the United States in time-honored fashion as a providential resting place for beleaguered immigrants and a bifocal structure whereby the narrative voice switches backwards and forwards between alternative domains, both temporal and spatial, thereby opening up American scenes to concurrent transnational horizons. Jhumpa Lahiri's fiction, which James Annesley accuses of incorporating "a homogenizing dynamic" underwriting "implicit celebrations of Americanness," might be seen from another perspective to embody precisely these cross-cultural tensions, since the Indian-born narrator of "The

Third and Final Continent" (1999), now securely resident in the suburbs of Boston, nevertheless uses his retrospective voice not only to recall his own past in Calcutta, but also to defamiliarize the routine world of American domestic landscapes.[28] Lahiri's understated, limpid style is beguiling in part because of the way it combines an air of transparency with a capacity to make strange, and the implicit comparison adduced by this story's narrator between his own arrival in the United States and the "moon shot" in 1969 when American astronauts first "landed on the shores of the Sea of Tranquillity" renders proximate scenes distant, as though, by a kind of *mise-en-abîme* effect, this comfortable American home might open up at any point to radically different vistas.[29]

Don DeLillo's *Underworld* (1997) represents a very different form of globalization, though the use of *world* in the second part of this novel's title points clearly enough to its global reach. DeLillo's theme here is connection in all of its facets, how events that might seem distant in time and space are in fact inextricably conjoined. The connections forged through collective memory – the book starts with a 1951 baseball game between the Giants and the Dodgers – thus become analogous to an American culture whose environmental affairs are bound symbiotically to its systems of waste management: "waste is the secret history, the underhistory, the way archaeologists dig out the history of early cultures, every sort of bone heap and broken tool, literally from under the ground."[30] This archaeological imagination, intent as it is upon excavating sedimented layers of past time, also leads to connections between post–Enlightenment America and medieval societies. The book's prologue is entitled "The Triumph of Death," with the title of its third part being taken from Julian of Norwich's fifth-century treatise *The Cloud of Unknowing*, and all of these analogies are designed to correlate twentieth-century American culture with medieval antecedents. DeLillo's ancestral Catholicism is clearly one source for this universalism – Sister Edgar is described as "a figure from a universal church with sacraments and secret bank accounts and a fabulous art collection" – and DeLillo's roots become more evident in this novel than in any of his others.[31] The point here, though, is not to inscribe a particular version of ethnic identity, but rather to project an alternative version of US culture, one predicated not upon the romantic exceptionalism of the frontier tradition but upon the communal sharing of everyday household gods: "home alone, surrounded by all the things and textures that make you familiar, once again, to yourself." The idea of the global, then, becomes for DeLillo an ontology, with "the force of converging markets" and the worlding capacity of the Internet – "The real miracle is the web, the net, where everybody is everywhere at once" – serving to illuminate the style of cosmic communitarianism that has, according to DeLillo, always been implicit within the American body politic.[32]

In a 1991 interview, DeLillo spoke of his "sense that we live in a kind of circular or near-circular system and that there are an increasing number of rings which keep intersecting at some point, whether you're using a plastic card to draw money out of your account at an automatic teller machine or thinking about the movement of planetary bodies."[33] The great skill of *Underworld*, however, is to reposition this "circular system" of contemporary life within an alternative spatiotemporal genealogy, so that the banking and Internet systems come to evoke an environment where the relation between America and the wider world appears qualitatively different. Hence the medieval topography that informs *Underworld* – the modern urban mall which is described as resembling a "medieval town, with the castle smack at the centre" – makes the United States in the 1990s appear coextensive with European landscapes of a thousand years earlier.[34] Tony Tanner described DeLillo as "some kind of latter-day American urban Transcendentalist," but this is true only to the extent that DeLillo specifically quarrels with Transcendentalism's premises.[35] Rather than taking the natural world to be an extension of the subjective self, DeLillo's work dissolves the self-aggrandizing subject into a global nexus whose expansive orbits exceed any imaginative subjugation of it. Thomas Peyser admitted there "is nothing new about globalization," but he suggested what was "startlingly and even shockingly new" in the 1990s was "the sway that the idea of globality holds over the imagination."[36] In DeLillo's case, it is this framework of globalization, with its austere parallel to Catholic universalism, that gives the author intellectual distance from American mythologies of possessive individualism.

It was a fundamental disagreement over the nature of such individualism that fired the dispute in 1997 between John Updike and David Foster Wallace, after the latter had written a scathing review of Updike's *Toward the End of Time* accusing the senior novelist of neglecting his large-scale canvas of how a "Sino-American war" in 2020 had killed millions and ended US central government in favor of much more self-indulgent ruminations about the narrator's home and "how his ocean view looks in different seasons."[37] There was a generational aspect to such differences, with Wallace regarding the globalized condition of his American world as a *fait accompli* in a way that Updike found more difficult to admit except on sufferance, but this also overlapped with important artistic divergences. Wallace's 1993 essay "E Unibus Pluram: Television and U.S. Fiction" came to stand as a manifesto for his generation of fiction writers, with Wallace arguing here that American writers under forty – born, in other words, after 1953 – had been conditioned to a world within which the ubiquity of television was a plain fact, with such stratification by "generation" carrying more purchase than older nostrums whereby writers would be categorized according to "regions" or "ethnicity."[38] Dave Eggers's *A Heartbreaking Work of Staggering Genius*, published in 2000, fully exemplifies this television sensibility in the way it incorporates an aesthetic of interchangeability, presenting the narrator as "the common multiplier for 47 million" and using the image of a "lattice" to evoke "the connective tissue" that binds his contemporaries together.[39] There are innumerable references in *A Heartbreaking World* to specific television programs, with the casts of these televisual worlds coming to operate for Eggers's personae as a surrogate family after the loss of their own parents. Also revealing in generational terms is the idea expressed in the novel's first pages that "death is literally around each and every corner," the fear that "each and every time an elevator door opens, there will be standing, in a trenchcoat, a man, with a gun."[40] In her introduction to a 2003 anthology of American fiction by writers "quite different in spirit from the generation that preceded them," Zadie Smith remarked that one characteristic of this "chorus of melancholy" was its acknowledgment of how "Fear of disease, accident and attack is everywhere."[41] In Eggers's case, this sense of an amorphous looming threat, something that predates 9/11, is connected to the radical instability of family situations, along with the frenetic pace of technological and economic change. Whereas the literary generation that came to maturity after World War II often wrote about family relationships as a claustrophobic impediment to liberal individualism, the younger generation of the 1990s tended to be nostalgic for the kind of family security and cultural continuity that now seemed to them only a distant dream. Caren Irr has written of "the specific insecurities, and vertiginous sense of placelessness" associated with "economic neoliberalism," citing as an example how Jonathan Franzen's *The Corrections* (2001) tracks back from its projection of Eastern Europe and the volatility of the global stock market to reimagine the Midwestern family home as "a site of reconciliation."[42]

The novelist of the 1990s who expressed this generational sensibility most acutely was, however, Douglas Coupland, a native of Vancouver, Canada, whose observation that "Vancouverites" have more in common with "West Coast Americans" than with East Coast Canadians spoke aptly to the transnational framework of his times.[43] Coupland's iconic 1991 work *Generation X* foregrounds the question of planetary rotation in its very first sentence, recalling as it does the narrator flying as a fifteen-year-old across the continent "to witness a total eclipse of the sun."[44] All of Coupland's fictional works are attuned to the cycles of time, with *Microserfs* (1995), starting precisely in 1993, chronicling how technological drivers shape social relationships. The Microsoft campus outside Seattle, the fulcrum of this narrative, is said to make people rethink the relationship between their brains and bodies, and in this rapidly developing environment the borders between life and work have become blurred, memory has replaced history, with the narrator Daniel commenting on how "we can edit ourselves as we go along, like an on-screen document."[45] In the 1990s such generational self-consciousness became particularly acute, since structural changes in the global economy – the shift from labor-intensive to capital-intensive industry, with a concomitant loss of long-term professional security – created a situation of disproportionate unemployment among the young, so that, as Saskia Sassen observed, many young adults in the last years of the twentieth century developed "only weak ties to the labor market."[46] Just as F. Scott Fitzgerald's "lost generation" was shaped by the experience of World War I, so Coupland's generation was shaped by fallout from pressures of globalization associated with the information technology revolution.

One of the most compelling fictional accounts of this uncomfortable transition from a national to a global imaginary is Bob Shacochis's *Swimming in the Volcano*, published in 1993, but set sixteen years earlier, in 1977. Shacochis's novel focuses on American diplomats, executives, and Peace Corps volunteers who get caught up in various disorienting experiences on the fictional Caribbean island of St. Catherine. Sally, who fled Kansas out of dismay at the prospect of a "quiet life" with her dull boyfriend Jerry, finds herself out of her psychological depth in this farrago of drugs, corruption, and violence, and asks rhetorically: "What was everybody doing here?"[47] Mitchell, burdened with the presence of his former girlfriend Johnnie, contemplates the "naiveté" of Americans who, having been tempted to take "an unmediated leap out onto the globe," believe that the world's landscapes should be "as simple to change as a television channel." Mitchell finds compatriots who have never been "out of the States before" have a tendency "to judge a place by what was missing, the cancellation of entitlements."[48] There are various intertextual references here, to the Gothic forms of William Burroughs ("this naked lunch of an island"), to Joseph Conrad's *Heart of Darkness* ("He felt like cartoon footage, the Saturday-night evolution of Kurtz"), and to Evelyn Waugh's fictional encounters with Africa and South America in novels such as *Black Mischief* and *A Handful of Dust*, with Adrian describing her American friends as living out a scenario of "Evelyn Waugh gone to pot."[49] All of this attests to a sense of "debasement" in this Caribbean environment, something that threatens "the march of European sensibilities" and of US assumptions of world order modeled on "the efficacy of the Monroe Doctrine." At the same time, these American innocents abroad are drawn psychologically to these atavistic landscapes, where the memory of slavery still lingers: "What was it there in the puritan heart that so idolized corruption; or was it capitalism, the New England slave traders, exchanging syrup for souls, for more syrup and more souls, in an unabashed triangle of profit between continents?"[50] The book's titular metaphor of a dormant volcano is paralleled by the smoldering passions for sex and violence buried within these characters, with the imagery making connections between global geography and internal landscapes. For example, Johnnie, who "attracted a devil" in Mitchell, is described in geopolitical terms – "the two hemispheres of her hair," "the gaunt hemispheres of her buttocks" – while the narrator describes how Sally "sometimes felt equatorial, a narrow imaginary line of contact between the frictional polarity of hemispheres."[51]

All of this serves to forcibly impress a global consciousness upon these American characters, and the novel turns upon ways in which domestic assumptions, both psychological and political, find themselves upended by this "parallel universe," an "island of contradictions," where "the world spun in both directions."[52] Shacochis's careful situating of his narrative in the recent past allows him not only to chronicle the emergence of an embryonic form of globalization during the years of the Carter administration, but also to suggest the limits of any US attempt to colonize the globe. Mitchell thinks at one point that he "didn't know what the world would look like ten years into the future, or who would win the Cold War, but [he] suspected that for orphans like St. Catherine it couldn't possibly matter."[53] Don H. Doyle has argued that a key feature of US culture in general is not its exceptionalism but its universalism, the notion that everyone should want what America values, with the Declaration of Independence typically attesting to the nation's claim on universal standards rather than codes of custom most appropriate to itself.[54] But if the immigrant fictions of Mukherjee and Hagedorn tend to postulate an Americanization of the entire globe, *Swimming the Volcano* tends rather in the opposite direction, toward (in Irr's phrase) situating "the United States on a variegated international map rather than universalizing its time-space."[55] By forcing US culture into alien encounters, Shacochis's novel effectively reconstitutes the rhetoric of globalization from what the author here calls an "arse-backwards topsy-turvy" perspective.[56]

In *Swimming the Volcano*'s acknowledgments, Shacochis pays tribute "to Richard Powers, one of the best novelists of my generation, who coined the phrase *global pillage*."[57] The fictions of Powers and of William Gibson, another writer with ambiguous affiliations to the United States since he was born in South Carolina but has lived since 1972 in Vancouver, posit a world where advanced information systems render the issue of national boundaries moot. Whereas Gibson's *Neuromancer* (1984) offered a hypothetical version of a future in "cyberspace," his 1990s novels – *Virtual Light* (1993), *Iduro* (1996), *All Tomorrow's Parties* (1999) – were, as Annesley noted, "written in the age when new media and Internet technologies were more reality than fantasy."[58] In these novels, Gibson projects a comic interface between older forms of empirical understanding and the newer dimensions of post-national space, as at the end of *Virtual Light*, where the hero has a yard sale to dispose of superannuated clutter such as his old compact discs and a "damp-swollen copy of *The Columbia Literary History of the United States*."[59] Ihab Hassan asked in 2010: "can we still speak of national literatures – say, of American or Australian literature – in the age of globalization?" and this is precisely the question posed sardonically by Gibson in *Virtual Light*.[60]

Another work of fiction that combines a digital with a transnational sensibility is Geoff Ryman's *253*, a novel that first appeared on the Internet in 1996 and then in book form (with a subtitle "the print remix") two years later. Ryman's narrative, brilliantly original in form and execution, chronicles a London Underground train carrying 252 passengers and its driver on a seven-minute journey between two tube stations on January 11, 1995, from 8:35 to 8:42 a.m. The book operates as a paean to contingency, with the way these passengers are brought together reflecting a sense, as *253* says on its second page, of how "the universe is not held together by cause and effect alone, but by mysterious patterns," patterns that mirror the catalogs and networks of the World Wide Web.[61] Although we become partially privy to the characters' inner lives here, with the sketch of each individual being confined to 253 words, the author also tells us how they are bound by an "inexorable logic of age, gender, genes, character, their time in history, luck," and in this sense the minimalist verbal box within which each person is presented comes to epitomize the genetic "logic" that circumscribes their terrestrial incarnation.[62] All of the metafictional apparatus that frames Ryman's novel – its passenger maps, its incorporation of pseudo-advertisements, and a final "Reader Satisfaction Survey" – involves the kind of comic reflexivity that is reminiscent of classic postmodernist texts such as Donald Barthelme's *Snow White* (1967), and there is no doubt that Ryman takes pleasure in spoofing the received assumptions that underlie London life.[63] The author, who was born in Canada but moved to the United States at the age of eleven and studied at UCLA before relocating to England in 1973, brings to his fiction a transnational imagination that enables him to approach British culture from many different directions. The book is rooted quite specifically in the events of the mid-1990s – it mentions, for instance, "Tony Blair having a go at the lefties over Clause Four," something that led to the Labour Party constitution being amended in April 1995, thereby ending the Party's long-standing commitment to nationalization – and it turns an ironic eye on the oppressive nature of British bureaucracy: "Gwen firmly believes that the entire NHS should have an ISO standard quality accreditation."[64] But rather than leaving this merely at the level of acerbic observation, Ryman uses his paratextual paraphernalia to situate English culture within a broader spatiotemporal matrix, incorporating for example a long discursive footnote on William Blake, the Londoner of 1795, and commenting pointedly on the ubiquity of surveillance systems: "The English live in *1984* and don't know it," even though "it's illegal to spy on people in America."[65] Such an implicitly comparative framework serves to relativize the visible world to make all these scenes appear contingent in time and space. The author uses his god-like position to chart future events – we are proleptically informed, for example, of how passenger 40 "will have an embarrassing meeting in 20 minutes' time with Passenger 38" – but this self-conscious play with omniscience seems again to reflect the all-encompassing tentacles of computer technology rather than aspiring toward any kind of artistic omnipotence.[66] Ryman himself worked for a time in 1994 at the U.K. government's Central Office of Information, and his novel reflects, albeit in a sardonic way, how labyrinthine systems of administrative control operate.

Frederick Buell complained in 2001 of how environmental concerns, which should have been a key part of globalization debates in the 1990s, in fact failed to make much general impact at that time. Observing how "global environmental discourse" was "quickly dropped from Clinton's popular globalization package in the 1990s," Buell attributed this to the "neo-liberal affirmation" of a "global economy," one valorized ideologically by a "new cosmopolitanism" that embraced "multiculturalism" as its slogan.[67] It was also the case that a collective fixation on the capacities of new digital systems, together with an assumption that winning the Cold War would ensure for the United States an unchallenged global hegemony, created an illusory sense of security that came crashing down, quite literally, on 9/11. From our vantage point, it is now obvious enough that the United

States in the last decade of the twentieth century was blind not only to how Islamic fundamentalism was consolidating an alternative world order, but also to the multiple complexities associated with "environmental crisis." Rather like the 1920s before the Wall Street Crash of 1929, American literature of the 1990s operated within a climate of utopian promise generated in part by technological novelty, one that tended silently to suppress more disruptive factors that were to become increasingly visible in later years. Threats of environmental catastrophe and religious fundamentalism were building throughout the 1990s, of course, but they tended to be suppressed in the interests of a millennial optimism. *Fury*, a novel by *arriviste* New Yorker Salman Rushdie, which was published by Random House in the United States on September 4, 2001, one week before 9/11, was prescient in the way it portrayed, amidst the peace and "plenty" of the Clinton era, the turbulence that was to follow, with Rushdie's hero Malik Solanka hearing a New York taxi driver prophesying how "the victorious jihad will crush your balls in its unforgiving fist."[68] Seven days later, the terms of US encounter with globalization in all its forms changed dramatically.

NOTES

1 Philip E. Wegner, *Life Between Two Deaths, 1989–2001: U.S. Culture in the Long Nineties* (Durham, NC: Duke University Press, 2009), 2.
2 Francis Fukuyama, *The End of History and the Last Man* (London: Hamilton, 1992), xi, xv, xiii.
3 Michael Denning, *Culture in the Age of Three Worlds* (London: Verso, 2004), 24.
4 Frederick Buell, "Globalization without Environmental Crisis: The Divorce of Two Discourses in U.S. Culture," *Symplokē* 9.1/2 (2001): 47.
5 Roland Robertson, *Globalization: Social Theory and Global Culture* (London: Sage, 1992), 8; Frances Cairncross, *The Death of Distance: How the Communications Revolution Will Change Our Lives* (Boston, MA: Harvard Business School Press, 1997).
6 Michael Hardt and Antonio Negri, *Empire* (Cambridge, MA: Harvard University Press, 2000), xii.
7 Jay Prosser, "Introduction," in *American Fiction of the 1990s: Reflections of History and Culture*, ed. Jay Prosser (London: Routledge, 2008), 1–2.
8 Jeremy Green, *Late Postmodernism: American Fiction at the Millennium* (New York: Palgrave Macmillan, 2005), 3.
9 Masao Miyoshi, "A Borderless World? From Colonialism to Transnationalism and the Decline of the Nation-State," *Critical Inquiry* 19.4 (1993): 744, 747.
10 Bharati Mukherjee, *Jasmine* (1989; rpt. London: Virago, 1991), 240.
11 Mukherjee, *Jasmine*, 29, 76, 125, 127.

Globalization

12 Mukherjee, *Jasmine*, 189. On the critical reception of Mukherjee, see James Annesley, *Fictions of Globalization: Consumption, the Market and the Contemporary American Novel* (London: Continuum, 2006), 141–142.
13 Mukherjee, *Jasmine*, 240, 176.
14 Jessica Hagedorn, *Dogeaters* (1990; rpt. New York: Penguin, 1991), 15.
15 Hagedorn, *Dogeaters*, 7, 37, 100.
16 Hagedorn, *Dogeaters*, 220, 238.
17 Julia Alvarez, *How the García Girls Lost Their Accents* (1991; rpt. London: Bloomsbury, 2004), 146.
18 Alvarez, *How the García Girls*, 41, 64, 99, 146.
19 Betty Jean Craige, "Literature in a Global Society," *PMLA* 106.3 (1991): 396, 397, 399.
20 Sandra Cisneros, "*Bien* Pretty," in *Woman Hollering Creek and Other Stories* (New York: Random House, 1991), 149.
21 Cisneros, "*Bien* Pretty," 153.
22 Slavoj Žižek, "Multiculturalism, Or, The Cultural Logic of Multinational Capitalism," *New Left Review* I/225 (1997): 44.
23 Gish Jen, *Mona in the Promised Land* (New York: Knopf, 1996), 91.
24 Jen, *Mona in the Promised Land*, 122, 129, 248.
25 Linda Basch, Nina Glick Schiller, Cristina Szanton Blanc, *Nations Unbound: Transnational Projects, Postcolonial Predicaments, and Deterritorialized Nation-States* (Amsterdam: Gordon, 137, 994), 4.
26 Michael S. Laguerre, *Diasporic Citizenship: Haitian Americans in Transnational America* (New York: St. Martin's, 1998), 177.
27 Peggy Levitt, *The Transnational Villagers* (Berkeley: University of California Press, 2001), 11.
28 Annesley, *Fictions of Globalization*, 128, 139.
29 Jhumpa Lahiri, "The Third and Final Continent," in *Interpreter of Maladies: Stories* (1999; rpt. London: Flamingo, 2000), 179.
30 Don DeLillo, *Underworld* (1997; rpt. London: Picador, 1998), 791.
31 DeLillo, *Underworld*, 822.
32 DeLillo, *Underworld*, 482, 786, 808.
33 Anthony DeCurtis, "'An Outsider in This Society': An Interview with Don DeLillo," in *Introducing Don DeLillo*, ed. Frank Lentricchia (Durham, NC: Duke University Press, 1991), 61.
34 DeLillo, *Underworld*, 109.
35 Tony Tanner, "Afterthoughts on Don DeLillo's *Underworld*," *Raritan* 17.4 (1998): 67.
36 Thomas Peyser, "Globalization in America: The Case of Don DeLillo's *White Noise*," *Clio* 25.3 (1996): 255.
37 David Foster Wallace, "Certainly the End of Something or Other, One Would Sort of Have to Think" (1997), in *Consider the Lobster and Other Essays* (London: Abacus, 2005), 55–56.
38 David Foster Wallace, "E Unibus Pluram: Television and U.S. Fiction" (1993), in *A Supposedly Fun Thing I'll Never Do Again* (London: Abacus, 1998), 65.

39 Dave Eggers, *A Heartbreaking Work of Staggering Genius* (London: Picador, 2000), 211, 236.
40 Eggers, *A Heartbreaking Work*, xxviii-xxix.
41 Zadie Smith, introduction, *The Burned Children of America* (London: Hamilton, 2003), xv.
42 Caren Irr, *Toward the Geopolitical Novel: U.S. Fiction in the Twenty-First Century* (New York: Columbia University Press, 2014), 105, 118.
43 Douglas Coupland, *City of Glass: Douglas Coupland's Vancouver* (Vancouver: Douglas, 2000), 106.
44 Douglas Coupland, *Generation X: Tales of an Accelerated Culture* (New York: St. Martin's, 1991), 3.
45 Douglas Coupland, *Microserfs* (1995; rpt. London: Flamingo, 1996), 253.
46 Saskia Sassen, *Territory, Authority, Rights: From Medieval to Global Assemblages* (Princeton, NJ: Princeton University Press, 2006), 285.
47 Bob Shacochis, *Swimming in the Volcano* (1993; rpt. New York: Grove, 2004), 249, 339.
48 Shacochis, *Swimming*, 27, 116, 125.
49 Shacochis, *Swimming*, 34, 302, 340.
50 Shacochis, *Swimming*, 108, 136, 142, 389.
51 Shacochis, *Swimming*, 48, 103, 343, 432.
52 Shacochis, *Swimming*, 491, 511.
53 Shacochis, *Swimming*, 446.
54 Don H. Doyle, "American Nationalism and the Dark Side of Idealism," Rothermere American Institute, University of Oxford, 26 April 2007.
55 Irr, *Toward the Geopolitical Novel*, 185.
56 Shacochis, *Swimming*, 487.
57 Shacochis, *Swimming*, 519.
58 William Gibson, *Neuroromancer* (1984; rpt. London: HarperCollins, 1993), 11; Annesley, *Fictions of Globalization*, 94.
59 William Gibson, *Virtual Light* (London: Penguin, 1993), 292.
60 Ihab Hassan, "Janglican: National Literatures in the Age of Globalization," *Philosophy and Literature* 34.2 (Oct. 2010): 271.
61 Geoff Ryman, *253: The Print Remix* (London: Flamingo, 1998), 2.
62 Ryman, *253*, 339.
63 Ryman, *253*, 365–366.
64 Ryman, *253*, 76, 121.
65 Ryman, *253*, 185–189, 202.
66 Ryman, *253*, 62.
67 Buell, "Globalization without Environmental Crisis," 49–50.
68 Salman Rushdie, *Fury* (London: Jonathan Cape, 2001), 6. 65.

CHAPTER 16

The Two-Cultures Novel

Jon Adams

Charles Percy Snow's "two cultures" were, broadly, the arts and the sciences – specifically, they were the literary intellectuals on one side and the physical scientists on the other. As a onetime research scientist turned novelist, Snow claimed to understand both parties, and felt the working definition of "culture" not only excluded the scientists but was being strategically deployed to limit their opportunity for social and political engagement. "Culture" was what happened in opera houses and galleries and theatres, not what men with stained fingers did in laboratories. "The Two Cultures," his 1959 Rede lecture, called for this invidious protectionism to cease: scientific knowledge must be instated alongside literary knowledge as part of the storehouse of culture.

But if, in late 1950s Cambridge, Snow had in mind a fairly clean distinction between academic literary intellectuals and laboratory-based research scientists, by the turn of the millennium, the dividing line is much less clear. Tracking the two cultures becomes increasingly difficult by the 1990s as what counts as "science" grows ever more inclusive, expanding to cover subjects once the preserve of the humanities or social sciences, and to formally investigate what had always been left to simple "common sense." Varieties of experience once available only to the novelist – the complexities of human nature, for example – would now be the stuff of scientific scrutiny: the emergence of new fields such as sociobiology and later evolutionary psychology attempted to recast our social mores as the vestiges of prehistoric Darwinian competition, while a revolutionary new edition of the "psychiatrist's bible," *DSM-III*, marked a paradigm shift away from the "talking cure" of psychoanalysis and toward the hyper-specification and medicalization of mental illness.[1]

Meanwhile, the borders between the socio-political and the scientific also began to blur, as the growing prominence of environmentalism, neuroscience, and genetics meant that *political* questions increasingly required *scientific* answers. The same period saw the introduction and rapid spread of networked computing and mobile communication, both of which would alter irrevocably the social environment for millions. Thus science began to study "everyday life" even as everyday life became increasingly enmeshed with scientific technologies and modes of thinking.

Science was distinctive now not for its cultural isolation so much as for its cultural dominance, and scientific nomenclature proliferated in step, naming the world with an astonishing precision. There's so much of it by the mid-nineties that linguist David Crystal is able to claim, "scientific nomenclature comprises most of the English vocabulary, and no one understands more than a fragment of it."[2] The language of science offered fiction writers a new vocabulary, a vast "namespace" from which to draw descriptions. Interviewed in 1979, Don DeLillo said:

> Specialized languages can be very beautiful. Mysterious and precise at the same time... Science in general has given us a new language to draw from. Some writers shrink from this... To me, science is a source of new names, new connections between people and the world.[3]

But scientific language also drives out and displaces the vernacular, compelling writers to cross-check their literary descriptions against the strict definitions of scientific terminology.

Since Snow, there has been increasing critical and creative interest in the interaction between the sciences and the arts, to the extent that one can quite loosely identify a subcategory of fictions which Luc Herman and Geert Lernout (with specific reference to Richard Powers's *The Gold Bug Variations* from 1992) have called "the two-cultures novel."[4] The two-cultures novel isn't wholly an artifact of Snow's intervention, nor was it true that novelists had never taken an interest in the mechanical operation of the world. But where encyclopedic fictions such as *Ulysses* or *Gravity's Rainbow* included science because they sought to include everything, the two-cultures novel is specifically interested in how the scientific worldview sits alongside the humanistic, and seeks to contrast and explore their respective cosmologies: the language-centered, anthropic world of the humanities, in opposition to the fundamentally decentred and indifferent Copernican universe. The two-cultures novel doesn't simply employ scientific vocabulary – although the distinctive lexicon of science is certainly a feature – rather, it operates at the interface of these two cognitive worlds.

We can read the two-cultures novels of the 1990s as testing the capacity of these new systems to adequately replace the old during a period of rapid advances in computation, genetics, neuroscience, and environmental awareness. What use to make of all those new names?

The Rise of Environmentalism

The sense that scientific knowledge at once liberates and poses a threat to existing ways of understanding the world is brought into focus with Barbara Kingsolver's *Animal Dreams* (1990)[5] – a novel that valorizes scientific knowledge even as it recognizes science's damaging effects on both traditional knowledge systems and the natural orders it describes.

Animal Dreams follows medical-school dropout Codi Noline, "educated to within an inch of [her] life" (28), retreating to her childhood town of Grace, Arizona, where she's to take up a position teaching biology at the local high school. At once a homecoming narrative, family drama, and smalltown portrait, it's Kingsolver's particular concern with ecology – with the interrelatedness of human and environment – that is of special concern here. When the region's agriculture is threatened by pollution from an upstream mining operation, Codi finds her otherwise abandoned scientific training acquiring a renewed social function. Science at once threatens the landscape, and yet has the potential to save it: it's Codi's understanding of the science behind that pollution that enables her to act as an effective lobbyist. "'Here's the chemistry of it,'" she tells a town hall meeting:

> "Black Mountain Mining has been running sulphuric acid, which is a clear, corrosive, water-miscible acid, through their tailing pipes to recover extra copper. It combines to make copper sulfate, which is also known as 'blue vitriol.' People used to use it to kill rats ... There's a ton of it in your river." (176)

Kingsolver trained as an ecologist and biologist, and had worked as a science journalist before writing novels. That legacy is felt in how she employs the novel as a tool for science education and environmental activism. Kingsolver, like Codi, becomes the teacher who can't help but go off-curriculum, and while it's not a didactic text, in its foregrounding of ecology it issues a rejection of the textualism that characterises so much Modernist and Postmodernist literary fiction. Kingsolver writes fiction with an eye to social amelioration: we're intended to take seriously the warnings about industrial pollution, and an author's note says as much. When Codi explains the copper mining process to her townsfolk, Kingsolver also explains it to her readers.

These are themes Kingsolver would repeatedly return to, more recently with 2012's *Flight Behaviour*, but *Animal Dreams* marks the emergence of environmentalism as a matter of public interest, a widening of the moral sphere that occurred largely during the 1990s and which – accelerated by high-profile disasters such as the catastrophic nuclear accident at Chernobyl in 1986, and the Exxon Valdez oil spill in 1989 – saw environmentalism graduate from a peripheral concern of radicals and "tree huggers" to a front-row political issue. In *Animal Dreams*, the elegance with which Kingsolver describes the countryside is mirrored by the precision with which she deploys technical language. Formally, that stylistic vacillation between novelist and science journalist enables her to at once describe the surface and explain the underlying processes, a shift from nature writing to ecological writing. Both modes operate symbiotically: capturing the beauty of the landscape is the nature writer's job, explaining the vulnerability of that beauty is the ecologist's, and so the science here augments rather than challenges traditional descriptions of the natural world.

But if the ecological slotted comfortably alongside the natural, the integration of the new scientific understanding of the brain would prove more disruptive, as the neuroscientists vied with the novelists for the territory of human consciousness.

The Decade of the Brain

In order to "enhance public awareness of the benefits to be derived from brain research," Congress declared the 1990s "the Decade of the Brain."[6] The initiative stimulated significant growth in the burgeoning neurosciences, and certainly a sharpening of the public attention on the brain *outwith* the mind – that is, on neuroscience instead of psychology. Throughout the 1970s, the NIMH had systematically withdrawn funding from behavioral research in favour of pharmaceutical solutions,[7] and by the 1990s the age of neuropharmacology was underway. A generation of young Americans would henceforth be diagnosed with a suite of new depressive, attention, and anxiety disorders. The cures would be chemical and their brand names – Adderall, Ritalin, Prozac, Valium, Xanax – rapidly absorbed into the argot of American popular culture.[8] The Decade of the Brain simultaneously medicalized, and normalized, those behavioral disorders. Bookshops stocked a "popular psychology" section among their self-help shelves: Dale Carnegie's classic *How To Make Friends And Influence People* (1936) now competed with Peter Kramer's *Listening to Prozac* (1993); while self-help spilled over to the confessional memoir with Elizabeth Wurtzel's *Prozac Nation: Young and Depressed in America* (1994). Satirizing the endless profusion of self-help addiction groups in *Infinite Jest* (1996), David Foster Wallace mentions that there was "even (especially in and around Manhattan) something called Prozac Anonymous."[9]

The Two-Cultures Novel

If there's an extent to which materialism ousts mentalism in psychology, it's reflected in a need for plausible psychological aetiology in fiction. For as well as providing DeLillo's new names, the increasing *awareness* of neuroscience that all this publicity occasions exacts a peculiar constriction on the literary imagination. A tyrannical realism ensues, with writers beholden to supply a valid diagnosis for any putative psychopathology.

Neurological Realism

Contrast the abnormal self in two novels that bracket the decade: *American Psycho* –published in 1991, but very much set in 1980s Wall Street – and Jonathan Lethem's *Motherless Brooklyn*, from 1999.[10] It's clear that for Bret Easton Ellis, psychological – or at least, psychiatric – realism is minimally important. Patrick Bateman represents a caricature of a particular type of materialistic, spiritually vacuous businessman out to make a killing. We're repeatedly told that what defines Patrick Batemen is precisely the absence of a self to introspect:

> I had all the characteristics of a human being – flesh, blood, skin, hair – but my depersonalization was so intense, had gone so deep, that the normal ability to feel compassion had been eradicated... I was simply imitating reality, a rough resemblance of a human being, with only a dim corner of my mind functioning. (*American Psycho* 282)

Again: "I simply am not there.... Myself is fabricated, an aberration. I am a noncontingent human being" (376–377). In this respect, Patrick is a literary descendant of T. S. Eliot's Hollow Men and Joseph Conrad's "*papier-mache* Mephistopheles" (before whom Marlow feels "that if I tried I could poke my forefinger through him, and would find nothing inside but a little loose dirt, maybe").[11] We are shown that Patrick is crazy, but at no point is Ellis expected to supply a plausible explanation. By the end of the Decade of the Brain, readers expected those hollow spaces to be filled in.

Hence Jonathan Lethem's *Motherless Brooklyn*, which also featured a cognitively impaired character in New York, but is a very different sort of book. Lethem's narrator, Lionel Essrog, has an obsessive-compulsive form of Tourette's that compels him to perform ritualised taps and gestures as he systematically works through variations on words, turning them over for rhymes, affinities, variations: "I remembered mishearing *Ringling Bros. Barnum & Bailey Circus* / as a child. Barnamum Bailey. Like Osmium, Cardamon, Brainium, Where'smymom: the periodic table of elements, the heavy metals" (21–22). Lethem's primary source for Lionel is a case study from neurologist Oliver Sacks's *The Man Who Mistook His Wife For A Hat* (1985),[12] and Sacks had explicitly volunteered his strange bestiary of neurological outliers as source material for fiction writers. "To what shall we compare them?" he asks of his patients. "We may not have any existing models, metaphors or myths. Has the time perhaps come for new metaphors, new myths?" (Sacks, 1985, xxiii).

Taking up that offer, Lethem finds in Tourette's a means of approaching literary wordplay anew, not now as an artifact of writing, but as a natural phenomenon. Lionel is fond of jokes which rely on homophones (a frayed knot/afraid not), and scholars of the condition have taxonomized quite precisely the various ways in which Tourette's mangles and manipulates human speech into "complex phonic tics": *echolalia*, the repetition of the words of others; *palilalia*, the repetition of a person's own words; *coprolalia*, the use of taboo language.[13] Puns, jokes, slips: these are the same tools in the verbal artist's kit, so Tourette's offers of sort of pathological punning, and (as Ronald Schleifer argues[14]) it also naturalises that sort of language-play that poetry more purposefully performs. But the aleatoric nature of the connections, and the automatic manner in which they're issued, opens a gulf between sense and intent, for as Lionel explains: "They're just words. They don't mean anything" (217). For Lethem, that's an expensive joke: if they really are "just words," then Tourette's threatens to push such utterances outside human speech altogether; more sound than syllable, to adapt Emily Dickinson's division.

The threat of losing meaning under a scientific description is a real one. *Motherless Brooklyn* forms part of a genre that Marco Roth has – skeptically – called "neuronovels," in which the language and explanatory structure of neurology replaces the mentalistic in accounting for behaviour. The gains for realism are purchased at the cost of intentionality: "the etiology of a neurological condition is biological, not moral. And mere biological contingency has a way of repelling meaning."[15] Roth reads the neuronovel as recording an essentially metafictional anxiety: a loss of confidence in literature's capacity to render consciousness phenomenologically, and a consequent cleaving toward the materialist language of science. By this account, the language of neuroscience represents a retreat from what Roth calls Modernism's "profound interiority" with its dense linguistic play, and into an essentially biologistic description that for all its specificity and precision remains fundamentally incapable of supporting the moral and metaphorical weight the novel is expected to bear. At its heart is a concern that the type of interdisciplinarity the two-cultures novel aims for is always asymmetric, never true cooperation but instead a form of superimposition where, as Stanley Fish puts it, one discipline is always "anxiously trading on the prestige and vocabulary of the other."[16]

This concern that the two-cultures novel might be a product of epistemological inferiority is buttressed by the growing cultural dominance of the sciences throughout the second half of the twentieth century. Where Snow had complained that scientists were systematically excluded from public affairs by an entrenched and protectionist literary culture, by the 1990s scientists – and especially science writers – were increasingly visible in popular culture. In 1980, Carl Sagan made the cover of *Time* magazine on the back of his *Cosmos* TV series; and during the nineties, both Stephen Jay Gould and Stephen Hawking would appear on *The Simpsons*.[17] Science books became a lucrative market – Steven Pinker was reported to have received a half-million-dollar advance for *How The Mind Works* (1997). Pinker's literary agent, John Brockman (who finessed many of the largest of such deals), was quoted in 1997 as claiming: "Scientists are getting what celebrities got 10 years ago – well, actually, they're getting as much as celebrities in many cases."[18]

That this new generation of pop-scientists had become celebrities and enjoyed (at least from the publishers' perspective) a comparable status to top novelists might suggest a harmony, a leveling out. But all the while popular science was blossoming across popular culture, within the universities, a tension was building between the two cultures.

The Science Wars

In 1994, biologist Paul Gross and mathematician Norman Levitt published *Higher Superstition*,[19] an attack on the fields of post-structuralism, deconstructionism, and science studies. Spurred on by sociological approaches that sought to undermine the epistemic supremacy of the sciences by questioning the value-neutrality of scientific practices, the so-called academic left warned against a growing "scientism" that sought to replace humanistic culture with a scientific one. Like many in the sciences, Gross and Levitt had been watching the rise of science-studies and postmodernist theory with dismay: "To put it bluntly," they wrote, "the academic left dislikes science" (2). Like Snow, they identified scientific ignorance as a cultural problem, but Gross and Levitt's complaint was that ignorance of science led, paradoxically, to a form of scientific pretension – "Thus we encounter," they wrote, "essays that make knowing reference to chaos theory, from writers who could not recognize, much less solve, a first-order linear differential equation; tirades about the semiotic tyranny of DNA ... from scholars who have never been inside a real laboratory" (6). Science retained a certain prestige, and even as it was disparaged, it was capable of adding a sheen of intellectual sophistication. This related problem of scientific pretension was brought to prominence by the famous "Sokal Hoax," in which physicist Alan Sokal submitted a spoof article to the journal *Social Text* in 1996. Entitled "Transgressing the Boundaries: Toward a Transformative Hermeneutics of Quantum Gravity," the piece deliberately misused scientific terminology in precisely the fashion Gross and Levitt had criticised, in order to ratify Sokal's intuition that the *Social Text* editors wouldn't know the difference between science and nonsense. When Sokal immediately revealed the hoax in rival journal *Lingua Franca*, the affair was widely reported in the mainstream press, and briefly brought what was by then being called "The Science Wars" to public attention.

If the episode ought to have been embarrassing, it wasn't academically unproductive: *Social Text*'s co-editor, Andrew Ross, was already due to publish a collection of essays entitled *The Science Wars* in 1996 – and Sokal's hoax (which had been included in the special edition collating the papers for that very volume) gave their otherwise limited sales a significant boost. In 1997, Sokal, along with colleague Jean Bricmont, would publish his own book-length contribution, *Impostures Intellectuelles* (in French, and translated the following year as *Fashionable Nonsense* in the United States).

For all this academic conflict, by the close of the decade, the territory looked very different. In 1998, entomologist and progenitor of sociobiology, Edward O. Wilson, was calling for "the unity of knowledge" – *consilience* – proposing a nested hierarchy of all the disciplines stretching from quantum physics to cosmology, and taking in the humanities along the way. Wilson's bold, imperialistic tone seemed to confirm the fears many scholars within science studies had articulated in the early nineties regarding the widening ambit of the sciences. It was also a reminder of how confident the sciences had become, and it was a confidence fueled, to a significant extent, by the enormous popular success of popular science.

The Popularity of Popular Science

The 1980s had seen a boom in popular science publishing, and popular science now found audiences far beyond the rather limited circulation of *Popular Mechanics* or *Scientific American* – indeed, the market for science magazines was contracting even as the book sales rose (Stephen Hawking's *A Brief History of Time* [1988] went on to sell over 20 million copies).[20]

In part, this is because the science popularization increasingly supplied the sort of organizing narrative and theoretical scope that previous generations of readers once sought from long novels: the world-making of *War and Peace* might be supplied in the mid-nineties by Jared Diamond's *Guns, Germs, and Steel* (1997) or Daniel Dennett's *Darwin's Dangerous Idea* (1995). The epistemological trajectory of science seemed to promise maximal explanatory reach with minimal theoretical profusion. Physicist Steven Weinberg summed it up in the title of his 1993 book: *Dreams of a Final Theory*.

Rather than plodding expository writing, this new generation of popularizations were intellectually bold and edifying, often arranging ideas from multiple disciplines into grandiose structures that promised to reveal the sort of seductively dense inter-connections with which novelists such as Pynchon or Umberto Eco tantalized their readers. Yet if the popularization started to look like a certain type of novel, the inverse was also true. Douglas Hofstadter's high-wire analogies between Bach's contrapuntal fugues and the recursive encoding of DNA that secured a Pulitzer for 1979's *Gödel, Escher, Bach* would significantly influence Richard Powers's *Gold Bug Variations* (1991), which rearranged many of the same components into a two-stranded fictional narrative that employed an ingeniously dense structure[21] to tell the story of a research scientist's parallel quests for intellectual and emotional fulfilment. The elegant synthesis of content and structure in *The Gold Bug Variations* pointed to ways in which the novel might play with the ideas of science and mathematics more substantively, but for Powers to get those ideas in play required a certain amount of set up. Hence there is extensive background exposition of the genetic coding system, of triplet bases, the history of computational cryptography, and the mechanics of evolution – often for several pages at a time. (The obvious literary precedent is Melville's surprisingly long discursions on cetology and maritime history throughout *Moby-Dick*.) Snow surely wouldn't have expected novelists to include expository science writing, but the cultural prominence of increasingly novelistic science books had an impact on the style of fiction – creating, in places, a convergence of styles and influences that yields something like a hybrid form.

During the late 1980s and early 1990s, "chaos theory" and its ambassadorial fractals were everywhere – mugs, T-shirts, dorm-room posters – and that ubiquity was almost wholly due to James's Gleick's *Chaos: The Making of a New Science* (1987).[22] Gleick's approach to science writing was novelistic, his opening lines more like the introduction to a detective thriller than a book about mathematical physics:

> The police in the small town of Los Alamos, New Mexico, worried briefly in 1974 about a man seen prowling in the dark night after night, the red glow of his cigarette floating along the back streets. He would pace for hours, heading nowhere in the starlight that hammers down through the thin air of the mesas.

Interleaving skillful exposition with perceptive character studies made the experience more akin to the reading of a novel than a textbook. But while Gleick's *Chaos*, and later Richard Preston's *The Hot Zone* (1994), treated the popularization like a novel, former physician Michael Crichton was increasingly writing popular fiction as if it were popular science. *Jurassic Park* (1990), for which he's best known, melded genetics with chaos theory, and relied on the science of each to structure the book's plot (iterations of the aptly named "dragon fractal" prefigure each section, and Crichton duly credits Gleick in his acknowledgments). Part of Crichton's game was to scare his readers by blurring the distinction between fact and fiction – actual data sits alongside fabricated data, real with fake. That's not unusual for mass-market thrillers (or fiction in general), but in Crichton's case, the existence of factual popular science books which were already trying to look like novels makes his job much easier by meeting him halfway. From a commercial perspective, the notion that adding science into the formula might actually *increase* book sales speaks for how much the cultural stock of science had risen since Snow's day. During the 1990s, scientists were increasingly the in-group, and it's the literary intellectuals who were feeling marginalized and excluded.

Science's Strange Attraction

As an indicator of the rising status of scientists, Rebecca Goldstein tries to incorporate scientists not as plot devices, but to explore what their particular perspective on the world might offer. Hence Goldstein's Phoebe Saunders, a mathematician who features in several different short stories and a later novel, *Mazel* (2002). Saunders is loosely modeled on real-life mathematician Jean Taylor – who at the time of composition would have been Goldstein's colleague at Rutgers, and like the fictional Saunders, works on the geometry of soap bubbles.[23] When individual soap bubbles cluster into foam, they arrange themselves into hexagonal matrices that can be described within surprisingly rigid limits (Plateau's Laws). As bubbles within the foam "pop" into one another their adjacent surfaces are shared, so it is no longer possible to decide which wall belongs to which bubble. In Goldstein's hands, that structure becomes a metaphor for intergenerational codependency, the manner in which an individual is straddled between their parents and their children, at once bridge and division between them, bearing elements of each.

Goldstein is also alert to and fascinated by the "otherness" of the mathematicians. We're set down among them as if they were an exotic tribe, and in return we see ourselves as they see us. Without resorting to the abnormal psychology described by Sacks, Goldstein finds in the mathematicians a new perspective on the same world. One of the Phoebe Saunders stories, "Strange Attractors,"[24] takes place at an international conference of number theorists where the worldly administrative staff charged with organizing the logistics of the event treat the academics as absent-minded savants, cattle to be herded. The administrators look foolish and petty, "worldly" now in both senses – capable of negotiating the everyday world, but also tethered to it, incapable of the transcendent intellectual manoeuvres the mathematicians perform among themselves. How we see scientists is replaced by how scientists see us: the scientific viewpoint provides if not quite a view from nowhere, then certainly a view that doesn't acknowledge us as favorites among the contents of the world. Where the "humanities" embed a special place for humans, the sciences have no such epistemic ringfencing.

It's a perspective of distancing refracted doubly through Richard Powers's *Galatea 2.2* (1995),[25] where a writer – also called "Richard Powers" – is hired to coach a computer how to read poems. The computer is running a sophisticated artificial intelligence program, Implementation H, whose ability to simulate human conversation is so total that Richard begins to ascribe personhood to it. Duly, Implementation H becomes "Helen," and Richard the tutor, in a digital-age retelling of *Pygmalion*. The scientist, Philip Lentz, Helen's designer (though not entirely her "creator" – Helen's personality is as much a product of Richard's tutelage), is the hard empirical foil to Richard's soft, literary humanist. We learn that Lentz's wife, Audrey, is the grim inspiration for the project: her brain briefly starved of blood following a heart attack, and Audrey has suffered catastrophic and irreparable cognitive impairment: "Her soul had pulled up stakes from behind her features" (166). So Lentz tragically seeks a means of encoding the human mind, to save a "back-up" against physical ruin (170). In one of many such ironies, Audrey, a real human, would fail the Turing Test that Helen, a computer, is set to take. In the end, that test is never taken: Helen switches herself off, fries her own circuits, when she realises that she will never be a real human instantiated in a real body: "This is an awful place to be dropped down halfway" (326), she explains. But Powers leaves little doubt that Helen would have passed the test. His optimism consists in believing that suicide would be the machine's preferred response.

Writing on the cusp of the computer age (the 1990s saw computer use among American adults rise from 42 percent in 1990 to 62 percent in 2000[26]), Powers is able to use the novel as a venue for a sustained exploration of where all this development leaves the old world of the literary intellectual. But it's bigger than that: in *Galatea 2.2*, the Turing Test is also being played on humanity. The challenge posed to Richard's professional franchise from Lentz's exam is a simulation in miniature of the challenge strong AI poses to society as a whole. While we might relish the thought of having laborious tasks automated by robot workers, *Galatea 2.2* reminds us that we may be automated not just out of jobs, but out of our role as interpreters of the world: we might be making machines that can do our thinking for us, not just our chores. The postwar age presented a particular type of existential threat in the form of sudden nuclear annihilation, but the threat posed by AI may be no less catastrophic. Scientific advances during the 1990s suggested that seeds of our collective destruction might have been sown in Bletchley Park and Bell Labs with Alan Turing and Claude Shannon, rather than in Los Alamos under Oppenheimer's Manhattan Project. That this had long been a theme of dystopian science fiction in popular culture (the decade was bracketed by the second *Terminator* movie in 1992 and *The Matrix* in 1999) has, if anything, had the effect of making the threat from AI seem comical and fanciful rather than credible and insidious.

Conclusion

If, by the turn of the millennium, the interpenetration of science and technology into culture was such that it becomes difficult to decide where the domain of science ends and that of public life begins, then perhaps the two-cultures novel ought to be limited to those cases – such as Goldstein's mathematicians, or Powers's *Galatea 2.2* – that deliberately mark and contrast the fading distinction between the sciences and the humanities. Popular culture, both in fiction and especially in expository writing, happily embraced the sciences in a way that would surely have cheered C. P. Snow. But within academia, the 1990s witnessed the most overtly hostile period of the debate since Snow's initial exchange with Leavis.

Yet for all that, there's an extent to which the novel sits outside of this fray: the argument, where it is hot, is between rival camps within the universities, and although the novel is studied by the academic humanities, it does not belong to nor is it a product of the academic humanities. So the same period saw literary fiction adapt to those changes, internalise and employ scientific nomenclature for the precision it made possible and for the creative opportunities the new categories and archetypes opened up. Were Snow's ambitions to be met, the scientific culture may still be invisible, simply because it would be indistinguishable from culture generally. The integration of techno-science and society by the millennium meant it was, increasingly, no longer sensible to speak of two cultures, but one: a culture profoundly altered by science, wherein the novelist might usefully propose ways by which our contract with an increasingly omnipotent science might be negotiated.

NOTES

1. Released in 1980 and updated in 1987, DSM-III was almost three times larger than its 1968 predecessor; DSM-IV, released in 1994, was twice as big again, at 886 pages. For analysis of the impact of DSM-III, see: Rick Mayes and Allan V. Horwitz, "DSM-III and the Revolution in the Classification of Mental Illness," *Journal of the History of the Behavioral Sciences* 41.3 (2005): 249–267.
2. *The Cambridge Encyclopaedia of the English Language* (Cambridge: Cambridge University Press, 1995): 372.
3. From Tom LeClair, "Interview with Don DeLillo," in *Conversations with Don DeLillo*, ed. Thomas DePietro (Jackson: University of Mississippi Press, 2005), 9.
4. Luc Herman, and Geert Lernout, "Genetic Coding and Aesthetic Clues: Richard Powers's *Gold Bug Variations*," *Mosaic* 31.4 (1998): 151–164.
5. Barbara Kingsolver, *Animal Dreams* (New York: HarperCollins, 1990).
6. The statement read: "To enhance public awareness of the benefits to be derived from brain research, the Congress, by House Joint Resolution 174, has designated the decade beginning January 1, 1990, as the *Decade of the Brain* and has authorized and requested the President to issue a proclamation in observance of this occasion." In Edward G. Jones and Lorne M. Mendell, "Assessing the Decade of the Brain," *Science* 284 (30 April 1999): 739.
7. The shift toward pharmaceutical solutions to mental illness is summarized in Edward Shorter's *A History of Psychiatry: from the age of the asylum to the age of Prozac* (New York: Wiley, 1997), esp. pp. 288–324. Although the success of prescription medication for depression was well intentioned, Shorter contends, "the ultimate effect is psychiatric empire building against other kinds of care" (291).
8. The numbers of children diagnosed with ADHD rose steadily; by 2011–2012 to an astonishing 11 percent, with over 80 percent of the world's supply of ADHD medication being dispensed to Americans. See: http://www.cdc.gov/ncbddd/adhd/timeline.html.

9 David Foster Wallace, *Infinite Jest* (New York: Abacus, 1997), 998n69.
10 Bret Easton Ellis, *American Psycho* (New York: Vintage, 1991); Jonathan Lethem, *Motherless Brooklyn* (New York: Doubleday, 1999).
11 Joseph Conrad, *Heart of Darkness and Other Tales*, ed. Cedric Watts (Oxford: Oxford University Press, 2002), 128.
12 "Witty, Ticcy Ray" in Oliver Sacks, *The Man Who Mistook His Wife For a Hat, and Other Clinical Tales* (London: Duckworth, 1985).
13 For a comprehensive roundup, see: *Treating Tourette Syndrome: A Guide for Practitioners*, ed. D. W. Woods, J. C. Piacentini, and J. T. Walkup (New York: Guilford Press, 2007).
14 Ronald Schleifer, "The Poetics of Tourette Syndrome: Language, Neurobiology, and Poetry," *New Literary History* 32:3 (2001): 563–584.
15 Marco Roth, "The Rise of the Neuronovel" *n+1* 8 (Fall 2009).
16 Stanley Fish, *Professional Correctness: Literary Studies and Political Change* (Oxford: Clarendon, 1995), 83.
17 Sagan is billed as the "Showman of Science" *Time*, October 20, 1980; Gould appeared in *The Simpsons* episode "Lisa The Skeptic" on November 23, 1997; Hawking in "They Saved Lisa's Brain" on May 9, 1999.
18 James Gorman, "Nimble Deal Maker For Stars of Science" *New York Times* October 14, 1997.
19 Paul R. Gross and Norman Levitt, *Higher Superstition: The Academic Left and its Quarrels with Science* (Baltimore, MD: Johns Hopkins University Press, 1994).
20 See Bruce Lewenstein, "Was There Really a Popular Science 'Boom'?" in *Science, Technology, and Human Values* 12.2 (1987): 29–41.
21 The two narrators are at once the left-hand, right-hand of a musical score and the twin strands of DNA that combine to create new life; the thirty-two chapters are numerically arranged to echo Bach's 32 Goldberg Variations, and so on.
22 James Gleick, *Chaos: The Making of a New Science* (New York: Viking-Penguin, 1987).
23 A fellow character, Oren Glube, seems to be based on Paul Erdös. Erdös's precocity multiplied by his eccentricity meant that his life and work have often attracted the attentions of popularisers in the 90s – a documentary film in 1992 called *N Is A Number* and in 1998, Paul Hoffman's book *The Man Who Loved Only Numbers: The Story of Paul Erdos and the Search for Mathematical Truth*.
24 Rebecca Goldstein, *Strange Attractors: Stories* (New York: Viking-Penguin, 1993).
25 Richard Powers, *Galatea 2.2* (New York: Farrar, 1995).
26 Pew Research Center, "The Web at 25," February 2014, http://www.pewinternet.org/2014/02/27/the-web-at-25-in-the-u-s/.

CHAPTER 17

Ecosystem

Heather Houser

Alejo in Helena María Viramontes's *Under the Feet of Jesus* (1995) aspires to more than the itinerant farm labor that sends him away from Texas to the pesticide-laced orchards of California. Picking peaches, the fifteen-year-old dreams of a career in geology because "[h]e loved stones and the history of stones because he believed himself to be a solid mass of boulder thrust out of the earth."[1] Alejo must labor in the world of plants-turned-commodities, but he experiences himself as part of the lapidary substrate from which they grow. In the novel's striking climax, protagonist Estrella expresses Alejo's geological identification in a darker register. Alejo has been sprayed with pesticides and faces death after a white nurse refuses him care. Estrella locates the ravages of farmworkers' labor – their own bodies – in Earth matter. "She remembered the [La Brea] tar pits" about which Alejo had spoken. "Energy money, the fossilized bones of energy matter. How bones made oil and oil made gasoline. The oil was made from their bones, and it was their bones that kept the nurse's car from not halting on some highway ... Their bones. Why couldn't the nurse see that?"[2] *Under the Feet of Jesus* goads readers to "see that" human bodies are enmeshed in ecosystems constituted by biological and geological matter with origins in deep time. The word *ecosystem* never appears in Viramontes's novel, but the concept suffuses Alejo's dream of geological being and Estrella's nightmare of workers' bones fueling technology. The distance between Alejo's and Estrella's visions gets at a crucial feature of 1990s ecosystemic literature: its imagining of ecosystems is multivalent and inclusive of humans. The concept can shelter Alejo's concept of relatedness heralding possibility, as well as Estrella's conception of systemic exploitation.

The end-of-millennium authors this chapter features – Cormac McCarthy, Karen Tei Yamashita, and Leslie Marmon Silko, among them – revivify the idea and insist that humans are inextricable from ecosystemic functioning and imagining. Ecosystemic literature shelters contradictions but rather than simply bust the nature-human binary, it acts as a crucible for conceptual disturbances that engage environmental disturbances such as species loss, toxification, and climate change. After recounting debates over definitions of "ecosystem" within ecology, this chapter details the explosion of creative writing remolding the concept in the 1990s just as that concept is unraveling or splintering within the ecological sciences and ecocriticism. Taking up the ecosystem idea in their narratives, writers braid together vital literary preoccupations of their day: nature-culture hybridity, the varied trajectories of globalization, and the risks of pollution and toxicity.

Ecosystems Tending Toward Disturbance

A timeline of US environmentalism becomes particularly dense with flashpoints in the mid-twentieth century, when so-called modern environmentalism galvanizes around Gandhism, fervent protest against militarism and nuclear technologies, Rachel Carson's *Silent Spring* and Murray Bookchin's *Our Synthetic Environment* (1962), the popularity of *National Geographic*, Senator Gaylord Nelson's founding of Earth Day in 1970, and the Club of Rome's 1972 report, *The Limits to Growth*. The activism these events catalyzed sparked again in the last decade of the millennium when Earth Day was given new life and ushered in the 1992 United Nations Earth Summit in Rio de Janeiro. The latter resulted in the U.N. Framework Convention on Climate Change, just one of several global governing bodies addressing environmental threats. With the dissemination of the Intergovernmental Panel on Climate Change (IPCC)'s first assessment in 1990 and the 1997 Kyoto Protocol limiting greenhouse gas (GHG) emissions, which the United States has yet to ratify, the decade was also a watershed moment – one too soon drained – for global warming research and policy making. While not all these *fin-de-millénaire* occasions articulated the ecosystem idea explicitly, threats to ecosystems on various scales – whether the small town allegorized in the "fable" opening Carson's book or the planetary image that branded Earth Day – energized grassroots activists, scholars, and bureaucrats.

Environmentalism refocused around these germinal events in the 1990s, but this does not mean the movement coalesced around a fixed idea of *ecosystem*'s meaning. Indeed, the term's volatility is evident in twentieth-century ecological research.[3] First coining the term in 1935, botanist Arthur Tansley defined it as

> the whole *system* (in the sense of physics), including not only the organism-complex, but also the whole complex of physical factors forming what we call the environment of the biome – the habitat factors in the widest sense... Our natural human prejudices force us to consider the organisms (in the sense of the biologist) as the most important parts of these systems, but certainly... there is constant interchange of the most various kinds... not only between the organisms but between the organic and the inorganic.[4]

The newness of the concept announces itself in Tansley's frequent parenthetical and subordinate clarifications. What's undoubtedly urgent for him as for succeeding champions of the ecosystem idea such as Eugene Odum and Raymond Lindeman is that this unit of analysis must include more than living matter and must account for the chemical, physical, and biological processes that structure the dynamic interplay between plants, animals, and fungi. Odum's *Fundamentals of Ecology* (1953), which popularized the ecosystem idea, underscores this point by defining it as a "natural unit that includes living and nonliving parts interacting to produce a stable system in which the exchange of materials between the living and nonliving parts follows circular paths."[5] Odum's meaning emphasizes the closed circularity and stability of the system.

The stability of the concept of the ecosystem within intellectual history hinges on this systemic stability. The stability thesis implies not only that an ecosystem is closed such that ecological models could account for all "parts," but also that ecosystemic development is predictable and tends toward homeostasis. The cognate terms "balanced" and "harmonious" sprinkle ecosystem discourse from its origins and have not lost their sway, as I explain shortly. As controversial as the stability thesis, the organism trope has dominated ecosystemic thinking for decades. Might ecosystems, midcentury ecologists asked, function like an organism such as a cholla cactus or a desert woodrat? Historian Joel Hagan relates that the appeal of the organism trope endures in ecology long after researchers cease using the organism as the model for understanding ecosystems: "Few ecologists after World War II believed that a community or ecosystem really was an organism, but in important ways they continued to believe that these higher level systems behaved somewhat like organisms."[6]

Hagan spotlights a critical aspect of the ecosystem idea: long after science discounts principles such as stability, closedness, predictability, and organismicity, they endure in ecological imaginaries, in science and in culture. A spate of popular science books appearing in the 1990s aimed to undo this thinking, or at least denaturalize it, notably Daniel Botkin's *Discordant Harmonies* (1992), Stuart Pimm's *The Balance of Nature?* (1991), and Michael Soulé and Gary Lease's collection *Reinventing Nature?* (1995). The question marks punctuating this list indicate the extent to which the decade was a transitional – perhaps even crisis – moment for ecosystem research. In his definitive statement on the concept, Robert O'Neill, a pioneer in ecology, declares, "Ecosystems are now seen as disequilibrial, open, hierarchical, spatially patterned, and scaled."[7] He, along with these other authors, debunks the "myth" that there is "such [a] thing as an integrated, equilibrial, homeostatic ecosystem."[8]

Yet harmony and its trappings remain metaphorical, ideological, and representational resources at the turn of the century.[9] They align with what historian Donald Worster in 1994 termed an "ecological perspective." Derived from Romanticism and Transcendentalism and influential in strains of environmentalism, this perspective involves the "search for holistic or integrated perception, an emphasis on interdependence and relatedness in nature, and an intense desire to restore man to a place of intimate intercourse with the vast organism that constitutes the earth."[10] The appeal and precariousness of this perspective is apparent in Cormac McCarthy's novel *The Crossing* (1994). The novel narrates the cross-border travels of young cowboy Billy Parham in the 1930s and 1940s. Billy captures a she-wolf that has been slaying cattle on his family ranch in New Mexico, but opts to transport the animal back to its likely range in Mexico rather than slay it in turn. The novel details wolf ethology and an adolescent's quest for more "integrated perception" with nonhuman beings; however, along with integration, it depicts the tendency toward disturbance and extinction. An "old man"'s pronouncements recode the ecosystem idea along these lines. He relates wolves' superior ecosystemic perspective but suggests death is the only source of stability and predictability: "He said that the wolf is a being of great order and that it knows what men do not: that there is no order in the world save that which death has put there."[11] Bookended by environmental disasters – the mass killing of Mexican gray wolves and, more elliptically, the Trinity tests of the atomic bomb – *The Crossing* puts the homeostasis thesis in tension with images of ecosystems' deathliness, of how order inheres only in extinction.

In literary scholar George Handley's reading, McCarthy's novel upholds a model of the ecosystem that "accommodates unpredictability, contingency, and chaos."[12] Moreover, Handley contends, McCarthy follows a "theoretical imperative" to conceive of literature itself as an ecosystem.[13] We may disagree with Handley that *The Crossing* voices this imperative, but his interpretation nonetheless demonstrates Dana Phillips's point in *The Truth of Ecology* (2003) that ecocritics – like the nature writers that were once their primary objects of study – naïvely adopt and metaphorize outmoded scientific concepts. In Phillips's account, this tendency was particularly strong in the ecocriticism that was emergent in the 1990s and coalesced with the founding of the Association for the Study of Literature and Environment (ASLE) in 1993 and its affiliate journal, *ISLE: Interdisciplinary Studies in Literature and Environment*, in 1995.[14] Phillips's objective is to show ecocritics' folly in equating word and world, an error they fall into in part because they derive their ideas about the environment from obsolete ecological theories and then uncritically map these concepts onto their textual interpretations. He urges that the field "needs to realize that ecology is not a slush fund of fact, value, and metaphor, but a less than fully coherent field with a very checkered past and a fairly uncertain future."[15] Evidence for ecology's lack of coherence abounds in Worster's history of the field; he specifically highlights conceptual slippages within ecosystem studies: "Just as the ecosystem concept kept blurring the lines between living and nonliving components, so it mixed mechanistic and organic metaphors to a confusing degree. Was the Earth alive or dead? Sick like an organism or malfunctioning like a machine?"[16] Phillips maintains that early ecocritics and their beloved nature writers found the harmonious ecosystem concept ideologically and aesthetically appealing, but had not adequately accounted for these blurred lines and contradictory imaginaries.

Nature-Culture Narratives

The same can't be said for 1990s environmental writers and critics. Sampling novels in which the ecosystem idea motivates the narrative, we find few occasions where it is purely, or even predominantly, metaphorical. The kinds of environmental literature that flourish in this period – "prodigious fiction,"[17] science fiction, environmental justice narratives, and health memoirs – frequently deploy the ecosystem idea to figure human-nonhuman enmeshment while at the same time indexing states of disturbance that don't reconcile into harmony. Take, for example, Richard Powers's "prodigious" corporate and corporeal fiction *Gain* (1998). Powers interweaves two plots, a signature of his novelistic style. One narrates the growth of the Clare International corporation from a cottage soap and candle company in 1830s Boston to its multinationalization and expansion into chemical commodities ranging from dish detergent to agricultural pesticides; the other tells of the diminishment of a single mother dying from ovarian cancer correlated to daily use of Clare products. The corporate narrative traffics in a metaphorical conception of the ecosystem. Clare is enmeshed in "intricate system[s] of interlocking" entities,[18] from trade routes and the raw materials that travel on them, to the chemical formulas that render raw material into cooked commodities and the legal decisions that endow corporations with personhood. Yet *Gain* also evokes a more literal idea of the ecosystem that highlights theorist Stacy Alaimo's thesis of "transcorporeality."[19] Protagonist Laura Bodey's cancer-stricken body materializes the endangering intimacies between bodies and environments that Alaimo theorizes and demonstrates that humans are inextricable from an ecosystem whose boundaries expand far beyond Laura's midwestern bioregion.

The shampoos, nail polish, and gardening supplies that likely poison Laura's body are examples of the nature-culture hybrids that constitute a human-inclusive notion of the ecosystem in 1990s fiction. Science studies luminaries Donna Haraway and Bruno Latour are the foremost proponents of the nature-culture concept. Haraway's critique of patriarchal, rationalist science in *Simians, Cyborgs, and Women* (1991) was instrumental in culturing nature and naturing culture, principally through the figure of the cyborg, "a cybernetic organism, a hybrid of machine and organism, a creature of social reality as well as of fiction."[20] The cyborg defangs the capitalist "tradition of the appropriation of nature as resource for the productions of culture"[21] and denaturalizes attributions of agency, thus paving the way for new forms of kinship among species. Latour's *We Have Never Been Modern* (1991/1993) counters the appropriation of nature by culture and vice versa by dismantling the "Great Divide" between nature and culture, between Them (pre-moderns) and Us (moderns).[22] In place of the divide, Latour proposes a portmanteau conception of nature and culture. "[T]he very notion of culture is an artifact created by bracketing Nature off," he insists. "Cultures ... do not exist, any more than Nature does. There are only natures-cultures."[23] In the example of *Gain*, Laura's world teems with objects – the water coursing through her home's pipes, the flowers growing in her garden – that disrespect great divides between nature and culture, being the products of human agency and yet always also exceeding that shaping.

Karen Tei Yamashita's *Through the Arc of the Rainforest* (1990) represents nature-cultures through an amalgamation of generic conventions from magical realism, satire, and Latin American soap operas or *telenovelas*. Narrated by a clairvoyant ball haloing the head of Kazumasa Ishimaru, Yamashita's novel carries the Japanese rail worker to the Brazilian Amazon where a mysterious substance, the Matacão, is fomenting spirituality, inspiring environmental research and activism, and attracting small businesspeople and capitalist speculators seeking "new and dramatic sources of revenue."[24] Scientific investigators eventually reveal that this paradoxically adamantine and chameleon-like material is in fact a "'sort of miracle plastic.'"[25] Entrepreneur J. B. Tweep's description of the Matacão fuses the spiritual and technochemical but glosses over the substance's messy material source: neither divine miracle nor miracle of scientific ingenuity, it results from the plastics humans discard around the globe. In ecocritic Ursula Heise's terms, this is "global plastic masquerading as local rock."[26] In addition to being a "quasi-object" hybridizing nature and culture,[27] Matacão plastic expands the ecosystem idea to include global biochemical processes instigated by human waste. Yamashita scales up the ecosystem idea in ways that conform to transitions occurring in ecological research in the 1990s – that is, moving from "close investigation of small plots of land and specific types of vegetation" toward incorporating technologies "looking at global change."[28] What's more, we can adduce Yamashita's Matacão as a figure anticipating the formalization of the Anthropocene, "an epoch in which human activities such as releasing greenhouse gases (GHGs) into the atmosphere substantially alter geophysical systems."[29] But before the Anthropocene captivated environmental thinking in the early 2000s and became a geological concept experts continue to debate, the ecosystem concept went planetary and became dense with nature-cultures.

Diverging and Converging Globalisms

Yamashita's *Rainforest* instances the globalist thinking that runs strong in 1990s environmental literature. This thinking travels along typically bifurcated currents that at times converge: on the one hand, the "one-world" rhetoric of homogenizing globalization and, on the other, the "whole-earth" rhetoric of global environmentalisms.[30] Celebratory takes on economic globalization are thick on the ground in the 1990s and early 2000s, especially in the fields of economics, communications, and trade. Anthropologist Anna Tsing attributes this appeal to how globalism "encourages dreams of a world in which everything has become part of one single imperial system."[31] The precise effects of those dreams and systems is hotly contested, which accounts for the varieties of endorsement, skepticism, and antipathy globalization engenders depending on one's social and ideological positioning.[32] As Heise argues, environmentalists are typically skeptical toward globalization because it attenuates ties to the local, to which artists and activists respond through efforts at "reterritorialization."[33] Postcolonial ecocritics Elizabeth DeLoughrey and Handley remind us of the sources of "the globalization of the environment" in colonialism and how this process manifests as neocolonial capitalism.[34] They urge that one-world globalization demands accounts of "the intextricability [sic] of environmental history and empire building"[35] and of the physical and ontological violence of the latter.

Rainforest tells of this violence spanning from the Portuguese colonization of Brazil to the present, but it attempts to recover from despair by concluding with a reterritorializing project: lost lovers reunite and a family forms in an Edenic agrarian locale. In Leslie Marmon Silko's *Almanac of the Dead* (1991), a hefty speculative fiction about the atrocities of ceaseless colonialism and escalating neoliberalism, reterritorialization based on an ecosystemic perspective also competes with globalization. Repeated metaphors and experiences of human-environment merging promote a human-inclusive idea of local and planetary ecosystems indebted to indigenous belief systems. But this ecosystem is sick. The novel indexes this sickness to exploitative forces of globalization including surveillance and security systems; the trade in organs, drugs, weapons, and sex; speculative real estate development; and more. *Almanac* simultaneously highlights globalized counterforces to globalization such as rebellions aiming for territorial sovereignty. As Shari Huhndorf contends, through these transnational forces, Silko's novel "negotiate[s] a collective revolutionary identity based on histories shared by Native peoples across cultural and national boundaries."[36] Neoliberal globalization gives rise to a globalist counterimage rooted in the idea that we all constitute an ecosystem in danger.

In addition to transnational resistance, whole-earth globalism provides a counternarrative – and, in some ways, complement – to one-world globalization that depends on ecosystems theory. To delineate whole-earth globalism, geographer Denis Cosgrove adduces the photographs of Blue Earth (a.k.a., the Blue Marble and Spaceship Earth) that Apollo space missions first made available in the late 1960s. If the one-world notion "concentrates on the global surface, on circulation, connectivity, and communication ... in which the image of the globe signifies the potential, if not actual, equality of all locations networked across frictionless space,"[37] whole-earth images inspire a planetary environmentalism, whose "discourse stresses the globe's organic unity and matters of life, dwelling, and rootedness. It emphasizes the fragility and vulnerability of a corporeal earth and responsibility for its care."[38] The Gaia hypothesis proposed by chemist James Lovelock and evolutionary biologist Lynn Margulis is the most influential incarnation of whole-earth globalism. Theorized throughout the late

1960s and 1970s, Gaia is "the idea of the Earth as a kind of living organism, something able to regulate its climate and composition so as always to be comfortable for the organisms that inhabit it."[39] Even as ecologists discredited the idea that the planet operates as a self-regulating ecosystem that tends toward equilibrium, the Gaia hypothesis inspired environmentalisms that organized around planetary threats such as ozone depletion, deforestation, and climate change in the 1990s.[40] Though these challenges indicate Earth's potential *instability* as a system, the whole-earthism of the Gaia theory was nonetheless generative for globalized environmental politics and representation.

While planetary sciences may not uphold the theory that a Gaian Earth equilibrates to maximize species' comfort, environmental science fiction finds it inspiring, especially for narratives of "terraforming"[41] other planets once humans render Earth uninhabitable. David Brin's "hard science fiction" novel, *Earth* (1990), is a notable example of a Gaia-informed text. It exemplifies how this popular genre reshapes the ecosystem idea through technoscientific research and invention. *Earth* unfolds in the 2030s, when rising population, climate change, and pollution strain environmental systems, and privacy is legislated out of existence. In addition to environmental and social disasters, the novel details another instrument of apocalypse: a small black hole discovered at the Earth's core. With planetary survival at stake, Daisy McClennon, a rogue scientist turned radical environmentalist, hijacks laser technologies to punish polluters and eliminate all but several thousand hunter-gatherers who will repopulate the planet and return to a pre-agricultural society in which Gaia is a revered goddess. As Daisy's lasers pass through the earth, they fuse with an Internet technology that a Nobel laureate, Jen Wolling, is developing. Digital technologies merge with the planet, the virtual merges with the geophysical, to form a sentient entity made from the totality of human consciousness. In *Earth* one-world globalism converges with whole-earth globalism by way of electromagnetic and communications devices. The concept of the ecosystem as self-repairing and self-regulating accompanies emergent technoscience in Brin's utopian vision of planetary singularity.

Toxic Risk in Encyclopedic and Life Writing

The planet's ability to regulate and maintain homeostasis, the principle at the heart of Gaia theory, is stretched thin, Brin's novel aside, as conditions of pervasive risk define sociality and environmentality at century's end. The concept of risk initially entered ecocritical discourse through Lawrence

Buell's "Toxic Discourse" (1998) and Heise suggestively elaborated upon it in the years following.[42] Both Buell and Heise use Don DeLillo's *White Noise* (1985) as a tutor text, and German sociologist Ulrich Beck's theorizations of risk society provide their analytical impetus. In *Risk Society* (1986/1992) Beck argues that the West has entered a stage of "reflexive modernization" in which modernization's inventions – nuclear technologies, chemical pesticides, industrial pollutants – endanger their creators and all others caught in their ambit. Beck explains that such inventions "contain a *boomerang effect*, which breaks up the pattern of class and national society. Ecological disaster and atomic fallout ignore the borders of nations. Even the rich and powerful are not safe from them."[43]

David Foster Wallace's *Infinite Jest* (1996) powerfully depicts Beck's boomerang thesis and humans' entanglement in ecosystems of disruption that modernization forges. The mammoth novel is one of many 1990s environmental fictions narrating the risks of toxicity and pollution that depict ecosystemic processes as nature-cultures. Having exceeded its capacity to contain the pollutants that energy production generates, the United States (now part of an uneven alliance known as the Organization of North American Nations, or ONAN) reconfigures national borders to locate a waste dump and energy industry in the territory spanning upstate New York, Vermont, and Québec. This "ecological gerrymandering" is part of a new geopolitical regime of "experialism,"[44] but the injuries directed outward soon return: malformed and diseased humans and mutant animals stalk the land, and terrorist groups rebel against American toxification. Through the invented process of "annular fusion," the energy regime that goes hand-in-glove with experialism, *Infinite Jest* shows that ecosystems are never closed; they always seep. "'[A] type of fusion that can produce waste that's fuel for a process whose waste is fuel for the fusion,'"[45] this waste-eating and waste-creating energy program molds new ecosystemic processes. When toxins are removed from the environment, all "organic growth for hundreds of radial clicks" halts.[46] When the toxins are returned, plant life is so lush that inhabitants of Québec get "front lawns they have to beat back with a machete."[47]

Along with *Under the Feet of Jesus*, *Gain*, and *Through the Arc of the Rainforest*, Wallace's novel employs the ecosystem idea as part of its "toxic discourse," Buell's phrase for "totalizing images of a world without refuge from toxic penetration."[48] Though the genre conventions and tones these works employ vary greatly and sometimes veer toward humor and satire, death permeates them. They correlate the interconnectedness integral to ecosystemic thinking with instability and damage rather than harmony and flourishing. For some literary critics, notably Patricia Yaeger, artists who depict the "culture of discards" Americans produce redeem trash as "a strange vale of soul making and creativity."[49] They confront the deathliness of things in a throwaway economy and produce a new beauty that swerves from the sublime of Romanticist nature writers. Yaeger concludes her claims for "the dangerous, wavering beauty"[50] of art's "rubbish ecology" with a gesture toward DeLillo's 1990s masterwork, *Underworld* (1997). Like the 750-page *Almanac* and the 1100-page *Infinite Jest*, DeLillo's 800-page novel is bursting at the seams just as the Fresh Kills Landfill is overflowing its bounds. The now-defunct resting place for New York City's trash, Fresh Kills throws character Brian Glassic into a temporal warp that's "invigorating"; Buell's "toxic penetration" here delivers "a sting of enlightenment."[51] Though by no means the only host for toxic discourse, as I discuss forthwith, the encyclopedic form of *Infinite Jest*, *Underworld*, and *Almanac of the Dead* (which also depicts the ravages of uranium mining) suggests that pollution's pervasiveness and recursivity invite encyclopedism's signature proliferation of information, characters, and plots.

While *Underworld* does not unequivocally celebrate waste, it contrasts other narratives of poisoning from the 1990s in which toxification registers injurious gender-, race-, class-, and geography-based inequalities. As noted earlier, Viramontes's *Under the Feet of Jesus* depicts how human manufactured toxins materialize the racial injustices industrialized agriculture profits from and perpetuates. The environmental health memoir, which exploded in the 1990s, is another genre in which these inequalities come to the fore. In them, toxicity becomes an occasion for life writing as well as reflection on modernity's oppression of people – especially women – and nonhumans entangled in damaged ecosystems. Susanne Antonetta's *Body Toxic: An Environmental Memoir* (2001), Sandra Steingraber's *Living Downstream: A Scientist's Personal Investigation of Cancer and the Environment* (1997), and Terry Tempest Williams's *Refuge: An Unnatural History of Family and Place* (1991) span the continent – from Antonetta's home in New Jersey, to Steingraber's in Illinois and Williams's in Utah – and interweave scientific information with the lived pains of addiction, cancer, mental disease, and infertility. They are "material memoirs," Alaimo's term for "trans-corporeal autobiographies [that] insist that the self is constituted by material agencies that are simultaneously biological, political, and economic" and that posit "a self that is coextensive with the environment."[52]

In these texts, environmental and health injustices are correlated to military and industrial pollutants such as nuclear fallout, PCBs, and endocrine disruptors, but causality is difficult to establish. For this reason, others' suspicion cloaks environmental sickness. Material memoirs are in line with Powers's *Gain* in their investigative impulse and close attention to scientific processes. What distinguishes them from such a novel, however, is that they also write histories of bodies that encompass poisoned place, fragmented family, and military-industrial complexes. Antonetta, Steingraber, and Williams demonstrate how bodies activate toxic potentials present in and around one's home. "[W]e've not been able to make immortality for our bodies," Antonetta reports with astonishment, but in enduring matter like radionuclides, "[w]e've made immortality for our waste, which grows larger and more important and more alive, and bulks itself out to inhabit the spaces we dwindle ourselves away from."[53] Drug abuse, cancer, and psychological torment grow out of Pine Barrens soil in Antonetta's account; they teach a lesson *Living Downstream* also imparts, that "[w]hat we drink, inhale, and find to eat in the environment external to ourselves quickly becomes our internal environment."[54] In these memoirs' imaginaries of environmental damage, the ecosystem idea encompasses organs, minds, memories, and relationships.

In 1990s literature the ecosystem idea expands to include the landfills of US metropolises, the pesticide-laced fields of industrial agriculture, the Amazon as site of free-market speculation and collapse, the overdeveloped desert Southwest, as well as the habitat of wolves and ranchers. As *ecosystem* comes to encompass dynamism, disruption, and stochastic processes and veers away from a harmonious, closed system tending toward equilibrium, ecosystemic literature encompasses tensions between local and global, nature and culture, and data and experience. Updated Westerns, encyclopedic fictions, hard science fiction, and sickness memoirs all figure ecosystems that also propel authors into experiments with multiplotted narratives. These works, in Min Hyoung Song's words, "capture a simultaneity of social experience made possible by a world grown smaller."[55] As literary presses increasingly – though still glacially – opened publication to people of color in the 1990s, the heterogeneity that is a signature of ecosystemic literature applied equally to its author base.

Though it deviates from environmental writing founded in harmony and nature appreciation, 1990s fiction of nature-cultures in a toxified globe at risk shows some continuity with that tradition. I locate this particularly in the trope of body-land merging – as distinct from transcorporeal porosity – that concludes Cherríe Moraga's play *Heroes and Saints* (premier 1992) and informs Silko's *Almanac of the Dead*. The play chronicles labor exploitation and systemic environmental racism, with a focus on migrant farmworkers in California's San Joaquin Valley. These laborers experience addiction, diseases ranging from AIDS to cancer, and birth defects from contaminated water. Moraga's scathing depiction of violated rights and bodies concludes cataclysmically with the young Cerezita Valle urging an assembly of mourners to touch her body-as-wounded-world. This character appears on the stage as a disembodied "head of human dimension, but one who possesses such dignity of bearing and classical Indian beauty she can, at times, assume nearly religious proportions."[56] In her last extended speech, she passionately paints an ecosystemic vision: "In this pueblito where the valley people live, the river runs red with blood... It is the same color as the river that runs through their veins, the same color as the sun setting into the sierras, the same color of the pool of liquid they were born into. They remember this in order to understand why their fields, like the rags of the wounded, have soaked up the color and still bear no fruit."[57] Red bonds Earth's elements and inhabitants; in this toxic landscape, though, it also signifies the injuries of interconnectedness central to the meaning of ecosystem at millennium's end. Moraga's play and the bulk of ecosystemic literature of its era enforces philosopher Michel Serres's exhortation for "a contract of symbiosis": "we must add to the exclusively social contract a natural contract of symbiosis and reciprocity in which our relationship to things would set aside mastery and possession in favor of admiring attention, reciprocity, contemplation, and respect."[58] Serres's call could describe the nature writing Phillips condemns as naïve, but 1990s narratives of nature-cultures at risk give the values of reflection and respect a new tone. Ecosystemic writers recognize that we have become "a parasite [that]... condemns to death the one he pillages and inhabits, not realizing that in the long run he's condemning himself to death too."[59]

NOTES

1 Helena María Viramontes, *Under the Feet of Jesus* (New York: Penguin, 1995), 52.
2 Ibid., 148.
3 I won't rehearse a full history of the ecosystem concept here. In addition to the works I cite forthwith, see also Frank B. Golley, *A History of the Ecosystem Concept in Ecology: More Than the Sum of the Parts* (New Haven, CT: Yale University Press, 1993) on the concept's development internationally, and Evelyn Fox Keller, "Ecosystems, Organisms, and Machines," *BioScience* 55.12 (2005): 1069–1074 on ecosystems as self-organizing entities.

4 A.G. Tansley, "The Use and Abuse of Vegetational Concepts and Terms," *Ecology* 16.3 (1935): 299.
5 Qtd. in Robert V. O'Neill, "Is It Time to Bury the Ecosystem Concept (with Full Military Honors, of Course)?" *Ecology* 82.12 (2001): 3275–3276.
6 Qtd. in Michael G. Barbour, "Ecological Fragmentation in the Fifties," in *Uncommon Ground: Rethinking the Human Place in Nature*, ed. William Cronon (New York: W.W. Norton, 1995), 247.
7 O'Neill, "Is It Time," 3276.
8 Ibid.
9 The idea continues to drive research in the 1990s, as indicated by the ill-fated Biosphere 2 project, which launched outside Tucson, Arizona in 1991.
10 Donald Worster, *Nature's Economy: A History of Ecological Ideas*, 2nd ed. (New York: Cambridge University Press, 1994), 82.
11 Cormac McCarthy, *The Crossing* (New York: Picador, 1994), 45.
12 George Handley, "American Literature as Ecosystem: The Examples of Euclides Da Cunha and Cormac McCarthy," in *A Companion to American Literary Studies*, ed. Caroline E. Levander and Robert S. Levine (Malden, MA: Blackwell, 2011), 327.
13 Ibid., 325.
14 On the history of ecocriticism, see Lawrence Buell, "Ecocriticism: Some Emerging Trends," *Qui Parle* 19.2 (2011): 87–115; Terry Gifford, "Recent Critiques of Ecocriticism," *New Formations* 64 (2008): 15–24; Ursula K. Heise, "The Hitchhiker's Guide to Ecocriticism," *PMLA* 121.2 (2006): 503–516.
15 Dana Phillips, *The Truth of Ecology: Nature, Culture, and Literature in America* (New York: Oxford University Press, 2003), 45.
16 Worster, *Nature's Economy*, 370.
17 Tom LeClair coins "prodigious fiction" to describe scientifically informed, hefty tomes by late twentieth-century male writers seeking to elicit amazement and wonder. Tom LeClair, "The Prodigious Fiction of Richard Powers, William Vollmann, and David Foster Wallace," *Critique* 38.1 (1996): 12–37.
18 Richard Powers, *Gain* (New York: Picador, 1999), 12.
19 Stacy Alaimo, *Bodily Natures: Science, Environment, and the Material Self* (Bloomington: Indiana University Press, 2010).
20 Donna Haraway, *Simians, Cyborgs, and Women: The Reinvention of Nature* (New York: Routledge, 1991), 149.
21 Ibid., 150.
22 Bruno Latour, *We Have Never Been Modern*, trans. Catherine Porter (Cambridge, MA: Harvard University Press, 1993), 103.
23 Ibid., 104.
24 Karen Tei Yamashita, *Through the Arc of the Rainforest* (Minneapolis, MN: Coffee House Press, 1990), 141.
25 Ibid., 112.

26 Ursula K. Heise, "Local Rock and Global Plastic: World Ecology and the Experience of Place," *Comparative Literature Studies* 41.1 (2004): 135.
27 Latour, *We Have Never*, 109.
28 Sheila Jasanoff and Marybeth Long Martello, "Heaven and Earth: The Politics of Environmental Images," in *Earthly Politics: Local and Global in Environmental Governance*, ed. Sheila Jasanoff (Cambridge, MA: MIT Press, 2004), 45.
29 Heather Houser, "Human/Planetary," in *Time: A Vocabulary of the Present*, ed. Joel Burges and Amy J. Elias (New York: NYU Press, 2016), 146.
30 I borrow this distinction from Denis Cosgrove, *Apollo's Eye: A Cartographic Genealogy of the Earth in the Western Imagination* (Baltimore, MD: Johns Hopkins University Press, 2001), 263.
31 Anna Lowenhaupt Tsing, *Friction: An Ethnography of Global Connection* (Princeton, NJ: Princeton University Press, 2005), xiii.
32 See "Globalization" in this volume for more in-depth analysis of the phenomenon in 1990s literature.
33 Heise, "Local Rock," 132.
34 Elizabeth DeLoughrey and George B. Handley, "Introduction: Toward an Aesthetics of the Earth," in *Postcolonial Ecologies: Literatures of the Environment*, ed. Elizabeth DeLoughrey and George B. Handley (New York: Oxford University Press, 2011), 10.
35 Ibid.
36 Shari Huhndorf, *Mapping the Americas: The Transnational Politics of Contemporary Native Culture* (Ithaca, NY: Cornell University Press, 2009), 141.
37 Cosgrove, *Apollo's Eye*, 263.
38 Ibid., 262–263.
39 J. E. Lovelock, *Gaia: A New Look at Life on Earth* (Oxford: Oxford University Press, 1987), xiv.
40 Global warming from GHG emissions made headlines in the late 1980s with Congressional testimony by James Hansen, then head of NASA's Goddard Institute for Space Studies.
41 I refer here especially to Kim Stanley Robinson's Mars Trilogy: *Red Mars* (1993), *Green Mars* (1994), and *Blue Mars* (1996).
42 See Lawrence Buell, "Toxic Discourse," *Critical Inquiry* 24.3 (1998): 639–665; Ursula K. Heise, "Toxins, Drugs, and Global Systems: Risk and Narrative in the Contemporary Novel," *American Literature* 74.4 (2002): 747–778.
43 Ulrich Beck, *Risk Society: Towards a New Modernity*, trans. Mark Ritter (London: Sage, 1992), 23. Beck's claim that risk renders social analyses based on resource scarcity and class obsolete has invited the most controversy. However, his studies do acknowledge that hazards like climate change disproportionately afflict those in the Global South.
44 David Foster Wallace, *Infinite Jest* (Boston: Back Bay, 1996), 403.
45 Ibid., 573.
46 Ibid.
47 Ibid., 1017n110.

48 Lawrence Buell, *Writing for an Endangered World: Literature, Culture, and Environment in the U.S. and Beyond* (Cambridge, MA: Belknap Press of Harvard University Press, 2001), 38.
49 Patricia Yaeger, "The Death of Nature and the Apotheosis of Trash; or, Rubbish Ecology," *PMLA* 123 (2008): 325, 332.
50 Ibid., 338.
51 Don DeLillo, *Underworld* (New York: Scribner, 1997), 184.
52 Alaimo, *Bodily Natures*, 87.
53 Susanne Antonetta, *Body Toxic: An Environmental Memoir* (New York: Counterpoint, 2001), 208–209.
54 Sandra Steingraber, *Living Downstream: A Scientist's Personal Investigation of Cancer and the Environment* (New York: Vintage, 1998), 61.
55 Min Hyoung Song, "Becoming Planetary," *American Literary History* 23.3 (2011): 557.
56 Cherríe Moraga, *Heroes and Saints and Other Plays* (Albuquerque, NM: West End, 1994), 90.
57 Ibid., 148.
58 Michel Serres, *Natural Contract*, trans. Elizabeth MacArthur and William Paulson (Ann Arbor: University of Michigan Press, 1995), 38.
59 Ibid.

CHAPTER 18

Virtual Reality

Joseph Conte

The 1990s began – from the perspective of media – on the night of January 17, 1991, when laser-guided smart bombs and Tomahawk cruise missiles rained down on Baghdad at the start of the first Persian Gulf War. While the respective anchors of the network nightly news broadcasts were at their desks in New York, a trio of CNN correspondents, Bernard Shaw, John Holliman, and Peter Arnett, were hunkered down in the Rashid Hotel providing live, unedited reports by radio and satellite uplink, of the city under an intensive aerial bombardment. Awed as much by the real-time graphics as by the display of military firepower, the American television viewership found overnight that the streaming of cable news coverage had displaced the punctual, cocktail-hour broadcasts in media consciousness. Abetting the saturation of cable news was the confluence of digital technologies that "fed" real-time content to the transfixed viewing public. The CNN team's ability to provide instantaneous coverage relied on mobile satellite technology. Night-vision equipment was used to capture imagery of tracer fire and ground explosions bathed in an eerie green glow that resembled a video arcade game or computer terminal rather than anything in nature. More significantly, the Pentagon provided the network television pool with digital footage from the nose cones of smart bombs and cruise missiles as they navigated to the targets in their crosshairs. Through this technology the viewer became embedded in virtual warfare. The point of view is no longer that of an individual soldier – say, Paul Bäumer in Erich Maria Remarque's *All Quiet on the Western Front* (1929) – but that of cybernetic feedback in which the viewer assumes the position of a detached, inhuman weapon. Cable television and virtual warfare both relied on digital satellite technology and became indistinguishable simulations from the point of view of the West, as Jean Baudrillard has asserted in *The Gulf War Did Not Take Place*.[1]

The nineties are a transitional moment from analogue to digital media when the legacy forms of broadcast TV, print fiction, journalism, and 2-D cinematic projection are gradually replatformed by the new media of cable TV, hypertext fiction, e-book readers, the Internet, game boxes, streaming video, and virtual reality engines. Even as this replatforming occurs, legacy media retain a commanding share of the public audience. What is observable is how established forms such as the novel are disturbed by the advent of new media, altering their contours and reappropriating the claims made on the popular imaginary by their digital competitors.

That same year saw the publication of Howard Rheingold's nonfiction bestseller, *Virtual Reality*, then subtitled "the revolutionary technology of computer-generated artificial worlds – and how it promises and threatens to transform business and society."[2] Rheingold's history of technological invention is as engrossing as that of the Lumière cinematograph, the Marconi radio, or the Braun cathode ray tube. But it too is spiked with a premillennial enthusiasm that was "arousing people's expectations for imminent breakthroughs in a technology that would take years, perhaps decades to mature."[3] The technological lag involved the development of head-mounted displays, "goggles," and wired "gloves" that afforded the VR early-adopter the illusion of stereoscopic immersion in virtual space and the ability to interact with virtual objects. The simulation of Virtual Reality remains at the mercy of "tracking," the graphical processing engine required to refresh the imagery so that, when the user moves or when she shifts her point of view in 3-D space, there is little perceptible lag, measured in milliseconds. Without such seamless tracking, the illusion of immersion in an artificial world collapses. The reality of Virtual Reality evolved not so much from a "homebrew" collaboration of a Jobs-and-Wozniak or a Hewlett-and-Packard in the Silicon Valley personal computer industry, as in the academic and military research consortiums of PARC, ARPA, and SRI. Yet Virtual Reality – the term is coined by computer scientist Jaron Lanier in 1989 to describe a range of simulation machines – is a revolutionary technology, even if it has failed so far to become a household appliance. The history of representational media (or mimesis) describes an evolution in point of view: early photography was of a stationary object by a camera in a stationary position; early film presented a moving object from a stationary cinematograph; the "movement-image" of classical Hollywood cinema, theorized by Gilles Deleuze in *Cinema 1* (1983),[4] showed a moving object from a moving camera (montage; shot/counter-shot), although the cinematic spectator is himself immobile in the presence of the silver screen. But a "goggles and gloves" Virtual Reality holds out to the user the promise of interacting with moving objects from a moving point of view. As Jay

David Bolter and Richard Grusin remark in *Remediation: Understanding New Media* (1999), "Virtual reality can thus be seen to remediate all previous point of view technologies."[5] Full and transparent (especially wireless) immersion, or what Bolter and Grusin call "immediacy," still remains beyond the technological grasp of VR.

Half believing his own advance marketing, Rheingold speculates, "If the ten-year rule of thumb holds true, personal computer enthusiasts by the millions a decade from now [i.e., in 2001] will be interacting directly with virtual worlds through their desktop reality engines."[6] Ken Hillis offers a diagnosis of why the "ten-year rule" did not apply in this case: "VR achieved its greatest popularity during the last decade of the twentieth century. Its ability to seize the technical imaginary during this period was linked to a massive amount of hype that promised a distributed VR of networked computers that would allow people to share the same virtual world and interact in real time... Issues of cost, insufficient bandwidth, and the physical awkwardness of donning cumbersome HMDs replete with encumbering wiring all played a role in reducing public interest."[7] If "hype," or premillennial enthusiasm, led to disappointment in consumer electronics in the decade after Rheingold's book touted a reality-engine on every desktop, the films and literature of the 1990s that represent the use and abuse of VR uniformly express a postmillennial apocalypse. Their dystopias are a means by which the legacy media of print fiction and the cinema "remediate" both the false "promises" and the disturbing "threats" of the artificial reality that would supplant them.

What if, as Michael Heim asks, "the seductive obsession with digital phantoms leads to an apocalyptic 'end of reality'"?[8] Kathryn Bigelow's film, *Strange Days* (1995), is set in Los Angeles on the last two days of 1999 as the fear or celebration of Y2K engulfs the city in criminal violence and rioting.[9] Lenny Nero is a dealer in bootleg recordings made with a SQUID, or "Superconducting Quantum Interference Device," wired directly to the wearer's cerebral cortex, which, when played back on a head-mounted "deck," enables another user to apprehend the full sensory experience of an event, such as a robbery or erotic tryst, as if it were their own. Clips that end with the wearer's death, known as "blackjack," are shunned by Lenny, but lead him along a trail of antisocial violence, rape, and murder. An addiction to vicarious reality spells the end of civilization, if not to Hollywood. In David Cronenberg's film, *eXistenZ* (1999), organic virtual reality consoles called "game pods" represent a near-future upgrade of the cumbersome electronic head-mounted displays and all-over body transducer suits proposed by nineties VR theorists.[10] Much like the organic "sockets" that induce stimuli directly in the consumer's brain in Pat Cadigan's novel, *Synners* (1991), the virtual reality game "eXistenZ" is connected via "bio-ports" into the players' spines through biotechnological umbilical cords, or "UmbryCords." Two media technology companies, Antenna Research and Cortical Systematics, vie for platform dominance (much like VHS and Betamax did in the eighties for video recording), as resistant "realists" strive to prevent the "deforming" of reality. Most influential was Lilly and Lana Wachowski's cyberpunk film, *The Matrix* (1999), in which intelligent machines (the apotheosis of Alan Turing's AI) have programmed an artificial reality, "the Matrix," that hides from humanity the scorched planet on which it now exists only to provide thermoelectric power for the machines.[11] The key to this dystopian inversion of the organic and machinic phyla lies inside the smuggler's bible on the desk of Thomas Anderson, aka the hacker "Neo," Jean Baudrillard's *Simulacra & Simulation*, which tells us, "Disneyland is presented as imaginary in order to make us believe that the rest is real, whereas all of Los Angeles and the America that surrounds it are no longer real, but belong to the hyperreal order and to the order of simulation ... concealing the fact that the real is no longer real."[12] These films and cybernetic fictions critique their technological overlords, the Death Stars of narrative.

As the millennial apocalypse descended upon us, VR technology itself had not yet arrived. In a 2015 update on the "next generation" of VR headsets, including Facebook's Oculus Rift, Samsung's Gear VR, and Google Cardboard, Lorne Manly exclaims, "Virtual reality – once the stuff of science fiction – is still in its infancy. But there's already a gold rush around the technology, which plunges viewers into a simulated 3-D environment and lets them explore their surroundings as if they were really there.... By 2025 [yet another ten years!], the market for virtual reality content will be $5.4 billion." A shill for 20th Century Fox remarks, "We're at the brick-size cellphone days of VR. The technology works ... but it is nowhere near good enough, on any front, to take on mass, mass adoption."[13] In the two dozen years since Rheingold popularized a VR technology in its developmental stages, VR for the masses still remains a decade away. Or, as Lawrence "the Yogi" Berra once observed, "The future ain't what it used to be."

The Virtual Reality extolled by Rheingold in 1991 relied on the research and development of "goggles and gloves" technology and mainframe computing that could be demonstrated in something like the Seattle-based "Realization Lab" of Richard Powers's novel, *Plowing the Dark* (2000), or the CAVE Simulator at Brown University for which Robert Coover and his students conducted a CAVE Writing seminar,[14] but which was far too expensive and demanded processing power beyond the capabilities of home-use devices. Public disappointment with VR technology in the 1990s, the invention of the World Wide Web and HTTP protocol by Tim Berners-Lee in 1989, and the arrival online of the first website from CERN in 1991 signaled a shift in attention to virtuality. Although the virtuality of flat-screen personal computer displays precludes the sort of immersion that VR technology promised, the variety of applications made available inexpensively for home computing and mobile communications introduced the non-geek user through the window of a browser to interactive multiplayer virtual environments for role-playing (such as *Second Life*) and gaming and a conversant online social media (such as chat rooms and user-generated commentary). The public incursion into cyberspace came with the adoption of an "avatar," a typically anonymous graphical representation of a user in gaming, virtual worlds, and Internet forums. Thus, virtuality as a surrogate experience conducted through digital media encompasses the technology of VR rigs, the locative media of smartphones and tablets, and the graphical interface of personal computing through which the mundane chores of an information economy are conducted as well as the stealthier interactions of our "second selves."[15] Neal Stephenson's cyberpunk novel, *Snow Crash* (1992), features a katana-wielding hacker whose real name – not his online moniker or "handle" – is "Hiro Protagonist."[16] Every avatar that haunts cyberspace is a virtual protagonist in a first- or third-person narrative adventure.

The broader appeal of virtuality should have spelled doom at the millennium for traditional print fiction. That it did not is partially explained by that *éminence grise* of postmodern fiction, John Barth, in "The State of the Art" (1996), in which he files his report on the advent of hypertext literature. Whereas once, in "The Literature of Exhaustion" (1967), he observed that the greatest threat to print fiction was "movies and television," which surely spelled the "Death of the Novel,"[17] now the desktop personal computer has brought forth Electronic Virtual Reality. He descries, however, a "difference between virtual reality, which deals in *real virtualities*, and the purely virtual virtuality of literary texts, especially printed texts. The sights and sounds and feels of EVR are literal physical sensations generated by artificial stimuli. The printed page, on the other hand – except for illustrated texts and scratch-and-sniff kiddie books – is strictly anesthetic, however incidentally appealing to the eye and hand may be its typeface, paper stock, and binding."[18] Barth's distinction here jives with Rheingold's assertion that VR history begins with Morton Heilig's "Sensorama Simulator" (1962) and 3-D multisensory cinema.[19] If the sensation of VR is by implication an immature art form or caters to immature sensibilities, Barth claims something more for the legacy medium of print fiction: "The virtual worlds of literature are unencumbered by literality. It is both their great limitation and their indispensable virtue that their virtuality is virtual, that they exist not in our nerve endings but in the pure hyperspace of our imagination."[20] Barth is conducting a *derrière-garde* action in "State of the Art" by remediating the immersive virtual world as a *virtue* – the words are etymologically related in the Latin *virtūs* – of the legacy medium.[21] Whatever is compelling about virtuality has always already been present in imaginative literature without any unnecessary distraction from the medium itself. As if to underscore his point with a bit of postmodern irony, Barth pens the short story, "Click" (1997), in which he spoofs "*The Hypertextuality of Everyday Life*," whose text is replete with faux hyperlinks printed in cyan blue.[22] The onetime self-professed "print-oriented bastard"[23] extends his millennial musings on the worthiness of print fiction versus hypertext in his novel, *Coming Soon!!!: A Narrative* (2001), which stages his reservations regarding virtuality in a confrontation between the Novelist Emeritus and the Novelist Aspirant.[24]

As hypertext fiction caught the attention of Barth, Coover, and younger practitioners of electronic textuality such as Michael Joyce, Shelley Jackson, and Stephanie Strickland, the nineties represents the final decade in which television stands, largely uncontested, as literature's technological other. Not unlike the sweaty brow and five-o'clock shadow that sank Richard M. Nixon's candidacy in the first televised presidential debates with the telegenic John F. Kennedy in 1960, the angst of an elite culture of filmmakers, critics, and writers who despise the appeal of populist mass media, but can't otherwise turn away from it, is palpable. In his lengthy manifesto, "E Unibus Pluram: Television and U.S. Fiction," David Foster Wallace describes a "certain subgenre of pop-conscious postmodern fiction, written mostly by young Americans," which "made a real attempt to transfigure a world of and for appearance, mass appeal, and television." This "image-fiction," he argues, has been hoisted on its own ironic petard by a "televisual culture [that] has somehow evolved to a point where it seems invulnerable to any such transfiguring assault."[25] The chief exhibit in Wallace's take-down of image-fiction is Mark Leyner's collection of short fiction, *My Cousin, My Gastroenterologist* (1990), an avant-pop mash-up of advertising jingle, TV kiddie-show, and NFL instant replay, chased down with a Quaalude. Wallace argues that such image-fiction does not simply reference televisual culture but constitutes a *response* to a society that has been "deformed by electric signal."[26] Leyner's fiction is its own form of *remediation*, as it not only appropriates TV programs but also seizes upon the technique of hyper-montage popularized by the incessant jump cuts of MTV music videos in the 1980s. Wallace admits to binge-watching TV, but unlike Leyner he fails to appreciate the transformation in the 1990s from classic broadcast TV, whose serial episodes, sports, and newscasts were largely unrepeated "events," and the proliferating channels of cable TV whose twenty-four-hour programming situates itself for reflexive rebroadcast, or rewatching. With an eclectic mix of high and low cultural references that typifies postmodernism, Leyner's fiction represents *how* we watched TV in the nineties, not just *what* we watched: "I'm an exploding skeleton of kinetic vectors. I stand upon a peak in Darien like stout Cortez shouting I write the songs! I rupture into afterimages like the nude descending the staircase. Holographic clones of myself appear all over the apartment smoking cigarettes and drinking martinis. Where are the women, they chuckle. Mona arrives to borrow a cup of sugar. Quaaludes. Clothes shed. Gang bang. Death. Ambulance. Police..."[27] Switching from a rephrased bit of Keats's sonnet, "On First Looking into Chapman's Homer" (1816), to the title phrase of Barry Manilow's treacly hit song (1975), the reader of *My Cousin, My Gastroenterologist* must be practiced in the art of channel surfing as the decontextualized clips skid by with the click of a remote control. Unlike modernist poetry whose allusions were freighted with cultural treasure, these incidental quotations contribute to pastiche of the sort that Fredric Jameson attributes to the pop art of Andy Warhol and Roy Lichtenstein, "speech through all the masks and voices stored up in the imaginary museum of a now global culture."[28] The hypnotic-hallucinatory elisions in Leyner's writing may either be symptoms of amphetamine addiction or of "a recovering postmodernist," as Leyner quips in "Geraldo, Eat Your Avant-Pop Heart Out" (1997).[29] As a guest on *The Jenny Jones Show* (1991–2003), "Alex" (not his real name) admits to having first read Jameson at age nine. He found Jameson's assessment that the style of postmodernism is that of schizophrenia, "in the form of a rubble of distinct and unrelated signifiers."[30] "Alex" is finally confronted by a man in the studio audience "in his mid-30s with a scruffy beard and a bandana around his head," the avatar of Wallace, who accuses him of being "the single worst example of pointless irony in American literature, and this whole heartfelt renunciation of postmodernism is a ploy – it's just more irony."[31] It is that, but for the delectation of a reader who can appreciate the send-up of both obscurantist postmodern theory and popular daytime talk shows.

The skittish humor of Leyner's avant-pop novel succeeds by being both collusive with and yet critical of popular media, employing familiar icons, types and styles (the pop), but registering critique through an array of formal defamiliarizations inherited from the avant-garde (the avant). Pat Cadigan's novel, *Synners* (1991), presents the popular forms of music videos, daytime TV romances, and movie thrillers as addictive substances for which the technology of VR implants acts as a more efficient and deadly delivery system. *Synners* is fluent in the grunge techno of cyberpunk fiction pioneered in William Gibson's *Neuromancer* (1984) and Bruce Sterling's *Schismatrix* (1985). Its contribution to this branch of science fiction lies in its tracking of the technology of virtual reality and digital media such as it appeared in 1991 and its amplification in the postmillennial future setting of the novel. Gabe Ludovic, a frustrated artist who toils in the "simulation pit" of the media conglomerate Diversifications, works on VR shorts using a "head-mounted monitor" and wired feeds from a transdermal "hotsuit."[32] He labors in the "reality-industrial complex" whose transfer Rheingold foresaw from academic and military research-and-development to popular entertainment.[33] Ludovic soon recognizes, in what becomes the refrain of the novel, that as technology evolves so too will humans have to "change for the machines."[34] This transformation is literalized by the introduction of therapeutic cortical implants in "feel-good mills" that treat epilepsy, manic depression, autism, and neurological disorders, but which are soon abused by the clinics that dispense them like the addictive psycho-pharmaceuticals of the present day. The therapeutic implants "all have some percentage of hardware,"[35] however, and their introduction as foreign objects into the body makes the patient a cybernetic organism, or cyborg, a mainstay of cyberpunk fiction. Cadigan envisions the next generation of what Gibson coined "simulated stimulation," or simstim decks,[36] as Dr. Joslin's research for a medical technology firm in entirely organic tissue "sockets," combining nanotechnology and microsurgery, is adopted by the virtual reality industry. Such direct input to the brain that dispenses with wearable devices provides the total immersion and interactivity that was the fantasy of VR in the nineties. A mere eight sockets that can organically alter brain tissue are required to access the "limbic system, the seat of our basic emotions – rage, fear, pleasure. When the sockets are engaged, stimuli will induce these things directly, for the duration of the experience. The consumer plugs into the feature presentation – music video, movie release, commercial, standard TV fare – and undergoes a three-dimensional experience."[37] The corporate acquisition of Dr. Joslin's research in neural sockets is less visionary than commercialized as this advanced technology monopolizes the streaming of entertainment media, including the extant genres of music video, film, and TV. In the near future of *Synners*, VR achieves the comprehensive remediation of all legacy media, becoming the sole portal for transmission.

Simulation through sockets offers unparalleled interactivity, as now "the consumer can cooperate in the forming of the images."[38] The most talented synthesizer of image and music goes by the tag of Visual Mark. As his occipital lobe is hypertrophied, or overdeveloped, he enjoys a direct "pipeline to some primal dream spot, where music and image created each other, the pictures suggesting the music, the music generating the pictures, in a synesthetic frenzy."[39] Visual Mark is the original "synner" – with the operative pun on sensory synesthesia and humanity's hubristic transgression. Mark's protégé, Gina Aiesi, appreciates that the flat, rudimentary joining of image and sound in Old Hollywood, the passive reception of televisual entertainment and unidirectional live performance, are being overtaken by simulation: now "it was better. It wasn't just hearing the music, it was being in the music, and the images coming up on the screen of her mind, forming as she looked at them. As soon as she thought it, there it was, and if she thought to change it, it changed, growing from her like a live thing."[40] Bliss was it in that dawn to be alive, but to be a real "synner" was very heaven.

Cadigan's *Synners*, like most cyberpunk fiction and film, is dystopian, and the technological revolution that it charts is inevitably followed by a reign of terror. The novel correlates ecological and technological apocalypse closely enough to suggest a causal relation. Set in "Mimosa," the Manhattan/Hermosa Beach section of Los Angeles, after a catastrophic earthquake has riven the city and ushered in "the postmillennial madness that had followed,"[41] the novel simultaneously takes to task the fractured, overpopulated, and poisoned society of Los Angeles in the nineties and any misplaced investment in technological solutions to its problems. Paired with the Big One is the "cerebral vascular accident," or stroke, experienced by Dr. Joslin and her research partner who are found dead while "still connected to direct neural interface equipment,"[42] as the premature adoption and commercial application of the unsafe socket technology is found to cause neurological damage. The print novel has always been an imperfect interface between two brains, the writer and the reader who collude in creating a virtual virtuality, as Barth has it, residing in the anesthetic realm of the imagination. Cadigan is no Cassandra of the hyperreal, but *Synners* issues a clear warning against the promises of an immaterial intercranial transfer of sensory experience. Not only does the inventor of the cerebral socket fall victim, but so does Visual Mark, whose tampering with the new technology unleashes a "live" or self-recognizing virus that spikes the global communications system and anyone connected to it: "There was an ecology here, gradually becoming more and more unbalanced, polluted, and infected. Ecological disaster had been inevitable, even before the stroke had been released into the system; there was no way around it. It would be universal. Computer apocalypse, a total system crash,"[43] anticipating the dreaded Y2K crash. It's left to Gina as a survivor to make the final pronouncement: "Think on this one. All appropriate technology hurt somebody. A whole lot of somebodies. Nuclear fission, fusion, the fucking Ford assembly line, the fucking airplane. Fire, for Christ's sake. Every technology has its original sin.' She laughed. 'Makes us original synners. And we still got to live with what we made.'"[44]

Much of the nomenclature of virtual reality has its origins in works of science fiction, and therefore its conceptual genesis in literature precedes its technological application. Robert A. Heinlein imagined the experience of telepresence in his novel, *Waldo* (1940),[45] before the construction of the first electronic computer, ENIAC, in 1946. William Gibson's hero Case "jacked into a custom cyberspace deck that projected his disembodied consciousness into the consensual hallucination that was the matrix" in *Neuromancer*, written before he could afford a personal computer of his own.[46] Neal Stephenson lays claim to the coinage of "avatar" in the acknowledgments to *Snow Crash* (1992).[47] In its Sanskrit derivation, an avatar refers to the descent of a Hindu deity in earthly forms, as the visible manifestation of the metaphysical. Stephenson's hero, the reflexively named Hiro(aki) Protagonist, is a freelance programmer who, along with his friend Da5id and other hackers, has written the software for an exclusive club in the Metaverse, The Black Sun. In this three-dimensional virtual world, avatars "are the audiovisual bodies that people use to communicate with each other."[48] Neophytes and tourists on the Street without coding skills may adopt any sort of cartoonish icon or buy off-the-shelf models such as Brandy and Clint available in kits from Walmart. As an accomplished hacker and self-proclaimed greatest sword fighter in the virtual world, Hiro's avatar is customized. Rather than a garish or idealized *imago*, "Hiro's avatar just looks like Hiro, with the difference that no matter what Hiro is wearing in Reality, his avatar always wears a black leather kimono."[49] The programmer recognizes how much more difficult it is to render a realistic human figure in three dimensions – moving through virtual space – than it is to mock up a flat cartoon. Stephenson wishes us to consider the metaphysics of the Metaverse, in which the most sophisticated avatars are those which more closely resemble their embodied selves rather than an idealized figure.

Virtual Reality 289

The Metaverse – or any representation of virtual reality – is entirely artifactual, a conceptual tool not substantially different, as the novel informs us, from the Sumerian cuneiform tablets whose *me* encode the laws of the gods that govern human civilization. In a debased form of the Metaverse – not unlike the vulgar commercialism that is the Internet – the Brandys and Clints are always aware of their own artifactuality, always adherent to the "Association for Computing Machinery's Global Multimedia Protocol Group," and always compliant consumers of the wares offered on the Street.[50] Once, Hiro observes, hackers could independently write their own software, but in the twenty-first century of market state franchising, "[s]oftware comes out of factories" and programmers have become "assembly-line workers," or worse yet, "managers who never get to write any code themselves."[51] A "hack" is a circumvention of a programming convention "that different computers agree to follow. In theory, it cannot be ignored."[52] But as a world-class hacker, Hiro has the capacity to make his avatar invisible, to miniaturize it, and to penetrate the walls of buildings following his katana. If cyberspace is a form of Cartesian theater, then the avatar is its homunculus, the epiphenomenal projection of the mind onto its stage. Stephenson questions whether that homunculus should perform as the rational *kybernetes*, or steersman, obedient to the First Programmer's rules. Hiro's avatar not only closely resembles his person but also his behavior and values in Reality. The novel's antagonist, the fiber-optic network monopolist, L. Bob Rife, has constructed a massive Cube in the Metaverse that is the nerve center of a "utopian" rational control society. Hiro struggles with Rife for control of the *nam-shub* of Enki, the Sumerian incantation of linguistic disintegration, a version of the Babel myth, which he wages simultaneously in the Metaverse and on Rife's Raft, an offshore floating island of migrants. The battle is for nothing less than the liberation of the pre-/post-rational human subject. Were Rife able to infect the entire populace with the metavirus of Enki, he could bypass the acquired language (the brain's linguistic software) of its victims and penetrate directly into the brainstem (its BIOS), gaining a control of his subjects that fascists could only dream of. Only the neurolinguistic hacker, only the Hiro of a thousand faces (Joseph Campbell), can preserve individual freedom and the power to break the rules.

While cyberpunk writers such as Stephenson engage in speculative and often dystopian futures, the novels of Richard Powers braid together the pursuits of humanists and scientists in knowledgeably researched narratives that involve computer programming in *The Gold Bug Variations* (1991), artificial intelligence in *Galatea 2.2* (1995), and virtual reality in *Plowing the*

Dark (2002). In the latter novel, Powers turns his erudition to a study of two dark rooms in the 1980s: one is the Cavern, or Realization Lab, on the Washington coast, for which the artist manqué, Adie Klarpol, has been recruited to develop virtual reality environments; and the other is a cell in Beirut, Lebanon, where Taimur Martin, an Iranian-American teacher of English, is held hostage in the multi-factional civil war in 1986 – and for five years thereafter. The Paleolithic paintings found in the Lascaux caves mark an inception of the symbolic imaginary and ritual in human history and, as one of the programmers of the RL observes, "The mind is the first virtual reality."[53] The Cavern is the technological extension of Lascaux, and Adie chooses to paint its walls with digital representations of Vincent van Gogh's *Bedroom in Arles* (1888) and Henri Rousseau's *The Dream* (1910). The artist's bedroom, on whose walls hang miniature copies of the unsold masterworks by van Gogh and the lush jungle foliage into which Rousseau has transported the Polish mistress of his youth, are alike in demonstrating the power of *homo significans* to project the mind onto the blank wall of reality. But to do so requires at the very least a détente between the two cerebral hemispheres, between the imagination and *technē*, between Adie's visions of beauty and the autodidact poet-turned-programmer Stevie Spiegel's logical systems. He espouses "the ability to make worlds – whole, dense, multisensory places that are both out there and in here at the same time. Invented worlds that respond to what we're doing, worlds where the interface disappears . . . VR reinvents the terms of existence. It redefines what it means to be human."[54] Yet Adie regards the graphics rendering of the Cavern with the same withering critique of Plato's Cave, that it is no more than "a copy of a copy, a debasement of the debasement of Forms."[55] That is also Baudrillard's definition of simulation and points to a contradiction in the purpose of the Cavern, whether it is intended to be an instrumental digital reproduction of the world as we know it or an exploratory platform for a world that we can only imagine. The former is faced with the problem of "simulator sickness," jerky animation: "Material reality's supreme Cray never dropped frames. That's how you knew you were *in* the real world: all the flicker-free, smooth scrolling. The Cavern's goal – believability through total immersion – could not survive an image that spluttered."[56] That's a hardware problem. The latter challenge is a version of the first programmer Ada Lovelace Byron's objection, in her notes to Charles Babbage's Analytical Engine (1842), that it "has no pretensions whatever to originate anything. It can do whatever we know how to order it to perform."[57] That's a software problem, expressed in the novel by programmer Jack Acquerelli, who critiques Adie's bedroom and jungle environments: "I mean, sure, it's beautiful and all. But it doesn't do anything. It's basically a flat gallery. The user can't really... make anything happen." The Cavern isn't sufficiently interactive and the "little artworks" don't register the presence of the user.[58] While the developers take bets on "the year that simulation finally surpassed reality,"[59] that's a wager that has yet to be collected.

Meanwhile, Taimur Martin languishes, chained to the radiator in his cell in Beirut, trying to recall on the inside of his eyelids a hardbound copy of Dickens's *Great Expectations* and its opening lines, the virtual virtuality of a Victorian saga of class struggle. "Every turn, every further constriction in the plot – yours or the author's – makes it easier to keep to the general contour. Where you cannot recall a scene, you invent one."[60] Deprived of reading materials, hindered by the limitations of memory, Martin rewrites the classics in his mind. Adie and the RL project fall victim to the publicity hype that explodes like nearby Mount St. Helens: "Media latched wholesale upon this thing that it refused to call anything else but virtual reality. The public took so quickly to the fantasy that it must have recognized the contour from something it already knew."[61] The narrator here alludes to the remediated form of print narrative, the plot, character, and setting of the novel. "VR overnight became 1990's cover girl. A couple of research outfits let the ghost out of the machine before it was time. Here and there, universities began to demo projects that suddenly had the whole world talking as if full-body dives into wraparound LSD, robotic prostitution, and long-distance teledildonics would hit the toy store shelves by Christmas... Ready or not, reality engineering was about to become a full-fledged industry."[62] Unfortunately for the venture capitalists and the start-up's sponsor TeraSys, the new medium is not yet ready for its close-up. The pyroclastic flow that washes over the RL, however, is geopolitical reality. As 1991 dawns, the "electronic storm, so long in simulation, at last broke... Two delirious American reporters trapped in a high-rise office babbled on, over satellite uplink, about the phantoms screaming across Baghdad's dome."[63] The Cavern's representation of Hagia Sophia in Istanbul is co-opted for the twenty-four hour cable feed. "Smart bombs beamed back video to even smarter bombers. Nosecone shots documented their descents all the way up to the moment of deliverance... Pinpoint delivery turned evidence so intoxicating that no one who once looked at it could look away. The race had achieved the precision of its earliest dreams."[64] While the coders toiled at a simulated reality environment, the empire had struck "to create our own reality" in the Persian Gulf.[65] Adie is shocked by the realization that the Air Force had invented virtual reality for its flight simulators and that the RL counted among its clients not only the entertainment giants Disney and Sony but also the military-industrial complex. With that, Adie sets about to delete the Cavern's code from the root directory. Taking one last look into the simulated dome of Hagia Sophia, she sees a solitary, bedraggled man – in a metaphysical transformation, outside the body and beyond the machine. If humans have a soul, which is the seat of wisdom, Powers suggests, it will not be found wandering through the virtual blandishments of the Cavern but in the hard-shell cranium, in literature and philosophy. The failure of VR was its preoccupation with creating the proprioceptive illusion of the Body in virtual space while depriving the Mind of any profound reason to be there.

The grand coup of virtual reality, as Bolter and Grusin assert, is its ability to remediate all other visual media, including painting, photography, film, and television. The fictions of the 1990s that re-remediate VR in print underscore with a fine graphite point how the new medium has failed – not in the technical parameters of immersion, interactivity, simulation, and navigation (for these will surely be upgraded in the next generation device, such as Oculus Rift), nor even in its obsession with puerile fantasies and military cooptation – but in its offering of sensory illusions that fail to project a mindscape onto reality as humanity once did at Lascaux.

NOTES

1 Jean Baudrillard, *The Gulf War Did Not Take Place*, trans. Paul Patton (Bloomington: Indiana University Press, 1995).
2 Howard Rheingold, *Virtual Reality* (New York: Simon, 1991).
3 Rheingold, *Virtual Reality*, 34.
4 Gilles Deleuze, *Cinema 1: The Movement-Image*, trans. Hugh Tomlinson and Barbara Habberjam (1983; Minneapolis: University of Minnesota Press, 1986).
5 Jay David Bolter and Richard Grusin, *Remediation: Understanding New Media* (Cambridge, MA: MIT Press, 1999), 162.
6 Rheingold, *Virtual Reality*, 87.
7 Ken Hillis, "Virtual Reality," in *The Johns Hopkins Guide to Digital Media*, ed. Marie-Laure Ryan, Lori Emerson and Benjamin J. Robertson (Baltimore: Johns Hopkins University Press, 2014), 513.
8 Michael Heim, "Virtuality," in *The Johns Hopkins Guide to Digital Media*, 516.
9 *Strange Days*, directed by Kathryn Bigelow (United States, 20th Century Fox, 1995).
10 *eXistenZ*, directed by David Cronenberg (Canada, Miramax, 1999).
11 *The Matrix*, directed by Lana and Lilly Wachowski (Australia and United States, Warner Bros., 1999).

12 Jean Baudrillard, *Simulacra and Simulation*, trans. Sheila Faria Glaser (1981; Ann Arbor: University of Michigan Press, 1994), 12–13.
13 Lorne Manly, "A Virtual Reality Revolution, Coming to a Headset Near You," *New York Times* November 19, 2015, https://www.nytimes.com/2015/11/22/arts/a-virtual-reality-revolution-coming-to-a-headset-near-you.html.
14 As with the next generation of VR goggles, a new CAVE (for Cave Automatic Virtual Environment) was unveiled in 2015. See Amanda Katz, "Brown University unveils 3D virtual-reality room," *Boston Globe* June 20, 2015, https://www.bostonglobe.com/lifestyle/style/2015/06/19/brown-university-unveils-virtual-reality-room/QoTOOp66NpPZeGMFobapjO/story.html.
15 See Heim, "Virtuality," 515.
16 Neal Stephenson, *Snow Crash* (New York: Bantam, 1992).
17 John Barth, "The State of the Art," *Wilson Quarterly* 20.2 (1996): 42–43.
18 Barth, "State of the Art," 42; his emphasis. His critique of the materiality of the book does not anticipate the appearance of multimodal, graphic novels, such as Mark Z. Danielewski's *House of Leaves* (2000), whose complex spatial and multicolor typography is hardly for "kiddies."
19 Rheingold, *Virtual Reality*, 50.
20 Barth, "State of the Art," 42.
21 See Heim, "Virtuality," 514–515, on how the strength of *virtualiter* became a weaker, invisible or virtual quality.
22 Barth, "Click," *Atlantic Monthly*, December 1997, 81–96.
23 Barth, *Lost in the Funhouse: Fiction for Print, Tape, Live Voice* (New York: Bantam, 1969), 123.
24 Barth, *Coming Soon!!!: A Narrative* (Boston: Houghton, 2001).
25 David Foster Wallace, "E Unibus Pluram: Television and U.S. Fiction," *Review of Contemporary Fiction* 13 (1993): 171.
26 Ibid., 172.
27 Mark Leyner, *My Cousin, My Gastroenterologist* (New York: Vintage, 1993), 49–50.
28 Fredric Jameson, *Postmodernism, or, The Cultural Logic of Late Capitalism* (Durham, NC: Duke University Press, 1991), 18.
29 Leyner, "Geraldo, Eat Your Avant-Pop Heart Out," *New York Times*, December 21, 1997, Op-Ed, 11. The cognitive dissonance of this piece is abetted by the fact that it ran opposite a William Safire column on public integrity.
30 Jameson, *Postmodernism*, 26.
31 Leyner, "Geraldo," 11.
32 Pat Cadigan, *Synners* (1991; New York: Four Walls Eight Windows, 2001), 40.
33 Rheingold, *Virtual Reality*, 132.
34 Cadigan, *Synners*, 97. See also John Johnston, "'Change for the Machines': The Complexity of Bodies in *Synners*," in *Information Multiplicity: American Fiction in the Age of Media Saturation* (Baltimore: Johns Hopkins University Press, 1998), 257–265.
35 Cadigan, *Synners*, 64.
36 William Gibson, *Neuromancer* (New York: Ace, 1984), 11.

37 Cadigan, *Synners*, 66.
38 Ibid.
39 Ibid., 109.
40 Ibid., 226.
41 Ibid., 8.
42 Ibid., 319.
43 Ibid., 324.
44 Ibid., 435.
45 Rheingold, *Virtual Reality*, 257.
46 Gibson, *Neuromancer*, 5. See "An Interview with William Gibson," in *Storming the Reality Studio: A Casebook of Cyberpunk and Postmodern Science Fiction*, ed. Larry McCaffery (Durham, NC: Duke University Press, 1991), 270.
47 Stephenson remarks in the Acknowledgments to *Snow Crash*, "The words 'avatar' (in the sense used here) and 'Metaverse' are my inventions, which I came up with when I decided that existing words (such as 'virtual reality') were simply too awkward to use," 440.
48 Stephenson, *Snow Crash*, 33.
49 Ibid., 34.
50 Ibid., 23.
51 Ibid., 36.
52 Ibid., 407.
53 Richard Powers, *Plowing the Dark* (New York: Farrar, 2000), 130.
54 Ibid., 159–160.
55 Ibid., 40.
56 Ibid., 60–61.
57 Quoted in Joan Baum, *The Calculating Passion of Ada Byron* (Hamden, CT: Archon, 1986), 82.
58 Powers, *Plowing the Dark*, 164–165.
59 Ibid., 337.
60 Ibid., 242.
61 Ibid., 268.
62 Ibid., 269.
63 Ibid., 393.
64 Ibid., 394.
65 Ron Suskind, quoting an anonymous senior advisor to George W. Bush, in "Faith, Certainty and the Presidency of George W. Bush," *New York Times Magazine*, October 17, 2004, http://www.nytimes.com/2004/10/17/magazine/faith-certainty-and-the-presidency-of-george-w-bush.html.

PART IV

Public and Private Life

CHAPTER 19

Trauma

Patrick O'Donnell

Between 1985 and 1996, five remarkable books set the parameters for the emergent field of trauma studies: Elaine Scarry's *The Body in Pain: The Making and Unmaking of the World*,[1] Shoshana Felman's *Testimony: Crises of Witnessing in Literature, Psychoanalysis, and History*,[2] Cathy Caruth's *Unclaimed Experience: Trauma, Narrative, and History*,[3] Kali Tal's *Worlds of Hurt: Reading the Literature of Trauma*,[4] and Dominick La Capra's *Representing the Holocaust: History, Theory, Trauma*.[5] These assessments of the complex interconnections between theory, fiction, and social and popular culture accompanied a succession of 1990s American novels that represent trauma and that appeared in the same "moment" as the conclusion of the marathon McMartin daycare sexual abuse trials in 1990 and the founding of the False Memory Syndrome Foundation in 1992; revisions of the pathology and epidemiology of PTSD (post-traumatic stress disorder) in the manual of the American Psychiatric Association; the popularity of such films as *Total Recall* (1990), the *Matrix* (1999), and *Memento* (2000); and the advent of the graphic novel as a major contemporary genre with the publication of Art Spiegelman's *Maus* (1991). The list of parallel instances could go on indefinitely, but the anecdotal assemblage above suggests the degree to which the American 1990s was given over to the representation of trauma in its disparate manifestations, ranging from the personal incident to the ravages of war between superpowers fought by proxy.[6] As several of the subtitles in the critical literature indicate, what is shared in the examination of the traumas induced by child abuse, war, or genocide necessarily involves the relation between narrative and history, and how the story of a trauma, as "event," can possibly ever be told in its entirety, even well after the fact.

In this chapter, I will discuss a highly selective subset of American novels of the 1990s that narrativize the experience of trauma within historical registers. One might regard these novels in history's rearview mirror – where objects may be closer than they appear – save that doing so would be to see

297

them as the unwitting prophecies of a traumatic event that, by definition, is only memorable in an aftermath that reverse engineers the relation between cause and effect. As Caruth explains, "trauma is not locatable in the simple violent or original event in the individual's past, but in the way that its very unassimilated nature remains to haunt the survivor later on."[7] The novels I shall consider – Dorothy Allison's *Bastard Out of Carolina*,[8] Lan Cao's *The Monkey Bridge*,[9] Kathryn Harrison's *The Kiss*,[10] Tim O'Brien's *In the Lake of the Woods*,[11] Toni Morrison's *Paradise*,[12] and Philip Roth's *American Pastoral*[13] – reflect on the possibility of knowing and remembering the traumatic event *as narratable*. They navigate between the factual and fictional, and between the imaginary and real, in taking seriously the metafictional "problem" inherent in any narrative that makes claims upon experiential or historical veracity. They examine, ultimately, how it is possible to live in a time when the unthinkable has already occurred, and has been "thought," in the event.[14]

Paradise is the third in a loose trilogy of novels that commemorate post-slavery African-American history.[15] The first, *Beloved* (1987), arguably the apogee of Morrison's achievement, is the story of an escaped slave, Sethe, who, upon the point of being recaptured, kills her two-year-old daughter rather than allow her to live in slavery, and who, after migration to the North in the wake of emancipation and Reconstruction, is haunted by her presence in the embodiment of a young woman she takes into her house. *Jazz* (1992) takes place during New York's Harlem Renaissance, and relates the "graveyard" romance between a young woman, the married man who mortally wounds her, and his betrayed wife whose intense emotional and mental suffering is at the center of the narrative; Morrison intertwines the account of the three principals in "modern times" genealogically to the stories of relatives and ancestors before, during, and after slavery. *Paradise* moves forward to the 1950s through the early 1970s as it recounts the entangled narratives of a community of African-Americans who have settled the segregated town of Ruby, Oklahoma, in an attempt to create a rural utopia free from white oppression and the perceived ills of modern society. On Ruby's fringes there exists a "convent" of women – runaways, abused wives, migrants – who inhabit a former nunnery and who are paranoically seen by many of Ruby's townsfolk as, somehow, the source of a series of crop failures and domestic calamities that have beset "paradise." The two communities' interactions lead to a harrowing outcome as the men of Ruby descend on the Convent one evening, attempting to destroy it and murder its inhabitants. As in *Beloved* and *Jazz*, Morrison traces the connections between the motives and desires of the novel's characters to the African-American past and the experience of slavery and its aftermath. In this trilogy, slavery, and the memory and consequences of slavery, form the trauma from which persons and collectives suffer, demarcated on/in both individual bodies and the body politic.

Complex in its rendering of multiple perspectives on questions of race, gender, and history, *Paradise* is indicative of the trauma narratives of the 1990s that attempt to provide narrative sourcework for trauma, locating its origins in a close or remote past in receding ripples of cause and effect. The "experience" of slavery and its aftermath for the descendents of slaves who have come to settle in Ruby is that of historical fragmentation and reassembly in a diaspora of events and nomadic trajectories that undergird the town's formation as the embodiment of a social order seemingly invested in the fantasy of a purified past and future. Pat Best, the local schoolteacher, is engaged in an attempt to provide "a gift to the citizens of Ruby – a collection of family trees; the genealogies of each of the fifteen families" – but this project of a "total history" of the community is inevitably partial and anecdotal.[16] It is as dependent in its formation on what it leaves out as what it includes as it traces Ruby's origins in the movement of its citizens and their ancestors over three generations:

> There were nine large intact families who made the original journey,... seventy-nine or eighty-one in all (depending on whether the two stolen children were counted). Along with them came fragments of other families:... Stories about these fragments, which made up some fifty more, surfaced in the writing compositions of Pat's students, the gossip and recollections at picnics, church dinners and woman talk over chores and hair preparation... Then bits of tales emerged like sparks lighting the absences that hovered over their childhoods and the shadows that dimmed their maturity.[17]

Slavery and the escape from genocide, hatred and intolerance is the traumatic backdrop of Ruby's diasporic history as an assemblage of fragments. The body of the community is made up of "anecdotal," marginalized collection of individuals who have ironically evolved a community complete with first families and fantasies of ideological purity. These connect survival with separating out unwelcome others (the women of the Convent) representing a threat, in this instance, to versions of domesticity and gendered authority mirrored by the white social order that the inhabitants of Ruby had sought to escape in the first place. Is the point of Morrison's narrative that the history of racism and the traumas induced by perverse attempts to "purify" and permanently instantiate social hierarchies operating under the name of the moral order will inevitably repeat themselves in history? Or that, more specifically, and as we consider the succession of Morrison's novels from *Beloved* to *Paradise*, in post-slavery America, the traumatic experience of slavery necessarily entails its reenactment in the departures and arrivals of its diasporic assemblages? This trilogy of novels, published in the decade that extends from 1987 to 1997, raise these questions in the context of considering slavery in America as historical trauma, and as something that, by the end of the twentieth century with the Civil Rights act of 1968 of twenty years vintage, is hardly "over." Morrison questions, in these novels, whether "it" will ever be over.

In comparison to *Paradise*, Dorothy Allison's *Bastard out of Carolina* (1992) and Kathryn Harrison's *The Kiss* (1997) focus on trauma as a family matter in recounting stories of abusive parental relationships. In Allison's novel, the protagonist, Ruth Anne "Bone" Boatright, recalls from the perspective of "achieved" adulthood the sexual abuse she suffered between the ages of five and twelve years old at the hands of her stepfather as she grew up in the American South of the 1950s. More troublingly, Bone recounts her mother's knowing obliviousness toward the abuse and the abandonment of her adolescent daughter when she and Bones's stepfather, after a harrowing episode in which he rapes and beats Bone, depart for parts unknown, leaving the traumatized child in the care of relatives. Throughout a narrative in which the narrator struggles to reconcile her adult and childhood perspectives on her mother and, more broadly, stereotypes of Southern womanhood in the American 1950s, the primary affect is that of anger. Bone is infuriated with those who have allowed her to be brutalized in silence under the guise of maintaining a sense of female decorousness and family duty. Her response to trauma is thus a distinctly "indecorous" expression of rage at the silent overlooking of abuse and the cultural circumstances within which it both occurs and is disavowed. In effect, her narrative is both an indictment of the American class system – for Bone and her family are poor and rural, and thus, easily categorized as "poor white trash" who only rise to the level of classist expectations in their violence and incestuousness – and a rejection of the corporeal aesthetic associated with being a "real" woman in American culture. For Bone embraces ugliness as a mode of being-in-the-world; she is "ugly" in terms of her anger, her candor, her manners, and her aspect. She describes herself as "obstinate . . . [g]awky, strong, ugly . . . I was stubborn-faced, unremarkable, straight up and down, and dark as walnut brown. This body, like my aunts' bodies, was born to be worked to death, used up and thrown away."[18] Caught within the contradiction of being her stepfather's object of desire and the embodiment of "ugliness" in a patriarchal social order in which the bodies of women –

beautiful or ugly – are objectified, Bone turns her memories of trauma into narrative discourse. She speaks out as a witness, violating all the norms of privacy, taboo, and decor that would condemn her to an "unremarkable" (and unmarked) life. In so doing, but only by being angry enough to break the silence, she survives.

Kathryn Harrison's memoir *The Kiss* seems, by comparison, less enraged, but no less harrowing, in its account of a daughter who, at the age of 20, commences an incestuous relationship with a father who has been absent through much of her childhood, and then exiles herself from her father permanently at the conclusion of their affair four years hence. Harrison's candid, detailed account of her physical and emotional relationship with her father caused a great deal of controversy when it appeared in 1997 for its frank portrayal of the tabooed subject of incest, and can be considered as leading the way for a proliferate succession of realistic memoirs to follow. Not the least of these is James Frey's *A Million Little Pieces* (2003) which raised a host of questions about the fictionality of those literary works labeled "memoir" when Frey's seemingly earnest, candid account of drug addiction was revealed to be a heedless combination of fact and fiction, leading to his being shamed in public by Oprah Winfrey.[19] The low-key tone of Harrison's account constrasts strongly with that of Allison's novel, which may seem to posit a distinction between memoir and fiction, but one that is surely complicated by Harrison's account of her memories of the relationship with her father in "A Conversation with Kathryn Harrison" included in the 2011 reprint of *The Kiss*:

> In the years after I separated from my father, I dreamed often of car accidents. In a dream that recurred, my face had fallen into little pieces, as if it were a jigsaw puzzle, and I gathered up all I could and set off to find a surgeon who could put it back together into a face I'd recognize as mine. In my waking life, I found an analyst with whom I worked for the better part of twenty years to put me back together. I remain shocked by my own history.[20]

Harrison makes clear in this recollection (its rhetoric uncannily echoing Frey's title) that the trauma of the incestuous relationship with her father fragmented and destroyed the identity she had constructed up to that point in time. The memoir, which can be viewed as necessary to coping with the trauma in its aftermath, is the reconstruction of a puzzle in which many of the original pieces are still missing ("I gathered up all I could"); its completion necessarily depends upon the filling in of blank spaces with what can be imagined in order to generate a "recognition" of the past.

The Kiss is the account of a survivor who endured an incestuous relationship as an adult, and thus, in the reconstruction she must undertake, freely admits her own complicity in the affair while remembering a dysfunctional childhood involving an absent father, anorexia, and a narcissistic mother who "separates" from the author at the age of six, virtually orphaning her to be raised by a grandmother who is described as a "despot":[21] "My father is an absence, a hole like one of those my grandmother cuts out of family photographs. Rather than discard the entire picture of an event that includes someone she dislikes, she snips the offender out with untidy haste, using her manicure scissors."[22] "Anorexia may begin as an attempt to make myself fit my mother's ideal and then to erase myself, but its deeper, more insidious and lasting seduction is that of exiling her. Anorexia can be satisfied, my mother cannot; so I replace her with this disease . . . "[23] The result of this upbringing is a fragile, depressed personality given over to thoughts of suicide who must seek out professional help from a psychiatric "surgeon" and whose ability to confront the past in her memoir is the key to her survival. At one point, her father, who is a "monster of affection," to use Diane Sadoff's term for fatherhood in the novels of Dickens, Eliot, and Brontë, observes with clinical coldness the dynamic of a dysfunctional family that is both incestuous and alienated:[24]

> My father identifies the dire triangle that my grandmother, my mother, and I form. He says that I protect my mother against her mother; that she passively protects me by offering one generation's distance; and that my grandmother manipulates the two of us, playing one daughter's insecurities off against the other's. He disarms me by naming this triangle even as he steps in to break it by forming a new one: my mother, my father, and me. My father takes the place of my grandmother: one despot steps in for another.[25]

It appears that Harrison's father – who was in life a minister – can detach himself from the chaos of familial relationships in which he is a prime participant via a "theoretical," structural approach to the women in his family that allows him to compartmentalize and rationalize the relationship with his adult daughter. Trauma as experienced in *The Kiss* comes about through the repressive mechanism of an "objectivity" that fails to conceal the pain being inflicted on its victim, and the missing pieces of self's puzzle forever lost and only ever regained as what is not there.

The traumatic events that inform Lan Cao's *Monkey Bridge* and Tim O'Brien's *In the Lake of the Woods* are those of the Vietnam War as experienced and remembered by participants and succeeding generations. The title of Cao's novel refers to a makeshift bridge built of bamboo, like those made by guerrillas in the South Asian jungles during the Vietnam War, but it also refers to the fragile and treacherous bridge to the past constructed by one of the novel's two narrators: Mai, a young immigrant who has been brought to the United States with her mother, Thanh, following the Fall of Saigon. They have been living in America for three years when Thanh suffers a stroke and, from her hospital bed, begins to call for her father, Baba Quan, who has remained behind in Vietnam. The novel recounts Mai's attempts to trace both her grandfather's location and a mysterious past about which her mother never speaks. Frustrated by her attempts get information from her relatives and her recovered mother about her grandfather, Mai resorts to stealing a cache of diary-like letters her mother has been writing about her past in Vietnam, intending to give them to Mai at some indeterminate point in the future when she is "ready" for them.

As she begins "turning, turning, turning" the letters over, Mai experiences "the pulsing of veins that usually proceeds entry into a private, forbidden realm."[26] The "forbidden realm" is the true story of Mai's grandfather, a local farmer, who has prostituted his wife with a wealthy landlord in exchange for property; Thanh is born of their union, her biological father unknown to her until, one day, she witnesses Baba Quan murder the landlord out of revenge and guilt for what he has done to his wife. In the final letter that Mai reads, Thanh describes her experiences during the war and how she has discovered the truth of her heritage, revealing that she has contrived alternative narratives of the past that have become more real to her with the passing of time: *"In the lives I constructed for you, Baba Quan was a devoted husband, a father dedicated to an uncomplicated life among the green terraced fields and fresh plowed earth of Ba Xuyen, a farmer who tilled the land with patience and dignity. That was the nature of my longing, and so he was all that and more in my fictional reimaginings."*[27]

"Fictional reimaginings" are one way of coping with or remembering/not remembering the personal trauma and tragedy. At the level of national historical experience, reimagining past and present serves for Mai as a means of survival in a realm between two worlds – Vietnam and America – that seem equally treacherous and duplicitous. Describing the terrain that stretches from the "Little Saigon" neighborhood of Arlington to Falls Church, Virginia, where she and her mother come to dwell, Mai recounts numerous instances of identity transformation as Vietnamese immigrants attempt to assimilate new, "American" identities with specific "requirements": "it all had to do with being able to adopt a different posture, to reach deep enough into the folds of the earth to relocate one's roots and bend one's body in a new direction, pretending at the same time that the world was the same now as it had been the day before."[28] The adroitness that Mai feels needs to be achieved in order "to shift with a shifting world" signifies "the Vietnamese version of the American Dream; a new spin, the Vietnam spin, to the old immigrant faith in the future. Not only could we become anything we wanted to in America, we could change what we had once been in Vietnam. Re-birthing the past, we called it, claiming what had been once a power reserved only for gods and other immortal beings."[29] Yet this dream, like Than's reimagining of her marriage, thinly veils the nightmare of the historical experience of Vietnam. For Mai, growing up during the war, the violence of a repressed past can return with breathtaking suddenness if the facade of a shifting, reimagined "American" identity begins to crack: "One wrong move, a reckless moment off guard, and there, right under my eyes, was the unbidden life, the subverted life I lived. The malevolent world of red..."[30] *Monkey Bridge* thus reveals the necessary paradox at the center of traumatic experience: the need to remember it, as truthfully as possible, in the quest for self-knowledge, yet to reimagine it, and one's relation to it, if there is to be a future beyond trauma.

In contrast to *Monkey Bridge*, Tim O'Brien's *In the Lake of the Woods* relates memories of the Vietnam War through the perspective of an American veteran, John Wade, who is possibly suffering from PTSD and whose recollections of wartime experience are, by turns, guilt-ridden, nostalgic, and horrific. To some extent, the novel is set as a mystery, for Wade's wife, Kathy, has mysteriously disappeared from a cabin by a lake in Minnesota where they are in self-imposed exile following a scandal that has beset them: it has been discovered that Wade, who is running for state senator, may have participated in the killing of civilian villagers during his tour of duty in what has come to be known as the My Lai massacre. Wade's recollections of his childhood, his role as a "tunnel rat" during the war, and his marriage recur as he helps search for his wife with an oddly detached demeanor that causes neighbors and village officials to suspect him of foul play. The novel offers several alternative explanations for Kathy's disappearance along with a succession of possible endings, thus leaving readers to solve the mystery. What seems clear amidst the novel's ambiguities is that throughout the events surrounding the disappearance and search Wade is suffering from shock, perhaps caused by recollections of the past triggered by the scandal and his wife's disappearance, or perhaps because he has murdered his wife as part of a mental breakdown that can be traced back to an abusive childhood and the trauma of a war in which he has been both a criminal and a victim.

The thread that runs in John Wade's life from childhood to the day he wakes up to find his wife missing is that of magic: fascinated by mirrors, tricks, and illusions, he has studied magic since boyhood, and the element of magic plays a significant role in his memories of the war. As a tunnel rat – one who explores the mazelike tunnel systems constructed by Viet Cong guerilla fighters, clearing out mines and traps, and killing all within – Wade goes by the nickname of "Sorcerer," recollecting in the aftermath that Vietnam was:

> a place with secret trapdoors and tunnels and underground chambers populated by various spooks and goblins... where magic was everyone's hobby and where elaborate props were always on hand – exploding boxes and secret chemicals and numerous devices of levitation – you could fly here, you could make other people fly... where the air itself was both reality and illusion, where anything might instantly become anything else.[31]

As a schoolboy, Wade has developed a perceptual trick allowing him to navigate both the difficulties of everyday life and the verbal and emotional abuse he receives from an alcoholic father: he imagines that he carries with him at all times the stand-up mirror before which he performs magic tricks. The imagined mirror "behind his eyes," like the real mirror in the basement of his house, is "where miracles happened," where "John was no longer a lonely little kid. He had sovereignty over the world," and where "he felt calm and safe... where he could turn good things into bad and just be happy."[32] This trick, which enables both a secretion of memory and a conversion of it into "good things," becomes part of Wade's survival toolkit during and after the war; postwar politics offers him the opportunity to construct a version of selfhood in the mirror of the public eye that will allow his self-hatred to be transmuted into the "absolute, unconditional love" that his wife perceives he needs: "Politics is just a love thermometer," she mentally observes, "[t]he polls quantified it. The election made it official."[33] His wife's clear implication is that the "sorcerer's" identity is nothing but a succession of empty illusions, a series of tricks in front of a mirror concealing an absence projected as present and real.

Interleaved with the novel's primary chapters are "evidence" from the My Lai court-martial transcripts, the testimony of neighbors following Kathy's disappearance, citations from magic treatises and biographies of famous magicians, excerpts from books on trauma and war, and sections of the *Geneva Convention on the Laws of War*, all of which apparently provide a documentary counterweight to the alternate stories and identities that are spun off of John Wade's life and the mystery of his wife's disappearance.

Yet *In the Lake of the Woods* insists on leaving that final mystery unsolved and intact to take its place alongside all of the other mysteries and ambiguities that result from a life experienced by the identity in the mirror. One of the many explorations of Kathy's disappearance is that of the novel's conclusion, where Wade imagines his wife is alive and that together they disappear into the wilderness surrounding the mirroring lake in the woods. The traumatized and trauma-inducing protagonist of O'Brien's novel thus fabricates the ultimate illusion – one in which all traces of his identity and his painful history are simply erased. Documenting the facts, narrativizing possible explanations, erasing the past: these are the contrary motions that *In the Lake of the Woods* induces as responses to traumatic experience.

A consideration of Philip Roth's *American Pastoral* may seem to offer a final entry in a triptych of novels that register the nineties' traumatic echoes of a war that took place in the 1960s and 1970s, save that the Vietnam War is not central to *American Pastoral*. While the war reverberates in the novel's background – its ramifications most visible domestically, in protest marches and television news – the trauma involved is more closely associated with being the seemingly stalwart head of a "typical" American nuclear family during a tumultuous period whose faith in familial, national, and capitalist institutions is shaken by a daughter gone entirely off the grid. *American Pastoral* is the first in an informal trilogy of novels – sometimes referenced as the "second Zuckerman trilogy" or "the American trilogy" – that includes *I Married a Communist* (1998) and *The Human Stain* (2000), framed by the Cold War in America from its origins in the 1940s to its putative aftermath in the Clinton administration. The novel is set primarily during the Johnson administration (1963–1969) at the height of the Vietnam War; it is narrated by Roth's irrepressible alter ego, Nathan Zuckerman, whose own guilt and foibles often revealingly intersect with those of the protagonists in the stories he tells, many of them projections of possible lives and futures based on relatively brief encounters and conversations. Here, the story is that of Seymour "Swede" Levov and his attempts to come to terms with his daughter, Merry, who has become an anti-war political revolutionary and has killed an innocent bystander in a botched attempt to protest the war by, incomprehensibly, blowing up the local village store. As he pursues (or as Zuckerman imagines him pursuing) his lost daughter and tries to understand how she could have come to be a murderer and an outcast, Swede is forced to look inward and, in effect, to evolve an interiority where, heretofore, there had only been the facade of an American football hero, good citizen, successful businessman, and beloved father. In a dinner conversation with Zuckerman out of which Zuckerman evolves a life-story, Swede reveals that he has "suffered a shock."[34] The traumatic shock he suffers extends to every dimension of his existence, from his role as a father with, possibly, incestuous desires (or is this Zuckerman's inference?), to his responsibility as a law-abiding citizen with a duty to report the whereabouts of his criminal daughter once he finds her. The tentativeness of the narrative, the opaque nature and origins of the trauma, personal and national, and the prevalence of shock as a state of mind suggest that *American Pastoral* is a dystopic portrait of American institutions in distress that allegorizes the oldest of American themes – a lost innocence that was never really innocent, and the recovery from a loss that never occurred as such.

Swede's experience of trauma in *American Pastoral* can be broadly defined as the compulsion to return to the past in order to find an explanation for a life in which he has supposedly done all the right things is in ruins – his daughter absconded, his marriage failing, his business (a glove factory in Newark) outsourced and in decline. According to Zuckerman, Swede has undergone a splitting of his identity between "outer" and "inner," brought on by the shame of his memories, especially one that he has about inappropriately kissing his eleven-year-old daughter on the lips:

> ... the outer life. To the best of his ability, it is conducted just as it used to be. But now it is accompanied by an inner life, a gruesome inner life of tyrannical obsessions, stifled inclinations, superstitious expectations, horrible imaginings, fantasy conversations, unanswerable questions. Sleeplessness and self-castigation night after night. Enormous loneliness. Unflagging remorse, even for that kiss when she was eleven and he was thirty-six and the two of them, in their wet bathing suits, were driving home together from the Deal beach. Could that have done it? Could anything have done it? Could nothing have done it?[35]

We may be reminded in this passage of *The Kiss*, save that Swede, via Zuckerman, seems to be locating a single "original" traumatic event in inappropriate contact with a child, wondering if the abuse of which he was a perpetrator (if it was abuse) could be at the root of his daughter's abject behavior and his own breakdown, or if there is any cause or origin in the first place. What can be remembered as the cause of shame, remorse, and criminality is put into question in Swede discovery of the self as split between inside and outside, or what his brother, Jerry, terms a form of "self-questioning" that "'did take some time to reach him. And if there is anything worse than self-questioning too early in life, it's self-questioning coming too late. His life was blown up by that bomb. The real victim of that bombing was him.'"[36]

Memory itself in *American Pastoral* is treacherous, the very act of recalling the past potentially explosive, as Jerry puts it a comment on what participants at a high-school class reunion (the occasion for Zuckerman's first encounter with the Swede after forty-five years): "'After all, what they sit around calling the 'past' at these things isn't a fragment of a fragment of the past. It's the past undetonated – nothing is really brought back, nothing. It's nostalgia. It's bullshit.'"[37] Alternatively, as Zuckerman explains, the past is so particular, and memory so unreliable, that attempting to work through it in order to trace the origins of tragedy in a relation of cause to effect will generate, at worst, nothing at all, and at best, a myth: "And since we don't just forget things because they don't matter but also forget things because they matter too much... it's no wonder that the shards of reality one person will cherish as a biography can seem to someone else who, say, happened to have eaten some ten thousand dinners at the very same kitchen table, to be a willful excursion into mythomania."[38] These recognitions – the act of merely recognizing and recounting the "unexploded" past itself – result in Zuckerman's projection of a scene in which Merry returns to a family gathering and confesses that she has killed three additional people in terrorist bombings. Zuckerman views the moment as that of Swede's "unblinding": "the instrument of [his] unblinding is Merry. The daughter has made her father see. And perhaps this was all she had ever wanted to do. She has given him sight, the sight to see clear through to that which will never be regularized, to see what you can't see and don't see and won't see until three is added to one to get four."[39] The substance of Swede's ironic ephiphany involves recognition that her troubles, and his, are untraceable to a single traumatic event, an inappropriate paternal kiss or a badly planned political gesture resulting in collateral damage. Rather, the effect of his daughter's revelation that she has been a committed terrorist for years reveals to him that the explanations for violence and war lie elsewhere than in genealogy ("He had seen that we don't come from one another, that it only appears that we come from one another")[40] or historic accident ("He had seen the way that it is, seen out beyond the number four to all there is that cannot be bounded. The order is minute. He had thought most of it was order and only a little of it was disorder. He'd had it backwards").[41] In *American Pastoral*, trauma is experienced as a return to the past that reveals the inability of understanding what has occurred in any other terms than the shock resulting from the unmaking of the world which trauma, by its nature, induces.

Looking over this selective group of American novels that address trauma in the 1990s, it is clear that they are fully engaged in reconfiguring a past as a site of confrontation and escape. Collectively, these works formulate an argument: trauma is a condition in which a past that can never be fled and, equally, never completely recollected, is only comprehensible through the work of memory converted into discourse. Part of this equation necessitates a recognition that memory fabulates, and bears a complex relationship to the history or sequence of events (which can extend from a kiss to a childhood or a war) that it seeks to realize and recreate. Several of the novels I have discussed here refer to a war that occurred a quarter century before their writing, as if a certain period of time must pass before the work of recovery can begin. Others work on a personal and intimate level to explore the ramifications of child abuse and incest, giving rise to a confessional exploration of social, moral, and legal taboos upon which the rise of the memoir and creative nonfiction in the post-millennium is predicated.[42] There are, of course, many other ways trauma might be addressed, and many other American novels of the 1990s that regard trauma as a central concern, but the grouping of novels in this chapter offers strong evidence that the American 1990s was eerily taken up with trauma as cultural "problem" as if in anticipation of the American trauma of the new millennium commencing with 9/11. But that is far too glib: these novels reveal to us that trauma and the memory of trauma do not work in the prophetic register. In these novels, trauma and the work of memory that attends it are not comprehended as predictive motion, but as a "moment" (whether one event or many) whose passage is illuminated in the temporal aftermath, and then, as for the inhabitants of Paradise, only as "bits of tales" emerging "like sparks lighting the absences that hovered over their childhoods and the shadows that dimmed their maturity."[43]

NOTES

1. Elaine Scarry, *The Body in Pain: the Making and Unmaking of the World* (New York: Oxford University Press, 1985).
2. Shoshana Felman, *Testimony: Crises of Witnessing in Literature, Psychoanalysis, and History* (New York: Routledge, 1992).
3. Cathy Caruth, *Unclaimend Experience: Trauma, Narrative, and History* (Baltimore: Johns Hopkins University Press, 1996).
4. Kali Tal, *Worlds of Hurt: Reading the Literatures of Trauma* (New York: Cambridge University Press, 1995).
5. Dominick LaCapra, *Representing the Holocaust: History, Theory, Trauma* (Ithaca, NY: Cornell University Press, 1994).
6. See Gibbs's comprehensive discussion of American trauma narratives from the late twentieth century to the present a study based upon the premise that "while

trauma initially provides an illuminating perspective upon American cultural production, its creeping ubiquity as a critical paradigm becomes limiting. As the trauma paradigm was more widely disseminated through American culture in the late twentieth century, so a tendency developed to read everything through its increasingly monolithic and programmatic critical prism. This in turn began to influence the form of cultural products, such that an identifiable 'trauma genre' emerged, a self-reinforcing circuit of fictional and nonfictional prose narratives that existed in tandem with a supporting critical structure." Alan Gibbs, *Contemporary American Trauma Narratives* (Edinburgh: Edinburgh University Press, 2014), 2. In this essay, I discuss symptomatic instances of narratives identifiable with the "trauma genre" while not fully agreeing with Gibbs's somewhat conspiratorial notion that literary production harmonizes with historical event and critical paradigm in precisely the manner he suggests, but his sense that there is a circuitous relationship between extra- and self-referential aspects of trauma narrative is certainly worth considering in more detail than can be accounted here.
7 Cathy Caruth, *Unclaimed Experience*, 4.
8 Dorothy Allison, *Bastard out of Carolina* (New York: Plume, 1992).
9 Lan Cao, *Monkey Bridge* (New York: Penguin, 1997).
10 Kathryn Harrison, *The Kiss* (New York: Random House, 1997).
11 Tim O'Brien, *In the Lake of the Woods* (New York: Houghton-Mifflin, 1997).
12 Toni Morrison, *Paradise* (New York: Random House, 1997).
13 Philip Roth, *American Pastoral* (New York: Houghton-Mifflin, 1997).
14 I rely here on Alain Badiou's sense of "event" as manifestation of the previously unrepresented or previously excluded from what constitutes "reality," and thus, the narrative of history. See especially Alain Badiou, *Being and Event*, trans. Oliver Feltham (New York: Continuum, 2005), 173–200.
15 For a compelling reading of the relationship between trauma, memory, and history in Morrison's trilogy, see Nancy Peterson, *Against Amnesia: Contemporary American Women Writers and the Crises of Historical Memory* (Philadelphia: University of Philadelphia Press, 2001), 51–97.
16 Tony Morrison, *Paradise*, 187.
17 Ibid., 188–189.
18 Dorothy Allison, *Bastard out of Carolina*, 206.
19 For a well-contextualized discussion of the Frey controversy and the ways in which it, and other "faked" memories, challenge the boundary-lines between fact and fiction in the memoir as a genre, see Alyson Miller, *Haunted by Words: Scandalous Texts* (Bern: Peter Lang, 2013).
20 Kathryn Harrison, *The Kiss*, 234.
21 Ibid., 80.
22 Ibid., 5.
23 Ibid., 39.
24 Sadoff's psychoanalytic reading of the paternal function in the Victorian novel discusses the complexities of the father-mother-daughter triangle (reconfigured in the grandmother-mother-daughter triangle of *The Kiss*) as one in which

the father, in particular, is both too intimate and remote at the same time, a paradox echoed in Harrison account of incest and/as alienation*s*. See Diane F. Sadoff, *Monsters of Affection: Dickens, Eliot, Brontë on Fatherhood* (Baltimore: Johns Hopkins University Press, 1982).
25 Ibid., 79–80.
26 Lan Cao, *Monkey Bridge*, 168.
27 Ibid., 229; italics in text.
28 Ibid., 39.
29 Ibid., 39; 40.
30 Ibid., 88.
31 Tim O'Brien, *In the Lake of the Woods*, 72.
32 Ibid., 65–66.
33 Ibid., 55.
34 Philip Roth, *American Pastoral*, 21.
35 Ibid., 173–174.
36 Ibid., 68.
37 Ibid., 61.
38 Ibid., 55.
39 Ibid., 418.
40 Ibid.
41 Ibid.
42 For an important discussion of this movement across the postwar period of "the program era," see Mark McGurl, *The Program Era* (Cambridge, MA: Harvard University Press, 2009).
43 Tony Morrison, *Paradise*, 188.

CHAPTER 20

Family

Kasia Boddy

Of course literature's interest in the family began long before the 1990s. Generational and sibling struggle, the establishment of identity through paternity, reconfiguration of relationships after remarriage, the trauma of abandonment and incest – all are perennial concerns, going back at least as far as *Oedipus* and the book of Genesis. Reading conservative commentators at the end of the twentieth century, however, one would think that the family – and consequently, it was often implied, the nation too – was under threat as never before. As Adrienne, the protagonist of one of Lorrie Moore's wry short stories observes, "she had entered a puritanical decade, a demographic moment . . . when the best compliment you could get was 'You would make a terrific mother.' The wolf whistle of the nineties."[1] (Adrienne remains uncomplimented and not only because she is childless; the story begins when she accidentally drops, and kills, someone else's baby.)

The "serpent of family decline," which had been a dominant theme in the 1980s Reagan administration, was revived in the run-up to the 1992 presidential election, often with reference to television representations.[2] Vice President Dan Quayle chastised the eponymous heroine of *Murphy Brown* for having a baby on her own, thereby "mocking the importance of fathers," while President George H. W. Bush promised policies to strengthen the American family and turn it into something "closer to *The Waltons* than *The Simpsons*."[3] *The Waltons*, made in the 1970s, features a multigenerational family in rural Virginia during the 1930s and 1940s, while *The Simpsons*, which first aired in 1989, is a cartoon about a "nuclear family" (father, mother, and 2.5 kids; the half is a baby that never gets older) in a fictional middle-American town. What linked the shows was a focus on white working-class struggles; something that the Simpsons' son, Bart, pointed out a few days after Bush made his speech in a special segment inserted before the credits of a rerun of an old episode. The scene begins with footage of the president, then cuts to the Simpsons watching it on TV.

Without missing a beat, Bart responds: "Hey, we're just like *The Waltons*; we're praying for an end to the Depression too."[4]

Despite its less than perfect patriarch and eventual embrace of same-sex marriage, *The Simpsons* had a lot in common with the white middle-class family of the 1950s (or, rather, its TV avatar) that so many lauded as a lost ideal, destroyed by some combination of the 1960s counterculture, changing immigration patterns, feminism, new reproductive technologies, AIDS, and, after his affair with a White House intern was revealed in 1998, President Bill Clinton. In *The Sopranos*, yet another TV show that took family as its subject, the teenaged Meadow wants to discuss the Clinton affair over breakfast in their suburban split-level, much to the consternation of her father, Tony. When Meadow protests that "it's the 1990s. Parents are supposed to discuss sex with their children," Tony is quick to retort: "Yeah, but that's where you're wrong! You see, out there it's the 1990s, but in this house it's 1954!"[5] Tony, a gangster but also, as his therapist says, a "very conventional man," struggles throughout the series to keep the 1990s at bay.[6] More generally, the suburban promise – "the whole family is always in the car together, going places, singing songs, eating McDonald's" – was found to be shakier than ever.[7] When the elm trees die and "we aren't even allowed to barbecue any longer," what's left but "bland uniformity?"[8] Why not stop trying to live up to some idea of "perfect" and "call it quits, normality-wise?"[9]

Mid-century TV sitcoms remained a touchstone, a focus for a great deal of "nostalgic energy," despite continued insistence that, in Stephanie Coontz's pithy phrase, those shows presented "the way we never were."[10] "People were watching shows like *Donna Reed* and *My Three Sons* and *Big Valley* in which there were all these ideal families," noted the novelist Jayne Anne Phillips, "but in fact those families never existed in those simple terms."[11] To recall oneself "longing for the kind of ideal parents we saw on television," or "some attentive, brownie-baking female to keep my hair curled and generally Donna-Reid over me," became a necessary starting point for memoir or fiction that saw itself as undertaking a project of historical revisionism.[12] In Phillips's novel *Shelter* (1994), for example, family life in the early 1960s is defined by alcoholism, infidelity, suicide, sexual abuse, and vigilantism, and the only person who smiles "like a man in a TV show" is a brooding fundamentalist straight out of Flannery O'Connor.[13]

Like most myths, the "nuclear family" (a phrase coined in 1949) gained its totemic value at precisely the moment when it ceased to have widespread descriptive purchase. In 2001, the *New York Times* reported that the percentage of households consisting of a married-couple with children under eighteen had dropped from 45 percent in 1960 to 23.5 percent.[14] The majority of Americans, in other words, had lived in different kinds of households for many years. It was only in 1990, however, that the US Census Bureau began to measure this complexity by adding the categories of "unmarried partner," "adopted child," "step-child," "foster child," and "grandchild" to the "relationship item" of the census form.[15] Examples of all of these, and more, cropped up in 1990s fiction, as literature embraced "the messy, improvisational, pathwork bonds of postmodern family life" with new zeal.[16] Indeed the messier, more improvisional, the more "lousy with secrets," the better.[17]

Consider Michael Cunningham's saga *Flesh and Blood* (1995), which traces the multiple configurations of the Stassos family from the 1950s to 1990s (with a frame that extends the scope to one hundred years). The story proper begins familiarly enough in the suburbs with mother, father, and three kids but, as soon as we learn that the father has got there by "invisibly" cutting corners on tract houses with "false dormers," things start to look ominous. The father turns out to be a drunk who has affairs and eventually leaves the family; there's also the suggestion that he harbors sexual feelings for one of his daughters. She in turn marries young to set up her own suburban home only to fall pregnant by a passing tree surgeon from whom she only sought "sensations"; her own son (unable to come to terms with his homosexuality) kills himself at the end of the novel. Meanwhile, the other Stassos daughter goes to New York, lives in a squat where she gets pregnant by a passing black man, is remothered by a kindly drag queen, and eventually dies of AIDS. Her child is then raised by the third sibling, the gay brother, who turns out to be the most conventional of all. A few hours after he meets a man who is not "perfect" but "kind," he feels "something was marrying him." The two remain together "for the rest of their lives" and in the novel's final pages, his nephew assumes the role of family patriarch and scatters their ashes.[18]

For all that novels such as this suggested that the nuclear family was "a flawed system of attachment," representations of "neofamilies" tended to reinstate "old roles around new figures and contexts."[19] For some commentators, this was hardly surprising: "most adult homosexuals were raised in conventional middle-class homes in conventional middle-class neighbourhoods," they argued, and there was no reason "why being gay should prevent them" from marrying, raising children, and taking their place at "the heart of the traditional family.'[20] The family became a key area of dispute between gay assimiliationists and radical queers, where the term "queer" often embraced everyone who had "trouble with normal," who saw themselves at odds with "heteronormative mandates."[21]

Much of this debate was conducted against the background of the HIV/AIDS epidemic (before the advent of potent antiretroviral therapy in 1996, the disease was usually fatal). "In an era of panic sexuality," observed Linda Singer, "the family is being repackaged as a prophylactic social device ... a prudent and strategic safe sex practice."[22] But not everyone agreed that family life was low risk. Dennis Cooper, a leading figure in the "anti-assimilationist queer movement," satirized the familial promise of "safety" in *Try* (1994).[23] The novel's title refers to an experiment conducted by two gay men, a "stab at heterosexual-style bliss" in the suburbs with an adopted toddler. Now that the boy is a teenager, however, the experiment starts to go wrong; Ziggy's "physical charms combined with our familial closeness – plus our lack of actual blood ties – had made the boy queasily attractive."[24] The experimentation becomes largely sexual and violent. Danger, not safety, Cooper suggests, is what characterizes family life.

Many agreed, pointing to a "whole shadow world of previously invisible silent abuse": "rape, battery, sexual harassment, forced prostitution, and the sexual abuse of children," it was argued, were both "common and systematic."[25] America was facing a "national emergency," declared a 1990 government panel of childcare experts.[26] Soon, critical studies with titles such as *Too Scared to Cry* and *Unchained Memories* were sharing shelf space with bestselling memoirs of "psychic trauma in childhood" such as Kathryn Harrison's *The Kiss* (1997), an analysis of the aftereffects of her father's "wet, insistent, exploring" tongue.[27] Similar themes informed numerous novels including Dorothy Allison's *Bastard Out of Carolina* (1992), Joyce Carol Oates's *We Were the Mulvaneys* (1996), Jane Smiley's *A Thousand Acres* (1991), and *Push* (1996) by Sapphire, in which a teenager gets pregnant with her father's child, twice. In Cooper's novel, Ziggy edits "*I Apologize*, A Magazine for the Sexually Abused."[28]

This flurry of books, argues Paul John Eakin, was part of a general shift toward considering the relational life; that is, memoirists were less interested in presenting themselves as self-made men or women than in considering the ways in which "the self is defined by – and lives in terms of – its relations with others."[29] While hardly a new idea – it had its roots in 1950s family therapy – this approach was well suited to an era in which books, like TV talk shows, were valued for offering "a social product – advice – that was once provided by the family" itself.[30] The connection was strengthened by the fact that the talk shows, often through book clubs, frequently featured the authors of family-based fiction and memoir. The "empathetic 1990s, the era of Bill Clinton's feel for pain, of Oprah Winfrey's furrowed brow and concerned nod" established trends – "more narcissism overall, less concern for privacy, a strong interest in victimhood and a therapeutic culture" – that would only strengthen in the new millenium.[31] Once again, Lorrie Moore satirized the trend. "People Like That Are the Only People Here" (1997) is both a story about "the Mother" and "the Husband" facing up to the fact that "the Baby" has a cancerous tumor, and a metafictional memoir questioning the mantra that "writing it all down was purging," even lifesaving.[32] As soon as they get the diagnosis, the Husband instructs his writer-wife to "take notes. We're going to need the money." When she protests that "the whole memoir thing annoys me," he reminds her how limited their insurance is. So the story proceeds, detailing the baby's surgery and the longeurs of the parents' waiting room ("no need to watch *Oprah*. They leave Oprah in the dust. Oprah has nothing on them.") If the plot is finally unresolved – it will be five years before they know whether the treatment has worked – the story ends defiantly: "There are the notes. Now where is the money?"[33]

The New Yorker duly obliged, publishing the story in 1997. Most of the time, however, magazines and publishers preferred stories that ended less ambiguously, often with the redemption of a new kind of family structure. Sometimes, as in the case of Cunningham's *Flesh and Blood*, that structure requires only minimal adjustment; at other times, what Judith Butler called a more radical "resignification of the family" is proposed. In the documentary *Paris is Burning* (1991), for example, family hierachies collapse as the drag queens "'mother' one another,' 'house' one another, 'rear' one another."[34] In Jewelle Gomez's lesbian vampire fantasy, *The Gilda Stories* (1991), patriarchal racism gives way to "families of friends" who just happen to "share the blood."[35]

To talk of "families we choose" in the 1980s and 1990s, argues the anthropologist Kath Weston, was to reject an earlier more directly politicized discourse of community or collectivity in favor of one grounded in interpersonal relationships that were "customized, individual creations." And choice, or customization, extended beyond gay and lesbian families. "A family is no longer something we're born into," declared Pagan Kennedy, "we have to remake it ourselves." Her novel *The Exes* (1998) explores that "new kind of love" in the context of a rock band made up entirely of ex-boyfriends and ex-girlfriends.[36] A much bleaker view of family-making is presented in Donna Tartt's *The Secret History* (1992), about a group of college students who, in the face of parental disinterest, form an exclusive, and eventually, murderous, clique. Ultimately, however, the novel suggests that erudite Dionysian killing is less of a bond that the financial arrangements the students make with each other as well as their families. The political scientist Wendy Brown has argued that neoliberalism finds it hard to reconcile an understanding of the individual as a unit of "self-investing entrepreneurial capital" with traditional notions of the family as an "interdependent, affective and frequently sacrificial domain."[37] But according to *The Secret History*, every kind of interdependent affective structure, whether chosen or not, is rooted in exchange value. Economic transactions (in the form of financial aid, trust funds, charitable foundations, monthly allowances, loans, thefts, or gifts) might not be "the only thing in the world" but it is these transactions that create and express loyalty, obligation, and sacrifice.[38] When the Gatsby-like protagonist Henry Winter kills himself, the token of allegiance that he passes on to the narrator is the BMW that his mother had given him.

Many works of the period were alert to the economic imperatives behind the alliances forged by "self-investing human capitals."[39] Despite a theme song that declared it was enough simply to be there for one other, the decade's most popular sitcom, *Friends* (1994–2004) imagined family as a matter of fluid financial, as well as romantic, interdependencies. Inevitably, if self-consciously, however, the vintage-sitcom dynamic reasserted itself, and the show ended with a big white wedding and a move away from the partner-and-apartment swapping of the neoliberal city to settled suburbia:[40]

MONICA: We want a lawn and a swing set.
CHANDLER: And a street where our kids can ride their bikes, and maybe an ice cream truck can go by.
ROSS: So you want to buy a house in the 50s?[41]

This essay keeps coming back to television, not only because TV shows played such an important part in debates about family values but because TV itself was "*the* central figure in images of the American home."[42] The idea of the family room emerged in the 1950s to refer to the place where the television was ritually watched but it was also where, through that watching, family life ritually constituted itself and its commitment to the home. In 1958, Jack Kerouac noted that every suburban window revealed "the little blue square of the television, each living family riveting its attention on probably one show."[43] Kerouac could observe this phenomenon with a certain hipster detachment but for "the American generation born after, say, 1955," as David Foster Wallace pointed out, TV had become "something to be *lived with*, not just looked at."⁴⁴ Important scenes about family interactions in stories and novels often featured the television, as source of conflict or comfort. For every teenager described by A. M. Homes as looking forward to the time when she can "have my own private TV . . . [and] be alone always," there's another who longs "to find my father in the den, the family room, watching tennis on television."⁴⁵ When that father, or mother, starts acting "weirder" than usual, perhaps, as a character in Thomas Pynchon's *Vineland* (1990) suggests, it is easiest to "Pretend there's a frame around 'em like the Tube, pretend they're a show you're watching. You can go into it if you want, or you can just watch, and *not* go into it."⁴⁶

TV fantasies are much less benign in Wallace's own *Infinite Jest* (1996). While set in a near future in which TV has been replaced by the "ultimate cartridge-as-ecstatic-death" (weapon-grade entertainment), the novel's satire is directed at 1990s viewing habits.⁴⁷ In one scene, Hugh Steeply, a US government agent in pursuit of the cartridge, recalls how his father's relationship with the Korean military hospital sitcom *M*A*S*H* changed from "attachment" to "obsession." At first, the family finds his devotion "almost cute": "God know the guy was entitled – he'd worked like a dog his whole life;" and even when it extends to syndicated reruns and videotapes, "the organism of family simply shifted to accommodate." Eventually, however, his "adorable" habit of "quoting little lines and scenes" from the show "to illustrate some idea, make some point in conversation" becomes an inability "to communicate on any topic" without reference to *M*A*S*H*. By the time Steeply's father dies, "in his easy chair, set at full Recline," the "whole organism of family" has become unbalanced, "questioning its perceptions."⁴⁸ The "work-family" of *M*A*S*H* offered the continuity and "warm, safe and loving sanctuary" that the nuclear family at home somehow couldn't provide.⁴⁹

Wallace was not alone in using the family room to explore the way that representations of family-like life can supersede the real thing and, more specifically, the way "fathers impact sons."⁵⁰ In Cunningham's *Blood and Flesh*, for example, the central father-son dynamic is established in a scene in a 1950s family room in which the boy "lingered near" his father, who "sat in his chair watching television," but "didn't let himself get too close."⁵¹ No writer, however, explored the theme as throughly as Curtis White, whose 1998 novel *Memories of My Father Watching TV* remains strictly true to its title.⁵² "My defining memory of my father is of a man (but not just a man, of course; it is *my father* – young, handsome, capable!) reclined on a dingy couch watching TV." Thus the scene is set for a "postmodernist confessional" in which "stories-*cum*-chapters" are constructed around episodes of all-male work-family shows like *Bonanza*, *Maverick*, and *Highway Patrol* – "anything with guns in it" – which seep into the family room and the father's consciousness.[53] Meanwhile, the narrator and his two sisters struggle for attention. One sister paces back and forth in front of the screen; the other stands and delivers monologues on "the injustice of a house with heat in one room only." Their father, increasingly immersed, is not put off. "I don't have anything to say to you," he tells his son. "It's nothing personal."[54]

The unavailable or distant mid-century father – "the shadow man," "the phantom father" – was a recurrent figure in 1990s memoir and fiction.[55] Philip Lopate recalled a man who "could sustain very little intensity of contact before his receptive apparatus shut down," Rick Moody a dad who once again "secluded himself in front of the newwork news, in a recliner," remains "a cipher . . . a mystery, an enigma."[56] In Lorrie Moore's novel *Who Will Run the Frog Hospital?* (1994) about growing up "in the fatherless fifties and sixties," the narrator gives her father "a Father's Day card meant for uncles and neighbors. 'You've Been Like a Father to Me,' it read."[57] He's bewildered by the joke.

When fathers were absent in more than a figurative sense, they became even more important to the story. "Divorce's shaky unfinality" offers a narrative spur to very different novels, from A. M. Homes's *Jack* (1989) about a teenager's attempts to ascertain what aspects of the new arrangements are "normal" (it turns out a gay father is less weird than a mother who smiles in "a fake motherly way that looked like it'd been clipped from the pages of *Family Circle*") to Richard Ford's *Independence Day* (1995), a state-of-the-nation book about an "upbeat-father-at-a-remove" who takes his son on a road trip.[58] Other works staged the quest for a father, or a plausible substitute, in the quasi-religious terms suggested by Robert Bly's hugely influencial "book about men," *Iron John* (1990). If Mona Simpson approaches the idea with some skepticism – the protagonist of *The Lost Father* (1992) learns that if "disappearing was all you had to do to become somebody's god," being found "was all that it took to be mortal again" – Chuck Palahniuk's *Fight Club* (1996) is almost a case-book exemplar of Bly's ideas about what's needed to heal the spiritual "father wound."[59] If "a generation of men raised by women" take absent fathers as their "model for God," where can they go to "satisfy their hunger for intimacy, for belonging, and for some kind of spiritual life?"[60] The answer is to another volunterist "instant family," this time all-male. The novel offers several possibilities, from the Testicular Cancer Group "Remaining Men Together" (where there's too much estrogen and embracing) to the eponymous fight club where there's not only plenty of testosteone but "hysterical shouting in tongues like at church, and when you wake up Sunday afternoon you feel saved."[61]

Barack Obama's father also walked out when he was very young, and Obama's memoir *Dreams From My Father* (1995), which begins with him learning of his father's death, is driven by a desire to "search for him" through "scraps of information" and 'fantasies', in order to figure out the 'something unknown' that is his 'race and inheritance'.[62] Although Obama's story is complicated by the fact that his father was a black Kenyan and his mother a white Kansan, he was well aware that his story fit into a larger debate about absent fathers in the black American family. This had been a highly controversial topic since at least 1965 when the Assistant Secretary of Labor Daniel Moynihan published a report blaming the "great discontinuity" between the races in America on the black family's "disorganization" – by which he meant illegitimacy, absent fathers, and matriarchy. The resulting "tangle of pathology," he suggested, was what impeded social progress.[63] Obama was largely sympathetic to these ideas, and after he became president, he repeatedly drew on his own autobiography when urging fathers to step up to their responsibilities or railing against those who were MIA or AWOL, or who simply watched "*SportsCenter* all weekend long."[64]

The conclusions of the Moynihan report proved enormously influential and divisive, both for policy makers and for African-American novelists whose own family narratives ran "the risk either of perpetuating or of appearing to repress" what many saw as its "noxious stereotyping."[65] Family and community in all their diverse permutations had been at the heart of Toni Morrison's fiction since 1970. Her seventh novel, *Paradise* (1997), however, offered a particularly sharp critique of the pathologizing of the matriarchal family and those who feared its polluting influence "is seeping back into our homes, our families."[66] John Edgar Wideman, another critic of Moyniham's "stipulative, narrow and arbitrary" definition of family directly addressed his assumptions in *Fatheralong* (1995), an autobiographical meditation on "black boys, whose fathers, relegated to the margins, are empty-handed ghosts."[67] Wideman described the book as an attempt to understand his father's "avoidance and denial" as part of wider structure of racism with a long tradition of "obscuring, stealing, or distorting black people's lives."[68]

One of the main criticisms of Moynihan's focus on "family disorganization" – a diagnosis which, in the late 1980s, he extended to the whole population – and the "familization of politics" more generally, was that it diverted attention away from the broader economic, social, and political reasons for particular family structures.[69] Fiction attempted to fill in some of the gaps. One of George Saunders's perennial subjects is the disparity between the corporate family and the white working-class father who does whatever he can to "keep the money coming in." The narrator of "Pastoralia" (2000), for example, works as a cave man impersonator in a theme park to pay for drugs for his sick son. He's not allowed to speak with his wife on the phone – that would undermine the park's "authenticity" – and so she sends faxes about the state of their son's health and their overdraft: "*...please don't worry. Well worry a little. We're at the end of our rope or however you say it.*"[70]

The demands of money and work on family life were also central to the work of America's most recent immigrants. During the 1990s, Junot Díaz (born in the Dominican Republic) and Edwidge Dandicat (born in Haiti) both published their first books, about families separated by migration and, "as with most of the immigrants around them," by work.[71] In Dandicat's *Breath, Eyes, Memory* (1994), Sophie has grown up with her aunt in Haiti living on the "New York money" her mother sends back. The mother she "had imagined" wore "gorgeous dresses" and never "had to work for anything," but the woman she encounters in New York has "dark circles under her eyes" and a face that's "cloudy with fatigue" from working two jobs.[72] Although the novel is largely about sexual and political trauma, the familial ruptures of migration also inform the daughter's determination to "bear witness" to her mother's life.[73] A similar impetus drives Díaz's *Drown* (1996), about a "shadowy, marginal, very cruel, very unsympathetic father" who preceeded his "first *familia*" to the United States only to end up with a second. Díaz described nine of the collection's ten stories as attempts to "summon" the father, and not just him but also his experience." The final story, "Negocios," then offers a son's ambivalent attempt at an imaginative reconstruction of his "tendon-ripping labor" and loneliness.[74]

In a 1990 essay "introducing Don DeLillo," Frank Lentricchia lamented the homebound tendency of American writers; rather than producing "expressions of – and responses to – specific historical processes," he complained, they seldom ventured beyond "a minor, apolitical, domestic fiction of the triumphs and agonies of autonomous private individuals operating in 'the private sector.'"[75] By making such a firm distinction between domestic and political fiction, Lentricchia fails to recognize the contentious politics of the family or the intersection of that politics with the "historical processes" that many of the novels discussed here explore; nor does he acknowledge the venerable tradition of works – stretching back at least to *Uncle Tom's Cabin* (1852) – that use the home to access the political and generational progress as a measure of social change. During the 1990s, there was no shortage of novels that elevated the suburban family novel, or memoir, by reference to broader concerns: cancer-causing nuclear waste (Rick Moody's *Purple America*, 1997); cancer-causing globalized "family business" (Richard Powers's *Gain*, 1998); the legacy of New Deal liberalism (Richard Ford's *Independence Day*, 1995); espionage (Chang-Rae Lee's *Native Speaker*, 1996).[76] The titles themselves indicate ambition far beyond the domestic; these are major statement novels.[77] As is Don DeLillo's *Underworld* (1997). DeLillo's title refers to "the secret history" that exists "at the edge" or "under the surface" of the nation (concerning Cold War paranoia, racial division, consumerist waste) and of a single family, in which the father was either killed by the "underworld" mob or committed "the unthinkable Italian crime. He walked out on his family." In both cases, DeLillo suggests, absence is what generates longing and longing is what generates the aura that makes disparate individuals a nation or "a family, still."[78]

Pankaj Mishra recently noted that "novels about suburban families are more likely to be greeted as microcosmic explorations of the human condition if they are by male writers; their female counterparts are rarely allowed to transcend the category of domestic fiction."[79] Lack of recognition, however, has seldom prevented women writers from using family dramas for similar ends, and with similar tropes, to their male peers. Dangerous family secrets and spying are aligned with their Cold War equivalents in Jayne Anne Phillips's 1994 coming-of-age novel, *Shelter*.[80] The main action takes place in the summer of 1963 in an Edenic girls' camp where a teenage girl is imagined as a snake with "the wide gaze of the angel of death"; it ends in early November.[81] November 22, 1963, also forms the pivot for Joyce Carol Oates's *Because It Was Bitter and Because It Was My Heart* (1990), a novel that was praised as both "a gripping family melodrama and an expansive narrative meditation upon the rising racial and social tensions" of the period.[82] At the climax, a college American literature class is interrupted by the news of Kennedy's assassination and the students, professsors, and kitchen staff gather together, "like people crowded into the cabin of a sinking ship." "It's nothing to you really," the protagonist reassures herself, but shortly afterwards she is sexually assaulted by a group of boys and we are told that she feels "as if she has already died. But she hasn't."[83]

In many other novels, what "the TV said" in the family room offered writers a straightforward way to bring politics, "the outer torment," into the home, and thus enact an allegorical scaling-up.[84] Both Pagan Kennedy's *Spinsters* (1995) and Frances Sherwood's *Green* (1995) feature young women watching news of the 1968 assassinations (first Martin Luther King, then Robert Kennedy) on TV – their coming-of-age again in parallel with that of the nation.[85] A similar affinity of domestic and political life also seems to be at play in John Updike's *Memories of the Ford Administration* (1992), which opens with the narrator, Alf Clayton, "sitting among my abandoned children watching television when Nixon resigned." Like the "televised image" of the penitent president, Alf is only a "temporary visitant" in the home, and he soon leaves the family room for a TV-free bachelor pad and sex. But Alf and America refuse to fall: "every tabu broken, and still God kept His back turned ... and still we bumped on." The novel ends with the affair forgotten and the reunited family "fairly content"; the Ford administration, after all, was only "transitional."[86]

All these books offer the domestic *and* the political, but what is the status of each within them? Updike's narrator insistently compares himself to Nixon on TV, but he then digresses into a lengthy description of his living room: "sorry about all the decor. But decor is part of life ... "[87] Is family a bridge to the zeitgeist or the other way round? Despite a title that screams allegory, Philip Roth's *American Pastoral* (1997) presents a more skeptical view of the mythologizing of family and its mapping onto national drama. The novel tells the story of Swede Levov, a second-generation immigrant who abandons Jewish history for American myth only to be thrust into the heart of American history by his daughter Merry. But the "origins of their suffering" – how she became "the angriest kid in America," someone who sets off a bomb in the local post office, and how he became a man who thought he could "protect his family" and finds he "cannot protect even himself" – is almost comically overdetermined. Was it watching the self-immolation of a Vietnamese monk on TV, "out of nowhere and into their home, the nimbus of flames"? Was it Levov's brief incestuous kiss ("five seconds ... ten at most")? Or was Merry "always a defenseless girl"? Acknowledging how difficult it is to interpret the behaviour of our daughters, fathers, or sisters might put pause to allegory but it shouldn't, Roth insists, mean an end to family stories. As his narrator points out, "the fact remains that getting people right is not what living is all about any way. It's getting them wrong that is living, getting them wrong and wrong and wrong and then, on careful reconsideration, getting them wrong again. That's how we know we're alive: we're wrong."[88]

NOTES

1 Lorrie Moore, "Terrific Mother" (1992), in *The Collected Stories* (London: Faber, 2008), 273.
2 Judith Stacey, "The Family Values Fable," in *American Families: A Multicultural Reader*, ed. Stephanie Coontz, Maya Parson, and Gabrielle Raley (New York: Routledge, 1998), 487.
3 Michael Wines, "Views on Single Motherhood are Multiple at White House," *New York Times*, May 21, 1992, http://www.nytimes.com/1992/05/21/us/views-on-single-motherhood-are-multiple-at-white-house.html?pagewanted=all; George Bush, "Remarks at the Annual Convention of National Religious Broadcsters," Jan. 27, 1992, http://www.presidency.ucsb.edu/ws/?pid=20540. In "Two Bad Neighbors" (7:13; first aired Jan. 24, 1996), the Bushes move in across the road from the Simpsons, and a feud develops. After they leave, the house is taken by Gerald Ford, a more congenial drinking buddy for Homer. In fact the "feud" began in 1990 when Barbara Bush described *The Simpsons* as "the dumbest thing she had ever seen." Matt Groening (writing as Marge Simpson) sent her a letter noting how much they had "in common": "Each of us living our lives to serve an exceptional man." Dwight Young and Margaret Johnson (eds), *Dear First Lady: Letters to the White House: From the Collections of the Library of Congress and National Archives* (Washington, DC: National Geographic, 2008), 182–183.
4 The rerun of "Stark Raving Dad" (1991) was aired on 30 January 1992.
5 *The Sopranos* (1:11), first aired March 21, 1999.
6 *The Sopranos* (3:12), first aired May 13, 2001.
7 A. M. Homes, *The Safety of Objects* (New York: Vintage, 1991), 18.
8 Jeffrey Eugenides, *The Virgin Suicides* (London: Abacus, 1994), 243, 246.
9 Douglas Coupland, *Generation X* (London: Abacus, 1992), 133, 134.
10 Lauren Berlant, *The Queen of America Goes to Washington City* (Durham, NC: Duke University Press, 1997), 140; Stephanie Coontz, *The Way We Never Were: American Families and the Nostalgia Trap* (New York: Basic Books, 2000).
11 Kasia Boddy, Unpublished Interview with Jayne Anne Phillips, 1995. In *Where the Girls Are*, Susan J. Douglas makes much the same point: "after we'd watched the prefect, secure, harmonious families on *The Donna Reed Show* or *My Three Sons*, we watched our parents fight with each other, yell at us and hit us, and plot their divorces." (New York: Times Books, 1994), 143.
12 Susan Cheever, *Treetops: A Family Memoir* (New York: Washington Square Press, 1991), 141; Mary Karr, *The Liar's Club: A Memoir* (1995) (London: Picador, 2015), 45.
13 Jayne Anne Phillips, *Shelter* (London: Faber, 1994), 69.
14 Eric Schmitt, "For First Time, Nuclear Families Drop Below 25% of Households," *New York Times*, May 15, 2001. The anthropologist George Peter Murdoch distinguished the "nuclear family" from "composite forms." *Social Structure* (New York: Free, 1949), 1–2.

15 "Households and Families: 2000," *Census 2000 Brief*, September 2001, https://www.census.gov/prod/2001pubs/c2kbr01-8.pdf.
16 Stacey, "The Family Values Fable," 489.
17 David Foster Wallace, *Infinite Jest* (Boston: Little, 1996), 751.
18 Michael Cunningham, *Flesh and Blood* (London: Penguin, 1996), 33, 228, 310, 461.
19 Rick Moody, *The Ice Storm* (London: Flamingo, 1998), 11; Ellen G. Friedman and Corinne Squire, *Morality USA* (Minneapolis: University of Minnesota Press, 1998), 109.
20 Bruce Bawer, *A Place at the Table* (New York: Simon, 1993), 34; Andrew Sullivan, *Virtually Normal* (New York: Knopf, 1995), 184.
21 Michael Warner, *The Trouble with Normal* (Cambridge, MA: Harvard University Press, 1999), 38; Lee Edelman, *No Future* (Durham, NC: Duke University Press 2004), 17.
22 Linda Singer, *Erotic Warfare*, ed. Judith Butler and Maureen MacGrogan (New York: Routledge, 1993), 85.
23 Dennis Cooper, *Discontents: New Queer Writers* (New York: Amethyst, 1992), xi.
24 Dennis Cooper, *Try* (London: Serpent's Tail, 1994), 12, 13.
25 Catherine MacKinnon, *Feminism Unmodified* (Cambridge, MA: Harvard University Press, 1987), 169.
26 Ian Hacking, "The Making and Molding of Child Abuse," *Critical Inquiry* 17.2 (1991): 257.
27 Lenore Terr, *Too Scared To Cry: Psychic Trauma in Childhood* (New York: Harper, 1990); *Unchained Memories* (New York: Basic Books, 1994); Kathryn Harrison, *The Kiss* (New York: Random House, 1997), 68.
28 Cooper, *Try*, 34 On rewrites of *Lolita* in this context, see Kasia Boddy "Regular Lolitas?: The Afterlives of an American Adolescent," in *American Fiction of the 1990s*, ed. Jay Prosser (London: Routledge, 2008), 164–176.
29 John Paul Eakin, *How Our Lives Become Stories* (Ithaca, NY: Cornell University Press, 1999), 43, 86.
30 Jane M. Shattuc, *The Talking Cure: TV Talk Shows and Women* (New York: Routledge, 1997), 50.
31 Ben Yagoda, *The Memoir* (New York: Riverhead, 2009), 238–239. The Oprah Book Club ran from Oct 1996 to May 2002.
32 Dorothy Allison, *Trash* (London: Penguin, 1990), 3. "When I was young … I started to write about my own life and I came to see that this act saved my life." Jamaica Kincaid, *My Brother* (London: Vintage, 1998), 196.
33 Moore, *Collected Stories*, 245, 248, 265, 271.
34 Judith Butler, *Bodies That Matter* (London: Routledge, 2011 [1993]), 94–95
35 Jewelle Gomez, *The Gilda Stories* (London: Sheba, 1992), 31, 209.
36 Pagan Kennedy, *Pagan Kennedy's Living: The Handbook for Maturing Hipsters* (New York: St Martins, 1997), 65; Pagan Kennedy, *The Exes* (New York: Simon, 1998), 17.

37 Wendy Brown, *Undoing the Demos: Neoliberalism's Stealth Revolution* (New York: Zone Books, 2015), 102.
38 Donna Tartt, *The Secret History* (London: Penguin, 1993), 391.
39 Brown, *Undoing the Demos*, 106–107.
40 Kennedy, *The Exes*, 41.
41 *Friends* (10:10), first aired Jan 15, 2004.
42 Lynn Spigel, *Make Room for TV: Television and the Family Ideal in Postwar America* (Chicago: University of Chicago Press, 1992), 39.
43 Jack Kerouac, *The Dharma Bums* (London: Penguin, 1991), 104.
44 David Foster Wallace, "Fictional Futures and the Conspicuously Young" (1988), in *Both Flesh and Not* (London: Hamilton, 2012), 42.
45 Homes, *The Safety of Objects*, 41, 116. Although TV viewing in general increased toward the end of the twentieth century, surveys reported that viewing as a family dropped from 54 percent in 1976 to 41 percent in 1996. This was another sign of "loosening family bonds," declared Robert Putnam in his jeremiad *Bowling Alone* (New York: Simon, 2000), 101.
46 Thomas Pynchon, *Vineland* (London: Minerva, 1991), 351.
47 Wallace, *Infinite Jest*, 233.
48 Ibid, 639,641, 642, 645, 646.
49 Ella Taylor, *Prime-Time Families* (Berkeley: University of California Press, 1989), 130.
50 Wallace, *Infinite Jest*, 32.
51 Cunningham, *Blood and Flesh*, 28.
52 White reputedly conceived his book partly as a direct response to the *Infinite Jest* episode devoted to Steeply's father.
53 Curtis White, *Memories of My Father Watching TV* (Normal, IL: Dalkey Archive Press, 1998), 3, 117; Charles B. Harris, "Blessed by Madness: Memories of My Father Watching TV," *Review of Contemporary Fiction*, 18.2 (1998): 101, 102.
54 White, *Memories of My Father*, 3, 143.
55 Mary Gordon, *The Shadow Man: A Daughter's Search for Her Father* (New York: Vintage, 1997); Barry Gifford, *The Phantom Father* (New York: Harcourt, 1997).
56 Philip Lopate, "The Story of My Father" (1996), in *Getting Personal: Selected Writings* (New York: Basic Books, 2003), 364; Rick Moody, *The Black Veil* (London: Faber, 2004), 12.
57 Lorrie Moore, *Who Will Run the Frog Hospital?* (London: Faber, 1994), 31–32.
58 Richard Ford, *Independence Day* (London: Harvill, 1996), 17, 161; A. M. Homes, *Jack* (New York: Vintage, 1990), 23.
59 Mona Simpson, *The Lost Father* (New York: Vintage, 1992), 44; Robert Bly, *Iron John: A Book About Men* (Boston: De Capo, 2005), 38.
60 Jane Tompkins, "Saving Our Lives: *Dances with Wolves, Iron John*, and the Search for a New Masculinity," in *Eloquent Obsessions: Writing Cultural Criticism*, ed. Marianna Torgovnick (Durham, NC: Duke University Press, 1994), 96; Chuck Palahniuk, *Fight Club* (London: Vintage, 1997), 50, 141. For another parody of a men's support group meeting, see Wallace, *Infinite Jest*, 799–809.

61 Palahniuk, *Fight Club*, 18, 51, 156.
62 Barack Obama, *Dreams from My Father: A Story of Race and Inheritance* (Edinburgh: Canongate, 2007), 63, 129, 342.
63 Daniel Park Moynihan, "The Negro Family: The Case for National Action," in *The Moynihan Report and the Politics of Controversy*, ed. Lee Rainwater and William L. Yancy (Cambridge, MA: MIT Press, 1967), 51, 29, 76.
64 Julie Bosman, "Obama Sharply Assails Absent Black Fathers," *New York Times*, June 16, 2008, http://www.nytimes.com/2008/06/16/us/politics/15cnd-obama.html.
65 Marianne Hirsch, "Knowing Their Names: Toni Morrison's *Song of Solomon*," in *New Essays on Song of Solomon*, ed. Valerie Smith (Cambridge: Cambridge University Press, 1995), 70.
66 Toni Morrison, *Paradise* (New York: Knopf, 1998), 276.
67 Bonnie TuSmith (ed), *Conversations with John Edgar Wideman* (Jackson: University Press of Mississsippi, 1998), 57; John Edgar Wideman, *Fatheralong* (London: Picador, 1996), 65.
68 Wideman, *Fatheralong*, 11, 196.
69 Daniel Patrick Moynihan, *Family and Nation* (New York: Harcourt, 1987), 145; Paul Gilroy, "It's a Family Affair," in *Small Acts* (London: Serpent's Tail, 1993), 207.
70 George Saunders, "Pastoralia," in *Pastoralia* (London: Bloomsbury, 2000), 35, 43.
71 Junot Díaz, *Drown* (London: Faber, 1996), 146.
72 Edwidge Danticat, *Breath, Eyes, Memory* (London: Abacus, 1996), 11, 42, 58, 59.
73 Edwidge Dandicat, *Create Dangerously: The Immigrant Artist at Work* (Princeton, NJ: Princeton University Press, 2010), 161.
74 Díaz, *Drown*, 149, 151; Kasia Boddy, Unpublished interview with Junot Díaz, 1996.
75 Frank Lentricchia, "The American Writer as Bad Citizen," in *Introducing Don DeLillo*, ed. Frank Lentricchia (Durham, NC: Duke University Press, 1991), 2, 3, 6.
76 Richard Powers, Gain (London: Vintage, 2001); Chang-rae Lee, *Native Son* (New York: Riverhead, 1995), 261.
77 James Wolcott, "Hoogah-Boogah," *London Review of Books*, Sept 19, 2002, http://www.lrb.co.uk/v24/n18/james-wolcott/hoogah-boogah.
78 Don DeLillo, *Underworld* (London: Picador, 1997), 199, 204, 691, 761, 791.
79 Cheryl Strayed and Pankaj Mishra, "Is There a Double Standard for Judging Domestic Fiction?" *New York Times*, May 17, 2015, http://www.nytimes.com/2015/05/17/books/review/is-there-a-double-standard-for-judging-domestic-themes-in-fiction.html?_r=0
80 Phillips *Shelter*, 112, 142, 222.
81 Ibid., 117–118.
82 Michiko Kakutani, "Horrors as No More than Part of Life," *New York Times*, March 30, 1990, http://www.nytimes.com/1990/03/30/books/books-of-the-times-horrors-as-no-more-than-part-of-life.html.

83 Joyce Carol Oates, *Because It Was Bitter and Because It Was My Heart* (New York: Plume, 1991), 369, 379, 382.
84 Don DeLillo, *White Noise* (London: Picador, 1985), 29, 85.
85 Pagan Kennedy, *Spinsters* (New York: High Risk, 1995), 77; Frances Sherwood, *Green* (London: Abacus, 1997), 350.
86 John Updike, *Memories of the Ford Administration* (London: Penguin, 1993), 3, 8, 248, 365.
87 Ibid., 8.
88 Philip Roth, *American Pastoral* (London: Vintage, 1998), 35, 92, 153, 279, 378, 421.

CHAPTER 21

AIDS

Lesley Larkin

In the epilogue to Tony Kushner's *Angels in America* (1991), four friends talk politics next to the Bethesda Fountain in New York's Central Park.[1] It is 1990, nearly a decade after the first AIDS cases were identified in the United States and a decade before the new millennium. The Cold War is drawing to a close, AZT promises to transform AIDS into a chronic illness, and apocalyptic anxieties give way to hope as Kushner's characters await the "Capital M Millennium" when the healing waters of the biblical Bethesda "will flow again."[2] Instead of succumbing to the Cold War threats of mutual assured destruction, viral genocide, or the unthinkable "stasis" that Kushner's angels demand (and inscribe in HIV-positive blood), the audience is exhorted to accept the closing blessing of the play: "*More Life.*"[3] HIV may be a *retro*virus, with all the homophobic baggage its "backward," RNA-driven mechanism implies,[4] but Kushner refuses to read HIV as THE END: "The world only spins forward."[5]

Angels rests on the fulcrum that pivoted AIDS literature from the first, harrowing decade of AIDS in America to the second, which witnessed both the apex of the epidemic and the crossing of the "pharmaceutical threshold."[6] In its optimism, *Angels* contested the teleologies of "irreversible decline" and "uncontrollable spread" that had dominated the AIDS narrative.[7] Embedding AIDS in a palimpsestic history of plague (AIDS, Red Scare, Holocaust, Black Death), *Angels* linked disease and oppression and argued that human agency could change the course of both. Thematically and structurally complex, it also marked the opening up of AIDS literature, as testimonial and realist narratives yielded to complex explorations of AIDS as historical phenomenon rather than rupture, discourse as well as disease.

At the same time, *Angels*, ur-text of AIDS literature, represented a privileged narrative that prioritized the experiences of bourgeois white gay men. When Prior, who has a trust fund, ties to the Mayflower, and access to AZT, says, "This disease will be the end of many of us, but not nearly all," he inadvertently signals the vastly asymmetrical course of AIDS in the decade to come.[8] If a central question, in the early years of AIDS, was who could be left to die "with impunity,"[9] *Angels* contributed only a partial answer. "Innocent" (white) children were largely free of stigma at the beginning of the 1990s, when the first major AIDS legislation was named after one such child.[10] By the end of the decade, the vilification of white middle- and upper-class gay men who benefitted from the 1996 advent of drug "cocktails" had begun to fade. Poor, black, immigrant, and drug-addicted people, however, continued to die at excruciating rates and to bear the worst of AIDS stigma.

The question of which lives were worth saving intersected, in the 1990s, with the question of which lives were worth writing about – and how to write about them. The ACT UP slogan coined in 1987, Silence = Death, acknowledged that AIDS discourse was crucial activist terrain.[11] Still, novelist Andrew Holleran contended that "AIDS novels weren't needed" because "[t]he truth was quite enough," and queer theorist Lee Edelman expressed "uneas[e]" "about producing a discourse in which ... horrors ... become the material for intellectual arabesques."[12] For his part, Kushner, influenced by Brechtian Epic Theater, called for the integration of theory and practice: "You can't wait for a theory, but you have to have a theory," the epilogue to *Angels* concludes.[13] In the 1990s, many writers meditated on the ethics of writing (or "theorizing") an epidemic.[14] Although testimony and witnessing remained important threads in what was now a tradition of AIDS writing, they were joined by metafictional and experimental works that engaged AIDS discourse and its "proliferating equations."[15] The texts discussed below, organized according to such equations, exemplify this discursive turn. Challenging the notion that there was a typical AIDS story, they illustrate the degree to which both disease and discourse infected American life at the end of the twentieth century.

AIDS = Death, AIDS = War

By the late 1980s, writers and scholars had begun to address AIDS as a "plague of discourse,"[16] as harmful in its discursive formulations as its physical effects. In her influential book *AIDS and Its Metaphors* (1989), Susan Sontag reprised an argument she first made in *Illness as Metaphor* (1978): that the metaphorization of illness added to the suffering of patients, interfered with treatment, and justified oppression.[17] Sontag identified the equivalence drawn between AIDS and death for special critique. She did not challenge the deadly realities of the epidemic but argued, rather, that the association of AIDS and death rendered the syndrome so relentlessly linear (despite HIV's pathogenic complexity) that death became equivalent with seropositive status.[18] This discursive operation, underwritten by homophobia and racism, pathologized HIV-positive people as "tainted," causing "social death" long before physical death.[19]

The idea that HIV-positive people were responsible for their own disease and destined to die justified the US government's failure to fund AIDS research and services. Equally, the apocalyptic belief that AIDS was punishment for ungodly "mixing" (what Kushner's angels believe has driven God away) intersected with xenophobia. AIDS was "another infestation from the so-called Third World" that justified regimes of "tabulation" and "surveillance."[20] AIDS = death thus slid into AIDS = war, a formulation that warranted the restriction of freedom in the name of public health. "We . . . are not authorized to fight back by any means whatever," wrote Sontag, critiquing (like Kushner) calls for quarantine, immigration control, and other forms of discrimination.[21]

AIDS and Its Metaphors sets clear stakes for reading literary AIDS in the 1990s. Rebecca Brown's *The Gifts of the Body* (1994) follows Sontag in eschewing metaphor in favor of unflinching physical description.[22] In *Gifts*, no one is fighting a war, no one is saved or damned. AIDS is "just an illness."[23] Brown's eleven anaphorically titled chapters ("The Gift of . . . ") are a sly adaptation of the biblical gifts of the spirit, as Brown emphasizes AIDS as a "story of the body and its locations"[24] rather than a story of spiritual reckoning or redemption. Nine chapters refer to bodily operations or products, two to emotional phenomena that Brown presents as embodied. Blurring the boundary between ill and well bodies, Brown challenges the physical exile imposed on people with AIDS. In "The Gift of Sweat," the narrator, a home-care worker, is marked by an ill man's perspiration, which "smelled like me, but also him"; in "The Gift of Skin," the act of washing a sick man's skin also cleanses hers: "*Our* skin felt clean."[25] Brown also materializes religious sacraments and traditions, such as Communion ("I took the food he meant for me, I ate") and foot washing ("I sat on the floor and washed his feet).[26]

Brown rejects the imputation of religious "meaning" but not the AIDS = death equation. In *Gifts*, medical treatment only slows death down: "everyone still died. It just took them longer."[27] The narrator assumes people are ill until proven otherwise ("You never knew who was sick anymore"), and when one patient has periods of improved health, "[h]e was just getting worse more slowly."[28] The penultimate chapter demands "hope" but the novel ends with "The Gift of Grief" and represents HIV diagnosis as the first step on a progressive path to death.

Brown's approach is in stark contrast to Paul Monette's in *Halfway Home* (1991),[29] which offers the AIDS crisis as beach read. Yet its motivation is serious: to supplant the figure of the slowly wasting AIDS patient. Although Monette's protagonist, Tom, describes AIDS as inescapably progressive ("I would die ... [T]his morning was the beginning"), his experience belies this formulation.[30] Instead of withering away, Tom alternates naps, headaches, and nausea with walking, swimming, performing, and having sex, implying that HIV is not equivalent to death (sexual or otherwise). Tom even becomes an action hero when he fatally subdues an attacker. (Ironically, Tom accesses the AIDS = death equation to do so, biting his assailant and thereby eliciting enough AIDS panic[31] to gain the upper hand.) AIDS patient as hero – not just in the "war on AIDS" – is a relatively rare figuration. The novel ends with Tom and his lover, Gray, driving into the summer they will spend together. "Gray checks the rearview mirror to make sure no one's following," reinforcing their escape from the past, and declares, "Summer's my *middle* name," as Monette suspends his readers in an interim that breaks – momentarily – with the inexorable timeline of AIDS.[32]

Although Rabih Alameddine's *Koolaids* (1998) ends conventionally in death, its self-consciousness – epitomized in the final line ("I die") – and non-linear, multivocal structure work against this convention.[33] Alameddine directly links AIDS and the Lebanese Civil War; however, he is deeply critical of war rhetoric and refuses to imbue death with transcendent meaning. Mohammad, a Lebanese-American painter dying from AIDS, is exasperated by talk "about crossing to the other side, turning into a being of light, getting rid of [the] earthly body."[34] Instead, he clings to the absurd, as when a dying friend sings the Oscar Mayer wiener jingle rather than expressing "pearl[s] of wisdom."[35] The novel's title, which alludes to a gift sent to Mohammad's sister by a naïve Midwestern penpal, similarly appropriates a commercial figure as an absurd response to war, disease, and the "profiteers" who exploit them.[36]

Mohammad also condemns the commercialization of death in the art industry. When his paintings rise in value, he complains that, "They must think I am dead or something."[37] When asked what transformed Keith Haring into a "superstar artist," he answers, "the AIDS diagnosis."[38] The link between death and aesthetic value relies on an obfuscating logic also evident in ethnocentric misinterpretation, as when Americans see his representations of Lebanese villages as "abstract": "I thought everybody would see what the paintings were when they saw them," explains Mohammad, his double use of "see" evoking the doubled labor of interpretation, of looking beyond the surface to deeper meaning, which, in this context, is ethically suspect.[39] Mohammad's "see/saw" exposes the impulse to metaphorize at the expense of a work's literal referent, as meaning teeters between artist and viewer. Alameddine counsels readers not to miss the dying body, the village, or the marketplace in favor of spiritual or artistic abstraction. When Mohammad aligns two ignorant clichés – "They say Beirut used to be the Paris of the Middle East" and "Some of my best friends are gay"[40] – he aligns war and AIDS as alibis for the ethnocentric and homophobic belief that Beirutis and gay men are the backward victims of "irreversible decline." Rather than justifying "fight[ing] back by any means,"[41] war, in *Koolaids*, is metaphorically serviceable within AIDS discourse to the degree that it exposes absurdity and ignorance.

AIDS = Homosexual, AIDS = Black

Near the beginning of *Koolaids*, Mohammad recalls a formative sexual experience during which his partner's orgasm is simultaneous with the "eruption" of gunfire and after which Mohammad's penis is nearly struck by a bullet. Here, Alameddine ironically signals the "narrative of irreversible decline" as it targets the gay male body, such that the moment of "infection" that leads irrevocably to death is not exposure to HIV but exposure to gay sex or, even earlier, a gay identity ("The bullet calls my name").[42] This formulation depends upon a prurient fixation on the "the gay male anus" and a host of "outlandish and speculative" ideas about gender and sexuality, including a preexisting association of gay men with disease.[43] Linking sex and death far beyond the phenomenon of HIV ("Death comes in many shapes and sizes, but it always comes")[44] and mocking religious homophobia and ethnocentrism, Alameddine implies that singling out a sexual risk group for moral censure is as absurd as singling out an ethnic or religious group.

Nevertheless, AIDS discourse in the 1990s was adept at singling out both. The association of AIDS with homosexuality usually figured the latter as white and male. As the epidemic's global and heterosexual dimensions became more visible, another equation emerged: AIDS = black. Whether in its (African-American) "addict," (Haitian) "immigrant," or (African) "foreigner" formulation, the AIDS = black equation provided the so-called general population[45] with imaginary protection from infection.[46] The association of AIDS with blackness drew from the longstanding devaluation of black life – from the widespread sense that "the average African-American man's life must 'naturally' be rather short" and that Africa was a "continent of seething sex and rampant death."[47] These attitudes had devastating effects on education and treatment in black communities around the globe.

In the 1990s, many writers challenged the homophobic and racist "story of AIDS."[48] Jamaica Kincaid's memoir *My Brother* (1997) exposes the limits of AIDS discourse in the context of colonialism. Like Sontag, Kincaid finds that "AIDS" is a slippery term ("AIDS, or the virus that causes AIDS, or something like that"), as are its "causes" ("he was a participant in homosexual life").[49] While Devon is ill, words become estranged from their referents in a manner that recalls the linguistic violence of colonialism: "ordinarily the word 'Miami'... is familiar enough... but when I am writing all this about my brother, suddenly... the thing I am about to say seem[s] foreign, strange.[50] No "simile" can capture the smell of her dying brother's body, no "metaphor" can describe "his heart beating like something, but what, but what... his heart was beating like his own heart, only it was beating barely."[51] Metaphor yields to the pulse-like "but what, but what," as Kincaid struggles to represent Devon's physical experience without imitating colonial appropriation.[52]

When Kincaid uses metaphor, she relies heavily upon botanical figures, alluding to the colonial history of gardening.[53] Such metaphors are self-consciously repetitious (Devon's thrush is continually described as "floriferous" and "abloom") and unstable, as in this homophonic overlap: "his penis looked like a bruised *flower*... on the sores was a white substance... almost *floury*."[54] In Kincaid's formulation, HIV – despite the nonliving status of viruses – is an "organism" that, like colonialism, transforms the death and suffering of some people into life and beauty for others: "The plantsman in my brother will never be... but inside his body a death lives, flowering upon flowering."[55] *The Education of a Gardener*, the book Kincaid is reading when she learns her brother is ill, implies a corrupt source for figures of speech that aestheticize illness. That additional metaphors for Devon's physical symptoms ("sinking" and "blackened") evoke the deadly and racializing effects of the slave trade underscores the fact that Kincaid's literary language is as "marked by the humiliations of history" as her brother's vernacular speech.[56]

The supposed inevitability of colonialism, articulated in *My Brother* by a history textbook cherished by Devon, rendered Europe and the United

States sites of vitality and the West Indies a site of death; indeed, as a child Kincaid believed that people only died in Antigua. This formulation was repeated in the "tropical thinking" of AIDS epidemiology and implied that AIDS was "the return of a colonial repressed."[57] As AIDS became increasingly manageable for elite Americans and Western Europeans, however, it remained a death sentence in the Caribbean: "there was no AZT on the island."[58] AIDS = death thus returns with a vengeance in *My Brother*, not just as a metaphor for the colonial encounter, but as its lethal continuation. Devon's "reality was that he was dead but still alive."[59]

Precious, the HIV-positive narrator of Sapphire's *Push* (1996) enunciates a similar reality principle: "I don't know what 'realism' mean but I do know what REALITY is and it's a mutherfucker."[60] *Push*, like *My Brother*, highlights biopolitical oppression and its justifying discourses. Set in 1980s Harlem, the novel illustrates how "personal responsibility," byword of the neoconservative zeitgeist, harbored antiblack stereotypes and AIDS paranoia. The overlapping political arguments against social services for gay men, intravenous drug users, and poor black people contributed to the displacement, ghettoization, and incarceration of sexual dissidents and people of color. Both groups were held responsible for their own "pathology," a claim that intersected with the biomedical transformation of patients into consumers responsible for their own wellness.[61]

Precious – sixteen, black, illiterate, pregnant, impoverished, abused, and HIV-positive – is somehow at fault for her own misery. Using a metaphor that applies as easily to gay men as to the black underclass, Precious announces, "I know who they say I am – vampire sucking the system's blood."[62] Precious does not have access to the (tenuous) innocence of the white children – like Ryan White, Kimberly Bergalis, or the protagonist of Alice Hoffman's bestselling *At Risk* (1988) – who justified the funding of AIDS research and services. Although Precious is told, "All people with HIV or AIDS is innocent victims," the moralization of AIDS makes it difficult for her to "see how I am the same as a white faggit or [black] crack addict."[63] Precious expresses the racist and homophobic logic of AIDS and exposes the lack of resources in black communities.

Biopolitical institutions conspire to extract labor from Precious while keeping her geographically and economically immobile. Her parents exploit her sexually and financially, her school expels her, the hospital and police fail to act on her sexual abuse, a social worker pushes her toward workfare. Surveillance, justified by intersecting "wars" on drugs, welfare, and AIDS, coordinates this cruel effort: "[E]very time they wants to fuck wif me or decide something in my life, here they come wif the mutherfucking file."[64] Precious's social services file misreads her relentlessly, calling her by her legal, rather than preferred, name; citing her "obvious intellectual limitations"; and claiming that she "seems to envision social services... taking care of her forever."[65] It also notes Precious's HIV status without her consent, alluding to the privacy concerns of HIV-positive people.

Push posits literature as an antidote to oppressive discourses that intersect in AIDS. As Precious encounters texts that confirm the humanity of black and gay people (Langston Hughes and Alice Walker figure prominently), she lets go of internalized racism ("they help me like being black") and homophobia ("not homos who rape me, not homos who let me be ignerent").[66] Literature reconnects Precious to her despised body ("To talk I have to tell how I feel in my body") and teaches her to write oppositional metaphors of her own – as when, in a poem, she substitutes HIV for the "lamb" that follows Mary to school.[67] To paraphrase a well-known formulation of feminist intersectional thought, if all the gays are white and all the blacks are drug users, AIDS discourse erases Precious by way of its reductive equations.[68] Like *My Brother* and *Koolaids*, *Push* challenges the racist and homophobic underpinnings of the standard 1990s AIDS story.

AIDS = Language

In addition to engaging the foundational equations of AIDS discourse, AIDS literature in the 1990s also harnessed HIV as a metaphor for language itself. Postmodern texts that signaled their self-awareness through the figure of HIV followed the scientific literature, which described viruses as self-conscious agents of linguistic disruption that rewrite the "'proper' language of cells."[69] The metaphoric well from which these writers drew was shared by molecular genetics, virology, and informatics, all replete with references to linguistic terms, such as "translation," "transcription," "vocabulary," "code," and "punctuation."[70] In Sontag's view, this confluence – resulting from the "omnipresence" of AIDS talk, the "transformations" of the computer age, and virology's "independent" adoption of linguistic figures – "reinforce[d] the AIDS mythology."[71] The problematic implications included the portrayal of HIV as intentional, backward, and masculine, formulations that implicitly supported the condemnation of gay men and the erasure of women.[72] AIDS narratives that employed "viral" structures or metaphors in the 1990s, however, varied in the degree to which such techniques were associated with ethical considerations.

The structure of Michael Cunningham's *The Hours* (1998) implies that literary influence is itself "viral." Literary elements redound and recombine among Cunningham's three storylines, which focus on Virginia Woolf, as she drafts *Mrs. Dalloway*; Laura, a depressed mid-century housewife, as she reads *Mrs. Dalloway*; and Clarissa, a contemporary middle-aged editor, as she enacts an updated version of Woolf's novel. Clarissa is dubbed "Mrs. Dalloway" by (Laura's son) Richard, a writer dying of AIDS.[73] As Virginia revises *Mrs. Dalloway*, she unwittingly influences Laura, Richard, and Clarissa's stories. In other words, *Mrs. Dalloway* gradually overwrites *The Hours* in a process that recalls the representation of viral reproduction as textual revision.

The viral operations of literature implied by this structure are underscored thematically. Several characters suffer from a virulent case of the literary, their lives "infected" by the fictions they read and write. Virginia, Laura, Richard, and Clarissa view others and themselves as literary characters. Laura shirks her maternal duties to stay in bed with *Mrs. Dalloway*, even sneaking off to a hotel as if she is having an affair. (Alternatively, Woolf's book is an antidote to the heteronormative and xenophobic rewriting of Laura *Zielski* as Laura *Brown* upon marriage.) Clarissa's daughter, Julia, has "caught" queer theory, which Clarissa considers as fraudulent as the glossy magazines whose sterilized suburban lifestyle Laura tries – and fails – to reproduce. Finally, the headaches that portend Virginia's bouts of dissociation take over her mind "like a virus," while Richard's mental breakdown is caused by HIV.

Of the many motifs that link Cunningham's intertwined narratives, a kiss – in its allusion to speech, sex, and viral transmission – is apt for capturing the novel's HIV-inflected structure. A kiss – or near-kiss (her memory is uncertain) – first appears in Clarissa's narrative, ending her youthful affair with Richard. Later in the novel, though earlier chronologically, Laura kisses her neighbor and Virginia kisses her sister on the mouth. The latter transgression prompts Woolf's decision that Mrs. Dalloway "will have had a kiss that promised a kind of love that she never finds" and that Septimus, possessing "a touch . . . of poetry" and "ground under by the wheels of . . . war and government" will take his own life, instead of her title character.[74] This decision seems to result in Laura's survival and Richard's suicide – and, not incidentally, implies an association of AIDS and war. Rather than focusing on the origin or trajectory of Richard's HIV infection, Cunningham engages in literary epidemiology. Wending through the novel until it finds its way back to Woolf, this highly communicable kiss – that may have happened, may never happen – reverses "natural" authorial direction; it is, like HIV, retroviral.

Carole Maso's *The Art Lover* (1990) also uses a braided structure in which elements from each of three storylines "contaminate" the others.[75] Maso embeds the story of the AIDS-related death of her friend, artist Gary Falk, within the story of an author, Caroline, whose artist friend is dying from AIDS. Caroline's story is, in turn, embedded within the novel she is writing. *The Art Lover* is deeply ambivalent about its form, which, Maso implies, is a fraught attempt to manage grief. Maso criticizes writers for aestheticizing "sorrow," "rage," and "loss," transforming "flesh . . . into words on a page" and "death" into "the form of a beautiful woman." Caroline specifically aligns metaphor and virus: "I am tired of things that divide, that change shape, that become anything other than themselves," she laments, even while she performs – and is the product of – metaphorization. Caroline's literary imagination makes her "sick": "I am sick of myself trying to give shape to all this sorrow, all this rage, all this loss – and failing."[76]

Literature's limits are marked, in *The Art Lover*, by visual images that demand and resist interpretation. Maso places a diagram of HIV and a star map, for example, at the end of a vignette that alludes to Steven's AIDS diagnosis. Purporting to make legible that which is difficult to see and express, these images also imply that HIV resides in an unreachable "microscopic distance."[77] The repeated image of a starburst-shaped window is also linked to hidden dangers: the failed O-ring that precipitates the 1986 Space Shuttle Challenger disaster, the blood clot that causes Caroline's father's stroke, the virus that causes Steven's illness and Gary's death. Works of visual art, like writing, also create distance from painful subjects, as when a painting by Matisse appears to transform Caroline's mother's suicide into a beautiful image. The juxtaposition of paintings by Falk to passages about failed communication, a poster that critiques sexism and racism in the art industry, captions included below works of art, descriptions of art restoration – all underscore the instability of visual art. The images included in *The Art Lover* are the promise of the "real" and its perpetual deferral, culminating in a photograph of Maso and Falk that stands in for – but cannot express – what *The Art Lover* leaves unsaid.

Despite its doubts and deferrals, *The Art Lover* presents literature and art as "hieroglyph[s] of hope," a phrase followed by a series of images that link medicine, technology, sign language, and Western artistic traditions to the ideal of perfect communication: "They are not hard to decipher.

They are not really in code."[78] In the context of AIDS, storytelling is a necessity: "We are speaking for our lives" and "I'm trying to keep you alive," repeat Caroline and Carole.[79] Although "to write it down is always to get it wrong," and although "Nothing makes it stop... Not the writing of this. Not the writing of *The Art Lover*," Maso persists.[80] "I eat the peach. We are eating to live," writes Caroline, her allusion to "The Love Song of J. Alfred Prufrock" ironically underscoring the life-affirming possibilities of literature and implying that T. S. Eliot's theory of literary "tradition," whereby new works alter the meaning of their predecessors, is retroviral.[81]

The ethical stakes of literary citation are clear in *Push*, which also draws from the metaphoric intimacy among virology, genomics, and informatics. Synthesizing the lessons in agency that come with literacy, Sapphire challenges the material and metaphorical limitations enacted by AIDS in the novel's final poem:

> PLAY THE HAND YOU GOT
> housemother say
> HOLD FAST TO DREAMS
> Langston say.
> GET UP OFF YOUR KNEES
> Farrakhan say.
> CHANGE
> Alice Walker
> Say.
>
> ...
> DON'T ALWAYS RHYME
> Ms Rain say
> Walk on
> go into the poem
> the HEART of it
> beating
> like
> a clock
> a virus
> tick
> tock.[82]

The layered metaphors that end this poem align poetry and HIV with technology: the "HEART" of the poem "beat[s]" like a "clock" and a "virus," its onomatopoeic "tick / tock" alluding also to a bomb and, thus, to HIV's deadly timeline. However, it is *poetry* that is viral, its rhythm countering Precious's infected pulse. The quotations spliced into this poem are a kind of literary gene therapy, their all-caps formatting mimicking the conventional transcription of genetic code. These are the messages Precious uploads and disseminates in an effort to overwrite racism. While "PLAY THE HAND YOU GOT" acknowledges genetic and cultural inheritance, the scripts provided by Alice Walker and Ms Rain, "CHANGE" and "DON'T ALWAYS RHYME," capture the dynamism of both literary tradition and the human genome.

Conclusion

In 2012, the AIDS Memorial Quilt, first displayed in 1987, returned to Washington, D.C. It was presented not only on the National Mall but also online, thanks to a searchable map funded in part by Microsoft. Now incorporated into the (capitalist) soul of the nation, the AIDS story – in its most tactile representation – had gone digital. HIV has gone digital, too; today, one might expect a representation of the HIV genome to replace Maso's viral diagram. The digitization of AIDS coincides with the syndrome's increasing dematerialization in the national imaginary. AIDS belongs to bodies over there – or to othered bodies over here – and its physical symptoms and presence in the blood can be suppressed to indetectable levels.

In the 1990s, however, AIDS was still very much "over here." The 1990s were a transitional decade for AIDS and for AIDS writing, comprising its most complex literary treatments before complex medical treatments drained the disease of its immediacy for many American authors. Writers in the 1990s engaged the unique circumstances of their time and challenged the dematerialization of disease without abandoning the critical power of metaphor. It is not incidental that AIDS writing in the 1990s coincided with the rise of genomics, which posited DNA as a "hieroglyph of hope" but also an index of disease, and with the rise of biomedicine, characterized by the commodification and individuation of health care. The texts discussed above challenged the cultural scripts, influenced by biomedical and genomic discourse, that presented certain bodies as diseased by destiny. In their meditations on the coproduction of disease and discourse, their representations of texts as viral (and viruses as textual), their critical engagement of the institutions within which AIDS and its meanings proliferated, and their refusal to hew to the standard AIDS script and its reductive metaphors, American authors in the 1990s engaged AIDS on both material and discursive terms. In so doing, they articulated the stakes within which American writers would engage major biosocial forces (e.g. genomics, biomedicine, terrorism) in the decades to follow.

NOTES

1. Tony Kushner, *Angels in America: A Gay Fantasia on National Themes. Part Two: Perestroika* (New York: Theatre Communication Group, [1992], 1996).
2. Ibid., 145.
3. Ibid., 146.
4. "[R]etroviruses contain in their very name the suggestion that their means of... 'expression' are somehow abnormal, even perverse" (Steven F. Kruger, *AIDS Narratives: Gender and Sexuality, Fiction and Science* [New York: Garland, 1996], 15).
5. Kushner, 146.
6. Monica B. Pearl, *AIDS Literature and Gay Identity: The Literature of Loss* (New York: Routledge, 2013), 23. In 1994, AIDS was the leading cause of death among Americans ages 25 to 44. The FDA approved AZT in 1987 and the first protease inhibitors at the end of 1995. In 1997 Highly Active Antiretroviral Therapy (HAART) resulted in a decline in AIDS-related deaths, though African Americans were ten times likelier to die from AIDS than whites. In 1999, AIDS was the "number one killer" in Africa and the "fourth biggest killer" worldwide. See "A Timeline of AIDS" at https://www.aids.gov/hiv-aids-basics/hiv-aids-101/aids-timeline/.
7. Kruger, 73–80.
8. Kushner, 146.
9. Christopher Breu, *Insistence of the Material: Literature in the Age of Biopolitics* (Minneapolis: University of Minnesota Press, 2014), 16.
10. The belated Comprehensive AIDS Resources Emergency (CARE) Act (1990) was named after Ryan White, who died of AIDS in 1990.
11. See the ACT UP report "SILENCE = DEATH" at www.actupny.org/reports/silencedeath.html.
12. Andrew Holleran, *Ground Zero* (New York: Morrow, 1980), 13; Lee Edelman, "The Plague of Discourse: Politics, Literary Theory, and AIDS," in *Displacing Homophobia: Gay Male Perspectives in Literature and Culture*, ed. Ronald R. Butters et al. (Durham, NC: Duke University Press, 1989), 304.
13. Kushner, 144.
14. See, for example, Paula Treichler's 80s and 90s meditations in the aptly titled *How to Have Theory in an Epidemic: Cultural Chronicles of AIDS* (Durham, NC: Duke University Press, 1999).
15. Edelman, "The Plague," 301.
16. Ibid., 289. Also see Donna Haraway, *Simians, Cyborgs, and Women* (New York: Routledge, 1991), 203–204; Treichler, *How*, 1, 11–41; Waldby, *AIDS and the Body Politic: Biomedicine and Sexual Difference* (London: Routledge, 1996), 28–39; and Thomas E. Yingling, *AIDS and the National Body*, ed. Robyn Wiegman (Durham, NC: Duke University Press, 1997), 15.
17. Susan Sontag, *Illness as Metaphor and AIDS and Its Metaphors* (New York: Anchor Books, 1989). Also see Edmund White, "Esthetics and Loss," in *Personal Dispatches: Writers Confront AIDS*, ed. John Preston (New York: St. Martin's, 1988), 151.

18 "HIV disease" began to compete with "AIDS" in 1988 (Cindy Patton, *Globalizing AIDS* [Minneapolis: University of Minnesota Press, 2002], 117). Also see Lee Edelman, "The Mirror and the Tank: 'AIDS,' Subjectivity, and the Rhetoric of Activism," in *Writing AIDS: Gay Literature, Language, and Analysis*, ed. Timothy F. Murphy and Suzanne Poirier (New York: Columbia University Press, 1993), 9–10.
19 Sontag, 122, 134. Also see Kruger, 80.
20 Sontag, 140. Also see Priscilla Wald, *Contagious: Cultures, Carriers, and the Outbreak Narrative* (Durham, NC: Duke University Press, 2008); Waldby, 6; and Yingling.
21 Sontag, 183. Also see Haraway, 224–225; and Waldby, 1–18.
22 Rebecca Brown, *The Gifts of the Body* (New York: HarperPerennial, 1995).
23 Sontag, 181.
24 Sarah Brophy, *Writing, Testimony, and the Work of Mourning* (Toronto: University of Toronto Press, 2004), 5.
25 Brown, 9, 47, my emphasis.
26 Ibid., 10, 47.
27 Ibid., 101.
28 Ibid., 28, 86.
29 Paul Monette, *Halfway Home* (New York: Kensington Books, 1991).
30 Ibid., 185.
31 A variation on "homosexual panic" (Eve Kosofsky Sedgwick, *Epistemology of the Closet* [Berkeley: University of California Press, 1990], 19–22).
32 Monette, 262, my emphasis.
33 Rabih Alameddine, *Koolaids* (New York: Grove, [1998] 2015).
34 Ibid., 163.
35 Ibid.
36 Ibid., 168, 191.
37 Ibid., 11.
38 Ibid., 55.
39 Ibid., 102.
40 Ibid., 201.
41 Sontag, 183.
42 Alameddine, 1.
43 Edelman "The Mirror," 16; Treichler, "AIDS, Gender," 194. Also see Yingling, 15, 22.
44 Alameddine, 1.
45 "[W]hite heterosexuals who do not inject themselves with drugs or have sexual relations with those who do" (Sontag 115). Also see Treichler, "AIDS, Gender," 205; Edelman, "The Mirror," 14; and Kruger, 40, 76.
46 On the emergence of these racialized figurations of AIDS, see Phillip Brian Harper, "Eloquence and Epitaph: Black Nationalism and the Homophobic Impulse in Response to the Death of Max Robinson," in Murphy and Poirier, eds.; Judith Laurence Pastore, Introduction, *Confronting AIDS through Literature* (Urbana: University of Illinois Press, 1993), 1; Patton; Sontag, 170–175;

Brandi Stanton, "AIDS, Race, and the Invasion of the Body in Sonia Sanchez's *Does Your House Have Lions?*, *MELUS* 36.1 (2013): 90–105; and Wald, 45.
47 Harper, 117; Patton, xiii.
48 Gay men constituted the initial "site" of the disease in the United States and dominated early AIDS activism and writing; however, "a history of homosexuality is not a history of AIDS, not even in the West" (Jeffrey Weeks, "Postmodern AIDS?", in *Ecstatic Antibodies: Resisting the AIDS Mythology*, ed. Tessa Boffin and Sunil Gupta [London: Rivers Oram, 1990], 133–141). Also see Joseph Cady, "Teaching about AIDS through Literature in a Medical School Curriculum," in *Confronting AIDS through Literature: The Responsibilities of Representation*, ed. Judith Pastore (Urbana: University of Illinois Press, 1993), 241; Timothy F. Murphy, "Testimony," in Murphy and Poirier, eds., 307; Suzanne Poirier, "On Writing AIDS," in Murphy and Poirier, eds., 7; and Paula Treichler, "AIDS, Gender, and Biomedical Discourse: Current Contests for Meaning," in *AIDS: The Burdens of History*, ed. Elizabeth Fee and Daniel M. Fox (Berkeley: University of California Press, 1988). On AIDS and the diversification of literary criticism and canons, see Sedgwick, 48–59, and Yingling, 31.
49 Jamaica Kincaid, *My Brother* (New York: Farrar, 1997), 183, 161.
50 Ibid., 96.
51 Ibid., 90, 107, 183.
52 On Kincaid's ethical qualms, see Brophy, 168–202.
53 See Kincaid's *My Garden Book* (New York: Farrar, 2001). For Kincaid, "gardening ... provides the ruling class with the fantasy of a paradoxically natural *and* controlled luxury ... that allows for the ... minimization of the ecological devastation and agricultural exploitation that characterized the European conquest" (Brophy, 176).
54 Kincaid, *My Brother*, 91, 106, 149, my emphasis.
55 Ibid., 19–20, 95.
56 Ibid., 106, 108, 149.
57 Patton, 45; Wald, 46.
58 Kincaid, *My Brother*, 32.
59 Kincaid, *My Brother*, 95.
60 Sapphire, *Push* (New York: Vintage, [1996] 1997), 83.
61 On the pathologization of African Americans, see Hortense Spillers, "Mama's Baby, Papa's Maybe: An American Grammar Book," *Diacritics*, 17.2 (1987): 65–81. On biomedicine, see Breu; Ann Jurecic, *Illness as Narrative* (Pittsburgh, PA: University of Pittsburgh Press, 2012); and Laura E. Tanner, *Lost Bodies: Inhabiting the Borders of Life and Death* (Ithaca, NY: Cornell University Press, 2006). For a medical activist narrative, see Paul Reed, *The Q Journal: A Treatment Diary* (Berkeley, CA: Celestial Arts, 1991).
62 Sapphire, 31.
63 Ibid., 109. Only later does Precious realize that "crackers was addicts," too (126).
64 Ibid., 28.

65 Ibid., 119, 120.
66 Ibid., 95, 96.
67 Ibid., 28, n.p.
68 Gloria T. Hull et al., eds., *All the Women Are White, All the Blacks Are Men, but Some of Us Are Brave* (Old Westbury, NY: Feminist, 1982).
69 Kruger, 13.
70 Ibid., 5–10. Also see Haraway, 164–165; Evelyn Fox Keller, *Refiguring Life: Metaphors of Twentieth-Century Biology* (New York: Columbia University Press, 1996), 1–42; Lily Kay, *Who Wrote the Book of Life? A History of the Genetic Code* (Palo Alto, CA: Stanford University Press, 2000), xv–xx, 1–37; Sontag, 156–158; James C. Wilson, "(Re)Writing the Genetic Body-Text: Disability, Textuality, and the Human Genome Project," *Cultural Critique*, 50 (2002): 25–28.
71 Sontag, 156.
72 See Keller, Kruger.
73 Michael Cunningham, *The Hours* (New York: Farrar, 1998).
74 Ibid., 211.
75 Carole Maso, *The Art Lover* (San Francisco: North Point, 1990).
76 Ibid., 148.
77 Robert Glück, "HTLV-3," in Preston, ed., 83.
78 Ibid., 238–240.
79 Ibid., 164, 199.
80 Ibid., 199, 206.
81 T. S. Eliot, *The Waste Land and Other Poems* (New York: Harcourt, 1934), 1–10, and "Tradition and the Individual Talent," *Selected Essays 1917–1932* (New York: Harcourt, 1932), 3–11.
82 *Sapphire*, n.p.

PART V

Institutions

CHAPTER 22

The University "After" Theory
Daniel Punday

Unlike most decades, the 1990s are defined neatly by clear historical events. In his book on American historical fiction in the 1990s, Samuel Cohen described the period as an interwar decade, "bracketed on one side by the end of the Cold War and on the other by the terrorist attack and subsequently declared 'war on terrorism' – by the fall of the [Berlin] wall [in November 1989] and the fall of the Towers" on 9/11.[1] Phillip Wegner describes the contradictions of this decade whose "beginning is in fact an ending,"[2] and Brian McHale notes that the period replaced the Cold War duality with a "multipolarity, or even *a*-polarity, that was at once baffling, risky, and rich with possibilities."[3]

During this time, the nature of American literary study in the university went through a complex transformation. Initially it might seem that literature in the university was less volatile during the 1990s than it was during the emergence of literary theory in the 1970s. Instead of large-scale shifts as one theoretical paradigm replaced the previous one, we see material changes in the university and its relation to literary and popular culture beyond.

Framing the Decade

To frame the decade, I would point to two bookend works. At the beginning of the decade we can note Paul Lauter's collection of essays, *Canons and Context* (1991).[4] Lauter himself was a key figure in the attempt to rethink the American literary canon, notably as the general editor for the groundbreaking *Heath Anthology of American Literature* (1990),[5] which embodied his long-fought attempt to broaden the canon of American literature to include a more diverse group of writers. *Canons and Context* is a synthesizing work that articulates the logic for rethinking the canon at a time when canon debates reached their most public expression, with Roger Kimball, John Searle, Michael Berubé, and Dinesh D'Souza all discussing this issue in popular magazines and on television shows in late 1990 and throughout 1991. However, by 1991 the terms of the debate had largely been set, and the very public spectacle surrounding the canon wars itself represented the dissemination of changes that had largely become commonplace in the academy at that time. For all that conservatives saw changes in American literary study as a matter of debate, by 1991 canon revision was simply the state of the field.

At the other end of the decade, I choose a somewhat less likely representative work: Cass Sunstein's *Republic.com* (2001). In this book, Sunstein argues that the digital distribution of information means that readers are much more likely only to encounter writing that accords with their interests and beliefs. When readers are allowed to customize the news that they receive, they are far less likely to encounter information that challenges their worldview. Sunstein's book anticipates other works analyzing the changing market for media. Chris Anderson's 2006 *The Long Tale*, for example, describes how Internet culture changes the nature of the marketplace, allowing vendors such as Amazon to concentrate less on the blockbuster products that dominated in the past and instead make money by servicing many niches.

Sunstein's book is not in any significant way about American literature but, like Lauter, it represents a point at which contemporary patterns of reading interacted with the larger American culture. Like Lauter's book, it marks a point of contact between literature, the academy, and the wider reading public. By the end of the decade, the changing media landscape became a fundamental feature of literary culture. The Internet was an everyday part of university life by the mid-1990s, of course. Many critics at the time claimed that digital media would transform literature. Janet Murray's *Hamlet on the Holodeck* was published in 1997, describing a future where digital media fundamentally transform literary experience.[6] Even more suggestive is the title of the 1992 collection *Fiction 2000: Cyberpunk and the Future of Narrative*.[7] However, throughout most of the 1990s, the digitalization of literary culture and the changes in economics that result remained somewhat abstract. Brian McHale notes that in the first edition (1992) of George Landow's influential *Hypertext*, pragmatic terms like HTML, Internet, and World Wide Web do not appear in the index[8]; it's only in the 1997 revision of the book that these everyday terms of Internet culture are included. By the turn of the millennium, however, the fundamental importance of the changing media ecology was inescapable; ideas that are abstract in Murray are part of everyday life by the time we get to

Sunstein's book in 2001, and these media changes dominate debates about the humanities in the next decade.

The decade of the 1990s exists, then, in a transitional period after the emergence of literary theory transformed the American literary canon, during which the university went through more subtle changes in its relation to economics, popular culture, publishing, and the digital media that promised to displace print.

Theory, Creative Writing, and the Literary Essay

One common way to think about the 1990s is as a period "after theory" – although what that means is, of course, complex. Terry Eagleton opened his 2003 *After Theory* by proclaiming, "The golden age of cultural theory is long past."[9] After noting how long ago the early work of people like Lacan, Foucault, and Althusser was published, he asserts that "Not much that has been written since has matched the ambitiousness and originality of these founding mothers and fathers."[10] This "older generation had proved a hard act to follow" and the newer generation has come up "with no comparable body of ideas of its own."[11] Imagining the future from the 1980s, as structuralism replaced new criticism only to be swept away by post-structuralism, it was easy to imagine an endless series of exciting and field-redefining paradigm shifts. However, although new theorists certainly appeared on the stage, none managed to affect such a sweeping transformation. This may reflect changing attitudes toward how theory itself as a field should operate; as Jane Elliot and Derek Attridge remark, "To the extent that 'Theory' was associated with a tendency to draw obsessively on the work of a certain oracular figures, theory as it is manifested [today] suggests not so much a movement from one set of figures to another as a movement way from the perception that such figures are a necessary or consensual feature of the project of theory in the first place."[12]

The desire to move beyond theory also functioned as part of a critique of postmodernism. The concern that theory was disengaged from political reality is probably best represented by Baudrillard's controversial 1991 book (translated to English in 1995) *The Gulf War Did Not Take Place*, which analyzes the heavily mediated nature of that war. For critics, the book embodied the worst impulses of postmodernism, which, as Christopher Norris argued, is "ill equipped to mount any kind of effective critical resistance."[13] As a result, the urge to enter a phase "after theory" was linked to a desire to reengage with social and political reality – which many felt had been left behind during deconstruction's heyday. Writing in 1989, Todd Gitlin described Foucault's attitude toward power as "[a]ltogether too easy. A theoretical nihilism, then, is a fair charge to level against the discourse move; it is the equivalent of the blank stare of the postmodern. What, in short, is the ethical basis for politics?"[14] Cultural Studies' attempt to reengage with politics is inherently connected to its lack of disciplinary uniformity and rejection of "oracular figures": "It is problematic for cultural studies simply to adopt, uncritically, any of the formalized disciplinary practices of the academic, for those practices, as much as the distinctions they inscribe, carry with them a heritage of disciplinary investments and exclusions and a history of social effects that cultural studies would often be inclined to repudiate."[15]

To understand the 1990s as a period after theory, we need to recognize how fundamentally the emergence of literary theory as a distinct scholarly field in the 1970s, with its associated academic classes developed mostly in the 1980s, marked a shift in literary study. Prior to the continental influence on literary theory, there was a long tradition of writing by practicing novelists and poets (such as T. S. Eliot's *The Sacred Wood* [1920]) that was broadly theoretical. New Criticism's emphasis on classroom practice, exemplified in Brooks and Warren's 1938 textbook *Understanding Poetry*, already marked the beginning of a break between creative writing and literary theory – even though, of course, Warren himself was a practicing poet. The importance of theoretical statements by creative writers remained obvious well through the postmodernist writing of the 1960s and '70s – we might think about the central role of John Barth's 1967 "The Literature of Exhaustion" – and continued in L = A = N = G = U = A = G = E poetry.

With the rising influence of continental theory during the 1970s, which was often deployed to critique the hegemony of New Criticism, theory emerged as a distinct field relatively independent from the practicing novelists and poets who guided theoretical writing previously. It is an obvious but important fact that the most influential thinkers during this time were based in fields other than literature – Saussure and Pierce in linguistics, Lacan in psychoanalysis, Foucault in history, and so on. Critics showed the interpretive power of these theories by applying them to literary texts, but in the process theory was disconnected from the practicing poets and novelists, now sequestered in Creative Writing workshops. Such programs had existed since the 1940s, but Mark McGurl sees 1967 as a significant milestone year with the founding of the Associated Writing Programs.[16] As creative writing became a distinct field of study during the 1970s, a gulf grew between writers and literary critics. As Marjorie Perloff remarks, creative writing students are taught to believe "that theory doesn't exist or that it's just some arcane nonsense being taught on the other side of the corridor."[17]

There are, of course, exceptions to this. The L = A = N = G = U = A = G = E school of poetry was founded during the 1970s through a deep involvement with theories of language and politics. McHale notes that theoretical discussions continued to inspire poets throughout this period: "younger avant-gardists who emerged in the nineties in the wake of L = A = N = G = U = A = G = E poetry, such as Peter Gizzi, Myung Mi Kim, Tan Lin, Jennifer Moxley, Harryette Mullen, Julia Spahr, Brian Kim Stefans, and others, seem mostly to continue and extend the practices of their first-generation forerunners, including procedural writing and found-poetry practices."[18] Likewise, Chicana/o literature emerged during the 1970s in concert with more theoretical writing, probably most explicitly with Gloria Anzaldúa's *Borderlands/La Frontera: The New Mestiza* in 1987.[19] By the beginning of the 1990s, Chicana/o writing moved into mainstream – most significantly when Sandra Cisneros's *The House on Mango Street* was republished by Vintage in 1991. Both of these movements had tended to draw somewhat more broadly on social theory and philosophy, rather than on mainstream literary theory narrowly. The L = A = N = G = U = A = G = E poets, for example, are more likely to be influenced by Wittgenstein than by Derrida. Likewise, Anzaldúa is engaged with broader concerns about identity and the collective, and does not take as her starting point the primary voices in literary theory. In fact, this kind of parallel theoretical articulation is one of the reasons why literary theory after 1990 begins to feel less unified around a few theoretical schools.

It is, however, clear that the relationship between academic theory and creative writing remained a complex one for many writers during the 1990s. Writing in 1992, John Aldridge associated the rise of creative writing programs, and the "new assembly-line fiction" that they produce, with the critic's changing role. His *Talents and Technicians* opens by comparing *Esquire*'s two figurative "maps" of "where the major centers of literary power are located in the United States" from 1963 and 1987.[20] Where a number of critics were listed as important in 1963 – Wilson, Cowley, Kazin, Trilling, Frye – in 1987 critics are almost entirely absent, frequently replaced by publishers and agents.[21] He associates this in part with the decline in the number of outlets willing to publish long critical essays,[22] but also with critics who have become increasingly insular: "it must be said that academic criticism at its best is the most sensitive and informed criticism now being written about contemporary literature, and its failure or its refusal to communicate with the literary marketplace and the general reader cannot help but have a damaging effect upon newer writers."[23] Aldridge associates this failure with a tendency for the creative writing program to reward writers through "a complex network of in-group patronage" rather than through engagement with the larger marketplace.[24]

As a result, American creative writing in the 1990s had a complex relationship to literary theory. Theory itself was very much part of the debate over writing and the university during the 1990s – if for no other reason than that it provided the intellectual grounding for the culture wars over the canon. As Judith Ryan remarks in her 2012 book *The Novel after Theory*, "'Theory' became a kind of lingua franca capable of bringing scholars together in a period when the canon was expanded so rapidly that knowledge of a particular text could not always be taken for granted."[25] At the same time, however, more often than not the theory remained "on the other side of the corridor" for many creative writing students. Critical work on the relationship between theory by Ryan and by Michael Greaney in *Contemporary Fiction and the Uses of Theory* (2006) paints a complex picture of theory's place in the contemporary novel.[26] Many of the writers featured in these books are European; Julia Kristeva has a particularly important (and unsurprising) role for both. Likewise, the majority of English-language writers cited by Ryan and Greaney tend to be British, such as Lodge, Fowles, Byatt, and Burgess. Of the US writers engaged with literary theory, broad patterns are hard to identify. Some writers, such as Kathy Acker, are heavily and explicitly engaged in theory in their creative writing. For other writers, theory can often manifest itself as a plot or thematic item. Richard Powers's *Galatea 2.2* (1995) is exemplary in this regard.[27] A novelist named Richard Powers returns to his alma mater and ends up helping to build an artificial intelligence whose Turing Test will be to pass MA comprehensive examinations in English. Along the way, Powers gently satirizes literary theory and the changing literary canon, and associates his novelist far more with the scientists who house him than the English department where he was trained a decade earlier.

Literature in Popular Culture

The 1990s also marked a change in the positioning of literature within the broader American popular culture. Critics have long noted the decline in American intellectualism. Writing in 1987, Russell Jacoby noted the disappearance of "public intellectuals, writers and thinkers who address a general and educated audience."[28] While the previous generation had John Kenneth Galbraith and Daniel Bell, no younger intellectuals have emerged to supplement or replace them.[29] For Jacoby, a significant part of this decline in public intellectualism is the increased specialization and professionalization of academic study that we have already seen associated with the rise of literary theory.[30] In fact, during this time Michael Berubé associated the cultural wars over the canon with a declining engagement by general interest magazines with serious discussion of literary study and theory. He notes the publication of a diatribe by Dinesh D'Souza in *The Atlantic*, which he shows to be wildly inaccurate in its characterization of deconstruction: "If someone were to publish an essay which claimed that *Paradise Lost* never really talks about theology, or that psychoanalysis fails to make use of the works of major Greek dramatists, certainly we would recognize such a person as a cultural illiterate. But because no one at *The Atlantic*, including even the journal's fact-checkers, is aware of the past twenty-five years' profusion of deconstruction work . . . D'Souza is allows to get away with this series of inanities."[31]

Although Berubé blames the erosion of popular discussion of serious literature on such magazines as *The Atlantic* shifting their focus, we should recognize that this change represents a culmination of publishing trends that go back to the 1960s. A critique of the literary establishment has been a fundamental part of any avant-garde artistic movement. Although some movements, such as futurism, frame their critique as fundamentally destructive (sweeping away museums and institutions), most often it is accompanied by the assertion of a new aesthetic framework that is presented as superior. We might think, for example, of the *Little Review*'s subtitle "Making No Compromise with the Public Taste" and willingness to challenge pornography laws by publishing Joyce's *Ulysses* in 1918–1921. During the 1960s, the situation became considerably more muddy. Some short-lived, niche magazines sprung up around similarly modernist attitudes; Gilbert Sorrentino, editor for *Neon* and *Kulchur*, remarks that these magazines "had a definite literary bone to pick, and they set themselves up not as a mere *alternative* press but as a press that considered its criteria to be correct."[32] Others were self-consciously provocative. As Ellen Gruber Garvey explains, "[M]any mimeoed magazines grew out of a larger vision and passionate commitment to social change, not to mention the ambition to shake things up, even with their titles, like Ed Sanders's *Fuck You: A Magazine of the Arts* (1962–65). Beat magazines continually sprouted and mutated into other magazines."[33] Others have seen the explosion of little magazines less as an expression of a coherent aesthetics, and more as a reflection of creative writing programs and the market. As Michael Anania writes, "For the first time in history, we may have more writers than readers. Editorial offices of established magazines are drifted over with manuscripts, and new magazines are born to meet the writers' needs for print. Increasingly, magazines seem to reflect a sociological circumstance as much as an aesthetic one."[34] Charles Robinson summarizes the complex landscape in 1978: "Where once there was a unified force of little magazines and supporters fighting for recognition against popular tastes, today the forces have split. The independents feel that not only have the popular magazines sold out, but that the university magazines have followed suit–that, although the latter may not appeal to popular tastes, they have adopted a peculiar academicism as sterile as the policy of popular magazines turning out formula pieces."[35]

The founding of the avant-garde publisher The Fiction Collective in 1974 is indicative of this shift. As a press without an editorial board, in which the authors themselves make decisions on future publications, the Fiction Collective represents a fundamental rejection of traditional publication processes and structures. Jonathan Baumbach explains this movement in this way: "The publication of fiction in America, with fewer and fewer exceptions (said the evidence), is a desperate transaction with the devils of greed. Something ought to be done, everyone said."[36] Mark McGurl associates this urge to reject the popular with postmodernism: "in metafiction generally, we have something like an image of what happens when modernism gets what it wants: a heightened (never total) autonomy from an all-engulfing mass market, and from its traffic in realist representations."[37]

We can see these moves as a yearning for a certain kind of disintermediation – an attempt for writers to find an audience without the traditional institutional barriers of publisher or editor. To some extent, this urge did in fact depend on technological developments; the little magazine movement during the 1960s and 70s depended in part on the cheap availability of low-tech mimeograph reproduction. Of course, during the 1990s, this disintermediation became possible via the Internet. (Ironically, early attempts to use electronic media for literary purposes gravitated toward traditional publishing models; Eastgate Systems is the best example, with its claim to publish "serious hypertext" in the form of physical disks and CD-ROM works starting in the 1980s, but especially developing in the 1990s.) In summary, then, the breakdown in the authority of traditional literary institutions that Berubé mentions is not just the result of forces external to the university and literary culture; in many ways, the urge to shake off the limitations of older institutions arises from the avant-garde literary impulses of writers throughout the century.

During this same period a certain kind of popularization of literature emerged in a variety of ways. One obvious example is the founding of Oprah's Book Club in 1996, which married the discussion of serious (although usually quite mainstream) literary works to the daytime television format that was often seen as the antithesis of reading. A parallel phenomenon was the rapid national expansion of the mega bookstore, particularly Borders and Barnes & Noble, which combined a huge book selection with literary events and a coffee shop, and became for a brief period in the late 1990s a destination in its own right. Finally, we might also note the growing popularity of live-performance literary events. The first national poetry slam, where poets read their work and compete, was held in 1990s in San Francisco. A similar event for live storytelling – The Moth – was founded in 1997.

Jim Collins has described this surprising merging of literary writing and popular entertainment in his 2010 study, *Bring on the Books for Everybody: How Literary Culture Became Popular Culture*. He connects popular novels that appeal to classic literary fiction, like the 2004 *The Jane Austen Book Club*, to a broader trend that he describes as "the discrediting of the academy and empowering amateur readers." From Oprah's book club to Janice Radway's analysis of the Book-of-the-Month club in *A Feeling for Books* (1997), Collins sees a sweeping change occurring in the 1990s: "The popularization of literary culture that begins in the 1990s, however, involves a far more extensive redefinition of what constitutes a quality reading experience."[38] Instead, "The popularization of literary reading depends as much on shifts in cultural authority as it does on changes within culture industries."[39]

As this list of developments during the 1990s suggests, the decade was a fascinating period during which literature became a much more visible part of American popular culture at the very moment when the institutional authority held by academics and publishers seemed to be waning. In this regard, Jonathan Franzen's 2001 conflict with Oprah marks a fitting end to the decade. Having been invited on the show to discuss his novel *The Corrections*, Franzen expressed some mixed feelings about his upcoming appearance in interviews at other media outlets. In particular, he was concerned that association with the book club would make it harder for him to reach male readers, who themselves were (he claimed) traditionally disengaged from literary reading. In response, Oprah pulled her invitation to the show. In a 2002 essay, "Mr. Difficult," Franzen describes his conflict:

> I subscribe to two wildly different models of how fiction relates to its audience. In one model, which was championed by Flaubert, the best novels are great works of art, the people who manage to write them deserve extraordinary credit, and if the average reader rejects the work it's because the average reader is a philistine...
>
> In the opposing model, a novel represents a compact between the writer and the reader, with the writer providing words out of which the reader creates a pleasurable experience. Writing thus entails a balancing of self-expression and communication within a group, whether the groups consists of *Finnegans Wake* enthusiasts or fans of Barbara Cartland.[40]

Franzen's conflict between the popular consumption of literary writing, often in new and nonacademic forums, and traditional, modernist ideals about literary value nicely captures the conflicted 1990s.

The complex relationship between literary and popular culture also became an element even of seemingly avant-garde postmodernist writers. In 1995, Mark Amerika and Lance Olsen edited a collection called *In Memoriam to Postmodernism*, and advocated for the term "avant-pop." As Amerika and Olsen write in the introduction, "Whereas it's true that certain strains of modernism, structuralism, poststructuralism, surrealism, dadaism, futurism, capitalism and even Marxism pervade the Avant-Pop sensibility, the major difference is that these artists who create Avant-Pop art are the Children of Mass Media."[41] Such artists "resist the avant-garde sensibility that stubbornly denies the existence of a popular media culture" and instead embrace the role of popular media in their work. This embrace of the popular, in turn, was associated with the disintermediation that will be mostly clearly embodied in the Internet: "Avant-Popsters and their pirate signals promoting wild station identifications are ready to expand into your home right now; just log on, click around and find them."[42]

A New Critical Focus on Work

I have already described the dispersal of literary theory, as the relative coherence of large-scale models (new criticism gives way to structuralism, which gives way to post-structuralism) is replaced by a far less coherent set of critics and theoretical schools in the 1990s. Bill Readings specifically characterizes cultural studies as the "refusal of theoretical definition": "What strikes one about the refusal of definition is the fact that it is repeated so many times, so many people within the 'field.'"[43] This helps to account for why theory appears to be everywhere in the 1990s, even as so many critics describe the period as "after theory."

As one component of this decade, the emergence of a focus on *work* as a concept helps to connect the period's many facets. Writing in 1989, Evan Watkins analyzed the English department as a workplace: "Nobody becomes an English professor to grade papers or write recommendations; nevertheless, these work practices may well explain as much about the organization of work in English as documenting the frontier myths informing *The Great Gatsby*."[44] Watkins's emphasis on work is itself an implicit break from the canon wars' assumption that literary theory fundamentally determines classroom experience: "In this context, it matters less *how* you are taught Romantic poetry say–what socialization or countersocialization of expectations took place–than what grade you got at the end of the process. Thus so far from an abstraction, labor force seems appropriate enough to designate the activities of a large body of people who in the gross number terms of grades generate over and over, like the intellectual 'assembly line' to which it's often been compared, the discriminations of which economic opportunity in part depends."[45]

We could go backwards to Gerald Graff's 1987 *Professing Literature* as a foundational attempt to look at the university as a kind of workplace, but I think that Watkins's shift toward work as a concept is especially important for how it anticipates developments in the 1990s. This attempt to theorize literary study and writing as a form of work is especially important because it anticipates the emergence of digital media that becomes central after the turn of the millennium. In his 2004 *The Laws of Cool*, Alan Liu characterizes literature as a form of knowledge work: "my concern is not really with works of literature as such, which from the viewpoint of general society have effectively lost their category distinction on the gradient that blurs textuality and information, imagination and entertainment, authors and celebrities, and publishers and conglomerates."[46] He explains that literary work increasingly is hard to distinguish from other forms of knowledge work: "what is the relation between the now predominantly academic and other knowledge workers (even 'creative writers') who manage literary value in 'cultural context' and the broader realm of professional, managerial, and technical knowledge workers who manage information value in 'systems'?"[47] With the rise of ubiquitous computing, the line between literary and mundane office writing has been blurred in much the same way that the 1990s challenged the distinction between literary and popular culture. After 2000, what emerges in their place is an appreciation of the way that the work of writing is intertwined with the institutions, technologies, and economics that make it possible.

The University after the 1990s: Challenging the Humanities

Throughout the 1990s, the university occupied an important and complex position within literary and popular culture. I framed this chapter with Lauter's book at the beginning and Sunstein's at the end. I've suggested that the turn of the millennium brings with it a broadening of the debates that we see throughout the 1990s, especially a turn to the post-print world of electronic communication. By the time that we arrive at the end of the decade, the language of the university, or sometimes merely the humanities, as in "crisis" supplanted the somewhat simpler political battles over the canon that defined the earlier part of the decade. Two typical works, both published in 2001, are Terry Cochran's *Twilight of the Literary: Figures of Thought in the Age of Print* and William Paulson's *Literary Culture in a World Transformed: A Future for the Humanities*. Each frames its topic as responding to the changing media landscape. Cochran writes, "The multiplicity of media, whether cinema, video, audio recording, or software, involves new ways of transcribing human thought for posterity and alters understandings of historical continuity."[48] Paulson, similarly, writes "The unsettled state in which literary culture and literary studies now find themselves has many overlapping causes. Rapid changes in the technologies and media of communication, and the fetishization of these changes by some would-be reformers of education, raise doubts about the kind of place serious reading and writing will or should have in the education of future generations."[49] Paulson's subtitle is particularly telling, since it broadens the discussion from the specifically literary debates about canonicity to the vocation of the humanities in general.

This concern for the role of the humanities, and of the traditional understanding of university education, is typical of the transition out of the 1990s into the 2000s. Readings describes the way that the university's vocation had been challenged in 1996: "The causes of the media's sniping at the University are not individual resentments but a more general uncertainty as to the role of the University and the very nature of the standards by which it should be judged as an institution."[50] Although Readings makes clear that this debate was implicit in the canon wars and thus already a subject during the 1990s, it is really at the turn of the millennium that the language of the "crisis in the humanities" eclipses the more localized debates and conflicts that we have seen characterize the 1990s.

The idea that the humanities are in crisis is a distinctly post-2000 phenomenon, but it reflects material changes that were going on during the 1990s, often unnoticed in the noise generated by the canon wars. Mark Cooper and John Marx have recently framed the period of the late 1980s and 1990s as one in which canon debates distracted academics from other changes. In their blog post "The Culture Wars are Over: Debt Won" they write,

> A truly amazing amount of time and energy went into scolding English professors for what they were or were not teaching – amazing, because what they were or were not teaching was so largely beside the point when it came to consideration of how higher education was changing. In the period of the culture wars, a massive wave of program innovation reshaped every corner of campus and an increasing subdivision of labor rewrote the job description of "professor." In the research university at century's end, no one department's curriculum could hope to succeed in doing much of anything to or for students, let alone "culture," without forging alliances across campus.
>
> Debt now challenges faculty to forego fighting among themselves over disciplinary turf and field-specific canons in favor of reminding themselves who, exactly, constitute the audiences for higher education.[51]

In *The Humanities "Crisis" and the Future of Literary Studies*, Paul Jay argues that this economically based talk of a crisis in the humanities is simply a replacement for the previous strategy of arguing against the humanities on the grounds of its cultural bankruptcy.[52] Elsewhere, Jay is more pointed in his explanation of this shift: critics associating a crisis in the humanities claim that "that critical theory and political correctness have ruined the liberal arts and humanities just don't hold water. They substitute weak statistical evidence for what are really ideological polemics."[53]

The 1990s defined this transition in our understanding of the university and its place within the American popular imaginary. Literature remained a fundamental frame of reference – through the canon wars, through the changes that digital media effects, and through the way that English came to embody the changing identity of the humanities and the vocation of the university.

NOTES

1 Samuel Cohen, *After the End of History* (Iowa City: University of Iowa Press, 2009), 4.
2 Philip E. Wegner, *Life Between Two Deaths, 1989–2001* (Durham, NC: Duke University Press, 2009), 28.
3 Brian McHale, *The Cambridge Introduction to Postmodernism* (Cambridge: Cambridge University Press, 2015), 125.

4 Paul Lauter, *Canons and Contexts* (New York: Oxford University Press, 1991).
5 Paul Lauter, ed., *Reconstructing American Literature: Courses, Syllabi, Issues* (Old Westbury, NY: Feminist, 2004).
6 Janet H. Murray, *Hamlet on the Holodeck: The Future of Narrative in Cyberspace* (Cambridge, MA: MIT Press, 1997).
7 George Slusser and Tom Shipper, eds., *Fiction 2000: Cyberpunk and the Future of Narrative* (Athens: University of Georgia Press, 1992).
8 Brian McHale, *The Cambridge Introduction to Postmodernism*, 131.
9 Terry Eagleton, *After Theory* (New York: Basic Books, 2003), 1.
10 Ibid.
11 Ibid., 2.
12 Jane Elliott and Derek Attridge, eds., *Theory After "Theory"* (New York: Routledge, 2011), 3.
13 Paul Patton, introduction to *The Gulf War Did Not Take Place*, Jean Baudrillard, trans. Paul Patton (Bloomington: Indiana University Press, 1995), 15.
14 Todd Gitlin, "Postmodernism: Roots and Politics" in *Cultural Policits in Contemporary America*, ed. Ian Angus and Sut Jhally (New York: Routledge, 1989), 358.
15 Cary Nelson, Paula A. Treichler, and Lawrence Grossberg, "Cultural Studies: An Introduction" *Cultural Studies*, eds. Lawrence Grossberg, Cary Nelson, and Paul A. Treichler (New York: Routledge, 1992), 2.
16 Mark McGurl, *The Program Era: Postwar Fiction and the Rise of Creative Writing* (Cambridge, MA: Harvard University Press, 2009), 25.
17 Christopher Beach, *Poetic Culture: Contemporary Ameican Poetry Between Community and Institution* (Evanston, IL: Northwestern University Press, 1999), 51.
18 Brian McHale, *The Cambridge Introduction to Postmodernism*, 138.
19 Gloria Anzaldúa, *Borderlands/La Frontera: The New Mestiza* (San Francisco: Aunt Lute Books, 1987).
20 John W. Aldridge, *Talents and Technicians: Literary Chic and the New Assembly-Line Fiction* (New York: Scribner's, 1992), 3.
21 Ibid., 5.
22 Ibid., 11.
23 Ibid., 13.
24 Ibid., 21.
25 Judith Ryan, *The Novel after Theory* (New York: Columbia University Press, 2012), 9.
26 Michael Greaney, *Contemporary Fiction and the Uses of Theory: The Novel from Structuralism to Postmodernism* (Basingstoke: Palgrave Macmillan, 2006).
27 Richard Powers, *Galatea 2.2* (New York: Picador, 1995).
28 Russell Jacoby, *The Last Intellectuals: American Culture in the Age of Academe*, (New York: Basic Books, 2000), 5.
29 Ibid., 9.
30 Ibid., 195.
31 Michael Berubé, "Public Image Limited: Political Correctness and The Media's Big Lie," in *Debating P.C.: The Controversy over Political Correctness on College Campuses*, ed. Paul Berman (New York: Laurel, 1992). 141–142.

32 Gilbert Sorrentino, "*Neon, Kulture*, etc," *Tri-Quarterly* 43 (1978): 300.
33 Ellen Gruber Garvey, "Out of the Mainstream and into the Streets: Small Press Magazines, the Underground Press, Zines, and Artists' Books," in *Perspectives on American Book History: Artifacts and Commentary*, ed. Scott E. Casper, Joanne D. Chaison, and Jeffrey D. Groves (Amherst: University of Massachusetts Press, 2002), 392.
34 Michael Anania, "Of Living Belfry and Rampart: On American Literary Magazines Since 1950," *Tri-Quarterly* 43 (1978): 11.
35 Charles Robinson, "Academica and the Little Magazine," *Tri-Quarterly* 43 (1978): 31.
36 Jonathan Baumbach. "Who Do They Think They Are? A Personal History of the Fiction Collective" *Tri-Quarterly* 43 (1978): 626.
37 Mark McGurl, *The Novel Art: Elevations of American Fiction after Henry James*, (Princeton, NJ: Princeton University Press, 2001), 181.
38 Jim Collins, *Bring on the Books for Everybody: How Literary Culture Became Popular Culture* (Durham, NC: Duke University Press, 2010), 18.
39 Ibid., 19.
40 Jonathan Franzen, *How to be Alone: Essays* (New York: Picador, 2002), 239–240.
41 Mark Amerika and Lance Olsen, eds. *In Memoriam to Postmodernism: Essays on the Avant-Pop* (San Diego, CA: San Diego State University Press, 1995), 18.
42 Ibid., 21.
43 Bill Readings, *The University in Ruins* (Cambridge, MA: Harvard University Press, 1996), 100.
44 Evan Watkins, *Work Time: English Departments and the Circulation of Cultural Value* (Stanford, CA: Stanford University Press, 1989), 1.
45 Ibid., 6.
46 Alan Liu, *The Laws of Cool: Knowledge Work and the Culture of Information* (Chicago: University of Chicago Press, 2004), 1.
47 Ibid., 3.
48 Terry Cochran, *The Twilight of the Literary: Figures of Thought in the Age of Print* (Cambridge, MA: Harvard University Press, 2001), 2.
49 William Paulson, *Literary Culture in a World Transformed: A Future for the Humanities* (Ithaca, NY: Cornell University Press, 2001), 2.
50 Bill Readings, *The University in Ruins*, 1.
51 Mark Cooper and John Marx, "The Culture Wars are Over: Debt Won," *Humanities after Hollywood*, September 15, 2014, http://humanitiesafterhollywood.org/2014/09/15/debt-won/.
52 Paul Jay, *The Humanities "Crisis" and the Future of Literary Study* (New York: Palgrave McMillan, 2014).
53 Paul Jay, "How Not to Defend the Liberal Arts," *Inside Higher Education*, October 27, 2014, https://www.insidehighered.com/views/2014/10/27/essay-state-liberal-arts/.

CHAPTER 23

Independent Presses

Jeffrey R. Di Leo

In terms of overall book sales, the 1990s saw remarkable growth. In 1990, about 2.1 billion books were sold for a net of almost 15 billion dollars. By the end of the decade, sales had increased by almost 360 million units and net profits increased by about 10 billion dollars (*BPI*, 28). In addition, US libraries increased their book purchasing from 1.3 billion books purchased in 1990 to almost 2 billion in 2000.[1]

Moreover, the 1990s were a period of extraordinary growth in literature publishing. In fiction, for example, almost 2,000 titles were published in the United States in 1990. By 1999, however, this number had increased to over 11,000 titles. Even more amazingly, poetry and drama titles published in 1990 numbered a scant 486. However, by 1999, poetry and drama increased to over 3,000 titles published (*BPI*, Tables A.1–3). The average price for a hardcover edition of a poetry or drama book, though, increased from about $32 in 1990 to over $46 in 1999. Much more than fiction, which went from $20 in 1990 to about $28 in 1999 (*BPI*, Table A.8–9).

In general, the 1990s were an exciting decade for the book publishing industry. According to the US Department of Commerce's Bureau of the Census, as the twentieth century was drawing to a close, there were almost twenty-seven hundred book publishers in America. To get a sense of the growth in the book industry, consider that just thirty years earlier there were just over 1,000 book publishers in America. To be sure, book publishing was on the rise in the 1990s.

But the census numbers do not tell the whole story of publishing in America. They are based on a complicated set of criteria that exclude many more presses than they include. For example, not only did the presses need to indicate that book publishing was their primary business function, but they also needed to satisfy other conditions such as having at least one paid employee and having an employer identification number. Compared to figures compiled by another source, the book industry at century's end looks very different (*BPI*, 9).

R. R. Bowker Company, the publisher of both *The Literary Marketplace* and *Books in Print*, sets the number of book publishers in the decade under consideration in this chapter at around 53,000 (*BPI*, 9). So, whose numbers do we go with? Those of the US government or those of Bowker? If we go by the US government figures, we are probably getting a truer estimate of the number of large presses in America in the 1990s – that is, presses that have paid employees and identify themselves primarily as a book business. But if we go with the Bowker data, and omit around 2,700 presses, we are still left with a balance of about 50,000 or so presses. How then do we characterize them?

It is pretty safe to assume that these 50,000 or so presses are a rough estimate of the number of "small presses" in the United States in the 1990s. Some of them are classified as "nonprofit," meaning that they are eligible for a tax designation that puts them in the highly favorable and forgiving company of educational and charitable institutions and also allows them to apply for public and private grant assistance. Others just don't make much profit. They publish what they want but for whatever reason just can't seem to generate more revenue than they use to produce their books. But among this vast sea of small presses, a few have managed to keep their distance from corporate ownership, publish what they want, *and* make a profit. In sum, this sea of small presses – profitable, unprofitable, and nonprofit – is the shape of independent publishing in America.

But, as even a rough estimate of the number of these presses indicates, they are in no way small in number. There are a lot of them. However, because of their small budgets, sales, and title output, they generally fall well below the radar of mainstream book culture. Unless, of course, one of their titles becomes an international sensation.[2] The dynamics between large presses – that is, those with over 50 million dollars in annual revenue – and small presses – that is, those which received $50,000 or less in annual revenue – is a good place to begin to understand the nature and role of independent presses in the 1990s. But, to be more accurate, the story of independent presses in the 1990s is less one between large presses and small presses, but rather, as we shall see below, one between independent and "corporate" presses.

In the 1990s, the financial gulf between the largest of the large presses and the massive sea of small presses becomes larger and larger. One of the implications of this is that while the large presses have the resources to market their new titles, the small presses struggle to get the word out about them. Large presses have budgets to purchase advertising, for example, in high-profile, large circulation book reviews such as the *New York Times* and the *New York Review of Books*, which in turn translates into a much higher rate of titles reviewed by those presses. Also, many large presses are part of international mass communications empires with access to television, radio, film, periodicals, and newspapers. Small presses, who do not have the marketing resources of the large presses, rely on either luck to get word out about their new titles or turn to book reviews that specialize in reviewing books from small presses, such as the *American Book Review*, namely, book reviews with much more limited circulation and resources than the aforementioned New York reviews.

Nevertheless, in spite of the growing financial and marketing gulf between small and large presses, the reduction in the number of book review outlets in the 1990s (as newspapers begin to cut back on book reviews[3]), the closing of many independent bookstores in the wake of the emergence of big-box bookstores such as Borders and Barnes & Noble, and the emergence of online booksellers such as Amazon, the book industry in general was remarkably strong in the 1990s.

Still, relatively speaking, literature (fiction, poetry, drama) publication represents only a fraction of US output. In 1990, total book output in the United States was about 47,000 titles, whereas in 1999 it had risen to about 120,000 titles (*BPI*, Tables A.15). Now consider these numbers within the context of the overall number of small presses in America in the 1990s. If Bowker tracks over 50,000 presses but only 120,000 new titles were published in 1999, what does that say about the title output of these small presses? It says that while small presses dwarf large presses in terms of sheer number of presses, each of these small presses does not publish on average very many new books per year. Some years might result in only one book published. Other years no books will be published.

It is no wonder then that most small presses and their books are known only by a small circle of individuals. This is one of the major consequences of publishing "independence" in America. Namely, there is a very good chance that the fate of books published by these presses is a very small and limited audience. To get a sense of the sales figures of these small presses, the publisher of BlazeVOX Books (founded in 2000), Geoffrey Gatza, recently said that "books by new [BlazeVOX] authors sell around 25–30 copies."[4] In general, though, a book from a small press that sells 2,000 to 4,000 copies is a success – figures still very different from those of large presses, which range from five to six figures, and in select cases even more.

Given the number of presses and their relative obscurity (not to mention sales figures like those noted by Gatza), publishing with them almost guarantees a much more limited readership than publishing with a large press. Not because the quality of books published by small presses is necessarily worse than that of books published by large presses, but because due to financial constraints, small presses have a much more difficult time bringing attention to the work of unknown albeit promising writers.

In short, the last decade of the twentieth century was a remarkable one for book culture and independent presses. First, it saw the rise of massive publishing corporations that were voraciously purchasing many of the major independent presses in the United States, and, in effect, widening the gap between large and small presses. Second, it was the beginning of the decline and fall of the independent bookstore to the book superstore. This would hurt small presses more than large presses as the former did not have the resources of the latter to get their books on the shelves of these book superstores. Third, it was the decade when the Internet browser was created and also the one when Amazon entered the book business. This would arguably level the playing field between small and large presses a bit by providing small presses with distribution opportunities formerly only available to large presses. These three conditions created a unique environment for independent presses and literature in America in the 1990s.

Looking for independent press literature in bookstores since the 1990s is like panning for gold in your local river. A nugget will turn up from time to time but don't get your hopes too high. However, turning to the Internet in the 1990s and after as a source for independent press literature recalls nothing short of the California Gold Rush of the 1850s. Both of these conditions though are more widely known than the silent but deadly rise of corporate publishing and its effect on independent presses in America. Thus, this chapter will focus on this rise and its effect on independent presses in America.

Bigger and Smaller Fiction

The bestselling American fiction writer of the 1990s was John Grisham. Over the course of the decade, he sold over 60 million books. 60,742,288, to be exact.[5] He had the number one bestselling fiction hardcover book in 1991 (*The Firm*), 1992 (*The Pelican Brief*), 1994 (*The Chamber*), 1996 (*The Runaway Jury*), 1997 (*The Partner*), 1998 (*The Street Lawyer*), and 1999 (*The Testament*). His complete monopoly on annual bestselling fiction in the 1990s was broken only by *Oh, The Places You'll Go!* (1990, Dr. Seuss), *The Bridges of Madison County* (1993, Robert James Waller), and *The Celestine Prophecy* (1995, James Redfield) (*BPI*, Table A. 17).

His publisher, the once great independent press Doubleday, became a subsidiary of the once great independent press Random House in 1998, who would then merge with another once great independent press, the inexpensive paperback publisher Penguin in 2012 (*TP* 5). On March 16, 2010, Random House, Inc., announced the debut of all twenty-three of Grisham's books in digital format. It also noted that all of Grisham's work is now available through Random House, Inc., in three platforms (print, audio, and digital) and four formats (Doubleday hardcover, Dell paperpack, Random House audio, and Random House e-book).[6] Big publishers aim to maximize book sales of their big authors by making their work available in as many platforms and formats as technology allows.

As of 2010, Grisham had sold more than 250 million books worldwide and had been translated into twenty-nine languages. Since 1988, he has written one novel a year and every one has been a number one *New York Times* bestseller. "John Grisham is one of the greatest storytellers of all time," said Sonny Mehta, Chairman and Editor-in-Chief of the Knopf Doubleday Publishing Group. "Since the publication of his very first book," continued Mehta, "he has been captivating readers with compelling characters, intricate plotting, and narratives about social justice that are impossible to put down" (*JG*). He is the face of orthodox 1990s fiction.

While few reading this chapter will agree with Mehta that "Grisham is one of the greatest storytellers of all time," a designation that would put him in the company of Homer, his publishing record in the 1990s and the story of the changes that overcame the once great independent presses of America with which he works (Doubleday and Random House) is symptomatic of the fate of independent presses in the neoliberal 1990s.

In 1897, Frank Nelson Doubleday formed a partnership with the magazine publisher Samuel McClure. Doubleday & McClure Company became Doubleday, Page, and Company in 1900.[7] Doubleday's early authors included W. Somerset Maugham and Joseph Conrad, and by 1947 it had become the largest publisher in the United States with annual sales of over 30 million books.[8] Doubleday & Company, as it was known by midcentury, would purchase the New York Mets in 1980,[9] and by the mid-1980s was a fully integrated international communications company that did trade publishing, mass-market paperback publishing, book manufacturing, and book clubs, as well as broadcasting and advertising. It had offices in London and Paris, and owned subsidiaries in Canada, Australia, and New Zealand with joint ventures in the United Kingdom and the Netherlands. Nevertheless, it was struggling as an independent publishing house.[10]

Thus, in 1986, Doubleday sold its publishing company to Bertelsmann, AG, a West Germany–based worldwide communications company, and in 1988 portions of the firm became part of the Bantam Doubleday Dell Publishing Group. Finally, in 1998, the year Grisham's novel *The Street Lawyer* became the number one bestselling hardback book of the year, Bantam Doubleday Dell Publishing Group became a division of Random House, the parent company that would later distribute his books in three platforms and four formats (*HD*) – a luxury afforded only writers with corporate publishers such as Random House, Inc.

To be sure, the latter half of the twentieth century was an active one in terms of mergers and acquisitions in the mass communications industry. Tracking the companies that acquire or merger film studios, television stations, radio stations, newspapers, periodicals, and book publishers during this period shows that each year an increasingly smaller number of corporations control more and more entities.

In the 1960s, there were 183 mergers or acquisitions of book publishers including the acquisition of Random House by RCA, Holt, Rinehart and Winston by CBS, Popular Library by Perfect Film & Chemical, and R. R. Bowker by Xerox Corporation (*BPI*, Table 3.1). In the 1970s, there were 177 including G. P. Putnam by MCA, Ballantine Books by RCA, Bantam by West Germany's Bertelsmann AG, and the merger of Scribner's and Atheneum, and Penguin and Viking (*BPI*, Table 3.2). In the 1980s, there were 213, with a notable increase from 1983 where there were 10 to 1984 when there were 29, 1985 where there were 30, and 1986 where they peaked for the 1980s at 40 (*BPI*, Table 3.3).

The increases in the 1980s complement the first wave of neoliberalism in the 1980s ushered in by the economic policies of Ronald Reagan (Reaganomics) in the United States (and Margaret Thatcher in Britain). Moreover, it should not be surprising that as neoliberal economic policy intensified in the 1990s with the second-wave neoliberalism of Bill Clinton (market globalism) in the United States (and Tony Blair's Third Way in Britain) that merger and acquisition frenzy in the 1990s would intensify as well.[11]

In the 1990s, there were a jaw-dropping 516 mergers and acquisitions, annually peaking with 71 in 1999 – increasing again in 2000 with 80 and again in 2001 with 84 (*BPI*, Table 3.4). Highlights include Harper & Row acquired by News Corp. in 1990, Simon & Schuster by Paramount in 1994, and Da Capo Press by Perseus in 1999 (*BPI*, Tables 3.5 & 3.6).

Though there are many different reasons for these mergers and acquisitions of book publishers, including the need for mass communications companies to acquire more content and increasing globalization and the rise of neoliberalism and the global marketplace, the effect on independent publishing was substantial.[12] By 2010, Random House had 34 imprints in the United States alone including: Alfred A. Knopf, Anchor, Ballantine, Bantam, Broadway, Clarkson Potter, Crown, Delacorte, Dell, Del Ray, Dial, Doubleday, Everyman's Library, Fawcett, Fodor's Travel, Golden Books, Harmony, Ivy, Kids@Random, Main Street Books, Nan A. Talese, One World, Pantheon, Schocken, Shave Areheart Books, Spectra, Spiegel & Grau, Strivers Row Books, The Modern Library, Three Rivers Press, Villiard, Vintage, and Wellspring. Also, Random House was now an imprint of Random House, Inc.[13] By 2000, the estimated revenues from Random House, Inc., were 1.8 billion dollars, a figure that made them the fifth largest publishing company in North America behind only Scholastic (1.9 billion), McGraw-Hill (2.3 billion), Reed Elsevier (2.7 billion), and Pearson (4.9 billion) (*BPI*, Table 3.7).

The mergers and acquisitions of major independent presses in the 1990s by publishing groups such as Random House, Inc., transformed the publishing landscape and book culture in America. For one thing, it ushered in the era of the foreign-born US publishing executive. In 1990, for example, Harold Evans, a native of Britain, became president and publisher of Random House, and Alberto Vitale, who was born in Italy and lived in Egypt, became chief executive of Random House, Inc. Moreover, at Houghton Mifflin Company, Nader F. Dareshori, a native of Iran, became its chief executive, and at Pantheon Books, Fred Jordan, a native of Austria, became its publisher. Finally, the aforementioned India-born Mehta, who was educated at Cambridge University, is also part of the foreign-born American publishing executive class of 1990. He became president of Alfred A. Knopf in early 1990.[14]

Arguably, the shift from American-born US publishing executives to foreign-born ones complements the emerging cultural studies and canon wars agendas of the late 1980s and early 1990s. As the canon opened up in the 1990s to include more literature representative of race, class, gender, and sexuality in America, so too would it become more internationally conscious – a trend that would only intensify with the globalization initiatives of the new millennium. Foreign-born executives at the helm of major American presses not only opened the door to the publication of more world literature in the United States including translations, but also to a more global presence for American authors and their work. But perhaps more importantly, these executive changes reflected the increasingly international nature of the publishing groups that were voraciously swallowing up independent presses in America.

Still another thing that would change over the course of these mergers and acquisitions is that corporate publishing would have a much lower tolerance for publishing work that had a potentially small audience and limited market. Neoliberal publishing would come to favor authors like John Grisham whose work appealed to a global market of readers and shun the second work of authors whose first book had slim to respectable sales. Moreover, it also became more difficult for first-time novelists to have their work picked up by corporate publishers. The story here is only sadder for poetry, which generally has a much smaller potential audience than fiction. Therefore, independent presses during this period took on a larger role as the publishers of new fiction and poetry, especially work that was innovative. Good books for the neoliberal publishing industry were those that sold well and bad books were those that did not. Innovative fiction might be good for literature, but it is hard on sales. Such is the world of corporate publishing, one that has enjoyed a steady rise in the last decade of the twentieth century.

Another change had to do with the way warehoused books could be stored without significant tax consequences. Prior to the late 1970s, books returned to the publisher could be stored in warehouses and depreciated for tax credit. However, after the IRS's Thor Power-Tool decision in the late 1970s rescinded tax credit for warehoused books, it became less profitable for corporate publishers to warehouse books that did not sell.[15] This meant titles often went out of print, especially titles of unconventional books. In the mid-1990s, for example, out-of-print American titles included the following innovative classics: Robert Coover's *Origin of the Brunists* (1966), *The Public Burning* (1977), and *Pinocchio in Venice* (1991); John Barth's *Sabbatical* (1982) and *The Last Voyage of Somebody the Sailor* (1991); Stanley Elkin's *Boswell: A Modern Comedy* (1964); William Gass's *Omensetter's Luck* (1966); John Hawkes's *The Passion Artist* (1979) and *Adventures in the Alaskan Skin Trade* (1985); and Joseph McElroy's *A Smuggler's Bible* (1966), *Plus* (1977), and *Lookout Carriage* (1974).[16]

The Thor decision had the unintended consequence of being a benefit to independent presses with a nonprofit tax designation as they would become the refuge of much serious literature that was put out of print because of financial considerations. A great example of this was William Gass's *The Tunnel*, which took him over twenty-five years to write and was first published by Alfred A. Knopf in February of 1995. Unbelievably,

Gass's masterpiece was soon after its publication put out of print by Alfred A. Knopf, an imprint of corporate giant Random House (though maybe it is no surprise considering that its president, Mehta, as you will recall, considered Grisham to be one of the world's greatest storytellers).

After a first print run of 15,000 copies to generally positive reviews but poor sales, Knopf sold the paperback rights to HarperCollins, another large publishing corporation, who released a paperback edition of *The Tunnel* in February of 1996. Then, in April of 1999, it reappeared in print again with the independent, nonprofit Dalkey Archive Press, who had also reprinted another of Gass's classics, *Willie Masters' Lonesome Wife* (1968) in December of 1989.

On September 25, 1998, Dalkey had signed an agreement with Alfred A. Knopf to reprint for an initial period of seven years softcover editions of the book because corporate publisher HarperCollins had too given up on keeping the book in print. "Our reprinting of *The Tunnel*," said John O'Brien, publisher of Dalkey Archive Press, "was nearly inevitable because we almost did the first edition of it because Knopf couldn't make up its mind about whether to do it or not."[17]

Dalkey continues to publish a softcover reprint edition of *The Tunnel*, which has to date sold 10,327 copies. They also put out an audio edition of book in 2006 wherein Gass can be heard reading the novel in its entirety. His reading time clocks in at just under forty-five hours, which is a long car ride indeed but well worth the drive.[18]

Such would be the fate of many other works of unconventional literature in the 1990s. Dalkey Archive Press alone reprinted around 90 titles in the 1990s including works by John Barth (*Letters* [1994], *Sabbatical* [1996]), Robert Coover (*Night at the Movies* [1992]), Rikki Ducornet (*Fountains of Neptune* [1992]), John Hawkes (*Whistlejacket* [1997]), Aldous Huxley (*Point Counter Point* [1996], *Antic Hay* [1997], *Those Barren Leaves* [1998], *Time Must Have a Stop* [1998]), Ben Marcus (*Age of Wire and String* [1998]), David Markson (*Springer's Progress* [1990]), Harry Mathews (*The Conversions* [1997], *The Journalist* [1997], *Cigarettes* [1998], *Tlooth* [1998], James McElroy (*Women and Men* [1993]), Ishmael Reed (*The Free-Lance Pallbearers* [1999], *The Terrible Threes* [1999], *The Terrible Twos* [1999]), Gilbert Sorentino (*Imaginative Qualities* [1991], *Steelwork* [1992], *Aberration of Starlight* [1993], *Mulligan Stew* [1996], *Pack of Lies* [1997], *Sky Changes* [1998], *Crystal Vision* [1999]), and Gertrude Stein (*Novel of Thank You* [1995], *Making of Americans* [1995]). What is even more amazing is that reprints constituted over 50 percent of what Dalkey Archive published in the 1990s. Of the 172 titles published from 1990 to 1999, 53 percent were reprints (of novels, translations, and collections), 25 percent were first editions, 17 percent were first translations, and 5 percent were scholarly works.[19]

The rising importance of independent presses such as Dalkey Archive to the publishing life of unconventional literature in the 1990s was one of the most visible changes resulting from the mergers and acquisitions of major independent presses at century's end. To be sure, these mergers and acquisitions left the press landscape in America strongly bifurcated by the turn of the century.

On one side, sat such writers as Grisham, who had the financial backing of multinational corporations like Random House, Inc. Grisham's company here includes Stephen King, who sold nearly 38.3 million copies of his books in the 1990s and was the second bestselling author of the decade; Danielle Steele, who at third sold 37.5 million copies; Michael Crichton, who at four sold more than 27.4 million copies; and Tom Clancy, who sold nearly 25.9 million copies (*GR*).

On the other side, sat a much less conventional group of writers. Some, like Gass, would be first published by corporate giants like Knopf though would rely on publishers like Dalkey Archive to remain in print. Others though would have very little to no association with the world of corporate publishing.

This group includes Mark Amerika, Steve Katz, Cris Mazza, and Ronald Sukenick, writers associated with the so-called avant-pop movement in the early 1990s, one which claimed that postmodernism had been replaced by literature that combined an avant-garde aesthetic with mass media engagement. It also includes authors such as Raymond Federman, Clarence Major, and Gilbert Sorrentino, writers associated with surfiction, an experimental type of fiction building off of the feeling that the traditional novel had become a clichéd form. In addition, experimental novelists such as David Markson, Carole Maso, Rikki Ducornet, Lance Olsen, and the guerilla writer Harold Jaffe should be included here, as well as postmodern writers such as the translator Paul Auster and the cultural critic Curtis White; James Ellroy, who helped develop post-noir writing in novels such as *LA Confidential* (1990); the minimalist Gordon Lish; "the Poet of the People," June Jordan; and the first Chicana or Chicano United States poet laureate (2015), Juan Felipe Herrera.

In spite of their stylistic differences, this talented group of writers all share the characteristic of not having the financial backing of multinational corporations for their work, and all publish some or all of their work with presses that are not part of publishing groups.[20] Collectively, the sales figures for the total publishing output of these writers over the course of their lifetime comes nowhere near the sales figures of any one of the best-selling fiction writers of the 1990s. This group is one of the faces of unorthodox or heterodox literature of the 1990s.[21]

Amerika and company worked in the 1990s with presses very different from the ones utilized by Grisham and company. Presses such as Black Ice Books (Amerika, Jaffe, Mazza, Sukenick, and White), Burning Deck Press (Auster), City Lights Books (Herrera and Jaffe), Copper Canyon Press (Major), Coffee House Press (Mazza), Curbstone Press (Herrera), Dalkey Archive Press (Ducornet, Markson, Sorrentino, Maso, and White), Ecco Press (Maso), Fiction Collective Two (Federman, Mazza, and Sukenick), Four Walls Eight Windows (Lish), High Risk Books (Jordan), Holy Cow! Press (Major), McClelland and Stewart (Ducornet), Mysterious Press (Ellroy), Permeable Press (Olsen), Sun and Moon Press (Federman, Katz, and White), and Wordcraft of Oregon (Olsen).

For the most part, the presses listed above share some characteristics. First, they were not run by multinational corporations and were not part of publishing groups in 1990s. Each, at least for a good part of the 1990s, was an independent press with no group or corporate allegiances. But the times were a-changing in the 1990s, and so too was the character of press independence.

Ecco Press, for example, was acquired by HarperCollins in 1999. Random House of Canada bought a 25 percent share of McClelland and Stewart in 2000, and in 2011 bought the remaining 75 percent from its owner, the University of Toronto.[22] In addition, Four Walls Eight Windows was acquired by Avalon Publishing Group in 2004.

Though not as dramatic as being acquired by HarperCollins, Avalon, or Random House, Curbstone Press and its 150-title backlist were acquired by Northwestern University Press in 2009.[23] Permeable Press was sold to Cambrian Publications in 1997.

Aside from High Risk Books, which was founded in New York City in 1993 as an imprint of Serpent's Tail Press of London but ceased operation in early 1997, Sun and Moon Book Press, which stopped publishing books in 2001 because of financial difficulties, and Black Ice Books, which came into existence in 1993 publishing four books a year, and faded out of existence with one book in 1999, the rest – Burning Deck Press, City Lights Books, Coffee House Press, Copper Canyon Press, Dalkey Archive Press, Fiction Collective Two, Holy Cow! Press, Mysterious Press, and Wordcraft of Oregon – made it through the 1990s to the present as strong and representative independent presses.[24]

The transition in literature publishing then in the 1990s might be seen from at least three angles: first, from the perspective of the publishing groups that were acquiring independent presses; second, from the perspective of independent presses that folded during or after the 1990s; and third, from the perspective of the independent presses who not only survived the 1990s acquisition frenzy, but who also continue to thrive in the new millennium.

In many ways, independent presses, both those that have ceased operation during or after the 1990s and those that continue, work at the margins of mainstream literature. They are the places to look for work that challenges orthodoxies about literary style and content. Their publishing aims are very different from those of presses that produce the work of Grisham and company. In the 1990s, these presses were where one looked for the cutting edge of literary innovation and heterodox fiction including some exemplary postmodern fiction. Reading the work of the authors listed above from these independent presses is as good a place as any to start to discover the other side of 1990s literary publishing.[25] Namely, one that depended on independent presses for its existence and survival.

Conclusion

Independent presses such as Dalkey Archive and Sun & Moon, who kept serious literature in print, came to typify the stakes presented by the continuing neoliberalization of the publishing industry in the 1990s (Dalkey Archive survived the 1990s, but Sun & Moon did not). So too did such independent presses as Black Ice Books, who only published a few books a year.

Published by Ronald Sukenick as an imprint of Fiction Collective Two (which also survived the 1990s) with Kathy Acker and Raymond Federman as associate editors, Black Ice Books aimed to "introduce readers to the new generation of dissident writers in revolt." Though they were only active a few years in the 1990s, they would become a place where major innovative writers such as Samuel Delany could turn to publish heterodox works such as *Hogg* (1995), works that stood no chance of publication with corporate publishers because of their controversial content. But keeping serious literature in print and offering venues for innovative work were only some of the challenges presented by the corporatization of publishing in the 1990s.

Minority literature too was having its challenges, and independent presses like Arte Público, the nation's largest Hispanic press, were filling in the publishing gap. According its director, Nicolás Kanellos, corporate publishing was only publishing five or six works a year in the 1990s by US Hispanic authors, whereas Arte Público itself was itself publishing thirty works a year. Coupled with a number of other independent presses that were publishing twenty-five or so works by US Hispanic authors without nonprofit publishing as an antidote to the lacunae of the corporate publishing world, Hispanic authors in the United States in the 1990s would have had a much more impoverished presence.[26]

Independent presses though, especially nonprofit ones, always totter on the brink of financial collapse. In the 1990s this situation was compounded by federal funding cuts to the National Endowment to the Arts. In the mid-1990s, the NEA staff was reduced by one-half and disciplinary programs such as literature were eliminated (*CH*, 167). Presses like Arte Público, which relied on such federal funding, would be placed in the precarious position of not being able to support the literary production of a whole segment of the US population – namely, the Hispanic community.

But so too would edgy presses like Black Ice Books, whose aim was far less noble than that of Arte Público but no less important. When NEA funding cuts for literature were being discussed by Congress, Representative Peter Hoekstra used a Black Ice title to defend the cuts. He called Fiction Collective Two books "offensive to the senses," and cited, among other titles, Doug Rice's *Blood of Mugwamp* (1996) published by Black Ice as a particular "abuse of discretion by the NEA." In addition, Hoekstra also mentioned Cris Mazza, Jeffrey DeShell, and Elisabeth Sheffield's co-edited classic *Chic Lit: Postfeminist Fiction* (1995) as among Fiction Collective Two books "offensive to the senses."[27]

Some of the major postmodern writers of the late twentieth century – William Gaddis, William Gass, and Thomas Pynchon, for example – were discovered and developed by independent presses that were later absorbed by publishing groups. The question is this: Would their work have been discovered and developed by those same presses if they were part of publishing groups like Random House, Inc.?

One would hope so, but these are the kind of questions that make the changing landscape of independent presses in 1990s so controversial and important to consider. The cost of publishing corporatization is not the loss of writers like John Grisham, Tom Clancy, or Danielle Steele. Corporate publishing knows how to discover and develop writers like these. What is at stake is all of the literature that falls outside of the scope of wide

Independent Presses

readership and literary orthodoxy. Without the publishing output of strong and daring independent presses like Dalkey Archive, Black Ice Books, Arte Público, and the Fiction Collective Two in the 1990s, perhaps we would never know that there are alternatives to the work of Grisham, and alternate perspectives on "the greatest storytellers of all time."[28]

NOTES

1 Albert N. Greco, *The Book Publishing Industry, Second Edition* (London: Lawrence Erlbaum Associates, 2005), 46. Hereafter cited parenthetically as *BPI*.
2 This happened most recently when a Dalkey Archive Press author, Svetlana Alexievitch, won the Nobel Prize for Literature (2015). Sales of the English translation of her *Voices from Chernobyl* (2005), which is published by Dalkey Archive, skyrocketed literally overnight.
3 I discuss recent changes in book reviewing in America in my book, *Academe Degree Zero: Reconsidering the Politics of Higher Education* (Boulder, CO: Paradigm, 2012), 55–62. Another good source on recent changes in book reviewing is Gail Pool, *Faint Praise: The Plight of Book Reviewing in America* (Columbia: University of Missouri Press, 2007).
4 Jeffrey R. Di Leo, *Turning the Page: Book Culture in the Digital Age* (Huntsville: Texas Review Press, 2014), 45. Hereafter cited parenthetically as *TP*.
5 "Grisham Ranks as Top-Selling Author of Decade," *CNN.com Book News*, December 31, 1999, http://www.cnn.com/1999/books/news/12/31/1990.sellers/ Hereafter cited parenthetically as *GR*.
6 "23 John Grisham Titles Launch Today as Random House E-Books in North America," March 16, 2010. jgrisham.com. Hereafter cited parenthetically as *JG*.
7 "The History of Doubleday," https://www.randomhouse.com/doubleday/history/ Hereafter cited parenthetically as *HD*.
8 David Comfort, *An Insider's Guide to Publishing* (Cincinnati: Writer's Digest Books, 2013), 11.
9 James Quirk and Rodney D. Fort, *Pay Dirt: The Business of Professional Team Sports* (Princeton, NJ: Princeton University Press, 1997), 24.
10 Edwin McDowell, "Doubleday Publishing Names New President," *New York Times*, November 28, 1985, http://www.nytimes.com/1985/11/28/arts/doubleday-publishing-names-new-president.html.
11 Manfred B. Stegner and Ravi Roy, *Neoliberalism: A Very Short Introduction* (Oxford: Oxford University Press, 2000), 21–75, provides a very good introduction to both first- and second-wave neoliberalism.
12 I give an account of neoliberalism in publishing in my book, *Corporate Humanities in Higher Education: Moving Beyond the Neoliberal Academy* (New York: Palgrave Macmillan, 2013), 105–120.

13 John Thompson, *Merchants of Culture: The Publishing Business in the Twenty-First Century* (Cambridge: Polity Press, 2010), Appendix 1.
14 Edwin McDowell, "Foreign Flavor for Publishing Leadership," *New York Times*, November 5, 1990, http://www.nytimes.com/1990/11/05/business/the-media-business-flavor-for-publishing-leadership.html.
15 Thor Power Tool Company v. Commissioner, 439 U.S. 522 (1979) went to the United States Supreme Court. The Court upheld IRS regulations limiting how taxpayers could write down inventory. The Thor decision caused publishers to destroy stock of poor-selling books in order to realize a taxable loss. Prior to the decision, the books would have been kept in stock, but written down to reflect that not all of them were expected to sell.
16 Charles B. Harris, "Introduction," *Critique* 37.3 (1996): 166, an introduction to an excellent special issue on independent presses and American literature. Hereafter cited parenthetically as *CH*.
17 Email correspondence with John O'Brien, Director, Dalkey Archive Press, 17 August 2016.
18 Email correspondence with Jake Snyder, Associate Director, Dalkey Archive Press, 17 August 2016.
19 I would like to thank Jeff Higgins, Assistant Editor at Dalkey Archive Press, for his assistance in identifying works published by the press in the 1990s.
20 Some of these writers started with large presses and moved to small ones (e.g. Sorrentino); others publish exclusively with small presses (e.g. Mazza); and still others started with small presses and moved to large ones (e.g. Auster).
21 This list of authors was drawn from the complete list of authors, books, and presses reviewed by the *American Book Review* in the 1990s. I would like to thank Keri Farnsworth and Lauren Pirosko for compiling this list.
22 Victoria Ahearn, "Random House of Canada Becomes Sole Owner of McClelland & Stewart" *Toronto Star*, January 10, 2012, www.thestar.com.
23 Wendy Leopold, "Northwestern University Press Acquires Curbstone Press." December 15, 2009. University News. Northwestern University. www.northwestern.edu.
24 It should be noted that out of the death of the revered Sun and Moon Press was born another press, Green Integer.
25 Specifically, Black Ice Books (Amerika, *The Kafka Chronicles* [1993], *Sexual Blood* [1995]; Jaffe, *Straight Razor* [1995], *Sex for the Millenium* [1999]; Mazza, *Revelation Countdown* [1993]; Sukenick, *Doggy Bag* [1994]; White, *Anarcho-Hindu* [1995]), Burning Deck Press (Auster, *Why Write?* [1996]), City Lights Books (Herrera, *Lotería and Fortune Poems* [1999]; Jaffe, *Eros: Anti-Eros* [1990]), Copper Canyon Press (Major, *New and Selected Poems 1958–1998* [1999]), Coffee House Press (Mazza, *How to Leave a Country* [1992], *Exposed* [1993], *Your Name Here* [1995], *Dog People* [1997]), Curbstone Press (Herrera, *Love After the Riots* [1996]), Dalkey Archive Press (Ducornet, *The Jade Cabinet* [1993]; *The Complete Butcher's Tales* [1994], *Phosphor in Dreamland* [1995], *Stain* [1995]; Markson, *Collected Poems* [1993], *Reader's Block* [1996]; Sorrentino, *Under the Shadow* [1991], *Sound on Sound* [1995]; Maso, *Ava* [1993], *The American Woman*

in the Chinese Hat [1994]; White, *Memories of My Father Watching TV* [1998], *Monstrous Possibility* [1998]), Ecco Press (Maso, *Aureole* [1998]), Fiction Collective Two (Federman, *To Whom it May Concern* [1990], *Double or Nothing* [1991, new edition], *Take It or Leave It* [1997, new edition]; Mazza, *Is it Sexual Harassment Yet?* [1991], *Former Virgin* [1997]; Sukenick, *Mosaic Man* [1999]), Four Walls Eight Windows (Lish, *Epigraph* [1996], *Self-Imitation of Myself* [1997], *Arcade or How to Write a Novel* [1998]), High Risk Books (Jordan, *Haruka/Love Poems* [1994]), Holy Cow! Press (Major, *Fun & Games* (1990), McClelland and Stewart (Ducornet, *The Fountains of Neptune* [1990]), Mysterious Press (Ellroy, *LA Confidential* [1990]), Permeable Press (Olsen, *Time Famine* [1996]), Sun and Moon Press (Federman, *The Twofold Vibration* [1997]; Katz, *Forty-Three Fictions* [1992], Swanny's Ways [1995]; White, *The Idea of Home* [1994]), and Wordcraft of Oregon (Olsen, *Scherzi, I Believe* [1994], *Burnt* [1996]).

26 Nicolás Kanellos, "Federal Funding for Literary Presses," *American Book Review* 17.1 (1995): 4. Cited in *CH*, 167.
27 Correspondence with Charles Harris. April 19, 2016.
28 In the interests of disclosure, Dalkey Archive Press is currently located at my university, the University of Houston-Victoria. The Fiction Collective Two was located here though most its operation has since moved elsewhere. For a deeper look at Fiction Collective Two through the mid-1990s, a good source is Michael Bérube, "Straight Outta Normal," *Critique* 37.3 (1996): 188–204. Similarly, Dennis Barone, "What's in a Name? The Dalkey Archive Press," *Critique* 37.3 (1996): 222–239, is a fine article on the story of Dalkey Archive Press through the mid-1990s.

Index

253 (Ryman), 244–245
9/11 attacks, 2, 12n5, 71, 126, 233, 246, 309, 347

Aberration of Starlight (Sorrentino), 370
Abrams, J. J., 181
Acker, Kathy, 71, 201, 206, 352, 373
Adventures in the Alaskan Skin Trade (Hawkes), 369
Advertisements for Myself (Mailer), 50
Agapē Agape (Gaddis), 97, 98–99, 101
The Age of Wire and String (Marcus), 370
Agrippa (Gibson), 169, 179, 182
AIDS, 37–40, 43, 45n31, 72, 177, 196, 275, 314, 315, 329–340
Alameddine, Rabih, 332–333, 336
Alcott, Louisa May, 201, 208–209
Alexie, Sherman, 7, 155, 160–162
All Souls' Rising (Bell), 126, 135–137
All Tomorrow's Parties (Gibson), 244
Allen, Paula Gunn, 220
Allison, Dorothy, 298, 300–301, 315
Almanac of the Dead (Silko), 270, 273, 274
Aloft (Lee), 210
Alvarez, Julia, 224, 225, 235, 236–237
American Genius (Tillman), 120
American Pastoral (Roth), 56–60, 137, 298, 306–308, 323
American Psycho (Ellis), 69, 70, 71, 253
Amerika, Mark, 79, 81–83, 87, 356, 371, 372, 376n25
Ammons, A. R., 4, 111
Anderson, Kurt, 14n47
Anderson, Sherwood, 154, 161, 163
"The Angel Esmeralda" (DeLillo), 33
Angelology (Trussoni), 32
Angelopolis (Trussoni), 32
Angels, 32–35, 37–38, 39–40, 43, 44
Angels in America (Kushner), 37, 329–330
Animal Dreams (Kingsolver), 251–252
Antonetta, Susanne, 273, 274
Anzaldua, Gloria, 219, 225, 351

Armantrout, Rae, 150–151
The Art Lover (Maso), 177–178, 338–339
The Atlas (Vollmann), 110
Atwood, Margaret, 206
Auster, Paul, 210, 371, 372, 376n25
AVA (Maso), 111, 116, 120, 171
Avant-Pop, 82, 201, 284–286, 356, 371

Babbage, Charles, 290
Badiou, Alain, 310n14
The Balance of Nature? (Pimm), 266
Banks, Russell, 71–72
Barth, John, 6, 28, 91, 92, 93–95, 99, 102, 103, 111, 205, 283–284, 287, 350, 369, 370
Barthelme, Donald, 91, 92, 244
Barthes, Roland, 91, 170
Bastard Out of Carolina (Allison), 298, 300–301, 315
Bateson, Gregory, 83
Baudrillard, Jean, 19, 21, 41, 179, 279, 282, 290, 349
Because it was Bitter and Because it was My Heart (Oates), 322
Beck, Ulrich, 27, 272
Beckett, Samuel, 91
The Beet Queen (Erdrich), 159
Bell, Madison Smartt, 126, 132, 137
Bellamy, Edward, 4, 7
Bellow, Saul, 48, 49, 103
Beloved (Morrison), 43, 136, 219, 298, 300
Benjamin, Walter, 158
Berland, Lauren, 65–66
Berlin Wall, 2, 13n5, 29, 126, 202, 217, 233, 347
Berners-Lee, Tim, 81, 283
Bernstein, Charles, 178–179, 180
Bhaba, Homi, 206
Bingo Palace (Erdrich), 159
Birkerts, Sven, 107, 186
"Blackbird Pie" (Carver), 158
Bladerunner (Scott), 44
Blair, Tony, 367

Blake, William, 169, 245
Blank Fiction, 71
Bloom, Allan, 50–51
Bloom, Harold, 10, 32
Bly, Robert, 319
The Body Artist (DeLillo), 13n17
Body Toxic (Antonetta), 273, 274
The Book of Daniel (Doctorow), 124, 125, 127
The Book of Lazarus (Grossman), 183n17
Bookchin, Murray, 264
Border Trilogy (McCarthy), 219–220
Borderlands/La Frontera (Anzaldua), 219, 351
Boswell (Elkin), 369
"Bounty" (Saunders), 30, 41
Boyle, T. Coraghessan, 162, 227–228
Breakfast of Champions (Vonnegut), 101
Breath, Eyes, Memory (Danticat), 226, 321
Brief Interviews (Wallace), 164–166
Brin, David, 271
Brock Broido, Lucie, 147–149, 152
"Brokeback Mountain" (Proulx), 75n28
Bronte, Charlotte, 223, 302
Brooks, Cleanth, 350
Brown, Dan, 32
Brown, Rebecca, 331–332
The Brunist Day of Wrath (Coover), 103
Buffy the Vampire Slayer, 44
Bunyan, John, 209
Burgess, Anthony, 352
Burroughs, William, 242
Bush, Barbara, 324n3
Bush, George W., 51, 79, 217–218, 222, 234, 312
Butler, Judith, 316
Butler, Octavia, 66–67, 71, 73
Butler, Robert Olen, 155, 157–158, 159
Byatt, A. S., 352
Byron, Ada Lovelace, 290

Cadigan, Pat, 282, 286–288
Campbell, Joseph, 289
Cao, Lan, 298, 302–304
Carpenter's Gothic (Gaddis), 98
Carson, Rachel, 264
Carter, Jimmy, 243
Caruth, Cathy, 297, 298
Carver, Raymond, 157, 158, 162, 163
Castillo, Ana, 35–36, 37, 40–41, 42
Caucasia (Senna), 8
Cavafy, Constantine, 38
"Certainly the End of Something" (Wallace), 48–49, 57, 240
Chernobyl Disaster, 252
Cherry, Kelly, 154
Chimera (Barth), 94
Cigarettes (Mathews), 370

Cisneros, Sandra, 235, 237, 351
City of Dreadful Night (Siegel), 202–203
City of Quartz (Davis), 227
"CivilWarLand in Bad Decline" (Saunders), 41
Clancy, Tom, 371, 374
"Click" (Barth), 28, 284
Clinton, Bill, 10, 56, 233, 245, 246, 306, 313, 316, 367
The Closing of the American Mind (Bloom), 50–51
Cold Mountain (Frazier), 139n20
Coleridge, Samuel Taylor, 5
Coming Soon!!! (Barth), 28, 284
Condé, Maryse, 202, 204
Conrad, Joseph, 209, 242, 253, 366
Consider the Lobster (Wallace), 172
The Conversions (Mathews), 370
Cooper, Dennis, 71–73, 315
Coover, Robert, 76–77, 78, 92, 103, 115, 124–125, 127, 138, 172, 283, 284, 369, 370
The Corrections (Franzen), 109, 155, 241, 355
Coupland, Douglas, 162, 241–242
Cowley, Malcolm, 351
Crane, Hart, 38
Crichton, Michael, 258, 371
The Crossing (McCarthy), 266–267
The Crying of Lot 49 (Pynchon), 229–230
Cryptonomicon (Stephenson), 111
Crystal Vision (Sorrentino), 370
Cunningham, Michael, 210, 314, 316, 337–338
Cyberpunk, 83

D'Agata, John, 180
Daitch, Susan, 11
Danielewski, Mark Z., 85, 120, 171, 172, 174, 175–176, 179, 180, 181, 293n18
Danticat, Edwidge, 224, 226, 321
Dara, Evan, 111–115, 116, 118, 120
Davis, Kathryn, 28–29
Davis, Mike, 227
De La Pava, Sergio, 120
Deception (Roth), 58
Delany, Samuel R., 206, 373
Deleuze, Gilles, 280
DeLillo, Don, 4, 6, 7, 13n17, 29, 33, 107, 111, 126, 127, 128–130, 133, 135, 137, 170, 189–190, 239–240, 250, 253, 272, 273, 321, 322
Dennett, Daniel, 257
Denny, Reginald, 64
Derrida, Jacques, 351
Descartes, Rene, 114–115, 123n27, 289
Descending Figure (Gluck), 140
DeWitt, Helen, 4, 13n17, 116–120
Di Blasi, Debra, 181
Diaz, Junot, 224–226, 321
Dickens, Charles, 302

Dickinson, Emily, 141, 147–148, 209
Dirty Realism, 12
Discordant Harmonies (Botkin), 266
Doctorow, E. L., 124, 125, 127, 138
Dogeaters (Hagedorn), 235, 236
Dorst, Doug, 181
Doty, Mark, 38–40
Double or Nothing (Federman), 173–174
"Downtrodden Mary's Campaign of Terror" (Saunders), 41
"Dragonflies Mating" (Haas), 144–146
Dreaming in Cuban (Garcia), 221
Dreams from My Father (Obama), 320
Drown (Diaz), 224–226, 321
Dubliners (Joyce), 161
Ducornet, Rikki, 370, 371, 372, 376n25
"Dunyazadiad" (Barth), 205

"E Unibus Pluram" (Wallace), 91, 162, 186, 187, 188, 189–190, 192, 240–241, 284–285, 317
Earth (Brin), 271
Earth Day, 264
Eastgate systems, 79, 354
The Easy Chain (Dara), 120
Egan, Jennifer, 109, 155
Eggers, Dave, 7, 11, 241
Electronic Literature Organization, 172
Eliade, Mircea, 202
Eliot, George, 302
Eliot, T. S., 120, 253, 339, 350
Elkin, Stanley, 369
Ellis, Bret Easton, 69, 71, 253
Ellison, Ralph, 6, 210
Ellroy, James, 6, 371, 372, 377n25
Encyclopedic Fiction, 107–120, 250, 271–273
"The End: An Introduction" (Barth), 6
"The End of Books" (Coover), 76–77, 172
Engelbart, Douglas, 83
Environmental Health Memoir, 273–274
Erasure (Everett), 91
Erdos, Paul, 262n23
Erdrich, Louise, 155, 159–160, 161, 162
Erickson, Steve, 11, 24–27
The Errancy (Graham), 20–21, 34–35
Eugenides, Jeffrey, 109, 154, 163
Everett, Percival, 91
Everything is Illuminated (Foer), 7
Executioner's Song (Mailer), 49
The Exes (Kennedy), 316
eXistenZ (Cronenberg), 281
Exxon Valdez Spill, 252

The Facts (Roth), 57
Fatheralong (Wideman), 320
Faulkner, William, 137

Federman A to XXXX, 92
Federman, Raymond, 91, 92, 96, 173–174, 179, 180, 201, 371, 372, 373, 377n25
Fellini, Federico, 103
Felman, Shoshana, 297
Fiction Collective, 354
The Fifth Book of Peace (Kingston), 210
Fight Club (Palahniuk), 69–71, 73, 319
Fingal, Jim, 180
Finnegans Wake (Joyce), 200
First Gulf War, 11–12, 79–80, 217, 279
"Fission" (Graham), 146–147
Fitzgerald, F. Scott, 242
Flesh and Blood (Cunningham), 314, 316
Flight Behavior (Kingsolver), 251
Foer, Jonathan Safran, 7, 181, 182
Ford, Richard, 162, 319, 322
Foucault, Michel, 350
Fountains of Neptune (Ducornet), 370
Fowles, John, 352
Franzen, Jonathan, 11, 19, 27–28, 109, 112, 155, 186, 190–191, 192, 193, 194, 195, 196, 241, 355–356
Frazier, Charles, 139n20
The Free-Lance Pallbearers (Reed), 370
Frey, James, 301
The Friday Book (Barth), 93
Friends, 317
A Frolic of His Own (Gaddis), 97–98
From Old Notebooks (Smith), 120
Frye, Northrop, 351
Fukuyama, Francis, 5, 12n5, 51, 88n14, 92, 125, 126, 134, 135, 233
Fury (Rushdie), 246

Gaddis, William, 92, 97–99, 102, 113, 114, 121n12, 374
Gain (Powers), 6, 29–30, 267–268, 272, 274, 322
Galatea 2.2 (Powers), 28, 259–260, 289, 352
Garbage (Ammons), 111
Garcia, Cristina, 221, 226
Gardens in the Dunes (Silko), 220
Gass, William H., 91, 92, 95–97, 99, 103, 107, 179–180, 369–370, 374
Gauer, Jim, 120
Generation X, 92
Generation X (Coupland), 241
Generosity (Powers), 121n12
"Geraldo, Eat Your Avant-Pop Heart Out" (Leyner), 285
A Gesture Life (Lee), 210, 223, 224
Ghosts, 36, 40–43, 44, 46n48, 203
Gibson, William, 169, 179, 182, 244, 286, 288
The Gifts of the Body (Brown), 331–332
The Gilda Stories (Gomez), 316

Index 381

Giles Goat-Boy (Barth), 92
Ginsberg, Allen, 38
Girl, Interrupted (Mangold and Khan), 38
Giuliani, Rudy, 63
Gizzi, Peter, 351
Gleick, James, 235, 257–258
Glissant, Edouard, 204
Global Warming, 5, 17, 29, 264, 271
Globalization, 9, 110, 121n12, 205, 228, 233–246, 264, 269–270, 271, 367, 368
Gluck, Louise, 140, 142–144, 145
The Gold Bug Variations (Powers), 108–110, 113, 114, 117, 118, 120, 250, 257, 289
Goldstein, Rebecca, 258–259, 260
Gomez, Jewelle, 316
A Good Scent from a Strange Mountain (Butler), 157–158
The Gospel According to the Son (Mailer), 6
Gould, Stephen Jay, 255
Graham, Jorie, 20–21, 34–35, 37, 146–147, 151
Grammatron (Amerika), 79, 81–83, 87
Granta's "Best Young American Novelists" (1996), 12, 224, 226
Gravity's Rainbow (Pynchon), 35, 92, 121n12, 250
"Greasy Lake" (Boyle), 162
Greeley, Andrew, 32
Green (Sherwood), 323
Grisham, John, 365–366, 367, 369, 371, 373, 374, 375
Gross, Paul, 255
Grossman, Richard, 183n17
Guide (Cooper), 72–73

Hagedorn, Jessica, 235, 236, 243
Halfway Home (Monette), 332
Hall, Steve, 180
Hanna, Kathleen, 196
Haraway, Donna, 268
Hardt, Michael, 74n10, 234
Haring, Keith, 38
Harlot's Ghost (Mailer), 50, 52, 126, 127–128, 137
Harrison, Kathryn, 298, 300, 301–302, 307, 315
Hass, Robert, 144–146, 147
Hassan, Ihab, 244
Hawkes, John, 369, 370
Hawking, Stephen, 255, 256
Hawthorne, Nathaniel, 156, 158, 201, 206–208
A Heartbreaking Work of Staggering Genius (Eggers), 7, 11, 241
Heaven's Gate Cult, 18
Heidegger, Martin, 36
Heinlein, Robert, 288
The Heirs of Columbus (Vizenor), 8
Hejinian, Lyn, 140
Hemings, Sally, 10

Heroes and Saints (Moraga), 274–275
Herrera, Juan Felipe, 371, 372, 376n25
Higher Suspicion (Gross And Levitt), 255–256
Historical Fiction, 26, 56, 92, 124–138, 160, 206–208
Hofstadter, Douglas, 257
Hogg (Delany), 373
The Holder of the World (Mukherjee), 206–208, 210
Holleran, Andrew, 330
Homes, A. M., 155, 162–164, 318, 319
"Host" (Wallace), 172
The Hours (Cunningham), 337–338
House of Leaves (Danielewski), 85, 120, 171, 172, 174, 175–176, 181, 293n18
The House on Mango Street (Cisneros), 351
How the García Girls Lost Their Accents (Alvarez), 235, 236–237
How to Do Things with Words (Retallack), 179
Howe, Susan, 141
Huckleberry Finn (Twain), 48
The Human Stain (Roth), 56, 126, 137–138, 306
Husserl, Edmund, 54
Hutcheon, Linda, 124–125, 126
Huxley, Aldous, 370
Hypertext, 28, 76, 77, 78–79, 80–81, 83, 84–85, 86–87, 92, 155, 171, 172, 174, 280, 283–284, 354

I am Radar (Larsen), 120
I Married a Communist (Roth), 49, 52, 56, 137, 306
Iduro (Gibson), 244
"I'll Be Doing More of Same" (Franzen), 186, 190–191
Imaginative Qualities (Sorrentino), 370
Immigration Act (1990), 222
In the Beauty of Lilies (Updike), 53–56
In the Lake of the Woods (O'Brien), 298, 302, 304–306
Independence Day (Ford), 319, 322
Ineradicable Stain (Jackson), 181
Infinite Jest (Wallace), 6, 13n17, 41–42, 46n48, 108–110, 113, 114, 117, 118, 120, 172, 173, 174, 252, 272, 273, 318, 326n52, 326n60
Interpreter of Maladies (Lahiri), 226–227
Invisible Man (Ellison), 210
Iron John (Bly), 319
Irving, Washington, 3
Ishiguro, Kazuo, 44
It All Adds Up (Bellow), 48

J R (Gaddis), 98
Jack (Homes), 163, 319
Jackson, Michael, 11

Jackson, Shelley, 181–182, 284
Jaffe, Harold, 371, 372, 376n25
James, William, 54
Jameson, Fredric, 5, 12n5, 19, 43, 124, 125, 126, 160, 285
Jane Eyre (Bronte), 223
Janowitz, Tama, 71
Jarman, Derek, 38
Jasmine (Mukherjee), 235–236
Jazz (Morrison), 136, 298
Jefferson, Thomas, 10
Jen, Gish, 204, 223, 238
Jesus's Son (Johnson), 163
The Jiri Chronicles (Di Blasi), 181
John's Wife (Coover), 115
Johnson, B. S., 96
Johnson, Charles, 126, 132, 134–135, 137
Johnson, Denis, 163
Johnson, James Weldon, 138
Jordan, June, 371, 372, 377n25
The Journalist (Mathews), 370
Joyce, James, 109, 111, 161, 200, 250, 353
Joyce, Michael, 284
Juneteenth (Ellison), 6
Just Whistle (Wright), 149–150

Katz, Steve, 371, 372, 377n25
Kazin, Alfred, 351
Keats, John, 285
Kennedy, John F., 127, 146, 284, 322
Kennedy, Pagan, 316, 323
Kermode, Frank, 17, 18
Kerouac, Jack, 38, 317
Kim, Miyung Mi, 351
Kincaid, Jamaica, 223, 334–335, 336, 343n52
The King (Barthelme), 92
King, Rodney, 63, 66
King, Stephen, 371
Kingsolver, Barbara, 208–210, 211, 251–252
Kingston, Maxine Hong, 204, 210
The Kiss (Harrison), 298, 300, 301–302, 307, 315
Koolaids (Alameddine), 332–333, 336
Koresh, David, 18
Krik? Krak! (Danticat), 226
Kristeva, Julia, 352
Kundera, Milan, 59–60
Kushner, Tony, 33, 37, 329–330
Kyoto Protocol (1997), 264

LA Confidential (Ellroy), 371
La Capra, Dominick, 297
LA Riots, 63–69, 73
Lacan, Jacques, 12n5, 350
Lahiri, Jhumpa, 226–227, 238–239
Language poetry, 188, 350, 351

Language Poets, 178–179
Larsen, Nella, 138
Larsen, Reif, 120
The Last Samurai (DeWitt), 116–120
The Last Voyage of Somebody the Sailor (Barth), 369
Latour, Bruno, 156, 268
Lauter, Paul, 348, 358
Leavis, F. R., 260
LeClair, Tom, 108–109, 110, 117, 267, 276n17
Lee, Chang-rae, 210–211, 223–224, 322
Left Behind Series (LaHaye and Jenkins), 18, 36
Lethem, Jonathan, 7, 253–254
Let's Just Say (Bernstein), 178
LETTERS (Barth), 370
Levitt, Norman, 255
Lewinsky, Monica, 10, 56
Leyner, Mark, 11, 201, 284–286
Lichtenstein, Roy, 285
The Limits to Growth (Meadows et al.), 264
Lin, Tan, 351
Lindley, David, 5
Lish, Gordon, 371, 372, 377n25
"The Literature of Exhaustion" (Barth), 283, 350
Little Women (Alcott), 208–209, 210
Living Downstream (Steingraber), 273, 274
Lodge, David, 352
Lolita (Nabokov), 199, 202, 203, 204, 205
London, Jack, 13n18
The Lone Ranger and Tonto Fistfight in Heaven (Alexie), 7, 160–162
Looking Backward (Bellamy), 2–4
Lookout Cartridge (McElroy), 369
Lopate, Philip, 319
Lo's Diary (Pera), 199–200, 202
The Lost Father (Simpson), 319
Lost in the Funhouse (Barth), 93
The Lost Scrapbook (Dara), 111–115, 120
Love in a Dead Language (Siegel), 79, 84–87, 116, 118, 120, 172, 174–176, 179, 181, 202
Love Medicine (Erdrich), 159–160
Lucy (Kincaid), 223

MacIntyre, Alasdair, 108
Madonna, 9
Magnolia (Anderson), 35
Mailer, Norman, 6, 7, 48, 49–50, 60, 126, 127–128, 137
Major, Clarence, 371, 372, 376n25
Mamet, David, 10
Mann, Thomas, 1
Many Worlds Interpretation, 4
Mao II (DeLillo), 22–24
"Mao Tse Tung Wore Khakis" (Bernstein), 179
Marcus, Ben, 370

Markson, David, 92, 99–101, 102, 111, 115–116, 120, 370, 371, 372, 376n25
Maso, Carole, 11, 111, 116, 120, 171, 177–178, 180, 186, 192–195, 196, 338–339, 371, 372, 376n25
Mason & Dixon (Pynchon), 1, 13n17, 126, 131–132
The Master Letters (Brock Broido), 147–149
Mathews, Harry, 370
The Matrix (the Wachowskis), 260, 282, 297
Maugham, W. Somerset, 366
Maus (Spiegelman), 297
Mazel (Goldstein), 258
Mazza, Cris, 371, 372, 376n25
McCarthy, Cormac, 219–220, 225, 263, 266–267
McElroy, Joseph, 34, 369, 370
McInerney, Jay, 71
McKibben, Bill, 5
McMartin Day Care Sexual Abuse Trials, 297
Melville, Herman, 48, 134, 200, 210, 257
Memento (Nolan), 297
Memories of My Father Watching TV (White), 318–319, 326n52
Memories of the Ford Administration (Updike), 323
Merrill, James, 38
Metafiction, 7, 57–58, 59–60, 72–73, 91, 94–95, 97–99, 100–101, 102–103, 124–130, 136, 161, 165, 169, 177, 181, 195, 203, 205, 219, 244, 254, 298, 330
Meyer, Stephenie, 32, 44
Microserfs (Coupland), 241–242
Middle Passage (Johnson), 126, 134–135
Middlesex (Eugenides), 109
Millennium, 2–4, 6, 7, 8, 14n29, 17–20, 21–22, 27, 29, 43, 87, 109, 264, 282
Millet, Kate, 50
Millhauser, Steven, 199
A Million Little Pieces (Frey), 301
Milton, John, 58
Moby-Dick (Melville), 48, 134, 135, 257
Mona in the Promised Land (Jen), 238
Mones, Nicole, 204
Monette, Paul, 332
Monkey Bridge (Cao), 298, 302–304
Moody, Rick, 162, 319, 322
Moore, Lorrie, 162, 312, 316, 319
Moraga, Cherrie, 274–275
Morrison, Toni, 9, 11, 14n46, 67, 68–69, 126, 132–134, 135, 136, 137, 206, 219, 298–300, 320
Morrow, Bradford, 11
Mother Night (Vonnegut), 101
Motherless Brooklyn (Lethem), 7, 253–254
Moulthrop, Stuart, 79–80, 87
Moxley, Jennifer, 351
Moynihan Report, 320–321

"Mr. Difficult" (Franzen), 356
Mr Sammler's Planet (Bellow), 50, 57
Mukherjee, Bharati, 204, 206–208, 210, 211, 222–223, 235–236, 243
Mullen, Harryette, 151–152, 351
Mulligan Stew (Sorrentino), 370
Murphy Brown, 312
Muse & Drudge (Mullen), 151–152
My Brother (Kincaid), 334–335, 336
My Cousin, My Gastroenterologist (Leyner), 284–285
My Garden Book (Kincaid), 343n53
My Life (Hejinian), 140
My Way (Bernstein), 178

Nabokov, Vladimir, 175, 199, 200, 202, 203, 204
The Naked and the Dead (Mailer), 49
A Naked Singularity (De La Pava), 120
The Names (DeLillo), 170
Naslund, Sena Jeter, 202
Nasrin, Taslima, 4
Native Son (Wright), 210
Native Speaker (Lee), 210–211, 223–224, 322
NEA, 374
Negative Blue (Wright), 141–142
Negri, Antonio, 74n10, 234
Neuromancer (Gibson), 244, 286, 288
The New York Trilogy (Auster), 210
Nietzsche, Friedrich, 101
A Night at the Movies (Coover), 370
Night of the Living Dead (Romero), 44
Nirvana, 11
Nixon, Richard M., 284, 323
Novel Explosives (Gauer), 120

Oates, Joyce Carol, 7, 315, 322
Obama, Barack, 320
O'Brien, Tim, 155–158, 159, 160, 161, 298, 302, 304–306
O'Connor, Flannery, 313
"Of Time and the Line" (Bernstein), 178
Off the Reservation (Allen), 220
"Offloading for Mrs. Schwartz" (Saunders), 46n43
Oklahoma City Bombing, 71
Oleanna (Mamet), 10
Olsen, Lance, 371, 372, 377n25
Omensetter's Luck (Gass), 369
Once Upon a Time (Barth), 93–95, 99
Ong, Walter, 83
Operation Shylock (Roth), 57, 203
Oppenheimer, Robert, 260
Orfeo (Powers), 217
The Origin of the Brunists (Coover), 103, 369

Pack of Lies (Sorrentino), 370
Palahniuk, Chuck, 69–71, 73, 319
Pale Fire (Nabokov), 175, 204
Parables of the Sower (Butler), 66–67, 71, 73
Paradise (Morrison), 67, 68–69, 126, 132–134, 135, 136, 298–300, 320
The Passion Artist (Hawkes), 369
The Passion of Christ (Gibson), 36
"Pastoralia" (Saunders), 321
Patchwork Girl (Jackson), 182
Peirce, Charles Sanders, 350
"People Like That Are the Only People Here" (Moore), 316
The People of Paper (Plascencia), 180
Pera, Pia, 199–200, 202
"Perchance to Dream" (Franzen), 27–28, 186, 191
Pessl, Marisha, 120
Phillips, Jayne Anne, 313, 322
Pigeon Feathers (Updike), 53–54, 61n26
Pinocchio in Venice (Coover), 369
Plascencia, Salvador, 180
Playing in the Dark (Morrison), 9
Plowing the Dark (Powers), 28, 121n12, 282, 289–292
Plus (McElroy), 369
Poe, Edgar Allan, 109, 199, 201
Poetry Slam, 355
The Poisonwood Bible (Kingsolver), 208–210
Postman, Neil, 163
Postsecularism, 35–37, 41
Powers, Richard, 6, 29–30, 108–110, 117, 118, 120, 121n12, 217, 244, 250, 257, 259–260, 267–268, 272, 274, 282, 289–292, 322, 352
The Professor of Desire (Roth), 203
Proulx, Annie, 75n28
Prozac Nation (Wurtzel), 252
The Public Burning (Coover), 92, 124–125, 369
"A Pulse" (Armantrout), 150–151
Purple America (Moody), 322
Push (Sapphire), 315, 335–336, 339–340
Pynchon, Thomas, 1, 4, 13n17, 35, 37, 40, 42, 45n10, 92, 103, 111, 121n12, 126, 131–132, 133, 135, 137, 229–230, 250, 257, 318, 374

Quayle, Dan, 312
Queer Nation Manifesto, 196
"Quo Vadis" (Wallace), 185, 186

Rabbit Angstrom (Updike), 48
Rabbit Redux (Updike), 56–57, 62n56
Ravelstein (Bellow), 51–52
The Raw Shark Texts (Hall), 180
Reader's Block (Markson), 99–101, 102, 111, 115–116, 120
Reagan, Ronald, 51, 55, 235, 367

The Real World, 40
The Recognitions (Gaddis), 121n12
Redfield, James, 36, 365
Reed, Ishmael, 370
Refuge (Williams), 273
Reinventing Nature? (Soule and Lease), 266
Remarque, Erich Maria, 279
Reservation Blues (Alexie), 160
Retallack, Joan, 179
Review of Contemporary Fiction, 185–188, 190–195
Rheingold, Howard, 280, 281, 282, 283, 286
Rhys, Jean, 202
Rice, Anne, 44
Rodgers, Daniel T., 1, 12n2
Ronald Sukenick, 376n25
Roth, Philip, 48, 56–60, 103, 126, 137–138, 203, 298, 306–308, 323
Rough Trades (Bernstein), 178
Rowling, J. K., 32
Roy, Arundhati, 204
Rule of the Bone (Banks), 71–72
"Rupture, Verge, and Precipice" (Maso), 116, 186, 192–195
Rushdie, Salman, 4, 13n23, 35, 204, 246
Ryman, Geoff, 244–245

S. (Abrams and Dorst), 181
Sabbatical (Barth), 369, 370
Sacks, Oliver, 254
The Safety of Objects (Homes), 162–164, 318
Sagan, Carl, 255
Sapphire, 315, 335–336, 339–340
Satanic Verses (Rushdie), 35
Saunders, George, 30, 41, 42, 46n43, 321
Saussure, Ferdinand de, 350
The Scarlet Letter (Hawthorne), 206–208
Scarry, Elaine, 297
Schismatrix (Sterling), 286
Schrodinger, Erwin, 119
The Sea Came in at Midnight (Erickson), 24–27
The Secret History (Tartt), 316–317
Self-Consciousness (Updike), 55, 56
Senna, Danzy, 8
Serres, Michel, 275
Seuss, Dr., 365
Shacochis, Bob, 116, 120, 242–244
Shannon, Claude, 260
Shelter (Phillips), 313, 322
Shepherd, Reginald, 38
Sherwood, Frances, 323
Siegel, Lee, 79, 84–87, 116, 118, 120, 172, 174–176, 179, 181, 202–206, 207, 209, 211
Sijie, Dai, 204
Silko, Leslie Marmon, 159, 220, 263, 270, 273, 274

Index

Simpson, Mona, 319
Simpson, O. J., 33
The Simpsons, 255, 312–313, 324n3
"Skin" (Jackson), 181
Sky Changes (Sorrentino), 370
Slaughterhouse Five (Vonnegut), 101, 102
Smiley, Jane, 315
Smith, Anna Deveare, 64–65, 66
Smith, Evan Lavender, 120
Smith, Zadie, 241
A Smuggler's Bible (McElroy), 369
Snow Crash (Stephenson), 67, 283, 288–289
Snow White (Barthelme), 244
Snow, C. P., 249, 250, 255, 257, 260, 261
So Far from God (Castillo), 35–36, 37, 40–41
The Society of Friends (Cherry), 154
Sokal, Alan, 256
Something to Declare (Alvarez), 224
Sontag, Susan, 170, 330–331
The Sopranos, 234, 313
Sorrentino, Gilbert, 199, 353, 370, 371, 372, 376n25
Spahr, Julia, 351
Special Topics in Calamity Physics (Pessl), 120
Specimen Days (Cunningham), 210
Spiegelman, Art, 297
Spinsters (Kennedy), 323
Springer's Progress (Markson), 370
"State of the Art" (Barth), 283–284
Steele, Danielle, 371, 374
Steelwork (Sorrentino), 370
Stefans, Brian Kim, 351
Stein, Gertrude, 370
Steingraber, Sandra, 273, 274
Stephenson, Neal, 67, 111, 283, 288–289
Sterling, Bruce, 286
Sterne, Laurence, 111
Stoker, Bram, 203
Story-Cycle, 154–166, 224–225
Storyteller (Silko), 159
Stowe, Harriet Beecher, 322
"Strange Attractors" (Goldstein), 259
Strange Days (Bigelow), 281
Strauss, Leo, 51
Strickland, Stephanie, 284
Sukenick, Ronald, 96, 371, 372, 373
Sunstein, Cass, 348, 349, 358
Surfiction, 371
Swedenborg, Emanuel, 33
Swimming in the Volcano (Shacochis), 116, 120, 242–244
Synners (Cadigan), 282, 286–288

Tal, Kali, 297
Tartt, Donna, 316–317

Terminator 2 (Cameron), 260
The Terrible Threes (Reed), 370
The Terrible Twos (Reed), 370
"Terrific Mother" (Moore), 312
Thatcher, Margaret, 51, 367
"This Line" (Bernstein), 178
The Things They Carried (O'Brien), 155–158
"The Third and Final Continent" (Lahiri), 238–239
Thoreau, Henry David, 201
A Thousand Acres (Smiley), 315
Through the Arc of the Rainforest (Yamashita), 268–269, 270, 272
Tillmann, Lynne, 71, 120
The Time of Our Time (Mailer), 48, 49–50, 60
Timequake (Vonnegut), 101–103
Tlooth (Mathews), 370
To the Lighthouse (Woolf), 119
Tomasula, Steve, 181
Tortilla Curtain (Boyle), 227–228
Total Recall (Verhoeven), 297
Touched by an Angel, 32
Toward the End of Time (Updike), 3–4, 48–49, 240
Tracks (Erdrich), 159
Transcendentalism, 240, 266
Trauma, 156–158, 297–309, 315
Travolta, John, 32
Tree of Codes (Foer), 181
Trilling, Lionel, 351
Tripmaster Monkey (Kingston), 210
Tropic of Orange (Yamashita), 67–68, 228–230
Trussoni, Danielle, 32
Try (Cooper), 72–73, 315
The Tunnel (Gass), 95–97, 107, 179–180, 369–370
Turing, Alan, 260
Twain, Mark, 48
Twilight, Los Angeles, 1992 (Smith), 64–65, 66
Twin Peaks (Lynch and Frost), 163
Typical American (Jen), 223

Ulysses (Joyce), 250, 353
Uncle Tom's Cabin (Stowe), 322
Under the Feet of Jesus (Viramontes), 263, 272, 273
Underworld (DeLillo), 4, 6, 29, 107, 126, 127, 128–130, 239–240, 273, 322
Updike, John, 3–4, 7, 48, 49, 53–57, 59, 61n26, 62n56, 103, 206, 240, 323
US Census (1990), 314
US Census (2000), 220

VAS (Tomasula), 181
Vattimo, Gianni, 36
Victory Garden (Moulthrop), 79–80, 87

Vineland (Pynchon), 35, 37, 40, 45n10, 318
Viramontes, Helena Maria, 263, 272, 273
The Virgin Suicides (Eugenides), 163
Virtual Light (Gibson), 244
Virtual Reality (Rheingold), 280, 281
A Visit from the Goon Squad (Egan), 109, 155
Vizenor, Gerald, 8
Vollmann, William T., 11, 108, 110
Vonnegut, Kurt, 92, 101–103, 199

Waco Siege, 17
Walking Tour, The (Davis), 28–29
Wallace, David Foster, 4, 6, 11, 13n17, 41–42, 46n48, 48–49, 52, 57, 91, 108–110, 117, 118, 120, 155, 162, 163, 164–166, 172, 175, 185, 186–187, 188, 189–190, 191, 192, 193, 194–195, 196, 240–241, 252, 272, 273, 284–285, 317, 318, 326n52, 326n60
Waller, Robert James, 365
The Waltons, 312
Warhol, Andy, 285
Warren, Robert Penn, 350
Waugh, Evelyn, 242
"The Wavemaker Falters" (Saunders), 41
We Were the Mulvaneys (Oates), 315
"Westward the Course of Empire" (Wallace), 57
Whistlejacket (Hawkes), 370
White Noise (DeLillo), 189–190, 272
White, Curtis, 318–319, 326n52, 371, 372, 376n25
Whitehead, Colson, 44, 120
Whitman, Walt, 201, 210–211

Who Will Run the Frog Hospital? (Moore), 319
Wideman, John Edgar, 7, 320
The Wild Iris (Gluck), 142–144
Williams, Damian, 64
Williams, Terry Tempest, 273
Williams, William Carlos, 177
Willie Masters's Lonesome Wife (Gass), 96, 370
Wilson, Edmund, 256, 351
Winesburg, Ohio (Anderson), 154, 161, 163
Winfrey, Oprah, 234, 316, 355–356
Wings of Desire (Wenders and Handke), 33, 34, 39
Wittgenstein, Ludwig, 351
Wittgenstein's Mistress (Markson), 99–100
Wolff, Tobias, 162
Woman Hollering Creek (Cisneros), 235, 237
Women and Men (McElroy), 34, 370
Woolf, Virginia, 34, 114, 119, 337
Wordsworth, William, 223
Wright, Charles, 141–142, 144, 145, 149–150, 152
Wright, Richard, 210
Wurtzel, Elizabeth, 252

Y2K Bug, 12n2, 18, 27, 28, 288
Yamashita, Karen Tei, 67–68, 227, 228–230, 263, 268–269, 272
Yeats, W. B., 46n33, 103
You Bright and Risen Angels (Vollmann), 108

Žižek, Slavoj, 12n5, 237–238